Strategic Management of Services in the Arab Gulf States

Strategic Management of Services in the Arab Gulf States

Company and Industry Cases

by M. Sami Kassem,
Ghazi M. Habib et al.

Walter de Gruyter · Berlin · New York 1989

Prof. *M. Sami Kassem*
The University of Toledo
College of Business Administration
Department of Management
Toledo, OH 43606 U.S.A.

Dr. *Ghazi Habib*
King Fahd University of Petroleum and Minerals
College of Industrial Management
Dharan 31261, Saudi Arabia

HD9987
P47
K37
1989

With 87 Exhibits

Library of Congress Cataloging-in-Publication Data

Kassem, M. Sami, 1938–
  Strategic management of services in the Arab Gulf states : company
and industry cases / by M. Sami Kassem, Ghazi M. Habib et al.
     p. cm.
  Bibliography: p.
  Includes index.
  ISBN 0-89925-386-5 (U.S.)
  1. Service industries -- Persian Gulf Region -- Management -- Case
studies.   I. Ghazi, M. Habib, 1950–   II. Title.
  HD9987.P47K37   1989   89-30563
  658.4'012'09536 -- dc 19   CIP

CIP-Kurztitelaufnahme der Deutschen Bibliothek

Strategic managment of services in the Arab Gulf states :
company and industry cases / by M. Sami Kassem ; Ghazi M.
Habib et al. – Berlin ; New York : de Gruyter, 1989
     ISBN 3-11-011449-6
NE: Kassem, M. Sami [Mitverf.]

⊚ Printed on acid free paper

Foreword

It is a pleasure to see the appearance of a book devoted entirely to service business practices in the Arab Gulf States.

For most U.S. businessmen and students, the international dimensions of business have become of central importance to success, and in some cases, to survival. Yet, a real in-depth understanding of business practice outside of the United States is often missing. This is particularly true the further one gets from the developed "western" world. International business is often viewed from the eyes of the beholder and not, as it should be, from the perspective of the country or region in which business is actually taking place.

The authors of this book combine the perspective of their own national backgrounds and on the spot working and research experience in the Gulf area, with long professional experience in the United States. They therefore look at the Arab world through Arab eyes – yet with the benefit of an additional perspective gained by working for many years outside of the Arab world.

The book is hard hitting in its criticism of many current management practices in the Gulf area, yet positive and creative in suggesting the scale of the opportunity that exists for change, as well as highlighting the very substantial progress that has already been accomplished. The authors make no bones about pointing out where change is imperative, and what forms it might take.

A major advantage of the book is that it is based on a considerable amount of new "case material" drawn from leading firms in the airline, hotel, financial, and health care industries. These cases provide the reader with direct insight into the history of the organizations, management practices, and functional activities of each subject firm. They allow discussion, not only of overall strategy and practices of the individual firm, but also a comparative analysis of several leading contenders in each of the four chosen service industries. The book fills a gap in the current literature by providing important insights into an area of the world which had developed a new economy based on oil revenues, yet shown its ability to survive also in the much harder economic conditions which prevail today. The authors suggest strongly that service industries are certainly going to play a critical role in these countries' economic future. With the rising political importance of the Islamic world, this in-depth view of the Arabian

Gulf service economy is an important building block in developing our overall understanding of what the economic future of the region may eventually look like.

Lausanne, March 1989

Derek F. Abell
Dean
IMEDE

Preface

The Arabian Gulf is a region of strategic importance to the world economy. It provides the world with oil, recycled petrodollars, and markets for consumer and capital goods.

The service sector is assuming a more important role in the economies of the Arab Gulf States. It employs over 60 % of the labor force and provides a market for the goods and services produced by domestic and foreign enterprises. Some students of economic development suggest that the service sector, if properly managed, could provide a vital source of national income second only to oil. They point to the experiences of Mexico and Egypt as pertinent examples. Others, equally sincere, are not as sure. They believe the effective management of the service sector is not an easy proposition. They argue that managers of Arab service organizations face far more constraints than their counterparts elsewhere. They must deal with: a) an imported, heterogeneous, and costly labor force, and b) a poorly trained, costly, and less motivated labor pool. In addition, they operate in a recessionary and turbulent environment characterized by: a) a sharp decline in the customer base, b) fierce competition, c) a host of government regulations and cultural barriers, and d) political instability and turmoil in the region.

What does the record show? How do Arab service organizations adapt themselves, both individually and collectively, to their contextual environment? Do they plan their future or do they just accept it as it comes? Do they develop their own "grand design" or "master strategy" to guide their future, or do they simply follow what is fashionable? What characterizes firms that try to master their environment as opposed to firms that more easily sway with the times? We pose these questions for our readers and will attempt to answer them based upon a thorough examination of the current management practices of 18 service organizations operating in the Arabian Gulf region. We invite the readers to formulate their own answers, compare them to ours, and arrive at their own theory of Arab management practices.

We believe the collection of case studies offered in this book is representative of the service industries found in the Arabian Gulf region. However, the bulk of information is derived from the Saudi Arabian experience.

As a group, the cases are exceptionally diverse. There are short and long cases, cases about large companies, and cases about both non-profit and profit-making organizations.

There are at least four features these cases have in common. First, they are all original cases focusing on strategic management issues, such as goal formation, social responsibility, strategy formulation, environmental analysis, and strategy evaluation and control. Second, they all have been written within the context of a severe economic recession caused by falling oil prices. Third, they are all grouped by their branch industry. This offers the student the opportunity to examine contrasting strategies of rivalling firms in managing economic decline and contraction. Finally, all the cases have been analyzed and discussed by students within the MBA curriculum of a major Saudi university. They have not been utilized, however, by audiences in the West. We therefore do invite our Western colleagues to share their feedback from students with us.

This book is designed to augment textbooks written by American academics specifically for American students and premised on the values of American business. Not unexpectedly, much of what is contained in such books is foreign to Arab students, including the language, events, situations, institutions, and concepts. This unfortunate situation often leads to the empty regurgitation of alien facts and concepts to pass exams which does little to help students come to grips with real business problems that are relevant to their world. What has been lacking, of course, are local texts and local cases which are culturally and situationally relevant. This book is designed to respond to that need.

The other major audience for this book consists of non-Arab students. Most business and management schools around the world have a course on business policy or strategic management. Some have specialized courses on the management of service operations and on international management. Business school professors, who are anxious to internationalize their courses, may find this book helpful in enriching their own perspective and that of their students.

It would have been difficult to prepare this book had it not been for the vision, support, and encouragement of His Excellency Dr. Bakr A. Bakr, Rector of King Fahd University of Petroleum and Minerals. He and his able assistants supported this project from inception through completion. His thoughtful feedback on the early draft of the book was most valuable.

Many other people have directly or indirectly supported this venture. We are particularly grateful to the leaders of the Arab enterprises discussed here, who agreed to cooperate with us and subject themselves and their organizations to our scrutiny. We are also grateful to our graduate students, who provided us with the raw material for some of the case studies included in this book. Technical feedback and editorial reviews were provided by Dr. Kate Gillispie of the University of Texas and by Dr. Bhal

Bhat and Dr. Thomas Sharkey of the University of Toledo. Richard Hobson, Jr., Aileen Smith, Linda Molenda, Craig Bickley, and Zosimo Bool deserve special thanks for their excellent help in producing the final manuscript.

Finally, we would like to dedicate this book to our parents and our immediate families. The former gave us the motivation to become academicians and authors. The latter provided us with inspiration and coped with our frustrations.

Toledo, Ohio
Dhahran, Saudi Arabia

M. Sami Kassem
Ghazi M. Habib

Table of Contents

Case Information Matrix XIX

Part I: Background

Chapter 1: Introduction 3
M. Sami Kassem

Overview 3
Rationale... 4
Focus 5
Methodology 6
Contributions.. 6
Plan of the Book... 6

Chapter 2: Understanding the Business Environment 9
M. Sami Kassem

Introduction 9
Physical and Geographic Environment 11
The Social and Cultural Setting 12
The Economic and Business Environment 13
Organizational and Administrative Setting 16
Summary and Conclusion.. 19

Chapter 3: Distinctive Aspects of Services in the Arab Gulf States.. 23
Ghazi M. Habib

Introduction 23
Characteristics of Services... 25
Services in the Arab Gulf States 27
Summary and Conclusion... 30

Part II: Industry Notes and Company Cases

Chapter 4: The Airline Industry 35

4.1 A Note on the Arab Airline Industry 35
M. Sami Kassem

Introduction 35
Present Status of Arab Carriers: A Statistical Profile 36
Industry Economics 37
Industry Structure 38
Entry and Exit Barriers 41
Economies of Scale 48
Suppliers 49
Competitors and Their Strategies 50
Buyers and Users of Airline Services 56
Substitutes 64
Conclusion 64

4.2 Saudi Arabian Airlines (Saudia) 69
M. Sami Kassem and Ghazi M. Habib

Introduction 69
Stages of Strategic Development 70
The Goals of Saudia 74
Organization 75
Financial Performance and Position 80
Personnel 80
Saudization of Jobs 80
Marketing 87
Marketing Channels 91
Saudia Pricing and Price Wars 91
Saudia's Future 95

4.3 Kuwait Airways Corporation (KAC) 98
M. Sami Kassem and Ghazi M. Habib

Introduction 98
Corporate Mission 98
Stages of Strategic Development 99
Organization 102
Functional Area Strategies 103
Marketing 106
Flight Operations 107
Money Matters at KAC 108
KAC's Future Direction 112

4.4 Gulf Air (GF).. 114
M. Sami Kassem and Ghazi M. Habib

Introduction 114
History.. 115
Gulf Leadership... 118
Management and Personnel 119
Finance 120
Operations... 125
Marketing 126
Pricing 128
Passenger Services.. 128
Competitor Profile 129
Strategic Planning at Gulf Air................................. 129
Facing the Remaining 1980s 131

4.5 Alia: The Royal Jordanian Airline – The First Twenty Years ... 134
M. Sami Kassem

Introduction 134
Alia's Mission 135
Stages of Strategic Development................................ 136
Organization... 140
Management Style 140
Personnel.. 142
Marketing 144
Financial Performance... 145
Facing Turbulent Times... 152

Chapter 5: Banking Industry 155

5.1 A Note on the Banking Industry............................. 155
Ghazi M. Habib

Introduction 155
Present Status of the Gulf Banking Industry................... 156
Industry Analysis 159
Entry and Exit Barriers... 170
Substitutes.. 171

5.2 National Commercial Bank (NCB)............................ 177
Ghazi M. Habib

Introduction 177
Objectives/Mission 178
History.. 178
Organization... 179

Services Portfolio 181
Personnel.. 182
Marketing.. 183
Finance 183
New Challenges 183

5.3 Saudi American Bank (SAMBA)............................... 188
Ghazi M. Habib

Introduction 188
Corporate Mission 189
Strategy.. 189
History... 189
Organizational Structure... 190
Personnel.. 193
Marketing.. 194
Finance 196
New Challenges 198

5.4 Saudi French Bank (BFS)...................................... 199
Mohamed S. Al Madhi and M. Sami Kassem

Introduction 199
History... 199
Mission 199
Management and Board of Directors 201
Bank Organization 201
Functional Area Strategies 205
Marketing.. 206
Financial Profile 207
Problems and Opportunities Facing the Banking Industry 207
Competition and Competitor Profiles 210
Adapting Strategy and Structure to Changing Times 212
Issues and Problems.. 212

5.5 Gulf International Bank (GIB)................................. 215
Anwar Yousif Abdulrahman

Introduction 215
Corporate Mission 215
History... 216
GIB's Organization... 217
Services Portfolio 217
Marketing.. 219
Personnel.. 222
Accounting 223
Finance 223

Challenges.. 223

5.6 "Bank Arabia" Computer Services............................ 228
M. Sami Kassem and Yousef Dashkouni

Part One 228
Questions for Part One 231
Part Two 231
Questions for Part Two 233
Part Three.. 233
Questions for Part Three...................................... 234
Part Four 234
Questions for Part Four 235
Part Five 236

Chapter 6: Lodging Industry 237

6.1 A Note on the Lodging Industry............................ 237
Ghazi M. Habib

Introduction 237
Industry Structure.. 238
Entry and Exit Barriers....................................... 242
Substitutes... 245
Cost and Revenue Structure.................................... 245

6.2 The Gulf Meridien (GM) 250
Prince Abdulaziz bin Salman Al-Saud

Introduction 250
The Hotel Industry in Saudi Arabia 251
Competitive Analysis 252
Internal Analysis... 254
Marketing.. 257
Financial Matters 262
Challenges Ahead 265

6.3 Al Gosaibi Hotel.. 266
M. Sami Kassem

Introduction 266
Overview 267
Personnel.. 268
Financial Position.. 268
Marketing.. 269
Home Office – Hotel Management Relation 269
The New General Manager 271

6.4 Al-Hamra Hotel.. 274
Eman Al Betairi and Ghazi M. Habib

Introduction 274
Hotel Organization... 275
Pricing 277
Competition 280
Personnel... 283
Finance 283
Challenges.. 285

Chapter 7: Health Care Industry 289

7.1 A Note on the Health Care Industry........................... 289
M. Sami Kassem

Introduction and Overview... 289
Competitive Structure of the Industry............................. 296
The Hospital Management Contract Segments......................... 306
The Market of Private Hospitals 308
Trends in the Health Care Industry 309

7.2 Al-Mana General Hospital..................................... 312
M. Sami Kassem

History... 312
The Business of Al-Mana 313
Service/Market Development.. 315
Management Philosophy... 318
Human Resources... 319
Marketing 321
Finance 323
Facilities and Equipment.. 325
The Future 325

7.3 Abdulla Fouad Hospital (AFH)................................. 328
Haman Al Otaibi and M. Sami Kassem

Introduction 328
Development of the Hospital....................................... 329
The Concept in Detail 330
Facilities 330
The Service Portfolio 331
Patient Classification and Its Impact on Clinics and Departments 333
Organization Structure.. 336
Hospital Personnel 338
Financial Issues 343

Competitive Analysis 344
The Future of Abdulla Fouad Hospital 346

7.4 Green Crescent Health Services Clinic (GC) 348
M. Sami Kassem

Introduction 348
Mission 349
GC Service Portfolio 350
Patient Mix 352
Charges and Fees 352
Management and Organization 354
Personnel 356
Marketing 356
Current Facilities 360
Finance 360
Future Directions 363

Chapter 8: Strategic Management in Different Industries 365

8.1 Saudi Consulting House (SCH) 365
Ghazi M. Habib

Introduction 365
Objectives/Mission 366
History 367
SCH's Organization 368
Marketing 371
Customer Mix 373
SCH's Competitors 373
Manpower Training 374
Finance 375
Challenges 375

8.2 Saudi Arabian International School (SAIS) – "The Dhahran
**   Academy" 380**
Gary Nosler and M. Sami Kassem

Introduction 380
Expatriate Education in Saudi Arabia 380
History of the Academy 381
Dhahran Academy's Mission 383
Customers' Analysis 383
Teachers and Staff 386
Governmental Regulation 386
Competitive Analysis 387

Organization Structure. 392
Outlook for the Future 393

8.3 "Alpha Data Soft" (ADS) 396
Abdulla Al-Sharif and M. Sami Kassem

History of "Alpha Data Soft". 396
Marketing 398
Operations. 399
Procurement 399
Financial Profile 400
Organization and Management. 401
The Computer Market in Saudi Arabia 401
Competition 404
The Future 406

Part III: Summary and Conclusions

Chapter 9: Strategic Management: Arabian Style
M. Sami Kassem

Chapter 9: Strategic Management: Arabian Style 411

Introduction 411
Strategy Formulation. 411
Organizational Structure. 420
Typology of Service Organizations. 425
Practical Implications. 429
Theoretical Implications 430

Appendix A: A Guide to the Case Method. 435

Appendix B: Questions for Discussion and Teaching Notes 441

Appendix C: Major GCC Currencies and Their Exchange Rates as
            of 11/11/1987. 475

Appendix D: List of Abbreviations. 477

About the Authors 479

Case Information Matrix

Case	Focus
The Arab Airline Industry	Factors that enhance the volatility of the Arab airline industry and that reduce its competitiveness
Saudi Arabian Airlines	Turning around a giant state-owned carrier
Kuwait Airways	Cost-containment turn-around strategies
Gulf Air	A regional airline is deciding to go global and expand its route network
Alia: Royal Jordanian	Strategic vision, longevity of executive tenure as determinants of business sucess
The Banking Industry	Identification of opportunities, threats and key success factors
National Commercial Bank	Service mix, separation of ownership and management
Saudi American Bank	Competitive weapon, strategy identification and evaluation
Saudi French Bank	Strategic evaluation and control, repositioning, restructuring
Gulf International Bank	Going global, diversification and branching strategies
Bank Arabia	Evolution of a matrix organization
The Hotel Industry	Identification of key success factors, opportunities, and threats
Al-Hamra Hotel	Retrenchment
Al Gosaibi Hotel	Executive leadership and changing times
Gulf Meridien	Firm-specific critical success factors plus choosing a management contract firm
The Health Care Industry	Identification of opportunities, threats, and key success factors
Al-Mana General Hospital	Social responsibility – Arabian style
Abdualla Fouad Hospital	Competitive strategies for an also-ran and a declining firm
Green Crescent Clinic	Liquidation as an endgame strategy: conditions for its optimal use, managing the process and confronting some of its inherent dilemmas
The Dhahran Academy	Competitiveness of American services in overseas markets. Identification of firm specific key success factors
Alpha Data Soft	Entrepreneurial management, competitive analysis; redefining the business
Saudi Consulting House	Strengths and weaknesses, strategy evaluation and control, firm-specific critical success factors

Industry	Complexity	Financial Data Ratios	Industry Conditions
Airline	High	No	Mature
Airline	High	Yes	Mature
Airline	Medium	Yes	Mature
Airline	High	Yes	Mature
Airline	Medium	Yes	Mature
Banking	Medium	Yes	Mature
Banking	Medium	Yes	Mature
Banking	Medium	Yes	Mature
Banking	Medium	Yes	Mature
Banking	Medium	Yes	Mature
Banking	Low	No	Mature
Hotel	Low	Yes	Declining
Hotel	Low	Yes	Declining
Hotel	Low	No	Declining
Hotel	Low	Yes	Declining
Health Care	High	No	Mature
Health Care	Medium	Yes	Mature
Health Care	Medium	Yes	Mature
Health Care	Medium	Yes	Mature
Private Schools	High	Yes	Mature
Computer Software	Medium	No	Emerging
Consulting	Medium	Yes	Growth/Global

Part I
Background

Chapter 1
Introduction

M. Sami Kassem

Overview

The Arab Gulf States play a key role in world politics and international
business. Accordingly, the need for an adequate understanding of the
region's business and management systems is great. Much has been written
about the geography, history, culture, politics, and even economics of the
Arabian Peninsula. Little analysis, however, has been undertaken from a
business point of view. Indeed, for many businessmen, the Arabian Gulf
region, particularly Saudi Arabia, remains a mystery in need of exploration
and worthy of systematic study. Our study represents one of relatively few
recent attempts to meet this need. It combines the scholarly approach of the
academician, curious about his subject for its own sake, with the pressing
and pragmatic need of the businessman. In so doing, this book constitutes a
threefold exercise. First, it surveys a few selected service industries in the
region and identifies the critical success variables for each. It also attempts
to determine where major industry players stand with respect to these
success variables. Second, in applying conventional strategic managment
concepts and theories to service enterprises in the Gulf area, this study aims
to bring a degree of critical analysis to current local thinking in business
and economics. Third, this study introduces business students – Arab and
non-Arab alike – to prevailing business practices peculiar to the Arabian
Gulf region.

For the purpose of this book, a service is defined as a deed or
performance that is intangible and non-standardized in nature, cannot be
possessed or inventoried, and is thus produced and consumed simultaneously. The service sectors under study here are: (1) commercial airlines,
(2) banking, (3) lodging, (4) health care, and (5) a miscellaneous group
of service enterprises, comprised of a consulting firm, a private school, and
a computer service organization.

Rationale

There are good reasons why this book focuses on the service sector. To begin with, no economy can survive without a service sector. (Riddle 1986: 28) Agriculture, mining, and manufacturing are the bricks of the economy. Services are the glue that holds them together – the industries that facilitate all economic transactions, and the engine that stimulates the production of goods. As a recent Egyptian experiment has shown, a nation cannot develop a viable fishing industry by simply acquiring a modern fishing fleet. As a minimum, it has to provide for both time and space utilities. Without first-class storage and transportation services, the fishing industry will be ill-fated.

Manufacturing is a popular diversification strategy among Arab policy makers. However, these policy makers need to be reminded of three facts. First, an over-emphasis on developing the manufacturing sector neglects the vital role played by the service sector, which is the prerequisite for all other sectors. Second, not all economies are blessed with a comparative advantage in their manufacturing sector. Third, an all-service-economy is a recession-free economy. Since the demand for services is more stable than that for manufacturing goods, service jobs expand rather than contract in recessions.[1]

While all sectors of an economy are important, the service is critical, particularly in the economies of the Arab Gulf States. More than 60% of the labor force in these states are gainfully employed in the service-related industries. Moreover, the Gulf States spend more than one-half of their budgets on services. The role of the service sector is expected to expand further.[2]

Another corollary reason for the pro-service bias of this book is that the marketing of services is little understood, particularly in the Arab Gulf States. A Gulf Arab not getting satisfactory service from a local bank can conceivably transact his financial business by mail, telex, or even home computer with a foreign bank located thousands of miles away. He does not have to subsidize inefficiencies of local banks or accept substandard service. Nor is he compelled to patronize his national airline if he feels that

---

[1] The recession-resistant nature of services is documented by the experience of the American economy during its last four recessions. For more details on the economic and social impact of service industries see J. L. Heskett (1986): *Managing in the Service Economy*, Boston, Mass.: Harvard Business School Press, Appendix B.

[2] The service economy thesis has three stages. First, as societies get richer, they develop new categories of needs (Engel's Law). Second, these new needs have to be met by services rather than by goods. Third, an increase in the demand for services leads to increased numbers in service employment. Thus, the service sector tends to predominate in the overall economy. For a detailed analysis of this thesis see J. Greshuny (1978: 69).

he can get a better fare, more reliable service, and a timelier connection from a foreign flag carrier. In a highly competitive service-oriented economy inefficient producers are soon weeded out, unless their inefficiencies are subsidized by the state. Even then, these producers – no matter how sheltered or protected they happen to be – may ultimately be forced out of the market by discriminating well-informed consumers.

Providing an understanding of what it takes to compete in such an economy is a major objective of this book. However, this study contains no quick and easy recipes to help businessmen market their services or invest their capital. Rather, it provides conceptual road maps or analytic frameworks which may help business practitioners and students alike to achieve a critical understanding of the risks and rewards, constraints and opportunities involved with operating the service sector of the evolving Gulf economy.

Focus

This study opts for focus and depth in preference to breadth. It covers selected enterprises in service industries: airlines, banking, lodging, health care, and a few others. There are good reasons for concentrating on these industries.

1) These industries are intensely competitive, characterized by:
   a. economies of scale;
   b. imaginative use of market segmentation;
   c. local ownership; and
   d. intensive use of foreign technology and management.
2) All four service industries are capital and labor-intensive industries. They are all characterized by high levels of employment. Moreover, the services each industry group provides touch a substantial portion of the local population. How well these industries are managed affects the livelihood and well-being of many thousands of people.
3) Such industries serve as indicators of the level of management sophistication, national prestige, and cultural value. A foreign business-man traveling to an Arabian Gulf city for the first time can catch a meaningful glimpse of the country, particularly if he arrives on Gulf Air, Kuwaiti Airways, or Saudia airline, changes money at a local bank, stays at a locally-owned hotel, or receives a medical check-up from a local hospital. These industries also reflect national and regional aspirations for Arab unity, regional cooperation, and economic integration within the Gulf Cooperation Council.

4) Although the four selected industries have a lot in common, they also differ from one another. These differences, as well as the similarities, merit our attention.

Methodology

This study utilizes a dual research methodology of library and field research. In surveying each of the selected industries and participating firms, we made heavy use of published data. This leg work enabled us to "walk the territory" and design a standard framework for data collection. In collecting data on each selected organization, we interviewed members of its management team, using semi-structured interviews. Both the primary and secondary data were then used in writing the "Case Study".

Contributions

This book makes some theoretical as well as practical contributions and enhances the understanding of the strategic management process in the Arab Gulf States. Specifically, it serves the following purposes:

1) It enhances the understanding of practitioners, academicians, and students of the nature, importance, and scope of the service industries in the Gulf States.
2) It attempts to identify differences in strategies and structures among key players within each selected service industry.
3) It provides Arab students with culturally relevant case studies which helps bring realism expeditiously and effectively into the classroom.
4) It raises the level of aspirations of Arab readers by exposing them to "success stories" from their own environment.
5) Finally, the book scrutinizes the applicability of Western management concepts to the Arab Gulf States.

Plan of the book

This book consists of three parts. Part I sets the stage. It surveys the distinctive characteristics of the Gulf business environment and the service firms operating in that environment. Chapter 2 outlines the basic physical, economic, socio-cultural, and macro-managerial factors that the Arab Gulf States have in common. It highlights those environmental constraints that are believed to have a direct bearing on the strategic choices of the sampled service firms. Chapter 3 differentiates between the service-producing and goods-producing industries. It outlines the universal characteristics of services and the special characteristics of service organizations in the Arabian Gulf region.

Part II is the crux of the book. In contrast to the preceding part which surveys the landscape, this part focuses on the forest and the trees. It consists of several chapters. Each examines a different service industry and the pattern of strategic adaptation followed by different member firms. The structure of each industry is analyzed in detail using Michael Porter's framework (1980). Key success factors and key trends are identified. Our aim throughout is to help the reader sort out the universal (industry-specific) from the related (region-specific) and the unique (firm-specific) patterns of strategic postures. The strategy followed by each firm is traced from its inception up to the time the case study was written. The resource profile unique to each firm is described in detail along with functional area strategies, using published data and selective interviews.

Two points need to be emphasized immediately. First, in preparing industry notes and writing case studies severe gaps in data were encountered. At times, relevant data on the status of each sampled industry in a given Arab Gulf State could not be found. We encountered similar difficulties in obtaining financial data on the sampled firms. Second, the issues and problems raised in each case study defy neat pigeonholing. The suggested focus for each – as indicated in the teaching notes – merely indicates major topic(s) for discussion. To a degree, the choice of focus is a matter of taste and personal preference of the instructor.

Part III is the conclusion. It is here where we can fit together the disjointed pieces of the Arabian puzzle. After analyzing the strategy and structure of the Arab service enterprise and relating these to their environmental context, the reader is invited to compare the Eastern with the Western approach to strategic management.

References

Greshuny, J. (1978): *After industrial society*, London: Macmillan.
Heskett, J.L. (1986): *Managing in the service economy*, Boston, Mass: Harvard Business School Press.
Porter, M.E. (1980): *Competitive strategy*, New York: Free Press.
Riddle, D.I. (1986): *Service-led growth*, New York: Praeger Publishers.

Chapter 2
Understanding the Business Environment

M. Sami Kassem

Introduction

Much like Western Europe, the Arabian Peninsula can be regarded as a distinctive cultural area. This is for two reasons. First, within the area there exists a pattern of life sufficiently different from the cultures of other regions to endow it with a character and personality of its own. Second, the way of life within the different countries of the Arabian Peninsula is generally uniform. With hardly an exception, people within the area speak Arabic, believe in Islam, and share the same physical habitat, mode of life, traditional values, and historic roots. Moreover, each of these states is experiencing the same economic, administrative, and modernization dilemmas. There hardly exists another region in the world whose constituent countries have so much in common as those of the Arabian Peninsula. These countries, which comprise the membership of the Gulf Cooperation Council (GCC)[1], are: Saudi Arabia, Kuwait, Bahrain, Qatar, the United Arab Emirates, and Oman (see Exhibit 1), North and South Yemen, while on the Arabian Peninsula, are not members of the GCC and are not included in this work.

To further grasp the ties that bind the GCC states, let us briefly examine the physical, socio-cultural, economic, and administrative setting of the GCC bloc.

---

[1] The Gulf Cooperation Council was officially formed in 1981 to coordinate and unify economic, industrial, educational and defense policies of the six member states. It is interesting to note that during the 1970's there had been several attempts to form a union composed in part of the states that would ultimately compose the GCC. Intra-regional rivalries and renewed conflicts aborted these earlier attempts.

The organization of the GCC closely resembles the political systems and hierarchies of the member states. The combined ministers of any single activity (such as health or education) may function as a council. The Supreme Council, composed of the six heads of state, is the top policy-making body of the GCC. The presidency of the group rotates every year in alphabetical order. The Supreme Council meets every six months and may also choose to meet for extraordinary sessions. Biannual meetings are commonly referred to as summit meetings. For further information on the history, composition, and policies of the GCC, see Anthony, (1982).

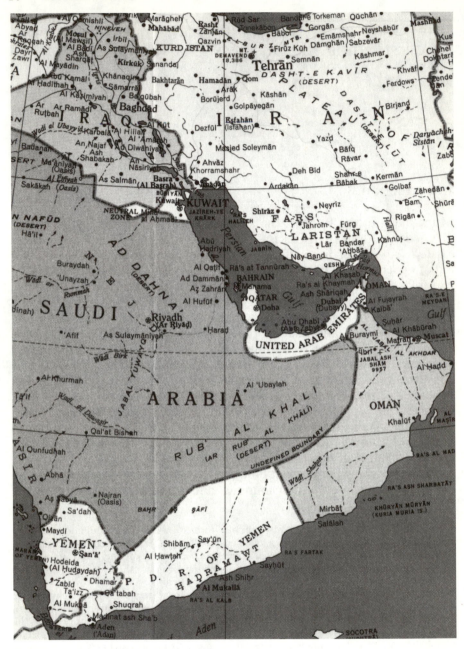

Exhibit 1   The Arab Gulf States
Source: New World Atlas © Copyright 1988 by Rand McNally & Company,
R. L. 88-S-190

Physical and Geographic Environment

The Arabian Peninsula as a whole contains some striking physical contrasts between mountains and flat plains, sandy deserts and rocky terrain, extreme heat and cold, oasis and desert, extreme aridity inland and extreme humidity on the coasts. Each of the countries of the peninsula has some of these contrasts as well in varying extent. Yet, the region as a whole is quite uniform, and each of its countries, with the exception of the island nation of Bahrain, is part of the same land mass. Bahrain's climate and topography is very close to that of the peninsula's eastern coastal region.

Climate and Land

Aridity is so characteristic of the area that the area has been called "the dry world." The most serious limiting factor to cultivation is not land but water. Lack of rainfall sharply limits the amount of cultivable land to an estimate 5% of the total area.

Mineral Resources

Apart from oil and natural gas, the mineral resources of the Arab Gulf States are generally of marginal importance. They are widely scattered, remotely located, difficult to extract, and generally uneconomical to exploit.

Geographic Importance

Another factor that influences the lives and destinies of the inhabitants of the region is its strategic importance in world business, and geopolitics. First, its often fresh and lucrative markets consume and test a lot of manufactured goods, services, and products arriving from all corners of the earth. Second, it has been the major supplier of oil and petrodollars to the industrialized economies of the world, and it contains about three quarters of the earth's proven oil reserves. Third, it is the location of the holy sites of Makkah and Medina in Saudi Arabia. More than one billion Muslims pray to Makkah five times a day. Last, but not least, the peninsula serves as a bridge between Europe and the Far East. Not unexpectedly, historically this region has been the center of great power rivalries and remains to be so today.

The Social and Cultural Setting

The common cultural heritage of the Arab Gulf States is characterized by:

The Islamic Tradition

The peninsula is the birthplace of Islam, which is the religion of more than 90 % of its population. In contrast to other religions, Islam is a way of life, prescribing not only man's relation to God but also his relation to his fellow men. It spells out man's obligations as a husband, father, employer, employee, borrower, lender, neighbor, and citizen. Islam, therefore, serves as a focal point for Arabian society and culture. An Islamic spirit permeates the entire region and all aspects of life – private, political, social, economic, and religious. In fact, the influence of Islam and its myriad social perscriptions in everyday life seems to be growing rather than waning (Dessouki (1982), El Ashker 1987, and Guillaume 1981).

The Arab Heritage

There are millions of people in the Gulf area who consider themselves Arabs, speaking a common language and sharing a common heritage. Although Islam is an essential part of this heritage, the Arabic tradition predates Islam and is not exclusively Islamic. Just as not all Muslims are Arabs, not all Arabs are Muslims. Nevertheless, the shared Arab heritage is the core of a vital force affecting most of the Arabian Peninsula today; Arab nationalism, Islamic fundamentalism, and the drive to regional cooperation are all aspects of this force.

Traditional Social Structure

Arabian society is basically a traditional society. It consists of three main types of people: nomads, in ever decreasing numbers, villagers, and townsmen, living in three kinds of mutually dependent communities – the tribal camp, the village, and the town or city. Economic and social institutions are relatively simple and organic. Traditionally, the village raised vegetables and fruits which were consumed by the townsmen and nomads; the nomads raised animals for food and transport to the villages and townsmen; and the latter produced and imported manufactured goods and served as middlemen in the barter between the villagers, the nomads, and others. This structure, while still present to a large extent, is changing rapidly with the industrialization of the area and the advent, for example, of large agribusiness replacing small farms.

However, traditional kinship groups, whether tribal or familial, remain of prime importance. The extended family is a basic social unit even in the larger urban centers. A folk type of culture predominates Arabian society: status is *ascribed* by such factors as age, sex, or family name, and is not necessarily *achieved*. Nevertheless, urbanization and industrialization have put stress on the traditional social fabric of the extended family.

The Economic and Business Environment

There are at least five important economic factors characterizing the GCC countries.

Over-dependence on Oil

Hydrocarbons will continue to propel the economies of the Arab Gulf States. However, the recent oil glut and the consequent decline in revenues have convinced the governments of the GCC countries to build economies which are less susceptible to the vagaries of the market.

A key strategic issue facing national planners is which sort of economies to build. Since agriculture development is not feasible in most of these states, industrialization seems to be the best way out. For instance, Saudi Arabia has already taken major steps in this direction, with the construction of energy-intensive industries such as petrochemicals, steel, fertilizer, and cement plants. Some Gulf economists argue that investing abroad, not at home, is the appropriate strategy for the area. They argue that the high cost of labor, management, imported technology, and raw materials outweighs the cheap cost of energy in the region; and they point to the small size of the domestic market, all of them are factors that put the area's industry at a competitive disadvantage. Kuwait and Oman are leading proponents of this alternative "international investment" strategy.

Shortage of Endogenous Labor

The GCC states depend heavily on imported labor to staff, operate and manage their organizations. The participation rate of the local component of the total labor force is as low as 15 % in the United Arab Emirates and as high as 21 % in Bahrain.

As the current recession continues, Gulf Arabs may become less reluctant to do the jobs that need to be done. Nevertheless, the GCC states continue to rely on Indians, Pakistanis, Bangladeshis, Thais, Koreans, Filipinos, and Sri Lankans in large numbers for unskilled and semi-skilled work. Other Arabs, Europeans, and Americans continue to perform many skilled and professional jobs. Expatriates have built the massive infrastructure projects, both huge and small manufacturing projects, and the large and small housing projects. Expatriates ("guest workers") continue to operate and maintain many of these projects, as well as countless small businesses. Their contribution helped speed up the economic and social development of the GCC states. For one thing, they expanded the size of the local labor market and improved its efficiency. They also expanded the size and broadened the offers of the GCC product markets. They enriched the quality of life of the Gulf Arabs. However, they also posed a threat to local culture and foreign currency reserves. GCC authorities saw in the recession an opportunity to send foreigners home in large numbers. Among those who remained, some are being replaced by cheaper substitutes, others by locals.

Shortage of Management Talents

Not only does the area's economy suffer from shortages of local labor but also of experienced management.

The GCC states have invested heavily in higher education. They have produced lots of engineers, geologists, scientists, accountants, economists, and statisticians, but few well-trained managers. Only a tiny minority of these managers are well-placed. This fact reinforces the suspicion that in this part of the world, managerial positions are primarily ascribed, not earned, particularly in the public sector.

As with skilled labor, the GCC states turn to the international markets to recruit the managers they need, and they have to pay a premium to attract them. They often must provide them with free luxury housing, schooling for their children, hospitalization, and air transportation to their homeland once or twice a year. The combined effect of these practices is to drive the payroll cost astronomically high. With this built-in handicap, it is no wonder that Gulf service organizations sometimes find it difficult to compete at home and abroad without government subsidies. Air carriers in the Gulf states are a case in point.

To minimize the risks of making wrong choices, some Gulf service organizations rely on long-established international firms to manage their local organizations on their behalf for a fee. The international management contract has been and will remain an accepted way of running complex service organizations particularly in this part of the world (Brook 1985).

Minor Role for the Private Sector

In contrast to its counterpart in the Western economies, the private sector plays a very minor – if not marginal – role in the GCC economies. In Saudi

Arabia, the dominant economy of the region, the private sector contributes about 20 % of the gross domestic product (GDP). It has not been given a chance to participate in the development of national economic plans. Instead, its role has been limited to the implementation of those plans. Even then, its role has been nominal, as in finding the right foreign partner to bid on a large-scale construction project. Once the project is completed, the partnership is usually dissolved.

Traditionally, trade has been in the hands of the private sector, and this is still true today. It has always been a respectable occupation for the Arabs. The Prophet Mohammed himself was a trader. Indeed, the merchant class has evolved into an elite – with business ventures and offices throughout the GCC states.

Nowadays, the private sector is flirting with small-scale manufacturing and service activities such as hotels, hospitals, and schools. This has been precipitated by government policy which offered private businessmen in selected high-priority sectors a set of financial incentives, ranging from interest-free loans and direct subsidies to duty-free imports, cheap electricity, and cheap developed land.

For several reasons, the private sector has not played a more vigorous role in the GCC economies. First, it does not have the capacity to do so. It lacks the technical skills, experience, and the requisite capital. Second, it also has a guarded attitude toward risks. Arab entrepreneurs generally seek quick, not distant, returns. Hence they shy away from long-term industrial projects in favor of short-term gains in trade. Last, but not least, government bureaucracies in the region tend to be unsympathetic, self-centered, and domineering, which deprives the private sector of its fair share of opportunities that are instead given away to the public sector.

Given the marginal role of the private sector in the GCC economies, the governments of these states have assumed the dominant role in the economy of these countries. Throughout the area, it is government that owns and operates the oil fields. It is the government that orchestrates development, through its direct involvement in and encouragement of business activities. The government is also the biggest employer. About six or seven out of ten employed Gulf nationals work for their respective governments. Finally, it is the government that regulates the operation of the local economy: banks, hospitals, commercial airlines, hotels, restaurants, the press, schools, and so on.

The GCC governments play the role of the industrialist and employer directly through their own bureaucracies and through a network of specialized public organizations and corporations. The latter approach has become most popular (Abdul Rahman 1982), since it grants each public organization the autonomy it needs to conduct its business with utmost flexibility and public accountability.

Abundance of Cheap Capital

In contrast to other developing countries, the GCC states are not short on capital, thanks to oil. Presently, some GCC countries are strapped for cash, but overall they still have plenty of reserve or other available capital to spend on financing government works and the private sector's high-priority investment projects. For instance, the recent decision of the Saudi government to pay 5 million (Saudi Riyals) (US$ 1.33 million) for every service station SASSCO builds on Saudi highways is proof that even in hard times the government plays a key role in stimulating local development and economic activity.

Organizational and Administrative Setting

Students of Arab management have identified a number of salient characteristics which collectively describe Arabian Gulf management systems. These characteristics can be grouped into two models discussed below.

Arab Organization Model: Bedoaucracy

The sociological indicators of the Arab organizational model, which is termed "bedoaucracy",[2] (derived from "Bedouin") are:

1) a moderate degree of vertical and horizontal specialization;
2) a low degree of coordination stemming from the exercise of personal authority and extensive use of committees;
3) a low degree of behavior formalization and highly "bendable" rules;
4) personnel decisions (i.e. selection, placement, promotion, compensation, etc.) based on flexible criteria subject to wide personal preferences and judgments and leading to overstaffing and disincentives to work hard or smart; and
5) a high degree of centralization of decision-making.

---

[2] We are not the first to coin this term. Just as it was natural for Max Weber to discover bureaucracy and develop its indicators, so it was for Arab students of Public Administration to discover bedoaucracy. Al Awaji (1971), Abdul Rahman (1982), Al Nimr and Palmer (1982), Al Hegelan and Palmer (1985) and Al Hashemi (1988) have all developed the theme that Arabia is a transitional society. Despite the introduction of modern organizations and methods, administrative behavior is still highly traditional. Consequently, overlapping of modern and traditional elements is a major feature of present-day Arabian bureaucracy. Other features include over-centralization of authority, overstaffing, personalization, formalization, nepotism, and corruption. These features continue to prevail because they are functional both to leaders and followers alike.

The underlying model of an organization for the Gulf Arabs is the tribe. Undisputed authority rests with the head of the tribe – the sheikh. Bedoaucracy is clearly a hybrid. It combines elements from both Western models of bureaucracy, with its emphasis on efficiency, and the traditional bedouin culture with its emphasis on tribal solidarity collective decision-making and communal welfare. This model worked well in old and large organizations operating in the relatively simple and stable environments of yesterday. As will be clearly seen in the case studies, it becomes a liability when used in the complex and turbulent business environments of today.

Arab Management Model

What are Arab managers from the Gulf like? How do they behave? How do they approach their jobs? The Gulf Arab manager tends to behave as follows[3]:

1) resists innovation and change;
2) seeks authority and likes to display bossiness;
3) averts responsibility and decision-making;
4) admires and respects his superiors;
5) plays favorites;
6) hates to plan, yet likes to control;
7) prefers secure to high-paying jobs;
8) motivates his subordinates by fear and negative strokes.

These behavioral tendencies seem to fit the cultural expectations facing a typical manager.

According to Hofstede (1980), cultural values impact all aspects of life, including work organizations and their management. By studying organization-related values in more than 50 countries for more than a decade, Hofstede isolated four dimensions of national culture which differentiate one culture from another. These dimensions apply to societies – not to the individuals – which each must answer in its attempt to organize the efforts of its members to achieve collective goals. These dimensions are:

1) Power distance: this concerns the issue of how society deals with the distribution of power among the haves (the powerful) and the have-nots (the powerless). This dimension is reflected in the values of both groups and relates to such issues as centralization of authority.
2) Uncertainty avoidance: the issue involved here is the way society deals with the future, the unknown, and the uncertain.

---

[3] This model is a composite which is based on the writings of several students of Arab management such as Badaway (1980); Muna (1980); Al Nimr and Al Mudaifer (1982); Al Hegelan and Palmer (1985), Saud (1985), and Kassem and Al Mudaifer (1987).

3) Individualism-collectivism: the cardinal issue involved here is the relation between the individual and his fellow teammates.
4) Masculinity-femininity: the issue here is how society deals with the distribution of roles between the sexes. This dimension also indicates the relative importance a society places on such "masculine" values as assertiveness, performance, and independence versus such "feminine" values as close personal relationships, cooperation, quality of life, and materialism.
5) Traditionalism-modernism: this scale is added by Kassem and Al Modaifer (1987) to capture the realities of the Arab world. It evaluates the extent to which a society socializes its members to seek innovation, universalism, and secularism or to reject these norms.

Kassem and Al Modaifer's findings (1987), are summarized in Exhibit 2. The data show that Saudis in comparison to Americans are high on power distance and uncertainty avoidance, and low on individualism, "masculine" values, and modernism.

Exhibit 2   The Saudi and American Cultural Maps Compared

| Dimension | Saudi Sample | | U.S. Sample | |
	Hofstede	Kassem	Hofstede	Kassem
Power distance	80	84	40	48
Uncertainty avoidance	68	64	46	10
Individualism	34	34	91	49
Masculine values	53	32	62	64
Traditionalism				
– Resistance to change*	–	9.7	–	13.7
– Particularism*	–	17.5	–	19.3
– Secularism*	–	20.1	–	30

* Low values mean high score
Source: Kassem and Al Modaifer (1987).

These findings, although slightly different from those of Hofstede, help explain the uniqueness of the Arab management system.

The high power distance scale explains the twin phenomena of excessive centralization and autocratic leadership. Gulf Arabs simply expect their leaders to lead them autocratically and to make decisions for them. In other words, centralization and autocracy are part of the mental programming of Arab managers and Arab employees alike. They are part of the same value system. The high uncertainty avoidance score tells us that Saudis do not tolerate uncertainty and ambiguity. They prefer to work with explicit rather than implicit rules. This reading of the Saudi cultural map explains the tendencies to delegate upward, to avert responsibility, to insist on multiple signatures and stamps, and to refer every minor matter to a committee.

The low individualism and by implication the high collectivism score explains the prevalence of particularism, nepotism, and favoritism – a phenomena which cannot be entirely stamped out by legislation or administrative reforms, no matter how carefully designed they happen to be. By contrast, the relative success of recent policies, aimed at putting local nationals in the driver's seat, can be explained by their local appeal. Simply put, these policies are culturally congruent.

Finally, the combination of high uncertainty avoidance with high power distance explains the ambivalence of Gulf Arab subordinates to their superiors. Having a powerful superior whom one can both praise and blame is an easy way of satisfying a strong need for avoiding uncertainty.

Summary and Conclusion

The foregoing makes it clear that meaningful similarities exist within the Arab Gulf States which render the region unique. No other region in the world of comparable size shares so many climatic, topographic, socio-cultural, economic, and administrative attributes.

It is only natural that the GCC states should form an economic union. They have learned that in union there are synergies – what economists call economies of scale. Each constituent state faces a series of challenges. None can face up to all these alone, hence, the case for the regional approach to socio-economic development. For instance, one of the toughest challenges facing the GCC states is diversifying away from oil. Fishing, agriculture, and tourism are not feasible strategic alternatives, whereas small-scale manufacturing, services, and foreign investment are. But these states cannot exploit any of these strategies successfully unless they pool their resources to achieve economies of scale in operation, marketing, maintenance, and training. Otherwise, their products and services will be priced out of the market. Airlines are a case in point.[4] GCC carriers cannot compete

---

[4] Arab airline industry displays the same consumption patterns of American hospitals. Within the UAE, for example, two contiguous states, Dubai and Sharjah, built international airports withing a few kilometers of each other. Likewise, both Bahrain and Dhahran have similar facilities although, in each case, one airport would be sufficient. Each

effectively with giant international carriers because of their relatively high cost structure. Should they cooperate by pooling costly facilities and operating joint flights, their cost structure could allow them to compete more effectively.

References

Abdul Rahman, O. (1982): *Oil bureaucracy and the development dilemma*, Kuwait: National Council for Culture, Arts, and Humanities.

Abdul Rahman, O. (1986): *The dilemma of development in the Arabian Peninsula*, Kent, England: Croom-Helm.

Al Ashker, A. A. (1987): *The islamic business enterprise*, Kent: U. K.: Croom-Helm.

Al Awaji, I. (1971): Bureaucracy and society in Saudi Arabia, Unpublished doctoral thesis, University of Virginia.

Al-Hashemi, Ibrahim (1988): Management development in transition: "The Gulf experience", *International Journal of Manpower*, 9:1:3–7.

Al Hegelan, A. and Palmer, M. (1985): Bureaucracy and development in Saudi Arabia, *The Middle East Journal*, 39,1: 48–68.

Al Jaffary, A. and Hollingsworth, A. T. (1983): An exploratory study of management practices in the Arabian Gulf, *Journal of International Business Studies*, Fall: 143–152.

Al Maney, A. J. (1981): Cultural traits of the Arabs: Growing interest for international management, *Management International Review*, 21: 10–18.

Al Nimr and Palmer, M. (1983): Bureaucracy and development in Saudi Arabia: A behavioral analysis, *Public Administration and Development*, 2: 93–104.

Al Qobaisi, A. (1985): Toward a comparative administration study of the Arabian Gulf States, *Journal of the Gulf and Arabian Peninsula Studies*, 42: 75–94.

Anastos, D., Bedos, A., and Seaman, B. (1980): The development of modern management practices in Saudi Arabia, *Columbia Journal of World Business*, Summer: 81–91.

Arab Gulf carrier operates a modern fleet, its own maintenance, catering, printing, technical and management training, and computer reservation facilities. Now the oil boom that caused this massive over-investment has ended, and inefficiencies that went unnoticed yesterday are more glaring today. Sharply reduced oil revenues and depressed traffic revenues are forcing industry officials to reconsider what they are doing. Ambitions are reappraised. Some operations are overhauled. Others are shut. Without some form of cooperative planning among Arab carriers, the outcome of this unsettling process may be bleak. For further details on the pros and cons of regionalism, see Sherif 1984.

Anderson, D. A. (1987): *Management education in developing countries*, Boulder, CO: Westview.

Anthony, J. D. (1982): The Gulf Cooperation Council, *Journal of South Asian and Middle Eastern Studies*, Summer.

Badawy, M. K. (1980): Styles of Middle Eastern managers, *California Management Review*, 21: 51–58.

Berque, J. (1964): *The Arabs* (Trans. Jean Stewart), New York: Praeger.

Birks, J. S. and Sinclair, C. A. (1980): *Arab manpower: The crisis of development*, New York: St. Martin's Press.

Chackerian, R. (1983): Public bureaucracy in Saudi Arabia: An empirical assessment of work group behavior, *International Review of Administrative Science*, 49: 3.

Dessouki, A. E. (1982): *Islamic resurgence in the Arab world*, New York: Praeger.

Fernea, E. W. and Fernea, R. A. (1985): *The Arab world: Personal encounters*, New York: Doubleday.

Guillaume, A. (1981): *Islam*, New York Penguin Books.

Hofstede, C. (1980): *Culture's consequences*, London: Sage.

Johany, A., Berne, M., and Mixon, W. (1987): *The Saudi Arabian economy*, Baltimore: Johns Hopkins University Press.

Jreisat, J. E. and Ghosheh, Z. (1986): *Administration and development in the Arab world*, An annoted bibliography, New York: Garland.

Kassem, M. and Al Modaifer, K. (1987): Bureaucracy and society in the Arab world: A replication and extension of Hofstede's value survey model, *Working Paper*, Dhahran: King Fahd University of Petroleum and Minerals.

Kubursi, A. (1984): *Industrialization and development in the Arab Gulf States*, London: Croom Helm.

Learner, D. (1958): *The passing of traditional society*, New York: The Free Press.

Mansfield, P. (1980): *The Arabs*, New York: Penguin Books.

Muna, F. (1980): *The Arab executives*, London: Macmillan.

Niblock, T., ed. (1980): *Social and economic development in the Arab Gulf*, New York: St. Martins Press.

Roukis, G. and Montana, P. (1986): *Workforce management in the Arabian Peninsula*, Westport, CT: Greenwood Press.

Saud, S. F. (1985): *Management & leadership styles of American, Arab and Southeast Asian managers*, Unpublished doctoral dissertation, U.S. International University.

Shabon, A. (1981): *The political, economic and labor climate in the countries of the Arabian Peninsula*, Research Report 9: Multinational Industrial Relations Series, Philadelphia: The Wharton School.

Sherif, A. (1984): The concept and practice of regionalism: The experience of the Arab carriers organization, *Regionalism in International Air Transportation*, Papers from an international conference organized by the M. I. T. under the auspices of Alia: The Royal Jordanian, Amman: Alia.

Wright, P. (1981): Doing business in Islamic markets, *Harvard Business Review*, Jan/Feb.

Wright, P. (1981): Organization behavior in Islamic firms, *Management International Review*, 21: 86–93.

Chapter 3
Distinctive Aspects of Services in the Arab Gulf States

Ghazi M. Habib

Introduction

In any economy, there are goods-producing industries, such as manufacturing, mining, construction, agriculture, forestry, and fishing, and there are service industries.

Classical theory describes economies as passing through three stages: the agrarian stage, manufacturing stage, and a stage of services. Levels of development often are equated with the stage an economy is in. Some countries may virtually skip the industrial phase altogether and become tertiary or service economies before becoming full-fledged industrial societies (Shelp et al. 1981).

Shelp (1985) asserts that a nation becomes a service economy when more than half of its work force is employed in productive intangible services.

Section C of Exhibit 1 shows that service industries account for a larger percentage of Western industrial countries' employment than any other major industry group. Shelp (1985) contends that if governmental services are included, approximately seven out of ten Americans are employed in the service sector. Furthermore, Linden (1978) estimates that more than 45% of the average U.S. family's budget is spent on services.

With regard to Arab countries, Exhibit 1 (section B) shows that in 1980, the service industries accounted for as little as 22% of employment in Sudan and Yemen Arab Republic, and as much as 62% in Lebanon and 64% in Jordan. Furthermore, it is noteworthy that the average annual growth rate of the labor force in these Arab countries is higher than in several leading industrial countries.

Exhibit 1 (Section A) shows the shifting composition of the labor force (1965–1980) in Kuwait, Oman, Saudi Arabia, and the United Arab Emirates. The World Bank report (1986) provides no statistics for either Bahrain or Qatar. The percentage of the labor force employed in service industries in Kuwait and the United Arab Emirates in 1980 was 67% and 57%, respectively. Given the similarity among the Arab Gulf States with

Exhibit 1   Changing Composition of the Labor Force in Arab and Selected Industrial Countries, 1965–1980

Country	Percent of Labor Force Agriculture Industry Service						Average Annual Growth of Labor Force (Percent)		
	1965	1980	1965	1980	1965	1980	1965–1973	1973–1984	1980–2000
A. Arab Gulf States									
Bahrain	–	–	–	–	–	–	–	–	–
Kuwait	1	2	34	32	64	67	5.3	6.9	3.1
Oman	62	50	15	22	23	28	–	–	–
Qatar	–	–	–	–	–	–	–	–	–
Saudi Arabia	68	49	11	14	21	37	3.9	5.9	3.2
United Arab Emirates	20	5	32	38	47	57	–	–	–
B. Arab countries									
Algeria	57	31	16	27	26	42	1.6	3.6	4.1
Egypt	55	46	14	20	30	34	2.1	2.5	2.5
Iraq	50	31	20	22	30	48	2.9	3.1	3.8
Jordan	36	10	26	26	37	64	2.6	1.6	4.7
Lebanon	28	11	25	27	47	62	2.5	– 0.1	2.1
Libya	40	18	21	30	39	53	3.6	4.1	4.1
Morocco	62	46	15	25	24	29	1.8	2.6	3.1
Somalia	81	76	6	8	13	16	3.8	2.6	2.6
Sudan	82	71	5	7	13	22	2.8	2.4	2.8
Syria	52	32	20	32	28	36	3.1	3.4	3.9
Tunisia	49	35	21	36	29	29	1.3	2.9	2.9
Yemen Arab Republic	79	69	7	9	14	22	1.0	2.1	3.2
Yemen, PDR	54	41	12	18	33	41	1.1	1.8	2.6
C. Selected industrial countries									
Canada	10	5	33	29	57	65	2.7	2.0	1.1
France	17	9	39	35	43	56	0.7	1.1	0.7
Germany, F.R.	10	6	48	44	42	50	0.3	0.8	– 0.1
Japan	26	11	32	34	42	55	1.7	1.1	0.7
United Kingdom	3	3	47	38	50	59	0.2	0.5	0.2
U.S.A.	5	4	35	31	60	66	1.9	1.6	0.9
USSR	33	20	33	39	33	41	0.7	1.1	0.5

* estimated
Source: The World Bank 1986: 238.

regard to economic conditions, work ethic, and the high average annual growth rate of the labor force, it is our estimate that if governmental services are included, more than 60 % of the work force in the Arab Gulf States of Bahrain, Kuwait, Oman, Qatar, Saudi Arabia, and the United Arab Emirates is, as of 1988, working in the service sector.

Before addressing particular aspects of services in these states, let us first examine some of the salient characteristics of services everywhere.

Characteristics of Services

A good is a tangible physical object, a device, a thing that can be created, inventoried, and possessed. A service is intangible and perishable. It is an occurrence, a process, a deed, a performance, an effort (Berry 1980, Sasser et al. 1978). Service organizations, such as airlines, hospitals, hotels, banks, consulting firms, schools, taxis, and barbershops, sell intangible products that can be consumed but not possessed. When a customer buys an airline ticket or a taxi ride, he or she is buying the right and the convenience of being transported from one place to another. In essence, the passenger has bought a service and the experience that comes with it, but he or she has bought no physical good that can be taken home at the final destination.

Shostack (1977) and Sasser et al. (1978) showed, separately, that there is a bipolar continuum comprised of tangible dominant physical goods, such as automobiles on one side, and intangible dominant services, such as teaching on the other. Shostack asserts that it is wrong to suggest that services are similar to goods except for intangibility. She argues that a service is rendered and experienced, but cannot be stored, touched, tasted, or tried on for size.

Inseparable Functions

Brown (1985) argues that production and consumption are literally inseparable when it comes to services. The lecturer delivers a speech while the audience consumes it simultaneously. A patient consumes a doctor's or dentist's service at the same time it is being produced.

Berry (1980) asserts that goods are generally produced first, then sold, and then consumed. By contrast, services are usually sold first, then produced and consumed at the same time. The telephone company sells the customer the right to make a long-distance call, the call itself is both produced and consumed when the customer dials the number.

The simultaneous production and consumption of services has important implications. First, it allows the provider to customize his service according to the customer's specifications. Second, because services are perishable and cannot be inventoried, synchronizing supply with demand becomes crucial. A vacant seat in an airplane or a vacant room in a hotel is wasted if unused at any given moment and cannot be stored for times of peak demand.

Problem of Quality Control

In an interview conducted in 1979 by Gary Knisely (1979) with James Schorr of Holiday Inn Inc., Schorr stated:

"A major difference between product marketing and service marketing is that we can't control the quality of our product as well as a P & G control engineer on a production line can control the quality of his product. When you buy a box of Tide, you can reasonably be 99 and 44/100 % sure that this stuff will work to get your clothes cleaned. When you buy a Holiday Inn room, you're sure at some lesser percentage that it will work to give you a good night's sleep without any hassle, or people banging on the walls and all the bad things that can happen to you in a hotel."

Lovelock (1984: 5) attributed the difficulty of controlling service quality to the involvement of both customers and service personnel in assembling the service that takes place under interactive real-time conditions.

Berry (1980) used Thomas' (1978) classification of services to suggest that people-based services tend to be less standardized and uniform than equipment-based services or goods-producing operations. Thus, in labor-intensive industries, customer contact personnel assume a tremendously important responsibility in producing and delivering the service. This necessitates recruiting the right personnel, training them well, motivating them, supervising them, and replacing the ones who do not maintain acceptable standards.

Evaluating Quality

Zeithaml (1981) contends that the intangibility, non-standardization, and functional inseparability of services make their quality harder to evaluate than the quality of goods. She identified three types of quality:

1) search qualities or the attributes that a consumer can determine prior to purchase, such as color and style;
2) experience qualities or the attributes that can be determined after a purchase or during consumption; and
3) credence qualities or the attributes which the consumer may find impossible to evaluate even after purchase and consumption, such as the appropriateness or necessity of a medical operation to remove one's tonsils.

Managing Supply and Demand

Because services are perishable and cannot be inventoried, the real challenge for a service manager is to find the best fit between supply (capacity) and demand. Sasser (1976) suggested the following options in managing demand:

1) Use a peak load pricing strategy as employed by telephone and airline companies.
2) Stimulate non-peak demand through price discounting, as hotels and airlines do.
3) Develop complimentary services to divert consumers away from bottleneck operations, such as providing game or TV entertainment while the consumer waits to be served in a restaurant or airline ticket office.
4) Create a central reservation system as utilized by hotels and airlines.

Sasser (1976) also suggested options for managing capacity or supply:

1) Use part-time employees.
2) Maximize efficiency through: (a) delivering essential tasks only during rush hours; (b) checking if certain skills are lacking or are inefficiently used; (c) redesigning the service delivery system; and (d) cross-training personnel to perform several tasks.
3) Delegate some of the tasks to the consumer, such as in self-service restaurants and other enterprises.
4) Share capacity with others.
5) Design the right capacity from the beginning.

Services in the Arab Gulf States

Economists contend that a nation becomes a service economy when more than half its work force is employed in producing intangible services (see Shelp et al. 1981). And since more than 60 % of the labor force in the Arab Gulf States are employed in service industries, technically, these states qualify as service economies.

Services are more important in the economies of the Arab Gulf States than is generally recognized and probably will gain more importance in the years ahead. The bulk of the work force is currently working in these industries, and Gulf governments spend most of their budgets on services. Furthermore, the rising affluence of the population of the region and the exposure of Gulf nationals to a variety of services when they visit Western developed countries are creating new categories of needs that are likely to be satisfied by services rather than goods (see Greshuny 1978).

Services in Arab Gulf States share the following characteristics.

Negative Social Connotations

Hospitality and service are part of the Arab culture, which honors those who serve others: "The servant of the group is their master." King Fahd of Saudi Arabia recently assumed the title servant or "custodian" of the two holy shrines – in Makkah and Medina. Islam, as the religion of the vast majority of Gulf citizens, stresses the importance of hospitability and serving others. However, in recent times, probably due to the rising affluence of Gulf citizens, the word "services" has begun to connote demeaning work. Many Gulf citizens, especially those with tribal heritage, refuse to engage in any service-related job, such as a hair-dresser, hotel or hospital receptionist, airline steward, laborer, technician, and many others. Ironically, they accept working as drivers, operators, secretaries, tea boys, messengers, and civil servants. In our judgment, occupational or career preferences in services in the Gulf states are affected by social status, degree of job independence, and the perception of whether the job is a "man's job" or "woman's job". This is particularly true in Saudi Arabia.

Built-In Cost Disadvantage

A number of factors, when taken together, have put the service industry in the Arab Gulf States at a comparative disadvantage. First, despite the huge geographic area of the Arab Gulf States, the total population of these states is only around 16 million. The vast bulk of both area and population lies within Saudi Arabia, which covers 2,150,000 square kilometers and has about 11.1 million people. Second, these states suffer from a shortage of skilled manpower and experienced managers, and from an immature local industrial and technological base. This has resulted in a need to import foreign labor, managers, technology and know-how, as well as equipment and spare parts at exorbitant prices.

Inadequate Marketing

The presence of numerous service enterprises in the region along with the declining market size due to the departure of many expatriates ("guest workers") in most of these states has several implications. First, only the fittest among the existing service organizations will survive. Second, marketing, as a way to synchronize supply and demand, becomes extremely important. Third, price wars become a common phenomenon in airlines, hotels, hospitals, consulting, and other service organizations. Finally, quality becomes a key success factor.

In the Arab Gulf region, marketing has not yet been discovered. As a function, it is often synonymous with sales. In status and power, it is often subservient to operations in many service organizations. In our judgment, the reason for this is that many managers in the region come from engineering backgrounds and have no formal education in management.

Additionally, little internal marketing takes place in most Arab Gulf organizations. That is, little is done to persuade personnel to provide the customer with a satisfactory level or quality of service. One executive in a leading service organization in the Gulf said that, despite huge investments in selecting and training customer-contact personnel, they still refuse to smile or be courteous to the customer. They are quick to remind their superiors that they are government employees whose task, as they perceive it, is to process customers' papers and not to perform public relations work.

Unevenness of Quality

Although unevenness of service quality is a universal problem, it takes on an added color in Gulf service organizations. Its sources are multiple: the high labor-intensity of many services, weak internal marketing, and a high turnover of foreign labor. To alleviate this problem, many Gulf service firms, especially airlines and banks, are resorting to automated machines as much as possible.

Regulation and Protectionism

One of the oldest arguments for protecting local industries from foreign substitutes suggests that initial output costs for a developing industry in a certain country may be so high that it renders the industry non-competitive in a deregulated market, but over a period of time the costs will decrease as operating efficiences are achieved (Daniels et al. 1983: 138). One can find examples of industries, such as commercial airlines and banking in Singapore and Japan, that have become competitive because of initial government protection. However, the danger is that a new industry will become dependent on subsidies and thus remain at only a static level of operating efficiency at a time when Gulf consumers are becoming better informed, and less committed to buying local goods and services unless they compare favorably with foreign substitutes, especially in terms of price.

Lack of Innovation

It is quite conspicuous that many Gulf service organizations adopt a strategy of risk-minimization by copying other businesses that have proven successful. This strategy has two pitfalls. First, Gulf firms that imitate other successful businesses typically do not conduct feasibility studies to find out whether the market has already reached a saturation point. Second, copying others can mean that firms have overlooked other more innovative opportunities including some that could prove to be very lucrative.

Summary and Conclusion

This comparative chapter has highlighted the importance and character-istics of the service sector in the Western and Arab Gulf worlds. We have argued that the Arab Gulf States are service societies where more than 60 % of their labor force is employed in service-related industries.

Intangibility, functional inseparability, perishability, and the difficulty of controlling quality are universal features which differentiate service from goods-producing industries. Service establishments in the Arab Gulf States are unique, however. They are characterized by (a) the absence of a service tradition, (b) high operating costs, (c) poor marketing, (d) an uneven quality, (e) a regulated market environment, and (f) lack of endogenous innovations.

References

Berry, L. L. (1980): Service marketing is different, *Business Week*, (May–June): 24–29.
Brown, S. W. (1985): Service marketing demands different approach, *D & B Reports*, (September/October): 52–53.
Chase, R. B. (1978): Where does the customer fit in a service organization, *Harvard Business Review*, 56,6 (November–December): 134–142.
Daniels, J., Orgam, E. Jr., Radebaugh, L. (1983): *International business environments and operations*, Addison-Wesley Publishing Co., Inc., Menlo Park, California.
Greshuny, J. (1978): *After industrial society*, London: Macmillan.
Gronroos, C. (1983): *Strategic management and marketing in the service sector*, Cambridge, Mass.: Marketing Science Institute.
Heskett, J. (1986): *Managing in the service economy*, Boston: Harvard Business School Press.

Heskett, J. (1987): Lessons in the service sector, *Harvard Business Review*, 65 (March/April): 118–126.

Judd, R.C. (1967): The case for redefining services, *Journal of Marketing*, 28 (January): 59.

Knisely, G. (1979): Greater marketing emphasis by Holiday Inn breaks mold, *Advertising Age*, January 15.

Linden, F. (1978): Service, please, *Across The Board*, 15,8 (August): 42.

Lovelock, Ch. H. (1980): Towards classification of services, in: *Theoretical developments in marketing*, C.W. Lamb and P.M. Dunne (Eds.), Chicago: American Marketing Association, 72–76.

Lovelock, Ch. H. (1983): Classifying services to gain strategic marketing insights, *Journal of Marketing*, 47,3 (Summer): 9–20.

Lovelock, Ch. H. (1984): Distinctive aspects of service marketing, in: *Services marketing*, Englewood Cliffs, NJ; Prentice-Hall, Inc.

Sasser, W.E. Jr. (1976): Match supply and demand in service industries, *Harvard Business Review*, 54,6 (November–December): 133.

Sasser, W.E., Olsen, R.R., and Wyckoff, D.D. (1978): *Management of service operations: Text and cases*, Boston: Allyn & Bacon.

Schmenner, W.R. (1986): How can service business survive and prosper, *Sloan Management Review*, 27,3 (Spring), 21–32.

Shelp, R. et al. (1981): *Services industries and economic development*, New York: Praeger Publishers.

Shelp, R. (1985): Service technology and economic development, *Economic Impact*, No. 25, 8–13.

Schostack, G. L. (1977): Breaking free from product marketing, *Journal of Marketing*, 41 (April): 73–80.

Thomas, D. R. E. (1978): Strategy is different in service business, *Harvard Business Review*, 56 (July–August): 158–165.

World Bank (1986): *World development report*, Washington, D.C.: World Bank.

Zeithaml, V. A. (1981): How consumer evaluation process differ between goods and services, in: *Marketing of services*, J.H. Donnelly and W.R. George, (eds.), Chicago: American Marketing Association.

Part II
Industry Notes and Company Cases

Chapter 4
The Airline Industry

4.1 A Note on the Arab Airline Industry

M. Sami Kassem

Introduction

Ours is a jet age. The modern airplane has replaced the ship, the railroad, and the automobile as the carrier of first preference, just as these displaced the camel. Man has always dreamed of flying, as if on an instinctive quest to bridge the distance between himself and his fellow man. In the 20th century, this dream came true.

Shortly before World War II, airplanes were used in the Middle East on a very limited basis, to transport mail between Cairo, Basra, and Jeddah. There was no way to get a letter quickly from Cairo to Riyadh, for example, except to have it shipped from Suez to Jeddah and then airmailed from Jeddah to Riyadh. There were very few airports in the Arab world, and no more than a single small airport in each nation.

After World War II, German JU52 planes were used to move precious goods and important dignitaries and VIPs, just as they were used before in moving "desert mail." With the revolution of rising expectations of the 1960s, the oil bonanza of the 1970s, and the advent of the jumbo jet, air travel turned from a luxury to an "essential undifferentiated commodity" affordable by the masses.

The commercial airline industry has been singled out by the policy-makers in developing nations, in general, and Arab countries, in particular, for special attention. To them, an important aspect of development was the ability to move people and goods from part of the country to another and, consequently, the reduction of differences in lifestyle between the city and the village. In many cases, as soon as a developing country secured its independence, it launched its national flag carrier, not only as a symbol of independence and national pride, but also as a way to link different parts of the nation together as well as the nation as a whole with the rest of the world.

Policymakers of developing nations – Arab countries included – expected their national flag carriers to be neither profitmakers nor chronic money-losers. At the same time, they often realized that the private sector of their respective economies was neither courageous nor altruistic enough to finance the proposed national airline. For this and other reasons to be discussed later, the governments of most developing nations were compelled to set up, finance, and operate their national flag carriers. Not unexpectedly, the newly-born airlines have been and still are guided not strictly by the logic of the marketplace, but by the developmental goals set by the political apparatus. In other words, many of these airlines were and still are run not as business enterprises but as public utilities like the telephone, electricity, and post.

This section explores the status, economics, structure, and trends of the Arab airlines industry. Although there are 18 members who belong to the Arab Air Carriers Organization (AACO), we shall limit ourselves by way of example and analysis to Saudia, Kuwait Airways, Alia, and Gulf Air. These carriers all operate as flag carriers in the service of their respective countries. They are all state-owned. Not all of them are profit-oriented, but all of them serve as instruments to achieve national, political, and social objectives. Finally, they all operate under a degree of state protection.

The airline industry is of strategic importance. While it accurately mirrors the aspirations, achievements, and frustrations of the Arab states, it also creates many jobs, absorbs large sums of capital, moves a lot of goods and people, and brings nations as well as people closer to one another.

Present Status of Arab Carriers: A Statistical Profile

A quick glance at Exhibit 1 shows that the Arab carriers have a combined fleet of 300 jets. By 1985, they had carried 33 million passengers, 391,000 tons of cargo, and achieved an average seat factor of about 58 % and a load factor of about 53 %. Even though their growth rate has been on the decline lately, these carriers grew at a healthy annual rate of 15 % over the 1973 to 1983 period – one of the highest growth rates in the international air transport industry.

Arab carriers employ about 81,000 persons, but a high percentage of these are non-Arabs. For instance, 35 % of the pilots, 50 % of the cabin crews, and 35 % of the engineers and technicians are foreigners – a fact that makes Arab carriers, in general, and Gulf carriers, in particular, less competitive than other international carriers. For instance, a European stewardess working for Saudia gets paid twice as much as she gets at home.

Exhibit 1   Arab Aircarriers – Statistical Profile (1985)

Airline	Fleet	No. of Employees (000)	No. of Passengers (000)	Cargo Tons	Passenger Load Factor %	Overall Load Factor %
Kuwait Airways	18	6.2	1,498	43,712	46.8	55
Saudia	101	25.5	10,795	165,556	47.3	60
Alia	16	4.5	1,290	40,620	51.6	57.1
Gulf Air	20	3.8	2,870	52,042	54.8	57.1
Egyptair	27	11.6	2,766	41,175	52.8	56.7
Syrian Air	14	3.3	476	4,492	53.7	57.5
Iraqi Air	N/A	N/A	N/A	N/A	N/A	N/A
Libyan Air	31	4.8	1,579	5,430	60.2	58.3
Sudan (Nile) Air	N/A	N/A	N/A	N/A	N/A	N/A
Middle East Air	14	4.8	501	15,573	46.3	46.4
Tunis Air	15	4.6	1,260	11,594	65.7	65.3
R.A. Maroc	18	4.1	1,114	15,999	52.2	58.3
Algerian Air	25	1.7	–	–	–	–

Source: IATA and carriers' 1986 Annual Reports.

If she is Asian or Middle Eastern (non-Saudi), she earns three times as much as she would in the same job in her own country.

In their route network, many Arab carriers are oriented more to international than domestic markets. For the last 10 years, they have contributed 6% of the total world air traffic. Three quarters of that contribution was devoted to traffic between the Arab countries and the rest of the world, particularly European countries. This pattern of outward orientation – strange as it is – explains why a Moroccan or Tunisian bound for Makkah may have to fly to Paris first and then connect to Jeddah. This suggests the failure of some Arab carriers to meet the regional and domestic needs of Arab passengers.

Industry Economics

The airline produces a service, sells it, deducts expenses, and either earns a profit or realizes a loss. One measurement of the core service an airline produces is the available seat kilometer (ASK) – one seat flown one kilometer. If that seat is filled by a paying passenger, it is called a revenue passenger kilometer (RPK). The actual relationship between ASK and RPK is expressed as a percentage termed the load factor. This is an important measure of a carrier's profitability: the higher the load factor, the greater the net income. Just as in lodging, the service an airline produces is a perishable one. Like an empty room in a hotel for a night, an empty seat on a flight cannot be stored and is lost forever as revenue.

Market share is another determinant of a carrier's profitability. A carrier attempting unilaterally to restrain capacity will suffer more than a proportionate loss in market share. By contrast, a carrier with greater capacity should be able to outperform the competition by substantially expanding its market share. For instance, a carrier competing on the Cairo/Jeddah route faces a dilemma: adding capacity during peak season (the Hajj or pilgrimage season and times when large numbers of Egyptian teachers travel to or from Saudi Arabia) decreases its load factor, even though it increases its market share.

The airline industry is one of high fixed costs. A carrier's costs are more directly related to the number of seats (ASK) flown over a given route. When it comes to costs, ASK per route is the unit of analysis. With respect to revenues, the passenger is the unit of analysis. Once a plane is scheduled to fly to a given destination, the total cost of that flight is substantially fixed, regardless of the number of passengers that plane is carrying.

Whereas costs are tied directly to ASK, revenues are related to (1) the number of passengers carried, (2) how far they are flown, and (3) how much each one pays per kilometer flown. These factors are measured in terms of RPK. The profitability of an airline is determined by the spread between the actual load factor and the break-even load factor (B.E.L.F.). The break-even load factor is calculated as follows:

$$\text{B.E.L.F} = \frac{\text{fixed costs (per flight)}}{\text{(revenue yield - unit variable cost)}}$$

Industry Structure

The thesis of this section is that Arab carriers need to change their operations in order to survive and prosper (Regionalism 1983). They need to convince their governments to open up their skies and airports to other Arab carriers and Arab passengers. Second, they have to learn to operate as business corporations whose primary objectives are to "create customers," serve them well, and earn a profit. They cannot expect to live indefinitely on government subsidies and/or the goodwill of customers, whose patience is not infinite.

Arab airlines are a mirror of the Arab nation, reflecting its fragmentation, frustration, and obsession with senseless regulations. These airlines have the following attributes:

1) With the exception of Saudia, they are all small in size. Individually, they cannot benefit from economies of scale in training, purchasing, maintenance, and operations. But collectively, they can.
2) With the exception of Middle East Air, they all are state-owned and state-run corporations. This has, all too often, led them to assume too much and function in a less than competitive manner.
3) With the exception of Saudia, they all are operating without the benefits of a sizeable domestic network. This built-in geographic handicap compels them to devote their energies and resources in the service of their international network, a fact which brings them in direct competition with the giant, experienced carriers of the Western world as well as with many lean, but well-managed carriers of the developing world (e. g., Singapore Airlines, Cathay Pacific).

In the absence of tight public accountability, the great majority of Arab carriers behave irresponsibly. Instead of linking parts of the Arab world together, they have lobbied for tighter regulations and more protectionism. Instead of serving the needs of the Arab traveler for high-quality service at competitive prices, they have offered sub-standard service at first-class prices. For instance, a Dhahran-Cairo passenger on Saudia is expected to pay a high price and spend a whole working day on the trip. Ironically enough, it would cost him less in both time and money (12 vs. 27 cents per mile) to fly to London than to Cairo or Amman. Unless that passenger is an expatriate employee returning home on a government ticket, many would be tempted to go to London using the services of a foreign flag carrier such as British Caledonian, Lufthansa, or Cathay Pacific. Those carriers often know more about the psychographics, demographics, and travel needs of the Arab passengers than Arab carriers themselves.

Who is the loser when passengers fly non-Arab carriers? In our example, Saudia loses a passenger. Thus, its planes will fly below capacity and its losses will multiply. It may then ask the government for more protection from the "unfair" practices of foreign competitors and for a fare hike to cover its losses. This can become a vicious circle, with higher prices leading, in turn, to further underutilization of the fleet.

In the process, the national economy of each Arab state gets hurt as the opportunity fades to deploy its resources efficiently. Arab tourism also suffers: as the load factor of the national flag carrier drops, so does the occupancy rate of hotels. Even the captive market that the state flag carrier often serves – i.e. government employees – is not invulnerable. It is constantly being pirated by aggressive foreign carriers and travel agents skilled in baiting government employees. For example, many expatriate employees working for a government agency in one oil-rich Arab country prefer to avail themselves of a regulation that allows them to cash in their

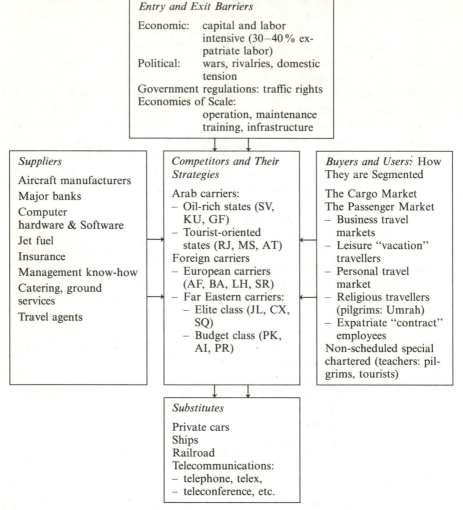

Entry and Exit Barriers

Economic: capital and labor intensive (30–40% expatriate labor)

Political: wars, rivalries, domestic tension

Government regulations: traffic rights

Economies of Scale: operation, maintenance training, infrastructure

Suppliers

Aircraft manufacturers

Major banks

Computer hardware & Software

Jet fuel

Insurance

Management know-how

Catering, ground services

Travel agents

Competitors and Their Strategies

Arab carriers:
– Oil-rich states (SV, KU, GF)
– Tourist-oriented states (RJ, MS, AT)

Foreign carriers
– European carriers (AF, BA, LH, SR)
– Far Eastern carriers:
  – Elite class (JL, CX, SQ)
  – Budget class (PK, AI, PR)

Buyers and Users: How They are Segmented

The Cargo Market

The Passenger Market
– Business travel markets
– Leisure "vacation" travellers
– Personal travel market
– Religious travellers (pilgrims: Umrah)
– Expatriate "contract" employees

Non-scheduled special chartered (teachers: pilgrims, tourists)

Substitutes

Private cars
Ships
Railroad
Telecommunications:
– telephone, telex,
– teleconference, etc.

Exhibit 2   Competitive Forces in the Arab Airline Industry

Note: Abbreviations explained in Exhibit 5
Source: Primary

assigned round-trip repatriation ticket on the national carrier for 50% of its face value. They turn around and buy a similar ticket from their favorite foreign carrier, getting the route and time they want and often saving money to boot. Asked why they are sometimes ungrateful about receiving paid tickets on the national carrier, these passengers often reply: "We hate to be taken for granted and treated like cargo. It's a shame. But we are human beings, too!"

Is there an answer to these problems? In our opinion, a massive but gradual restructuring of the Arab airline industry and dramatic strategic alignment by its members are needed. This would involve a reorientation to the principles of free-market economics and learning from the experience of others. Arab governments hold the key to the revitalization of their airline industry (Ghandour 1979a). Individually, each must ultimately sell its flag carrier to the private sector. Collectively, they must loosen their grip on the movement of Arab people and aircraft throughout the Arab world.

However, it is not necessary for Arab governments to blindly follow the Americans' lead and open their skies to all kinds of commercial traffic. But as a mature industry, the Arab airlines have to stand more on their merits and become less dependent on government support.

The Arab airline industry has its own distinctive underlying structure. A brief analysis of that structure provides the economic rationale for our conclusions. It also helps identify the critical factors that impact the airline industry and affect its performance.

According to Porter (1980), competitiveness and profitability depend on five basic forces, which are shown in Exhibit 2. Each of these is treated below.

Entry and Exit Barriers

Economic Factors

The airline industry is capital-intensive. The purchase of a single modern long-haul aircraft (such as B747-400) represents a US $ 100 million capital outlay. This is an amount beyond the cash capabilities of most airlines of developing countries. Entering international money markets to borrow the necessary funds can be extremely difficult and, at times, fruitless if international interest rates and domestic political risks are high. This has prompted Mr. Ali Ghandour, Alias's chief executive officer, to say, "I found myself working hard for the banks!" (Ghandour 1980)

Some airlines' underutilization of capacity and their efforts to generate cash by selling aircraft made many used planes available in the international market at bargain prices. Planes, unlike cars, are built to last for 12 to 15 years. Executives of Arab carriers have been reluctant, though, to buy anything except the latest aircraft on the market.

The airline industry is not only capital-intensive, but also labor-intensive. Aircraft need to be manned while airborne and serviced, loaded, and unloaded while on the ground. Moreover, ticket sales, boarding, and disembarking services are all labor-intensive activities requiring numerous personnel at widely dispersed urban and airport locations. The availability of the right number and right quality of cockpit and cabin crew, as well as technical, maintenance, sales, customer service, administrative, and managerial personnel, is critical to success. Since these talents are in short supply in the Gulf states, they have to be imported – along with the aircraft – at a premium. The importing carrier has to provide for the orientation, housing, and transportation of foreign personnel and their families, as well as schooling for their children. This tends to put Arab carriers, particularly in the Gulf, at a severe cost disadvantage. Thus, whereas labor costs represent about one-third of the total operating costs of major American and European carriers, they represent about one-half for Gulf carriers.

This cost differential is perhaps the main reason that Gulf carriers cannot and will not be able to innovate low-fare strategies for years to come. They also will not be able to join the price war which is going on in their backyard and sustain it for a long period of time without incurring heavy losses. As long as some Gulf carriers refrain from heavily investing in the training of personnel – pilots, aircraft mechanics, avionics, and mechanical engineers – chances are there will not be the equivalent of "People Express" in Arabia.

Political Factors

The Middle East is plagued by continual strife, political uncertainty, and economic dislocation. The area is affected by at least three problems: the Arab-Israeli conflict, the Iran-Iraq war, and intra- and inter-Arab rivalry. These problems have taken their toll and left a permanent mark on the Arab airline industry. They have affected the movement of people and goods, changed the faces of nations, and established the norms of Arab airline operations (e. g., excessive delays due to extensive security checks, exorbitant insurance premiums, unusually high fuel bill). Everything an Arab airline does, every decision it makes, is dictated by the highly volatile situation in this part of the world.

To illustrate the debilitating effect of inter-Arab rivalry, let us consider the case of Gulf Air (GF). GF is to the Gulf states what SAS is to the Scandinavian countries. As of late, GF has been threatened by a disagreement among its partners. The Bahrain-based carrier is owned by the governments of Bahrain, Abu Dhabi, Qatar, and Oman. Until recently, it was a leading money-maker. Weakening economic conditions in the Gulf states have hurt the airline which saw its profits decline from US $ 51 million in 1984 to a loss of $ 6 million and $ 7.6 million in 1986 and 1987 respectively. In an effort to rationalize operations and cut costs, GF drastically reduced frequencies to and from Dubai, Qatar, and Oman – a move which alienated and outraged those states, particularly Dubai. It saw the service cutbacks as too much of a penalty to pay for issuing temporary operating permits (TOPs) to some non-Arab carriers – to the detriment of Gulf Air routes. Dubai retaliated by starting its own carrier – "Emirates." Similarly, both Oman and Abu Dhabi plan to pursue a more independent aviation policy, a move which might further hurt GF's profitability in years to come. Emirates has already forced GF to switch more services away from popular Dubai to nearby, but less accessible, Sharjah. Other problems could surface as the new airline's proposed European route network gets under way by mid-1987. To add insult to injury, Emirates is looking to involve both the cities of Fujairah and Ral Al-Khaimah in the new setup – supposedly to achieve economies of scale.

Another overriding concern is the Arab-Israeli problem. Until the Palestinian problem is settled, and until the Arab states learn to live together in synergistic cooperation, it will be difficult to achieve permanent peace in the Middle East and for all airlines in the region to operate economically. Alia chairman, Ali Ghandour, an articulate spokesman for the Arab airline industry, summed up the impact of the unstable political situation in the Middle East on the area's airlines:

Until we have peace, there can be no real strategic business planning. We find ourselves buying aircraft not on the basis of pure economy or comfort but after detailed consideration of such factors as range and ability to operate under adverse conditions. So, you see, without peace we must live each day, as it comes; the victims of perpetual crisis management. (Ghandour 1979 b)

Government Regulation

The international airline industry is not characterized by high economic barriers to entry. However, non-economic considerations greatly complicate the entry process. It would be relatively easy to get a new airliner off the ground if there were no controls on entry. The newcomer does not have to own the "road" over which its equipment travels, nor the terminals (i. e. airports). The equipment can be bought on credit or leased, and the crew can be hired in the international market. The entry barriers seem so few that even small and less fortunate Gulf states have jumped into the business as of late. All it takes for the newcomer to enter the business or for an existing airline to expand into a new market (i.e., a pair of cities) is to obtain commercial traffic rights on the chosen route or sector. These rights or "freedoms" (see Exhibit 3) can be obtained only through inter-governmental negotiations, which are typically influenced by political considerations. Bilateral agreements resulting from these negotiations are typically modeled after the Bermuda I agreement, and usually spell out the

Exhibit 3   Types of Traffic Rights: The Six Freedoms

To get a new airline off the ground, many rules and regulations have to be met. The most important ones of these are commercial traffic rights on the airline's targeted routes. These rights are based on the recommendations of the International Conference on Civil Aviation held in Chicago in 1944 and are commonly known as the Six Freedoms. They are shown here in their simplest form. Take contracting states, A and B.

Freedom One: The right to fly from state A through the airspace of state B.

Freedom Two: The right to touch-down in state B, not to pick-up or disembark passengers but for emergency landings or other technical reasons.

Freedoms one and two are generally referred to as the "*technical freedoms*" or "*technical rights*."

Freedom Three: The right to carry commercial traffic from state A to state B.

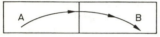

Freedom Four: The right to carry commerical traffic from state B to state A.

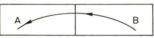

Freedom Five: The right to carry commercial traffic from state A to state B plus "fill up" traffic from or via intermediate states.

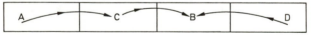

Freedom Six: The right to carry commercial traffic from state B to state A from or via intermediate states.

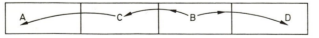

city-pairs to be served, amount of capacity, flight frequency, type of aircraft, and departure times.

As for the regulation of rates, in the past the practice was to have the airlines concerned agree between themselves on the fares and cargo rates they will charge or have these fares established by IATA (the International Air Transport Association), subject to ratification by the concerned governments. This is essentially how the "airline game" has been played over the last 40 years or so.

The industry is now witnessing a new game called deregulation. Although American in conception, the new game caught many carriers – giant and small, Arab and non-Arab – unprepared. To understand the new game and evaluate its impact on Arab carriers, let us first examine the regulation era.

Simply put, regulation means government intervention in the working of the industry. Such intervention remains one of the most controversial issues facing aviation policymakers at the present time (Levine, 1987). However, its effect on the strategic management function of commercial airlines is indispensable. For the last 40 years, government regulation has touched every aspect of the industry: market entry and exit, the type of service provided (scheduled vs. charter), capacity, frequency, and pricing. Why has the airline industry been so tightly regulated throughout its history?

There are two sets of answers or arguments for regulation. The first is akin to those invoked for other modes of domestic public transportation. Under this set of arguments, regulation aims to:

1) safeguard public safety;
2) offer protection to scheduled services;
3) maintain industry stability by limiting entry and prevent wasteful duplication, overcapacity, too many empty seats, and resultant fare wars;
4) maintain a wide route network;
5) maintain air service on thinly traveled (unprofitable) routes; and
6) promote regional accessibility within a country.

The other set of arguments relates to airlines' international services. It includes the following two major provisos or regulatory principles:

1) Each state has a sovereign right to its airspace. No foreign flag carrier can penetrate that airspace unless it is authorized to do so and issued "a foreign air carrier permit."
2) Like the steel, petrochemicals, and electronics industries, airlines are susceptible to the infant industry phenomenon, in which new entrants face major obstacles. Substantial differences in the efficiency and competitive ability between participants in the airline industry point to this fact, which partially explains why IATA's list of the 10 most productive airlines has never included a Third World carrier. Free competition from giant carriers with superior service and lower costs may result in heavy losses to the infant carrier. These fears, real or

imagined, have led small developing nations to regulate competition and often subsidize, directly or indirectly, the operations of their flag carriers. This practice, in turn, has prompted established airlines from more developed countries to complain that they face unfair competition brought on by subsidization and other government practices, such as requirements that citizens use the national airline. Regulated competition has almost always proved to be the best way out under these circumstances.

What has been the impact of regulation on the airlines of developing countries?

In the past, newly established carriers of the developing countries were not pleased with the way the airline game was played. They suffered from restrictions on capacity and flight frequency. The developed countries kept the newcomers on the periphery of the game. Ali Ghandour, a pragmatic advocate of regional cooperation, noted in a speech before the Middle East Civil Aviation Conference in June 1979:

For several years we were flying 707's on certain routes with a Caravelle capacity, i.e., maximum of 82 seats out of 150. 58 % seat factor was our ceiling. And even third and fourth freedoms were denied to us except subject to heavy royalties to be paid by Alia to major airlines of the advanced and industrialized or oil-rich countries. All those empty seats and royalties must be paid for by somebody by way of losses, higher fares, or government subsidies. *(Ghandor 1979a)*

Whereas the airlines of developing countries suffered from such costly restrictions, they enjoyed IATA's multinational system of setting fares. According to that system, fares were determined with an eye toward offsetting costs instead of stimulating growth. Consequently, fares ended up higher than they would otherwise have been under more competitive conditions. Understandably, both new and established carriers seemed quite happy with the system. The least efficient carriers felt comfortable with the protection they were getting from IATA, while the most efficient carriers of developed countries stood to reap undue gains.

Thus, the financial interests of the airlines were well-served, but only at a cost. IATA's regulations and controls had the effect of dulling management's ability to see new opportunities and exploit them. Management lost its freedom to respond quickly to changing market conditions the more it became involved in inter-carrier and inter-governmental negotiation and compromise. There is now a feeling that such inflexibility brought on many problems which in the future can only be avoided by less rigid controls.

Since the Chicago conference of 1945, the economies of Western Europe and Japan have recovered and boomed, as have the economies of most developing countries. Air travel has ceased to be an American monopoly.

The advent of the Jumbo jet, coupled with rising living standards around the world, revolutionized and expanded the international air travel market. Pent-up demand for air travel at a reasonable price made it possible for charter companies to enter the field on a large scale, tapping the newly developed mass market. These "non-skeds" (non-scheduled) demonstrated that the demand for international air travel is relatively price-elastic.

These changes in the market prompted the U.S. government to deregulate its domestic airline industry in 1975. The success of the domestic experiment encouraged the administration of President Jimmy Carter to unilaterally deregulate international air transportation with the passage by the U.S. Congress of the Airline Deregulation Act of 1978. This bombshell set in motion a complete transformation of the world airline industry. It removed all market-entry barriers and fare controls.

The response of Arab carriers to deregulation has been uneven. Carriers of the oil-rich states have fought it staunchly. They ignored the trend toward reduced fares. In their drive to "clean up" their markets, they blacklisted travel agents suspected of dumping foreign carriers' tickets. This protectionist urge stems from the fact that most of their networks are made up of thin routes with seasonal peaks and limited room for growth. They cater primarily to expatriate employees from neighboring Arab and Asian countries who travel annually at their employers' expense. Travel on these routes is restricted by visas. Fares are higher on these routes to cover the cost of empty seats in the low season or on "dead hauls" to pick up passengers traveling primarily in only one direction.

By contrast, airlines of tourist-oriented Arab countries (e. g., Egypt and Jordan) resigned themselves to deregulation and tried to adapt. Quietly, they joined the discounting wave to stimulate traffic on dense routes. They relaxed restrictions on visas. They added new long-haul routes, particularly to America, to their network. Quietly, they capitalized on their geographic location and touristic appeal to compete for fifth and sixth freedom traffic (see Exhibit 3). Alia and Egyptair are good cases in point.

Fortunately, Arab carriers do not have to choose between the extremes of rigid protectionism and unbridled competition. Both extremes are equally bad for them. The former suits nations with thin international routes, while the latter suits countries with developed airlines, well-established routes, and open skies. Since Arab countries do not strictly fit either profile, they would be better off adapting themselves to the new game, at least in the short run. In the long run, it behooves them to pool their resources, experiment with joint ventures to reduce unit costs, operate long routes, diversify their gateways, tap new markets, and create integrated computerized reservations system that are responsive to the needs of their volatile environments.

Economies of Scale

Probably the greatest amount of academic interest in airlines as business has centered on the question of economies of scale. Nevertheless, the issue has been somewhat muted in the airline industry itself, because government protection has taken the edge off market forces that otherwise would help determine the optimal size of the carriers. Yet, even in a protectionist environment, the issue of economies of scale is important. It affects the efficiency and profitability of both protected and unprotected carriers. Clearly, unprotected European carriers with lower average costs have a large competitive advantage over Gulf carriers that have diseconomies of scale but enjoy certain protection from their governments.

Saudia, one of the world's 10 largest airlines, if well-structured and well-managed, should have the lowest operating costs among Arab carriers. To achieve this, perhaps it should consider spinning off parts of its system into more manageable entities (domestic, international, cargo) to avoid diseconomies of scale. The experience of Alia, which has been more profitable than Saudia for the last 20 years, points to the efficacy of this approach. Both Alia and Saudia are government-owned carriers, but their size and management differ substantially. Alia is financially healthier, not only because it is leanly run but also because its management is business-like and relatively unimpeded by uneconomic structures. Moreover, the Jordanian government has relaxed all visa restrictions, something that is not likely to happen soon in Saudi Arabia – beyond the Gulf Cooperation Council states – which have already relaxed visa restrictions for each other's citizens.

Admittedly, recent evidence fails to substantiate any systematic relationship between average costs and airline size. Nonetheless, economic logic suggests that economies of scale do exist in air transport operations. For instance, an aircraft's operating costs decrease as its seating capacity increases (giving rise to the familiar U-shape cost curve). Likewise, the costs per kilometer decrease as stage length increases (see Appendix 1). These economies are achieved because the marginal costs of labor, fuel and capital become lower as aircraft capacity increases. There are also costs associated with starting and ending a flight stage. As a result, the airline planner must look for efficient routing – large on board loads to and from high-yield markets. There can also be economies of scale in passenger and aircraft handling at larger and busier stations with more efficient use of facilities and labor. Such economies can be achieved in maintenance and crew training: the larger the size of the fleet, the lower the maintenance costs per aircraft, and the lower the training costs per pilot and crew member.

Suppliers

Airline suppliers provide the industry with an array of products and services (see Exhibit 2).

Aircraft manufacturers are obviously a key group of suppliers. They provide aircraft, spare parts, and often training devices and maintenance technology. They are a concentrated group who can and do exert significant bargaining power over the airline industry.

Banks and financial institutions are another key resource for the airline industry. This group includes numerous suppliers of capital with no single source being a major provider. The purchase of even a single wide-bodied aircraft can involve a syndicate of several domestic and international banks.

A modern airline, like a modern international bank, cannot function without sophisticated information technology. Computerized reservations systems (CRS) provide a carrier with a powerful anti-competitive weapon (Gilbert, 1988; Copeland et al., 1988), i.e. the instant booking of airline seats, hotels and hire cars at given rates. American mainframe manufacturers dominate the hardware scene, while subsidiaries of major American carriers (e.g. Covia and AMR) provide the software.

Of all the supplier groups, fuel companies have the greatest impact on the airline industry. They know there is no substitute for jet fuel. In the oil-producing Gulf states, the jet-fuel bill surprisingly represents about 50% of the total operating costs of GCC carriers, against an industrywide average of 25%.

Insurance companies are another concentrated group of suppliers who have considerable bargaining power over Arab air carriers. Political instability and the escalation of the Gulf War increase the risk of plane hijackings. The insurance premiums for Arab carriers are raised accordingly.

Other supplier groups are not as concentrated and, as such, do not exert significant bargaining power. Management consulting firms, aircraft maintenance companies, catering firms, aircraft leasing firms, advertising and travel agencies fall into this category.

Travel agents are the most numerous and visible providers of airline services. Deregulation of the global airline industry has increased both the number of carriers serving the Arab world and those passengers who now go fare shopping. The channels of distribution for services have also altered greatly. Some indigenous carriers have intensified efforts to rid local markets of unfair dumping by foreign carriers, placing the latter under pressure to abide by the law. These have transferred the booking and selling of seats and tickets from their city ticket offices (CTOs) to travel agencies, whose share of all tickets sold has risen from 50% to 85% since 1975. The remainder are government tickets issued by CTOs of the respective flag carrier.

In the Arab world, travel agencies are mostly small, individually owned, and neither franchised nor fully computerized. Often dependent on telephone and couriers, these agents make use of personal local contacts to reserve scarce seats before these are released to the computer system.

Competitors and Their Strategies

According to Porter (1980), eight factors promote competition in an industry:

(1) numerous competitors,
(2) competitors of roughly equal size and power,
(3) slow industry growth,
(4) lack of differentiation in service,
(5) high fixed costs,
(6) high exit barriers,
(7) perishability of the product, and
(8) a diversity of rival strategies.

The Arab airline industry exhibits most of these characteristics. It is experiencing competition in a way it has never seen before. About 40 air carriers – Arab and foreign alike – are battling fiercely to expand their customers' base in order to improve rapidly deteriorating load factors. Once a genteel, clubbish, and discrete service industry, whose members competed primarily on service and scheduling, airlines have become aggressively competitive over the past few years. While the Arab air travel market was once one of the fastest-growing markets in the world, it is now one of the slowest. "It is a war out there, and it is going to get worse before it gets better," an industry spokesman noted.

The reasons behind this pessimistic forecast are as follows: first, the weakened economy of the Gulf states hurts airlines directly in several ways. Demand for leisure and business air travel has slowed. Many travelers simply postpone or cancel their travel plans, spend their vacations close to home, or, if they do travel by air, shift from first or business class to economy class. The economic slowdown also has caused employers to send expatriate workers home permanently, thus depriving Gulf-based carriers of their "core market."

Second, Gulf carriers have a lot of excess capacity resulting from over-sized, under-utilized fleets.

Finally, competing international-class carriers are making passenger pickup stops at airports in the Gulf countries at marginal cost on their way to or from the Far East (Gimson 1986).

Despite the economic slowdown in oil-exporting states, the Arab air travel market in general is worth about US $ 7 billion. The lion's share of it (about US $ 5 billion) is taken by non-Arab carriers. Let us attempt to learn why.

Arab Carriers

There are two groups of Arab carriers. The first is made up of carriers who belong to the oil-rich states: Saudia (SV), Gulf Air (GF), Kuwait Airways (KU), and Emirates Air. With the exception of Emirates, they all have a fairly extensive international route network, ultra-modern fleet, and unusually high-cost structure. These carriers are handicapped by security considerations and visa restrictions, a fact which prevents them from developing transit passenger traffic. Promotional strategies frequently used by giant international carriers are of little value to the GCC carriers.

The second group is made up of carriers that belong to the tourist-oriented Arab countries (e. g., Alia, Egypt Air, Middle East Air, Royal Air Maroc). Virtually all of them are deprived of a domestic market and, therefore, must concentrate on international routes. As pointed out earlier, they compete for the tourist, transit, and labor traffic. Alia is the most notable member of this group and the most aggressive one of all Arab carriers. It was the first one to see deregulation as an opportunity to expand its network and innovate low fares. It is, for example, the first Arab carrier to fly to New York, Chicago, and Los Angeles. It is also the top Arab carrier in terms of profitability.

Non-Arab Carriers

There are two groups of non-Arab carriers who share in the US $ 5 billion Arab market. Both groups are aggressive marketers. Because of their comparatively low-cost structure, they are able to promote fare wars and innovate new services (e. g., business class, special hostesses for unaccompanied minors, Hajj meals for pilgrims). Both types thrive on fifth and sixth freedom traffic to fill their planes, which in turn enables them to offer competitive fares.

The Giant European Carriers

This group is made up of the elite carriers of the Western world (e. g., Air France, Lufthansa, Swissair, British Airways, and KLM). It is they who collectively wrote the book on the airline game, developed its rules, and perfected its service standards. It is they who developed the technology and have the aircraft, trained pilots, skilled mechanics, experienced cabin crews, and efficient management systems that glue all these pieces together. It is they who span the globe more frequently than others. In short, it is they who have the upper hand in the airline game. They cannot afford to lose.

These carriers are serious about their business. Take Swissair for example: it has six sales offices in Egypt (five in Cairo, one in Alexandria), and five in Saudi Arabia (two in the Eastern Province, one in Riyadh, and two in Jeddah). By contrast, Egypt Air has only two offices in Switzerland. Likewise, Saudia has only two.

The Far Eastern Carriers

This group has become strategically important, particularly in the Gulf passenger market. It is made up of two subgroups:

1) *The elite carriers* (e.g., Singapore Airlines, Cathay Pacific, and Japan Airlines): this subgroup appeals to business travelers who appreciate both superior service and competitive fares.
2) *The budget carriers* (Pakistan International, Air India, Thai Air, Philippine Airlines, Korean Air, etc.): these carriers belong to the labor-surplus countries. As such, they capitalize on the labor traffic emanating from or destined to their base cities. They capitalize on their low-cost position to offer budget fares, decent service, and direct nonstop flights to major GCC capitals.

How Do the Players Compete?

Low Fares

Air carriers compete by offering lower fares and better services than their competitors. Deregulation probably is here to stay, and victory will go to those carriers who manage to cut their operating costs the most (Lynch 1984). Arab carriers, in general, and Gulf carriers, in particular, are endangered because of their high cost structure and relatively poor service image. For an analysis of how selected Arab carriers compare with their foreign counterparts on selected cost items, see Exhibit 4.

Better Services

Service is another key competitive weapon. To the majority of Arab carriers, it is still a slogan, but to most international-class carriers, it is a "religion."

4.1 A Note on the Arab Airline Industry   53

Exhibit 4   Arab Vs. Foreign Carriers – Cost Comparison (1984)

Carrier	Total Wage Bill US$ (000)	No. of Employees	Average Wage ($)	Maintenance expense per aircraft hour	PAX service expense in $ (000)	RPK's (000)	PAX service exp. per RPK in cents	GAE in $ (000)	Total operating Expense	GAE as % of total oper. exp.
Singapore	200,168	9,948	20,121	830	154,059	20,890,300	0.74	19,858	1,299,294	1.5%
KLM	447,163	19,193	23,298	1,130	118,667	17,980,645	0.66	67,998	1,514,701	4.5%
British A.	882,545	36,096	24,450	n.d.	n.d.	34,206,000	n.d.	n.d.	n.d.	n.d.
Alia	51,520	4,760	11,490	611	25,250	3,610,191	0.7	10,378	269,480	3.9%
Gulf Air	139,203	4,623	30,110	1,634	49,010	785,796	0.62	42,000	785,470	5.2%

PAX = Passenger
GAE = General & Administrative expenses
RPK = Revenue passenger Kilometer

Source: Primary, based on data compiled from the 1984 Annual Report of the four respective carriers.

Exhibit 5   A Composite Profile of Air Carriers operating in the Arab Passenger Market

Type of Carrier	Fare discount		Service					Safety
	intra-Arab	Other places	frequency	layovers	punctuality	inflight	ground	
Arab:								
1. Tourist-oriented countries: MS, ME, RJ	D	B	C	D	C	C	C	D
2. Oil-rich countries: SV, KU, GF	D	D	C	D	B	B	D	B
Foreign: "Non-Arab"								
1. Giants: SR, LH, KL, SQ, CX	–	B	A	A	A	A	A	A
2. 3rd Word: AI, PK, CA	–	A	C	C	B	B	C	B

Legend: $\dfrac{\text{High   Low}}{\text{A B C D}}$

Notes:

– Top rated airlines by our respondents are the European and Far Eastern Airlines.
– Ratings for each carrier may show some variation by respondents' nationality.
– The majority of Arab carriers were given an average (C) rating by our respondents.
– None of the Arab carriers was given an excellent (A) rating.

Airline Code:

AI	Air India	GF	Gulf Air
AF	Air France	JL	Japan Airlines
BA	British Airways	KL	KLM (Royal Dutch Airlines)
BR	British Caledonian	KU	Kuwait Airways
CX	Cathay Pacific	LH	Lufthansa
CA	China Airways	ME	Middle East Airlines

MS	Egypt Air
PK	Pakistan Int'l Airways
RJ	Royal Jordanian
SV	Saudi Arabian Airlines
SQ	Singapore Airlines
SR	Swiss Air

Source: Field Survey of Travelers' opinion – taken at Dhahran Airport, May 1986.

Even though each airline that competes in the Arab market has its own views of what constitutes good service, the fact remains that there are common ingredients an air traveler expects to get when he buys a ticket. What are these common ingredients? An independent survey conducted by the International Travel Research Institute on a large sample of Middle Eastern travelers in 1982–83 showed that out of 17 factors believed to be influential in travelers' choice of airlines, the following were the most decisive (Middle East Traveller 1983):

– good in-flight service;
– punctuality;
– convenient scheduling;
– safety.

Another independent study was conducted in the summer of 1986 by one of the authors on a group of Arab frequent travelers out of Dhahran and a few European airports. Respondents were asked to rate their favorite airline according to a number of factors. A composite profile of air carriers competing in the Arab marketplace is given in Exhibit 5. Although ours was a very limited convenient sample compared with the aforementioned study (67 against 821 respondents), the two studies are almost identical in their findings.

Another large-scale survey was conducted by Saudi Arabian Airlines in 1985. In response to a question about what passengers think is important when they select their favorite airline, the following list emerged as the 10 most important considerations among about 2,000 respondents:

1) good in-flight service;
2) safety;
3) flight attendants;
4) catering;
5) on-time performance;
6) ground service;
7) facilities/comfort;
8) prior good experience with airline;
9) competency of pilots and crew;
10) type of aircraft.

How do Arab carriers rate according to these factors? A 1986 survey conducted by students at the University of Petroleum and Minerals (later renamed King Fahd University of Petroleum and Minerals, KFUPM) tried to answer this question. It sampled a group of 142 international passengers out of Dhahran International Airport and asked them to rank their favorite Arab carrier according to 30 service factors. Using the semantic differential methodology, the study ranked Kuwait Airways first among respondents, followed by Saudia, Gulf Air, and Alia (see Exhibit 6). In contrast to the other three studies, the KFUPM study helps determine strengths and weaknesses of each carrier covered by the survey.

Why are Arab carriers not doing a good job servicing their customers? There are many possible reasons for this. First, there is a lack of motivation among customer service personnel who believe that rewards and promotions have nothing to do with efforts and performance. Second, there is a lack of service tradition in the Arab world, particularly in the public sector. Customer service personnel honestly believe they do not have to lean over backwards to serve their customers. Accordingly, it is the customer who has to do the bending.

Buyers and Users of Airline Services

In view of the vast mass of land that the Arab world occupies and the fact that the region relies heavily on imported goods, it is not surprising that many of the region's air carriers earn about 10–15 % of their operating revenue from freight. The flow of air freight in the region has pronounced directional imbalances. For example, of all freight traffic moving in and out of the Saudi-European market, about 95 % moves in the direction of Saudi Arabia and only 5 % to Europe. Air carriers compete for cargo business with surface transport on all routes. This is in marked contrast to air passenger business which has almost no competition from surface carriers on long-haul routes.

Two types of goods are shipped by air freight: emergency items or perishables (e. g., meat, dairy products, medical items, fruits, vegetables, newspapers, and magazines) and routine non-perishable goods (e. g., jewelry, fashionable wear, spare parts, and goods with high value-to-weight ratios for which air freight offers the advantage of speedy delivery). The price elasticity of the second category of goods is considerably greater than for either emergency or perishable items, because cheaper surface transport is a viable substitute for air freight of routine non-perishables.

Given the heat and the rugged terrain of the desert, the endless security checks at overland Arab borders, the imperfect surface transport system, and the dependence of the region on imports, it is expected than air freight will compensate for the drop in passenger traffic and continue to be in unusually high demand for years to come. Take 1984 as an example of the shape of things to come in the post oil-boom era. On the Middle East-Far East routes, passenger traffic registered an 11 % increase, while freight grew by 36 %. The comparable growth rates elsewhere in the world were 9 % for passengers and 14 % for freight.

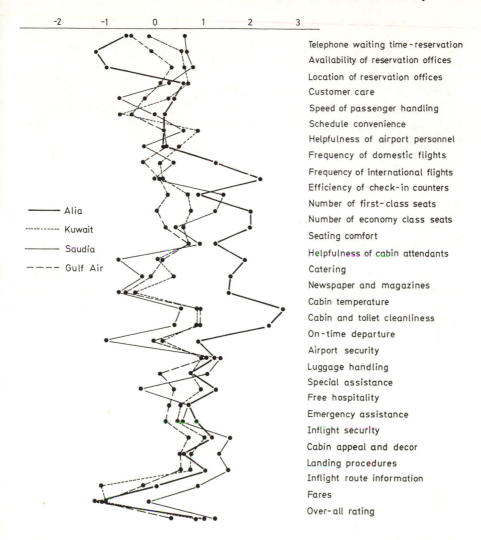

Exhibit 6   Passengers' rating of the Performance of Selected Arab Carriers

Source: A survey of the Service Performance of Selected Arab Carriers, unpublished student survey supervised by Dr. Ghazi Habib of the King Fahd University of Petroleum & Minerals, Spring, 1986.

The Air Passenger Market

In looking at the passenger market, it is useful to segment it into six categories: business travelers, leisure travelers, those who travel for personal reasons, those who travel for religious reasons, those who work abroad, and those who are studying abroad.

The balance of this section will describe the peculiar characteristics of each segment, profile the prototype passenger for each category, survey trends associated with each, and suggest the implications of these trends for airline management.

The Business Travel Market

This market segment was the foundation of the early stage of growth in the Gulf airline industry and remains important today. However, due to the completion of most infrastructure projects in the oil-rich stages, the sharp decline in oil prices, and the resulting slump in the region's economy, business travel declined sharply by the mid-1980s. Today, business travel represents one-sixth to one-fifth of the total travel market in terms of number of bookings.

There are at least three distinct features of the business market:

1) Business travelers do not pay their own fares and therefore are more inclined to travel first-class.
2) Business travelers often cannot predict in advance the timing of their trips.
3) Business travelers tend to travel by air more extensively than others. To airlines, the business traveler is the most valued customer.

The price of business travel is inelastic. Nevertheless, in the current business recession, the budget for business travel among business in the Gulf has not been curtailed very much. There have been cutbacks in some cases, however, as some businessmen are buying cheaper economy-class tickets. Since someone else is paying for the trip, the status-conscious Arab traveler will be attracted to patronize foreign carriers who offer VIP in-flight service, frequent flights, and seat availability. Knowing this, some world-class carriers specializing in business travelers offer their regular customers a variety of incentives, such as frequent-flyer bonuses or a seat upgrade, i.e., a first class seat for a business class fare or a business class seat for an economy fare.

Available evidence from one airline suggests that business travelers are predominantly middle-aged men from their early 30s to early 50s.

The Leisure Travel Market

The leisure (pleasure) market segment is strategically important to all air carriers. Arab carriers are no exception. Arab and non-Arab carriers serving the region assign around 80–85% of their seats to economy class passengers, suggesting a strong presence of leisure travelers.

The leisure segment exhibits a number of features which totally distinguish it from business travel.

1) The vacationing or leisure traveler almost always pays his or her own fare.
2) He or she usually does not travel alone, but with a family.
3) He or she is not pressed for time.

The implication of the above is that any increase in air fares or visa charges will have a negative multiplier effect, extending to all members of a given family who are traveling for leisure. Not all of the tourist-oriented countries in the region know that lesson. The fact is that demand for leisure is always likely to be price- and income-elastic. Strong support for this proposition comes from the large gains in traffic at Cairo airport during the early mid-1980s, which followed fare reductions (made possible through heavy discounting and a decline in the value of the Egyptian pound).

The leisure market also differs from the business market in terms of customer profile. The vacation market divides much more evenly between males and females. The trip-generation rate among school-age children is low. These rates rise sharply for the 19–27 age group, then fall sharply for families with young children. The rates go up again for middle-aged adults with older children, then decline, as one would expect, among the elderly.

The contrast in the service requirements of business and leisure travelers is also striking. Since vacationing travelers are paying for the trip out of their own pockets, they shop for a bargain fare. Therefore, it is not surprising that giant international carriers (e.g., Swissair and Lufthansa) capitalize on this fact by innovating cheaper fares on their dense routes.

Arab tourists have a variety of preferred destinations. For example, Saudi men like to travel to Manila and Bangkok. Saudi families like to travel to Switzerland, Spain, and London and emphasize shopping in their visits. Geneva and Malaga have replaced Cairo and Beirut as favorite destinations. Istanbul and Vienna are becoming popular.

Two major problems facing Arab tourists are the language barrier and the devaluation of the dollar (currencies of many Arab countries, but not all, are pegged to the dollar).

Given the fact that leisure travel is heavily concentrated in the early part of the weekend, in the summertime, and around the Muslim Eid holidays (national vacations), there are few reasons why Arab carriers cannot meet the needs of the vacation traveler more efficiently and at lower costs than they can meet the requirements of the business traveler. Less expensive cabin service, higher seat loads, and the ability to package all-inclusive tours to popular destinations are all helpful in this respect. This is how the Arab carriers can stimulate a mass-travel market to the benefit of everyone – the traveling public, the hotel operator, the air carrier, and the government or taxpayer who is subsidizing the flag carrier.

The Personal Travel Market

This segment of the air travel market is the smallest of all. It is made up of people who travel on their own time, pay for their way out of their own pocket, but have tighter timing and routing constraints than leisure travelers. An example of personal travel is a trip brought about by an urgent and unpredictable family matter such as death or illness.

The service needs of these travelers are similar to those of the business traveler. Seat availability and flight frequency are very important. The unpredictable nature of this market and the high level of service it requires means that it can only be supplied at a premium price.

The Religious Travel Market (Hajj and Umra)

In terms of size, the Hajj and Umra market (to and from Makkah) is growing very rapidly. Yet, it is not receiving as much attention from Arab carriers as it possibly merits. It shares many of the characteristics of the vacationing market segment, namely:

1) The Hajj traveler almost always pays his own fare.
2) He does not travel alone but with his family.
3) He is not pressed for time.
4) He is a repeat traveler.

However, in contrast to the leisure travel segment, the Hajj segment is concentrated in time and space. Additionally, it is fare- and income-inelastic.

Given the hardship in performing this religious ritual, it is not surprising to find that the trip generation-rate tends to be very high among Muslim men and women who are faithful, 35–60 years old, and physically fit. It is very low among children, unmarried young women, and adults below age 35 or older than 60.

Since travelers making the Hajj or Umra require entry visas to the Kingdom of Saudi Arabia – which may take a couple of weeks to obtain – the trip requires planning. Hence, frequency is a less important consideration for this market segment. In contrast to the leisure traveler who is paying for a non-essential, but highly desirable service, the Hajji or pilgrim feels to some degree that he is buying a "ticket to paradise" or reserving a seat in heaven. Therefore, Hajj travel is always more likely to be price- and income-inelastic.

Hajj operations are mutually beneficial to both the Muslim community and the airlines. Out of the approximately 2 million pilgrims who traveled to Makkah in 1982, 1.2 million arrived from within Saudi Arabia, while about 855,000 came from abroad. Of the latter, 56,000 arrived by sea, 174,000 overland and 626,000 (or 31 % of all Hajj travelers) by air. Travel by air is thus becoming the major mode of transportation. It allows the pilgrims to do with less luggage and shortens their absence from home and work. Besides, it is available at a full range of prices. A large part of the Muslim population who would otherwise have little prospect of making the pilgrimage to Makkah can now hope to do so because of affordable air travel.

Since performance of the Hajj is a religious requirement of every capable Muslim, at least once in a lifetime, and since the time for its performance each year is fixed, unlike Umra, the lesser pilgrimage, any airline that is equipped to meet the special needs of this market successfully is likely to come out ahead of its competitors. It can charge a standard fare for a sensible standard service using a jumbo aircraft. It can reorganize itself temporarily into a charter-like carrier and advertise its schedule and fares ahead of time. The economy-minded carrier can build a market share and utilize its fleet efficiently through marginal costing concepts.

The strategic significance of the Hajj market is evidenced by the fact that the national flag carrier of virtually every Muslim country considers the Hajj market as a "natural" monopoly; something they do not want to share with Saudia or any other carrier (see Exhibit 7).

The "Guest Worker" Market

Guest or expatriate workers constitute the dominant segment of the passenger market in the Gulf Arab countries. This segment makes up anywhere from 50–60 % of the economy class passengers of Arab and Asian carriers serving the region. Its relative size is stable, but its actual size has been on the decline in the post-oil boom. The oil-poor countries like Egypt, Jordan, the Philippines, and Pakistan are the leading exporters of manpower to the Gulf nations, who are in great need of manpower. Together, they import around 5 million workers. These workers (technicians, teachers, engineers, nurses, doctors, accountants, truck drivers, pilots, housemaids) are invited to come on a temporary work visa and are usually given an annual repatriation ticket by their employers to their country of origin. They are a slightly declining market segment, due to the

62   M. Sami Kassem

Exhibit 7   Number of Pilgrims Carried

Carrier	1982	1983
Air Afrique	12,300	7,600
Air Canada	11,450	9,160
Air France	10,798	8,265
Alia	4,862	8,370
Garuda	55,281	49,950
Ghana Airways	250	500
Gulf Air	3,800	4,730
Icelandair	70,000	70,000
Iran Air	90,000	102,000
Kuwait Airways	3,051	4,406
Nigeria Airways	78,448	80,763
Pakistan International Airways	43,500	47,650
Saudia Arabia Airlines	68,170	86,975
Syrian Arab Airlines	24,078	37,238
Tunis Air	17,878	13,603
Yemen Airways	28,447	54,444

Source: Gulf Air Magazine, 1985: 24.

completion of large-scale infrastructure projects and weakened economic conditions of the region due to oil oversupply in the world market. Also, higher paid expatriate workers from some Arab and European countries are being gradually replaced by cheaper Arab and South Asian labor.

In any case, guest workers still offer a lucrative market for both Arab and Far Eastern carriers serving the region. For one thing, guest workers will be around for years to come. The more expensive workers will be sent home, but they will be replaced by less expensive ones. Also, since holidays of expatriate workers often do not coincide with the seasonal Muslim Eid times, the air travel of these workers can help area airlines even out the peaks and troughs in demand. Finally, these travelers do not go home empty-handed. They take along many items purchased tax-free in the host countries of the Gulf. This translates into millions of dollars worth of excess-luggage revenues for the airlines.

About 3 million of the 5 million guest workers employed by the oil-rich Gulf states are Muslims. Their families back home may come to visit them and perform the Hajj or Umra at the same time, further expanding the air travel market.

The guest worker market and freight markets have some similar characteristics, a fact that may lead airline officials to unintentionally process guest workers as cargo rather than human beings.

The guest worker market is, to a great extent, a concentrated one, in that decision-making is in the hands of a small number of government and private-sector officials (heads of directorates of education and public health, as well as heads of personnel and manpower recruitment agencies in the private sector).

On guest workers' routes, directional imbalance is the most common situation. For example, planes carrying Egyptian teachers to Cairo from Saudi Arabia often return empty.

The guest worker hardly ever buys his own ticket. Yet, unless he is a company executive, a heart surgeon, or another highly-paid professional, he is not offered a first-class ticket. If he is a laborer, he is grouped with others to qualify for a "group fare" – almost like cargo.

The guest worker's time is not his own. It is his employer's time. The implication of this is that guest workers' travel is price-inelastic.

Some guest workers, especially in the professional and skilled manpower categories, are like business travelers. They travel extensively and, as such, are discriminating consumers of airline services. If an air carrier innocently mistreats them, or performs below standard, it may lose them forever as customers. This is a powerful lesson to Saudia, Kuwait Air, and Gulf Air. These guest workers are also very time-conscious. Seat availability and flight frequency are important considerations to them.

Finally, a word about the profile of the guest worker is in order. He is typically in the prime of his life, 35–45 years old, male, bilingual, and at least a high school graduate. A carrier that treats this traveler as a human being and is sensitive and appreciative of his special travel needs can win a loyal customer.

Student Travel Market

This market segment is made up of both nationals and non-citizens (whose parents are guest workers) who are studying abroad. These students traveling to or from school usually do not pay the cost of air travel themselves. Their government, employer, or parents sponsor them.

Since nearly all Gulf states now have well-developed educational institutions, and since many employers have stopped paying overseas educational stipends for dependents of their employees; this once lucrative market segment has shrunk considerably. Nevertheless, some carriers continue to specialize in handling the needs of students (special escort, reduced fares, in-flight attention, and post-flight handling). Such is the case with Swissair, British Caledonian, and KLM.

Substitutes

A key factor influencing profitability of the Arab airline industry is what economists call the "substitution effect." They argue that the traveler is willing to pay a certain fare for a certain run, but once the fare exceeds a certain level, he will attempt to substitute a less expensive mode of transportation (e. g., car, ship, train). This phenomenon exists in the Arab airline industry, particularly in domestic, intra-region operations, and with respect to the vacationing or leisure traveler.

The Arab market for airline service has many such "substitutes." Arab travelers, for example, often fly in groups with friends or relatives and, as a result, find it much cheaper to drive a car or take a boat rather than fly. Arab pilgrims are a case in point. Another example is vacationers from Dhahran heading for Riyadh or Bahrain, from Cairo heading for Alexandria, or from Jeddah heading for Medina. The availability of inexpensive gasoline, superhighways, private automobiles, public inter-city buses, and, to a lesser extent in the Gulf, frequent and reliable train service make airlines vulnerable to the substitution effects, especially on short and medium routes.

Reliable long-distance telephone links, telex services, automated document transmission, and teleconferencing are all important here. There is now the suggestion that the present level of business air travel is no more than a transient phase that will pass as the communications revolution speeds up and spreads, obviating the need for a significant proportion of business travel.

However, no one can predict accurately how advances in telecommunication technology will ultimately influence the growth in business travel. For the moment, though, one thing is certain for the Arab businessman. There is no substitute for direct, face-to-face, eye-to-eye contact.

It is safe to conclude that the immediate future will not see any significant decline in the actual number of either the leisure or business travelers in the Gulf region due to the substitution effect per se.

Conclusion

The following set of observations seem relevant to strategic planning for Arab air carriers as they prepare for the 1990s:

1) Demand is relatively and predictably seasonal. Air traffic reaches its peak between the two Eid holidays. It drops after the pilgrimage and evaporates in September with the opening of schools.
2) Business travel will continue to decline, not because of substitutions, but due to a combination of factors that include depressed oil prices, the

completion of infrastructure projects and, to some extent, rapid advances in telecommunication technology.

3) Idle capacity continues to plague Arab carriers. This phenomenon is caused by the return of part of the guest workers to their homeland, the acquisition of new wide-bodied aircraft, artificially high intraregional prices, and the aggressive marketing practices of foreign-flag carriers who have managed to switch the loyalties of some Arab passengers away from their national flag airline to a foreign flag competitor.

4) A predicted increase in idle capacity will undoubtedly hurt Arab carriers in many ways. For one thing, it will eventually translate into lower profits or higher losses. For another, it will impede the ability of Arab carriers to enter new markets, thereby perpetuating the dependence of most of these carriers on government subsidies and protectionism. Privatization – selling the national carrier to private investors who run it as a business, not as a government agency – is often offered as a way to cope with rising idle capacity. Given the above-mentioned entry barriers and the prevailing Arab trading mentality, it is questionable whether privatization alone will be the answer to the headaches of Arab air carriers. Alia's experience clearly suggests that it is not a matter of who owns the airline that makes a difference in performance, but who runs it, (Hammer and Hinterhuber, 1988).

5) The salvation of Arab carriers, therefore, will come not from their privatization but from the willingness and capacity of their executives to pool and share their costly resources wisely. If and when there are strong pressures to do so, economies of scale in financing, purchasing, training, computerization, maintenance, and joint operations of long-haul routes will materialize. Idle capacity will no longer be a problem. Unit cost will be drastically reduced. Besides, once the benefits of joint cooperation are realized, Arab airline executives might be tempted to lobby for an open skies policy. This would mark a new chapter in the history of Arab commercial aviation.

6) Travel barriers have been virtually eliminated for GCC nationals traveling between the GCC countries. Egypt and Jordan, both tourist-oriented countries, maintain an open door policy for Arab and non-Arab visitors. However, the majority of Arab states have not yet eased visa restrictions across the board for most nationalities, which inhibits the free movement of people in and out of their countries and rigidifies their air travel markets.

Appendix: Basic Principles in Air Transport Economics[1]

If we are to clarify our thinking about air transport economics, it is necessary to return to a few basic definitions and principles. There is some degree of confusion amongst regulators, academics, and airline managers which inhibits rational discussion of the economic operation of air transport markets. I will briefly touch on some of these essential to the argument that regional rather than bilateral negotiation will be superior in bringing about economic efficiency.

A. *Markets* for passenger in air transportation are defined by demand. They are characterized by a city pair, origin-destination, by a class of service, and by trip purpose such as business/pleasure. Passengers are generally residents of either the origin or destination region, and are demanding a round trip service.

B. A *route* is an itinerary followed by an aircraft which provides nonstop, multistop, or connecting service to many markets simultaneously. The scheduled carriers do not make supply decisions on a market-by-market basis, but rather over a network of cyclic routings to be followed by the aircraft. There generally is a small set of markets in some region for which supply decisions are made.

C. The *costs* of providing scheduled service to a market cannot be determined without making an arbitrary allocation. It is possible to identify aircraft costs incurred (cost per departure, cost per route station), operating costs (cost per aircraft visit, cost per passenger), and system operating costs (cost per dollar of revenue, cost per ticket sold), but these have to be allocated against various services simultaneously produced by scheduled route operations.

D. The *marginal cost* of adding an incremental passenger to a service, once it has been scheduled, is essentially zero. Since average costs are arbitrary, and short-term marginal costs are zero, there is no guidance from cost information in establishing prices to be charged for various services.

E. *Economies of scale* exist in air transport operations. For the aircraft operating costs, the costs/seat (for a given stage length) decrease as seating capacity is increased; and the costs/mile (for a given seating capacity) decrease as stage length is increased. These are due to technological reasons – we use fewer resources in terms of labor, fuel, and capital as we build and operate a larger capacity aircraft, and there are increased costs in starting

---

[1] Excerpt from Robert W. Simpson, The Economic Rational for Regionalism, in: *Regionalism in International Air Transportation: Cooperation & Competition*, (Amman, Jordan: Alia, The Royal Jordanian Airlines, 1984).

and ending a flight stage. As a result the airline scheduler must look for efficient routings which have large on-board loads on route segments of longer stage lengths. As well, there can be economies of scale in passenger and aircraft handling costs at larger and busier stations due to more efficient use of labor and facilities.

F. *Economies of scope* are very strong in scheduled aid transportation. This is a term used by economists to describe a situation where a firm in one market finds itself in an advantageous position in othe markets. Because of the economies of scale mentioned above, scheduled carriers find themselves interested in routings and connecting patterns of service which allow them to use large aircraft and keep their stations busy serving a larger set of related markets.

As a result of the above characteristics, the airline planner is faced with a complex problem in finding an efficient pattern of service. He must simultaneously select aircraft size, range, routing patterns, frequency of service, and price in markets. These are all strongly interrelated over regions of his network. The complexity of this problem only arises when restrictions on these variables are removed. Historically, the problem has been handled sequentially, and certain variables are not free for the planner to consider. This prevents finding optimal or even good solutions in some cases.

G. *Alternative routings* may exist which supply competitive service offers to demand in a given market. This creates need for establishing a coherent set of prices for all markets in a network of services. By combining services in other markets and their prices, the consumer creates an alternative. A bilateral determination of price and service in a market affects similar decisions by consumers in other markets.

References

Civil Aeronautics Board: *Handbook of airlines statistics*, Washington, D. C:
Copeland, D. and McKenney (1988): "Airline reservations systems: lessons from history" *MIS Quarterly*. 12:3:353–373
Ghandour, A. (1979a): Airline planning in the 80's: A paper presented at the Middle East Civil Aviation Conference, June 4–8, Amman: Alia P.R. Dept.
Ghandour, A. (1979b): Politics in the Middle East: Its effects on air transportation and communication: Address before the Council for World Affairs, Los Angeles, Sept. 10.

Ghandour, A. (1980): The economic position of civil aviation in the Middle East: Paper presented at the International Civil Aviation Conference II, New York City, April 29–30, Amman: Alia P. R. Dept.

Ghandour, A. (1983): The role of air carriers in developing air transport in the Arab world: A paper presented at the Civil Aviation Forum sponsored by the Arab League Civil Aviation Council, Rabat, July 7–11, Amman: Alia P. R. Dept.

Gary Gimson (1986): More freedom for region's airlines, *Middle East Transport and Telecommunications*, 64, (March/April): 11–14.

Gilbert, Lee (1988). "Building 21st Century Interorganizational systems: Information technology-based alliances in Pacific Rim airlines." Eighth Annual Strategic Management Society Conference. Amsterdam October 17–20, 1988.

Gulf Air (1985): The Hajj – IATA's role, *Gulf Air*, 25 (August): 24.

Hamer, R. and Hinterhuber, H. (1988). "Policies and strategies in the privatization debate." Eighth Annual Strategic Management Society Conference. Amsterdam October 18, 1988.

IATA (1984): *Annual Report*,

IATA (1986): *Annual Report*,

Kassem, M. S. and Bhatt, Bah (1988). "Survival strategies for state-owned airlines: the case of Arabian Gulf carriers: in Proceedings of the International Conference on Services Marketing, sponsored by the Academy of Marketing Science, Cleveland, Ohio. Volume V, October 1988, pp. 126–136.

Kramon, G. (1987): Low ratings for U.S. airlines, *New York Times*, November 4.

Levine, M. E. (1987) "Airline competition in deregulated markets: theory, firm strategy and public policy." *Yale Journal of Regulation*, 4, 393–494.

Lynch, J. (1984): *Airlines organizations in the 1980's:* An industry report on strategies and structures for coping with change, London: Macmillan.

The Middle East air traveller (1983): AACO seminar: Seattle, Washington: Boeing Commercial Airplane Company. (This report provides an excellent summary of the INTRAMAR PROJECT of the International Travel Research Institute.)

Porter, M. E. (1980): *Competitive strategy*, New York: Free Press.

Rieger, Fritz (1987) "The influence of national culture on organizational structure, process and strategic decision-making: A study of international airlines." Unpublished doctoral dissertation. McGill University, Montreal.

Regionalism (1983): Regionalism in international air transportation: Cooperation and competition Proceedings of an international conference organized by MIT and held in Amman (April 19–21, Amman: Alia P. R. Dept.

4.2   Saudi Arabian Airlines (Saudia)

M. Sami Kassem and Ghazi M. Habib

Introduction

Saudia, the national airline of Saudi Arabia, is one of the world's major airlines. Its on-time performance and sheer size place it among the top 15 airlines in the world. During 1985, 94% of Saudia's scheduled flights, which averaged 300 per day, departed on time, while on-time termination averaged 90%. It carried 12 million passengers and 172 million tons of cargo and employed 25,600 persons. It has an ultra-modern fleet of 101 aircrafts, half of which is less than three years old.

Apart from its impressive punctuality and size, Saudia is a sensitive mirror of Saudi society. Its history reflects the transformation of the country from the camel age to the jet and space age, from a closed society to one fully in touch with the world, from a society which has relied heavily on foreign labor to one that is educating, training, and utilizing its own citizens more and more, even in high-tech fields.

Saudia is a leader among Arab carriers. It owns and operates one-third of the Arab fleet (100 of 300 aircrafts), employs one-half of its work force (26,000 of 52,000), and serves as many passengers as all other Arab carriers combined (about 12 million). It has the largest domestic network in the Arab world. It also has the largest and most modern in-house maintenance, catering, and training capability. Saudia's operations also are the most computerized, from its reservation system to ticketing, departure control, luggage-tracing, cargo-tracking, and flight simulator training.

However, size and technical sophistication are not automatic business assets. Saudia's average unit cost is high, while its load factor and profitability are relatively low. Nowadays, these are matters of concern to Saudia's executives and board members who are contemplating ways to improve the situation.

Stages of Strategic Development

Saudia's history can be divided into four stages, outlined below:

Domestic Growth (1945–1962)

Lacking anything even remotely resembling a national highway system in a country the size of Western Europe, Saudi Arabia quickly became dependent on air travel, soon after its age of oil dawned in 1938. King Abd al-'Aziz Al Sa'ud, the founder of the Kingdom of Saudi Arabia, envisioned air transport as a way to link the nation's distant parts and unify its people. When U.S. president Franklin D. Roosevelt gave him a DC-3 Dakota aircraft as a gift in 1945, it was quickly put into service to carry passengers and mail between the three major cities of Jeddah, Riyadh, and Dhahran. In 1947, two additional DC-3s were bought to launch a regular service and cope with the increasing demand for air transport.

By 1949, the Kingdom had expanded its modest fleet to include five DC-4s and five Bristol freighters. The nucleus of a national airline was by now in place.

Air service was extended to the Arab capitals as early as 1947, starting with Amman, then Cairo, Baghdad, Khartoum, and Beirut. It catered to pilgrims from these Arab capitals. To meet the needs of this growing regional network, the fleet grew to include five DC-4s, five Bristol freighters, and ten Corvair 340s. Early in the 1960s, the network reached some European capitals. Two B-720 jets were added to the fleet.

Beginning in 1946, the year it was founded, Saudia had a technical management contract with Trans World Airlines (TWA), which has lent key technical personnel, given technical advice, and acted as a purchasing agent and personnel recruiter for Saudia in the United States and Europe. This agreement was broadened in 1966 to allow for the active participation of TWA in the operation and management of all Saudia's departments. This agreement expired on Sept. 30, 1986.

Controlled Growth (1962–1972)

In 1963, the government nationalized Saudia and converted it into a corporation that was to conduct its activities as a commercial enterprise. It also sponsored some of Saudia's training activities aimed at preparing a new generation of Saudi pilots, technicians, and administrators. By 1966, the company added three DC-3s and another 3 DC-9s to its fleet. It joined Arab Air Carriers Organization (AACO) in 1965 and the International Air Transport Association (IATA) in 1967.

By 1967 Saudia had extended its Arab network to include Tunis, through

Beirut. A few months afterwards, the carrier began a regular weekly service to Geneva, Frankfurt, and London.

Continuing expansion on the international front led to the purchase of two B-707s in 1968. The introduction of this new generation of jets gave Saudia the ability to offer nonstop service from Jeddah to London, Rome, and Algiers. It also made it possible for the carrier to start an all-cargo service in 1971 between the Kingdom and Europe, connecting to transatlantic routes. In 1972, the B-737 jet took over as the workhorse of Saudia's domestic routes and the B-707 as the workhorse for its international network. Saudia now operates 19 B-737s and 2 B-707s. This stage marked the introduction of not only jets, but also high-speed IBM 370/20 computers to Saudia's finance and administrative division.

Explosive Growth (1973–1982)

During this decade, Saudia's growth was phenomenal and unparalleled within the airline industry. As it grew, its impact on Saudi society also increased. It served increasingly as a prime mover of people, vital equipment, farm animals, and industrial products to the Kingdom. Travelers (businessmen, workers, technicians, consultants) came by the planeload from all corners of the earth to join the construction boom of the 1970s.

As can be readily seen in Exhibit 1, passenger traffic increased tenfold, freight twelvefold, and mail ninefold. To handle this growth, Saudia purchased two Lockheed L-1011s in 1975, followed by a number of B-747s in 1981. It then launched a nonstop service between Jeddah and New York. It also started a nonstop freight service using a B-747F. Its work force grew fivefold, from 4,265 in 1972 to 23,730 employees in 1982. Its route network mushroomed to include over 46 international destinations and 26 domestic ones. With the exception of New York and Casablanca, the East provided all the new destinations in the international network (i.e., Manila, Singapore, Bangkok, and New Delhi).

The rapidly expanding Saudi economy required laborers from the East to build the nation's infrastructure and heavy equipment and livestock from the industrialized West and Japan for industrial and agricultural development programs. Saudia carried them all.

Stable Growth (1982-Present)

The present stage of Saudia's development is characterized by stable growth and a shift in focus from routes and services to manpower development and cost control, or from extensive to intensive development. In terms of routes, just three Far Eastern destinations have been added,

Revenue Passengers Carried (in thousands)
    900 1,100 1,300 1,800 3,100 4,900 6,500 8,000 9,500 9,400

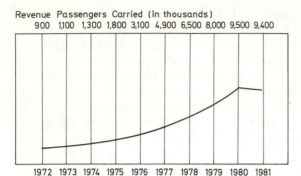

    1972 1973 1974 1975 1976 1977 1978 1979 1980 1981

Haj Passengers Carried (in thousands)
    118   130   116   102   165   108   89   99   37   113

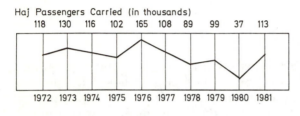

    1972 1973 1974 1975 1976 1977 1978 1979 1980 1981

Passenger Revenues
(Saudi Riyals in millions)
    758 1,283 1,906 2,324 3,159 3,774

    1976 1977 1978 1979 1980 1981

Freight Kgs. Boarded (in millions)
    8   12   17   21   29   38   49   61   72   100

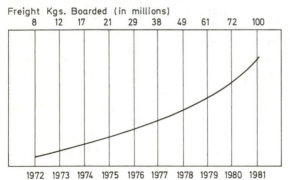

    1972 1973 1974 1975 1976 1977 1978 1979 1980 1981

Freight Revenues
(Saudi Riyals in millions)
    187 230 310 425 506 648

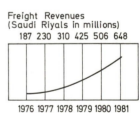

    1976 1977 1978 1979 1980 1981

Mail Kgs. Boarded (in thousands)
    800 1,100 1,300 1,500 2,000 2,600 2,700 4,600 5,500 7,400

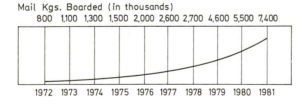

    1972 1973 1974 1975 1976 1977 1978 1979 1980 1981

Exhibit 1   Comperative Statistics: The boom Years

Source: Saudia Annual Report 1981

namely Seoul, Jakarta, and Colombo, reflecting a continued reliance on relatively inexpensive labor throughout the Saudi economy.

Meanwhile, Saudia's overall passenger traffic has continued to increase. Saudia carried 11.6 million passengers in 1984, compared with 11.4 million in 1983. Whereas domestic traffic declined by 4%, international traffic increased by 7.3% – mostly from increases in Asian markets.

Load factors, however, declined somewhat from 1983 to 1984. The passenger load factor dropped from 65% to 63% and the weight load factor from 49% to 48%. Fortunately, Saudia's break-even load factor also decreased from 48% to 47%.

The drop in load factors is the result of a combination of factors. Whereas Saudia increased the size of its fleet and frequency of flights on some routes, passenger demand did not keep pace. Business travel declined following the completion of the Kingdom's infrastructure projects. Moreover, a large reduction in demand for labor – Saudia's core market segment – followed the sharp decline in the Kingdom's oil revenues. In addition, undeclared fare wars fought by Saudia's competitors in international air travel markets and the availability in Saudi Arabia of attractive substitutes to domestic air transport, namely, inter-city public buses, private cars, or taxis, and the Dammam-Riyadh rail road, helped dampen passenger demand.

By contrast, Saudia cargo business has continued to show healthy growth. Cargo uplift amounted to 172 million kilograms in 1984 against 163 million in 1983 and 139 in 1982. This expansion is reflected in Saudia's freight revenues, which increased by 6% over the period. The carrier operates three all-cargo aircrafts: two B-747s and one DC-8F.

Saudia has made massive investments in equipment, spare parts, and technology. It purchased eleven Airbus 300-600s in 1981 for use on both domestic and international routes. It received ten B-747s as a gift from the Royal Court. It purchased two sophisticated and expensive flight simulators, one for the B-747 and the other for the A300-600s. Finally, it opened a US $20 million jet engine facility to test aircraft engines that have been overhauled and repaired at Saudia's workshops.

A key strategic emphasis of the current stage is a drive to cut costs without curtailing Saudia's expansion programs or the development of its human resources. This concern for improving operational efficiency has led to increased computerization. Today, the automated management of information extends to virtually every area of Saudia's operation. It has computerized many of the vital functions, such as tracking cargo consignments, making reservations, issuing tickets, managing the inventory of aircraft spare parts, flight operations, accounts payable, and the payroll. Saudia's aim is to streamline routine work, reduce costs, and improve the quality of passenger service.

One key indicator of service quality is punctuality. Saudia has maintained an enviable record in this regard. About 91 % of its flights have originated on time. To achieve that remarkable record, Saudia has invested heavily in variables, that affect dispatch reliability, such as fleet maintenance, catering, and training. These vital services lend themselves to economies of scale. Faced with the classic make-or-buy question, Saudia has recently opted for the former. For a long time, it purchased many of these serives from independent contractors. Lately, however, Saudia has found that it has more to gain by providing these services itself. For instance, it has developed its in-house engineering and maintenance capability to the point that – despite the heterogeneity of its sizeable fleet – nearly all major airframe, engine, and power plant overhauls are carried out in its own ultramodern facilities, which employ about 5,000 persons.

Similarly, Saudia has invested perhaps more than any other airline in the world in developing its skilled manpower. It has established one of the most comprehensive training programs in the industry covering all aspects of running a modern commercial airline. The twin goal of all these programs is to improve the quality of passenger service both on ground and in the air and to develop the skills of Saudi nationals to the point where Saudia can function independently of foreign assistance.

The Goals of Saudia

The Saudi government has charted the following goals for Saudia:

National and International Goals

1) contribute to the economic and industrial development of the Kingdom;
2) contribute to the social development of the Kingdom by linking remote towns and villages with urban centers through an efficient air transport system;
3) link the Kingdom with friendly nations around the globe;
4) expand and improve the transport of pilgrims to the holy places.

Social Goals

1) serve Saudi society by employing and training Saudi nationals;
2) build and maintain good employee relations by providing adequate fringe benefits such as training, education, and ample compensation;
3) generate a cadre of Saudi employees who are expert in the latest airline technologies.

Business Goals

1) increase revenues while containing expenses to become financially self-sufficient;
2) expand the route network in response to public demand without sacrificing the quality of service;
3) increase Saudia's share of the international travel market by offering competitive services;
4) emerge a leader in the air transport industry by acquiring modern technologies and improving the delivery of services;
5) operate and manage the airline as a business enterprise capable of standing on its own feet and financing its own obligations.

Organization

The job of Saudia's board of directors is to oversee the achievement of the above-listed objectives, to evaluate top management's performance, and to authorize budgets and financing. The eleven men on Saudia's board collectively discharge this reponsibility as representatives of the "public interest." As shown in Exhibit 2, the board includes both high government officials and prominent businessmen, all well-qualified to oversee the corporate goals listed in the preceding section.

Exhibit 3 shows the current managerial structure of Saudia. It approximates the "machine bureaucracy" typical of the airline industry. Three corollary observations can be made:

1) At the corporate level, Saudia is organized along functional lines with an executive vice-president in charge of each of the four major functions. Each of these functions – except marketing – is also organized along functional lines. Marketing is organized on a geographic basis.
2) Saudia has a tall, pyramid-like structure. The head of each of the four functional units (executive vice-president) has a number of vice-presidents reporting to him. Each of these vice-presidents, in turn, has five to six general managers reporting to him and so on down to the level of unit manager.
3) Decision-making tends to be centralized. For example, many passengers' service matters are referred first to office managers, then to the district or regional manager, and finally to the head office in Jeddah. This can create an exasperating slowness in response time, an inherent danger of any rigidly centralized bureaucracy. But it can be particularly pernicious to businesses that sell their product or service directly to the public.

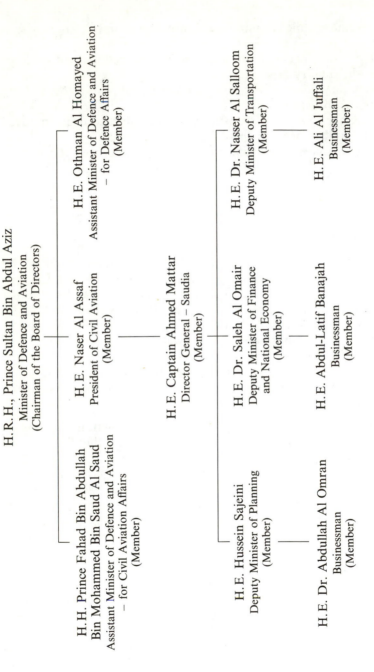

Exhibit 2   Board of Directors

Source: 1984 Saudia Annual Report.

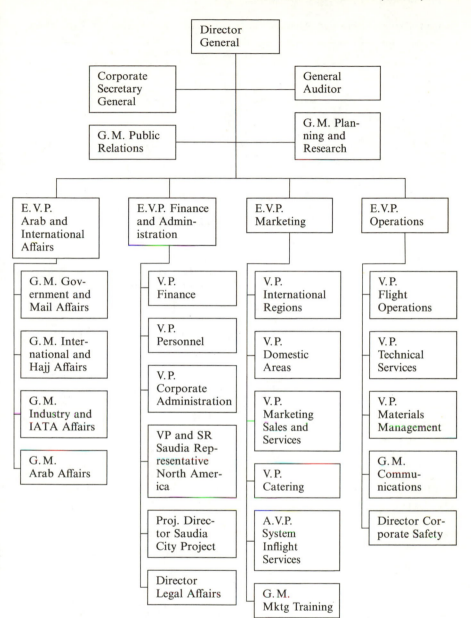

Exhibit 3   Saudia Corporate Organization – August 1986

Exhibit 4   Saudi Arabian Airlines Corp. – Operating Revenues and Expenses

System Operating Results		Decade in Statistics (Saudi Riyals Millions)					
Operating Revenues Transport	1984	% Disb	1983	% Disb	1982	% Disb	1981
Passenger	5,737.5	77.3	5,213.7	75.0	5,040.6	77.1	3,774.4
Cargo Revenue	762.8	10.3	728.7	10.5	713.2	10.9	647.5
Mail Revenue	109.2	1.5	101.1	1.5	73.4	1.1	50.8
Hajj Charters	60.4	0.8	82.8	1.2	50.2	0.8	70.5
Special Flights	151.0	2.0	145.9	2.1	101.8	1.6	75.7
	6,820.9	91.9	6.272.2	90.3	5,979.2	91.5	4,618.9
Transport Related Revenue							
Hajj Royalties	68.2	0.9	75.0	1.1	71.0	1.1	68.4
Other Misc. Rev.	537.0	7.2	600.9	8.6	483.1	7.4	303.3
Total	7,426.1	100.0	6,948.1	100.0	6,533.3	100.0	4,990.6
Operating Expenses							
Salaries and Wages	2,385.1	32.7	2,130.4	31.0	2,173.5	31.3	1,905.5
Fuel and Oil	720.1	9.9	557.1	8.1	542.9	7.8	510.5
Depreciation	827.8	11.4	795.2	11.6	680.5	9.8	459.9
Gen. Svcs. Purchased	523.9	7.2	565.0	8.2	679.0	9.8	543.2
Rentals and Landings	489.8	6.7	636.9	9.3	571.4	8.2	725.9
Food Expenses	92.4	2.6	191.1	2.8	229.0	3.3	192.7
Traffic Commission	491.9	6.8	392.0	5.7	320.7	4.6	229.7
Maintenance Materials	82.1	2.5	168.0	2.4	151.6	2.2	121.7
Taxes			27.0	0.4	19.9	0.3	20.3
Other	1,474.5	20.2	1,410.6	20.5	1,570.0	22.7	1,144.3
Total	7,287.6	100.0	6,873.3	100.0	6,938.5	100.0	5,853.7
Operating Income/(Loss)	138.5		74.8		(405.2)		(863.1)

Non-Operating Revenue/(Expenses)	1984	1983	1982
Interest Expenses	(287.9)	(237.6)	(244.2)
Capitalized Interest	44.6	19.4	46.8
Foreign Exchange Adjustments	(77.3)	(108.9)	(22.4)
Gain on Disposal of Equipment Net	0.2	–	–
Other Net	18.9	32.2	46.1
Total Non-Operating Revenue (Expenses)	(301.5)	(294.9)	(173.7)
Net Income/(Loss) Before Government Contribution	(163.0)	(220.1)	(578.9)
Government Contribution	543.0	410.0	450.0
Net Income (Loss)	380.0	189.9	(128.9)

Note: For 1980 & 1981, the portion of additional capital payments representing subsidization of domestic traffic amounting to SR 290,000,000 and SR 52,000,000 respectively was credited to passenger revenue.

Source: *Decade in Statistics*, Published Corporate Document, (Saudia 1983): 5.

for the year ending Dec. 31, 1975 through 1984

% Disb	1980	% Disb	1979	% Disb	1978	% Disb	1977	% Disb	1976	% Disb	1975	% Disb
75.6	3,158.7	74.9	2,324.1	72.72	1,906.7	73.88	1,283.6	71.15	758.8	65.02	450.1	61.00
13.0	505.8	12.0	425.5	13.31	310.9	12.05	230.3	12.77	187.1	16.03	118.5	16.06
1.0	39.6	0.9	26.9	0.84	17.4	0.67	14.5	0.80	10.5	0.90	7.2	0.98
1.4	43.6	1.0	39.0	1.22	32.9	1.27	28.4	1.57	53.1	4.55	40.0	5.42
1.5	84.5	2.0	73.9	2.31	58.0	2.25	43.7	2.42	82.9	7.11	52.9	7.17
92.5	3,832.2	90.8	2,889.4	90.40	2,325.9	90.12	1,600.5	88.71	1,092.4	93.61	668.7	90.63
1.4	60.0	1.4	52.1	1.63	44.5	1.73	54.9	3.04	35.8	3.07	49.4	6.70
6.1	327.5	7.8	254.8	7.97	210.4	8.15	148.8	8.25	38.8	3.32	19.7	2.67
100.0	4,219.7	100.0	3,196.3	100.0	2,580.8	100.0	1,804.2	100.0	1,167.0	100.0	737.8	100.0
32.6	1,232.1	27.2	954.9	27.81	752.0	27.47	529.6	26.87	319.7	24.99	217.3	28.54
8.7	419.3	9.2	323.4	9.42	197.9	7.23	167.2	8.48	122.3	9.56	80.1	10.52
7.9	292.3	6.4	246.8	7.19	192.6	7.04	147.4	7.48	86.5	6.76	54.5	7.16
9.3	557.5	12.3	322.1	9.38	304.4	11.12	217.9	11.05	124.3	9.71	72.3	9.50
12.4	710.2	15.7	527.9	15.37	318.4	11.63	278.8	14.14	175.4	13.71	119.3	15.67
3.3	158.5	3.5	135.6	3.95	123.0	4.49	99.0	5.02	53.0	4.14	24.9	3.27
3.9	196.5	4.3	130.7	3.81	90.8	3.32	61.7	3.13	41.2	3.22	21.7	2.85
2.1	49.0	1.1	47.0	1.37	37.5	1.37	40.2	2.04	24.8	1.94	15.8	2.07
0.3	15.1	0.3	12.4	0.36	10.1	0.37	8.0	0.41	5.3	0.41	6.5	0.85
19.5	906.7	20.0	732.8	21.34	710.7	25.96	421.5	21.38	327.0	25.56	149.0	19.57
100.0	4.537.2	100.0	3,433.6	100.00	2,737.4	100.00	1,971.3	100.00	1,279.5	100.0	761.4	100.00
	(317.5)		(237.3)		(156.6)		(167.1)		(112.5)		(23.6)	
1981		1980		1979		1978		1977		1976		1975
(56.6)		(1.3)		(0.2)		(0.6)		(2.3)		(4.3)		(4.5)
38.1		–		–		–		–		–		–
(34.3)		0.6		(18.9)		(5.1)		(42.5)		(21.8)		(3.9)
–		–		–		–		–		–		–
5.2		84.1		46.1		0.8		12.8		16.3		6.8
(47.6)		83.4		27.0		(4.9)		(32.0)		(9.8)		(1.6)
(910.7)		(234.1)		(210.3)		(161.5)		(199.1)		(122.3)		(25.2)
308.0		–		–		–		–		–		27.0
(602.7)		(234.1)		(210.3)		(161.5)		(199.1)		(122.3)		1.8

Financial Performance and Position

Financial information on Saudia is presented in Exhibits 4 through 6.

Where does Saudia's money go? Exhibit 4 provides the answer. It shows that the payroll is the largest expense category, and one that has risen over time. Fuel accounts for about 10 % of total expenses. While this is the lowest ratio in the industry, it ranks as Saudia's second largest expense. Depreciation accounts for another 10 % of Saudia's operating budget.

Saudia is doing its best to improve its cash flow situation (see Exhibit 6). It is trying to develop new sources of transport-related revenues (e. g., catering, maintenance facilities).

At the same time, it is working on collecting its receivables from outside and inside the Kingdom so that it will be able to fulfill its financial obligations toward banks and government agencies.

Personnel

Saudia is one of the largest and most desirable employers in Saudi Arabia. Exhibit 7 shows the phenomenal growth in the size of its labor force over the past decade. There was a fourfold increase during the 1975–1984 period, with the largest annual percentage increase taking place in 1976. The marketing area of Saudia grew the fastest. Its employees rose from 2,768 in 1975 to 11,654 in December 1985. This is also the largest occupational category of employees at the airline.

Whereas the size of the work force increased fourfold from 1975 to 1984, productivity only slightly more than doubled during the past 10 years. Available tonne kilometers (ATK) per employee rose from 80,400 in 1975 to 165,700 in 1984. Revenue per employee – another indicator of employee productivity in airlines – rose from SR 112,900 to SR 300,300. In terms of a third indicator, number of employees per aircraft, Saudia compares well with airlines from labor-short societies and very favorably with airlines from labor-surplus societies. Saudia had 272 employees per aircraft, compared with 219 for Pan American, 260 for British Airways, 249 for Japan Airlines, 983 for Air India, and 612 for Pakistan International.

Saudization of Jobs

Twenty years ago seven out of ten Saudia employees were non-Saudis. Ten years ago, the ratio was six out of ten. Now, it is five out of ten.

Exhibit 5   Balance Sheets Saudi Arabian Airlines Corporation (Saudi Riyals in thousands)

Assets	1985*	1984*	1983*
Current Assets:			
Cash	218,657	134,800	380,284
Cash in foreign countries not available for immediate use	232,938	245,250	241,555
Accounts receivable, less allowance for doubtful accounts of 130, 134 and 115,000	2,666,152	2,206,651	1,802,544
Spare parts, materials, and supplies, less allowance for obsolescence of 229,102 and 171,194	817,758	670,399	633,533
Prepaid expenses	58,253	59,140	96,920
Other	169,229	288,954	–
Total Current Assets	4,162,987	3,605,194	3,154,836
Property and Equipment, at cost:			
Flight equipment		8,499,497	6,412,479
Advances on flight equipment purchase contracts	10,520,021	184,376	447,707
Ground equipment	1,169,296	1,048,472	947,726
Land, buildings, and improvements	3,431,019	3,507,084	3,247,184
	15,120,336	13,239,429	11,055,096
Less: accumulated depreciation	4,266,300	3,672,234	2,918,308
Net Property and Equipment	10,854,036	9,567,195	8,136,788
Total Assets	15,017,023	13,172,389	11,291,624
Liabilities and Equity			
Current Liabilities:			
Air traffic liability	895,398	1,035,809	1,195,163
Accounts payable and accrued expenses	2,059,533	1,146,539	1,139,915
Current maturities of long-term debt	1,687,665	1,468,477	730,884
Bank overdrafts	2,091,137	2,135,101	1,419,360
Total Current Liabilities	6,733,733	5,785,926	4,485,322
Long-term Debt	4,983,235	5,770,896	5,595,957
Other Long-term Liabilities	217,786	187,660	162,410
Deferred Income	1,824,028		
Equity of the Kingdom of Saudi Arabia			
Balance at January 1	1,427,907	1,047,935	857,975
Net income/(loss)	(169,666)	79,972	189,960
Balance at December 31	1,258,241	1,427,907	1,047,935
Total Liabilities and Equity	15,017,023	13,172,389	11,291,624

* Year endet December 31.   Source: Annual Reports.

Exhibit 6   Statements of Changes in Financial Position Saudi Arabian Airlines
Corporation (Saudi Riyals in thousands)

	1985*	1984*	1983*
Source of funds:			
Net Income	(169,666)	379,972	189,960
Items which do not use (provide) working capital:			
Depreciation	631,960	760,824	755,496
(Gain) on disposal of equipment, net	(732)	(213)	(6,416)
Funds provided from operation	461,562	1,140,583	939,040
Increase in long-term debt	–	174,939	–
Proceeds from disposal of equipment	6,359	1,393	44,241
Increase in other long-term liabilities	30,126	25,250	16,282
Increase in deferred income	1,824,028	–	–
	2,322,075	1,342,165	999,569
Application of funds:			
Additions to property and equipment	1,924,428	2,192,411	259,532
Reduction in long-term debt	787,661	–	749,365
	2,712,089	2,192,411	1,008,897
Net increase in working capital deficit	(390,014)	(850,246)	(9,334)
Changes in components of working capital deficit:			
Increase (decrease) in current assets:			
Cash	83,857	(245,484)	131,246
Cash in foreign countries not available for immediate use	(12,312)	3,695	(56,981)
Accounts receivable	459,501	404,107	574,284
Spare parts, materials, and supplies	147,359	36,866	33,995
Prepaid expenses	(887)	(37,780)	(31,191)
Other	(119,725)	288,954	–
	557,793	450,358	651,353
Increase (decrease) in current liabilities:			
Air traffic liability	140,411	159,354	(413,702)
Accounts payable and accrued expenses	(912,994)	(6,624)	(242,297)
Current maturities of long-term debt	(219,188)	(737,593)	(208,859)
Bank overdrafts	43,964	(715,741)	204,171
	(947,807)	(1,300,604)	(660,687)
Net increase in working capital deficit	(390,014)	(850,246)	(9,334)

* Year ended December 31.
Source: Annual Reports.

Exhibit 7 Growth in Size and Composition of Saudia's Work Force by Occupational Category

Employees at Year End	1985	1984	1983	1982	1981	1980	1979	1978	1977	1976	1975
Marketing	11,654	11,236	10,486	10,734	10,182	8,633	7,363	6,014	4,961	4,037	2,768
Technical services	5,246	4,895	4,391	4,616	4,279	3,399	3,235	2,561	2,362	2,000	1,674
Flight operations and communications	2,835	2,685	2,509	2,509	2,407	2,062	1,780	1,418	1,233	950	821
Others	5,811	5,916	5,968	5,871	5,578	4,681	3,622	2,664	2,210	1,715	1,273
Total	25,546	24,732	23,354	23,730	22,446	18,775	16,000	12,657	10,766	8,702	6,536
Increase over previous year (%)		5.9	(1.6)	5.7	20.0	17.3	26.4	17.6	23.7	33.1	24.0
Employee Productivity											
Revenue per employee (SR 000)	283,988	300,3	297,5	275,3	222,3	225,3	199,8	203,9	167,6	134,1	112,9
ATK per employee (000)	163,141	165,7	160,4	138,8	132,3	141,2	163,8	143,5	126,8	97,3	80,4

Source: Saudia Annual Reports 1975–1984.

Exhibit 8   Saudization of Jobs: Actual Head Count by Nationality Groups 1985, November 1985

	Saudi	ME/FE	European	American	T.W.A.	Expat Cab. Crew	OOK Local	total	Unfilled	Budgeted
Executive	45 0.18%	19 0.07%	–	–	–	–	–	64 0.25%	08	72
Audit and Security	358 1.40%	40 0.16%	–	–	–	01	–	399 1.56%	12	411
Public Relations	28 0.11%	18 0.07%	01 –	02 0.01%	–	–	–	49 0.19%	02	51
Plng. and Research	28 0.11%	27 0.11%	03 0.01%	03 0.01%	03 0.01%	–	–	64 0.25%	14	78
Arab and Int'l Aff.	778 3.04%	194 0.76%	–	–	–	–	–	972 3.80%	30	1002
EVP Fin. and Admin.	24 0.09%	31 0.12%	01	01	–	–	04 0.02%	61 0.24%	09	70
Data Services	176 0.69%	86 0.34%	52 0.20%	52 0.20%	–	–	–	366 1.43%	98	464
Corp. Admin.	473 1.85%	553 2.16%	65 0.25%	87 0.34%	–	–	07 0.03%	1185 4.63%	160	1345
Personnel	217 0.85%	167 0.65%	11 0.04%	07 0.03%	–	–	42 0.16%	444 1.73%	37	481

	1	2	3	4	5	6	7	8	9	10
Mktg. Sales and Svcs.	335 1.31%	142 0.55%	39 0.15%	5 0.02%	03 0.01%	–	06 0.02%	530 2.07%	41	571
Intl. Regions	87 0.34%	20 0.08%	–	–	–	–	1863 7.28%	1970 7.70%	137	2107
Domestic Areas	4764 18.61%	758 2.96%	09 0.04%	2 0.01%	02 0.01%	–	–	5535 21.62%	240	5775
Sys. Inflt. Svcs.	497 1.94%	58 0.23%	07 0.03%	02 0.01%	03 0.01%	2833 11.07%	45 0.18%	3445 13.46%	143	3588
EVP Operations and Corporate Safety	14 0.05%	09 0.04%	01	07 0.03%	01	–	–	32 0.12%	05	37
Technical Svcs.	2452 9.58	1631 6.37%	533 2.08%	430 1.68%	37 0.14%	–	172 0.67%	5255 20.53%	768	6023
Mat. Mgnt.	292 1.14%	256 1.00%	07 0.03%	18 0.07%	01	–	53 0.21%	627 2.45%	52	679
Flight Operations	1082 4.23%	432 1.69%	242 0.95%	360 1.41%	03 0.01%	–	98 0.38%	2217 8.66%	187	2404
Communications	430 1.68%	117 0.46%	60 0.23%	14 0.05%	–	–	–	621 2.43%	61	682
Total	13237 51.71%	4906 19.16%	1040 4.06%	1000 3.91%	54 0.21%	2833 11.07%	2528 9.88%	25598 100.0%	2161	27759

Source: Unpublished internal document; Manpower Control: Saudia, 1985.

National planners in Saudi Arabia realize the importance of investment in human resources. The third development plan (1980–1985) for the Kingdom and the corporate plan for Saudia both gave manpower development the highest priority. Training is viewed as a way to increase the size and quality of the national labor force and reduce dependence upon expatriate manpower. In Saudia's case, this goal was enunciated early on. A royal decree was issued in 1965, shortly after Saudia became an independent legal entity, which stipulated that educational institutions should be established to train Saudi nationals in all aspects of commercial aviation and airline administration. Today, Saudia's aviation training is so comprehensive that in 1983 the carrier won the World Aerospace Education Award.

Two principles guide the Saudization of jobs at Saudia. First, Saudization – or replacing foreign contract workers with Saudi nationals – is a long-term process that cannot be achieved overnight. It takes years to train a B747 pilot, a flight engineer, or a strategic planner, for example. Second, there are jobs that cannot be performed by Saudi nationals, either because of local tradition (e.g., stewardesses) or foreign labor laws (personnel stationed outside the Kingdom). These jobs account for about one-fourth of Saudia's total manpower pool.

Given the enormity and complexity of the task, training at Saudia is handled by the respective line organization. Thus, corporate training and development, the largest of Saudia's training areas, is supervised by the corporate administration division; marketing training by the marketing division; and technical communications and flight operations by the operations division.

Each year several hundred trainees are sent abroad to attend programs leading to internationally recognized qualifications, such as the pilot certificate. At home, Saudia training departments provide courses for both new recruits and experienced staff covering a wide range of managerial and technical skills. For instance, during 1983 about two-thirds of the marketing division, or 7,247 employees, took at least one course in marketing airline services.

As a result of its massive training effort, Saudia has achieved steady progress toward the goal of Saudization, despite rapid expansion of its operations. Saudis now make up about 51% of the entire work force. About 52% of its flight crewmen are Saudis, as are 78% of the first officers, 46% of the in-Kingdom technical services personnel, 77% of finance division employees, and 82% of employees in the marketing division, excluding the out-of-Kingdom staff (see Exhibit 8).

Marketing

Marketing is the most critical function of any commercial airline. At Saudia, however, marketing is still limited to handling the routine activities of making reservations, selling tickets, and following through with the customer until his or her final destination is reached. This is mainly a reactive rather than proactive strategy. However, as the airline further matures, a full-fledged marketing program may eventually take shape. Nevertheless, it would be wrong to assume that Saudia can or should pattern its marketing program along the lines of other big international carriers. Its prohibition against serving alcoholic beverages can, for example, be viewed as a marketing constraint. However, this can also be viewed as a marketing opportunity to attract not only Muslim passengers from around the world, but also a presumably large non-Muslim segment that is health-conscious or otherwise indifferent to the issue if Saudia can offer other good services at competitive prices. In any case, Saudia will have to eventually devise means to attract new customers, satisfy their changing needs, earn their loyalty, and improve its market share if it is to continue to grow. For instance, unlike its Kuwaiti sister or other airlines outside the Gulf region, Saudia has not introduced an in-flight telephone service. It also has not promoted religious tourism inside or outside the Kingdom. A direct Dhahran-Medina weekend service, for example, at bargain fares has never been contemplated. However, one can assume that continued competitive pressure will lead Saudia into such marketing directions, barring any sudden increase in government protection, which is unlikely.

Passenger Mix

Exhibit 9 shows that the bulk of Saudia's passengers (44%) are government employees (contract workers). These travelers neither pay for their tickets, nor do they have the discretionary choice of normal consumers to shop around for the best service at the most affordable price.

Leisure travelers make up 27% of Saudia's passengers. They constitute the second largest market segment. Since these people pay for their own tickets, they respond favorably to promotional fares and shop around before they buy their tickets.

Business travelers make up about 9% of Saudia's passengers. Virtually none pay for their tickets, and nearly all of them have a noticeable preference for first-class seats. Expatriate employees in Saudi Arabia and "Umra" travelers to Makkah constitute slightly over 10% of Saudia passengers. Whereas the local employer usually pays for the tickets of expatriate travelers to or from the Kingdom, nearly all Umra travelers pay their way. The latter two groups share of Saudia's overall passenger market

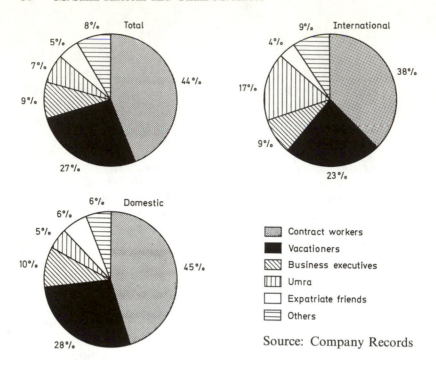

Exhibit 9 · 1987 Market Segments (Jan-Mar). Passenger Mix

is on the decline: there are fewer expatriates for economic reasons, but the reasons why there are also fewer Umra passengers are unknown.

Service Portfolio

Saudia offers the following types of service: passenger (domestic, international, charter, and Hajj), cargo (scheduled/charter), excess luggage, mail, and catering.

Passenger Service

The bulk of Saudia's operating revenue (77%) comes from scheduled passenger service. Only 3% comes from non-scheduled passenger service, such as the seasonal transport of Egyptian teachers and foreign pilgrims to and from the Kingdom. In contrast to other Arab carriers, Saudia operates a sizeable domestic network, which serves 23 destinations. Although the domestic network represents 70% of Saudia's operations, it only generates

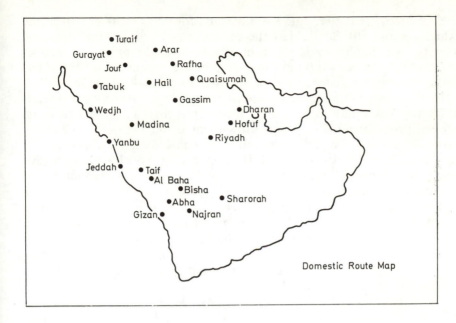

Domestic Route Map

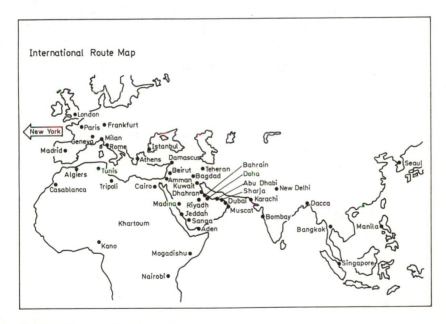

International Route Map

Exhibit 10   Saudia Route Map

28 % of its operating revenue and accounts for 43 % of its expenses (see Exhibits 9 and 10). Saudia has the exclusive right to run this domestic network as a public service. It cannot raise the fare or discontinue its services to a given city without top government's approval. In 1985, it has carried 8.5 million passengers on this network against 8.3 million in 1984.

Saudia also operates a sizeable international passenger network. It calls on 40 major international cities on four continents. This segment of its business generates 72 % of its operating income and 57 % of its operating expenses. Saudia competes with about 40 international carriers who legitimately carry third- and fourth-freedom traffic and who are aggressive enough to carry fifth- and sixth-freedom traffic from the Kingdom's three international gateways (Dhahran, Riyadh, and Jeddah). In contrast to the domestic network, the international network is not only carrying its own weight, but is growing at a robust pace, particularly in the Middle Eastern and Far Eastern markets. In 1985, Saudia carried 3.5 million international passengers against 3.2 million in 1984 and about 3.6 million in 1986. This amounts to about 48 % of the total international traffic market to the Kingdom originating from abroad.

The charter and Hajj markets are less significant but potentially profitable. Land-air packages targeted to Saudi vacationers during summer and winter holidays could be a valuable source of revenue if they were priced and promoted properly. Similarly, Umra and Hajj packages, organized in cooperation with leading Mutawafeen (religious tour guides) and hotel operators and targeted to Muslim minorities in North America and Western Europe, could also be a valuable source of revenue.

Cargo Service

Cargo traffic growth has slowed world-wide and Kingdom-wide in recent years. During the period 1980–1983, Saudia's cargo service grew at double-digit rates, then slowed to 9 % (see Exhibit 11).

Exhibit 11   Saudia's Cargo Traffic

Year	Cargo Brdg (kg million)	Change Rate	Cargo Sales (SR million)	Change Rate
1980	70	–	N/A	–
1981	94	16%	N/A	–
1982	126	34%	N/A	–
1983	156	24%	644	–
1984	162	4%	644	–
1985	177	9%	758	15%

Source: Saudia Marketing Plan (1986): 24.

Marketing Channels

Saudia sells its services directly through its city ticket offices (CTOs) spread throughout the Kingdom and around the world. They are equipped with state of the art computers that allow for automatic booking, fare calculation, and issuing of tickets.

Presently, about 35% to 40% of Saudia tickets are sold through its CTOs, compared with 46% in 1983 and 59% in 1981 (Saudia Marketing Plan 1986). The remaining 60% to 65% are issued and sold by travel agencies, or general sales agents (GSAs) in the Kingdom and in the major cities Saudia calls on abroad. These agents normally charge 5% to 10% of the value of the tickets they write. Usually they split their commission with their customers to attract and retain them, particularly when writing international tickets. Domestic service customers do not have a choice except to fly Saudia, and, even then, they expect to get 2% to 3% off the published fare.

In recognition of the important role of travel agents, Saudia has rented them computers that have direct access to the airline's computer reservation system in Dhahran, Jeddah, and Riyadh. This enables travel agents to make and quickly confirm reservations, and retrieve for their clients the latest flight information, as well as information about car rentals, hotels, and other services.

Saudia Pricing and Price Wars

Saudia prides itself on being a respected member of the International Air Transport Association (IATA).

IATA provides ancillary services to carriers on a pooled basis (e.g., acting as a clearing house, offering management development courses). Until several years ago, it also helped set and stabilize air fares.

The passage of the Air Deregulation Act in the United States in 1978 set in motion the transformation of the American and then the international airline industry. This act has effectively removed all market entry barriers and fare controls. It allowed American carriers to set their own fares, a move which dealt a severe blow to IATA and other fare regulators.

Different carriers opposed the Deregulation Act for different reasons. Those from most developing nations banded together, rallied behind IATA, and kept on operating as if nothing had changed. Saudia was one of those carriers. It perceived deregulation as a threat and continued to abide by rules set under the IATA protective umbrella. Saudia labeled the new rules "unfair," "unauthorized," "illegal,", and "illegitimate."

Saudia's initial insistence on not discounting fares in the face of what it regarded as unfair competition led to some erosion of its share of the international travel market – the backbone of its most profitable sector (see Exhibit 12). It complained to IATA about the "illegal" practices of foreign-based carriers, but to no avail. Frustrated, it launched a "cease and desist" campaign against individual travel agents who were suspected of participating in "price wars." However, this campaign, which was conducted with the blessing of Saudi Civil Aviation Authority and local police, did not put a stop to "illegal discounting."

Exhibit 12   Saudia's Share of the International Travel Market (Percentage)

Year	To and from Jeddah	Riyadh	Dhahran	All Sectors
1981	–	–	–	47.8
1982	46.7	100.0	12.5	47.4
1983	45.1	99.6	10.4	48.5
1984	47.4	90.5	12.3	49.4
1985	48.1	89.1	14.1	51.5

Source: Saudia unpublished data.

In a desperate move to halt the forfeiture of passengers to its foreign competitors, Saudia reluctantly and selectively joined them in the discounting game. Only lately has Saudia introduced promotional fares on selected dense routes (e. g., Paris, London, New York). However, these fares, often subject to restrictions, may have been too little too late. Time will tell how Saudia adapts to the increasingly competitive international environment.

Saudia has made remarkable progress in certain service areas. Its inflight meals, computerized reservation system, and on-time departure performance are well-regarded in the airline industry. However, its on-ground customer service leaves much to be desired, as survey results show.

Company and independent passenger surveys consistently single out preflight services as Saudia's most serious problem area. Based on results of a 1985 company-sponsored passenger survey answered by 2,000 respondents, Saudia has found that:

1) Most passengers are not regularly ticketed at CTOs.
2) More than half of the respondents ticketed in the CTOs rate the behavior of ticketing personnel as good or very good.
3) The efficiency of the check-in-personnel has gotten worse, whereas the behavior of the personnel has slightly improved since 1984.

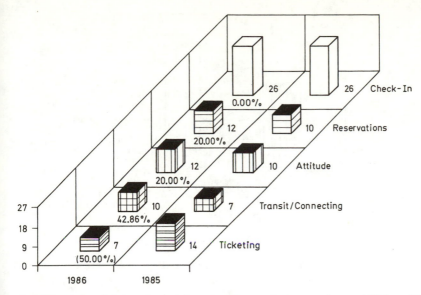

Exhibit 13 A   Major Complaints On-Ground: Comparison – 1986 vs. 1985

Source: System Quality Assurance and Performance Evaluation Travel Impression Reports (Jeddah: Saudi Arabian Airless Corp., 1986)

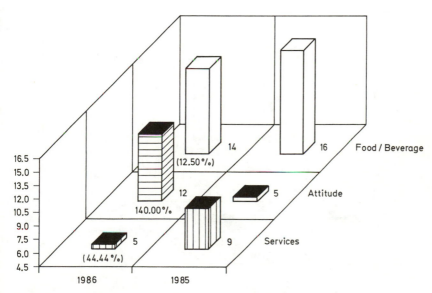

Exhibit 13 B   Major Complaints On-Board: Comparison – 1986 vs. 1985

Source: see Exhibit 13 A

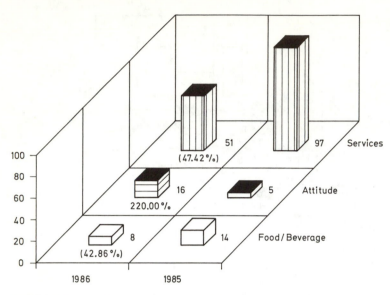

Exhibit 14 A   Major Compliments On-Board: Comparison – 1986 vs. 1985
Source: see Exhibit 13 A

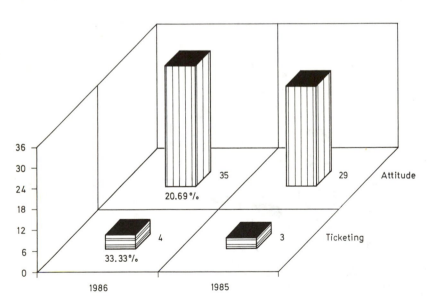

Exhibit 14 B   Major Compliments On-Ground: Comparison – 1986 vs. 1985
Source: see Exhibit 13 A

4) Saudia received its *lowest* ratings (see Exhibits 13 A and 13 B):
   - from Westerners on beverage selection (Islam prohibits the serving and drinking of alcoholic beverages);
   - from Arabs on food selection; particularly on domestic flights; and
   - on in-flight entertainment, including the selection of magazines and newspapers.
5) Saudia received its *highest* ratings (see Exhibit 14 A and 14 B) on the performance of its cabin attendants, the majority of whom are non-Saudis.
6) Saudia's recitation of travel prayer at takeoff is highly rated by Muslim travelers.

In another unpublished company-sponsored survey, a select group of travel agents were recently invited by Saudia to sample its international First-Class service. Those discriminating travelers were impressed by Saudia's in-flight service. However, when it came to service on the ground, they were not equally impressed.

The Manila-based International Travel Research Institute in its INTRAMAR Project gave Saudia only an average rating on passenger service (The Middle East air traveler 1983). Its findings confirm airport statistics (see Exhibit 12) which show that Saudia is not the most preferred carrier even in its own base cities. A recent study by students at King Fahd University of Petroleum and Minerals surveyed a select group of international passengers at Dhahran International Airport to determine the relative ranking of Gulf Cooperation Council carriers on a number of service-related factors. Using the semantic differential methodology, this study ranked Kuwait Airways first overall, followed by Saudia, Gulf Air, and Alia.

Saudia officials acknowledge an inconsistency in the quality of service offered to their customers. They attribute this to: the demotivation, apathetic and even discourteous attitude of some customer service personnel; weak supervision; the absence of a service tradition in the wider Saudi culture; and an over-protective civil service code which makes it tough for a manager to fire a Saudia employee.

Saudia's Future

Saudia is the biggest airline in the Arab world. It has achieved spectacular growth in its route network, capacity, passenger traffic, cargo tonnage, and work force. It has exemplary punctuality, fleet maintenance, and operational technology. Its impact on the local economy has been immense, indeed.

Yet, the downturn in the Gulf region's economy, political instability in the region, and a sluggish corporate culture all pose serious challenges to Saudia. Specific challenges facing Saudia include:

1) Excess capacity in the marketplace.
2) The air traffic market has undergone depression due to the sharply lower number of guest workers in Saudi Arabia, since the completion of basic infrastructure projects and the decline in oil production and revenues, as well as massive cuts in imports, which has depressed the air cargo market.
3) The combined effect of the above trends, plus deregulation of the world airline industry, have given rise to intense competition among the 40 or more international carriers serving the Kingdom.
4) Personnel salaries in the airline industry are steadily rising, putting most Arab carriers at a competitive disadvantage vis-à-vis Third World carriers.
5) Other expenses such as fuel, landing fees, taxes, and insurance premiums are also rising.
6) International economic instability has resulted in the devaluation of the Saudi riyal vis-à-vis the yen and European currencies.
7) Political instability in the Middle East and Far East has resulted in the closure of Lebanon and Iran as viable markets for Saudia.
8) Land transportation that connects Saudi Arabia with Bahrain, Kuwait, Jordan, and Turkey has improved.
9) A worsening cash-flow situation exists due to low load factors and heavy use of leveraging or debt-financing.

Saudia's caretakers are concerned about the possible impact of these factors on the health and direction of their company. They are not sure whether the retrenchment track that the company is on right now is a strong enough medicine for Saudia's ailments.

Saudia is entertaining some long-term proposals designed to revitalize the carrier and make it more competitive. These proposals include:

1) restructuring the company by splitting it into a few manageable units (e. g., international, domestic, cargo, catering, etc.);
2) privatizing or denationalizing the company by selling the assets of each of the smaller units to private investors or to its employees;
3) improving the productivity of available resources, including people, planes, and facilities;
4) changing the present strategy to include one or more of the following:
   – match competition by introducing lower fares and more and better service;
   – introduce more point-to-point destinations;

- expand international service to Japan, Rio de Janeiro, and Muslim Africa; and
- diversify into new passenger and non-passenger operations. These might include charter tours, handling foreign carrier accounts in the Kingdom's international airports, aircraft rental, airport hotels, restaurants, and car rental.

An industry study published in 1984 concluded that carriers best positioned to emerge from the present turmoil would be the ones that control their operating expenses wisely, utilize their employees and their aircraft intelligently, finance their expansions internally, and treat their customers courteously (Lynch 1984). Whether Saudia meets these criteria may ultimately depend on its ability to react quickly given its present size. Giant airlines such as Saudia are like large battleships. Both have enormous momentum once they get going, but can be slow to change directions. In the dynamic environment of today's airline industry, maneuverability may be the ultimate key to success.

References

Lynch, J. (1984): *Airline organizations in the 1980's: An industry report on strategies and structures for coping with change*, London: Macmillan.
Manpower Control (1985): *Manpower control*, (December).
The Middle East air traveller (1983): An AACO seminar conducted by Boeing Commercial Airplane Company, Seattle: Washington, November 1983.
Saudia Annual Report (1975–1984): *Annual report – Statistical supplement*, Saudi Arabian Airline (undated internal report).
Saudia Annual Report (1981): *Annual report*.
Saudia Marketing Plan (1986): Marketing plan, Unpublished corporate document, Saudia.
System quality assurance and performance evaluation travel impression reports, Saudia, 1986.

4.3   Kuwait Airways Corporation (KAC)

M. Sami Kassem and Ghazi M. Habib

Introduction

One morning in February 1953, two Kuwaiti entrepreneurs met, and their discussion ended in the birth of an idea. They soon organized a meeting with a group of prominent businessmen who discussed the formation of a national airline company. In less than 30 years, this company has grown from an infant regional carrier – specializing in providing a fast and reliable means of transporting the manpower needed by the burgeoning oil industry – into a respectable international airline with a route network covering 42 major cities, 128 offices around the world, a staff numbering 6,700 employees, and an ultramodern fleet of 19 wide-bodied aircraft.

As the company was building its infrastructural facilities and modernizing its fleet, the economic and political landscape of the Gulf states was deteriorating. Consequently, the region's airline industry encountered many difficulties, including severe competition, economic recession, fare wars, currency fluctuations, and the Gulf war.

As a result of these hard times, KAC began to feel the growing pains of indigestion. Its management is trying a little of almost everything: suspending service to war-zone cities (Beirut, Baghdad, and Teheran), trimming costs, cutting capacity, discounting fares, borrowing money, and selling aircraft.

This case study describes some of the tough strategic choices being made to effect KAC's recovery. It provides the reader with an opportunity to evaluate the soundness of each alternative, identify the various internal and external obstacles associated with each, and recommend better ways of coping with the present recession.

Corporate Mission

KAC is a public corporation constituted and regulated under Law 21 of 1965. Article 1 of that law states that Kuwait Airways is considered a public institution, wholly owned by the government of the state of Kuwait, yet it has its own separate legal entity and operates of a commercial basis.

Article 2 specifies the mission of KAC as performing all activities pertaining to civilian air transportation and operating all services connected with commercial air traffic in Kuwait, such as maintenance hangars, engine overhaul shops, catering, ground handling, etc.

Stages of Strategic Development

Four stages in the evolutions of KAC's strategy can be identified. Stage 1 (1954–1964) saw the birth of a regional carrier; stage 2 (1964–1977) was characterized by rapid expansion into the jet age; stage 3 (1978–1983) involved extensive growth in infrastructure, and the current stage 4 (1984–present) is a period of both intensive development and retrenchment to cope with the turbulent environment. Management has indicated that it would consider the company successful if it steers a steady course out of the present inhospitable environment without going into the red or having to lay off a massive number of employees.

The Birth of a Regional Airline (1954–1964)

A group of prominent Kuwaiti businessmen saw an opportunity to transport workers and technicians from nearby labor-rich countries to Kuwait where they were needed in the booming oil industry. They formed a company with a capital of Kuwaiti Dinar (KD) 150,000 and less than a dozen employees. They bought an old DC-3 and on May 17, 1954, started a thrice weekly service to Basra, Iraq. Shortly afterwards, three more regional routes were added: Jerusalem, Damascus, and Abadan. There was no airport to speak of in Kuwait at that time. The plane landed on a sandy runway that is today known as the Nouzha air strip. There was neither a control tower nor a maintenance facility – only a small wireless radio in a tent that was set up by the runway. Later on, routine maintenance check-ups were done in the open on a concrete slab just big enough for a small aircraft.

Recognizing the need of the infant company for money to buy additional aircraft to meet increasing passenger demand, the government acquired a 50% interest in the company for KD 200,000. As a result, the company's capital was doubled, and its name changed to Kuwait Airways Corporation in 1955. More aircraft (Handy Pages, DC-4s, Viscounts) were added to its fleet of three DC-3s. New routes were opened to Bahrain, Cairo, and

Dhahran in 1957 and to Bombay, Karachi, and Doha in 1959. Two landmarks of this stage were:

1) the signing of two consecutive management contract agreements with BOAC, the first in 1954 and the other in 1958; and
2) the arrival of a tough competitor on the scene with a better product and a modern fleet. Its name was "Trans Arabian Airways" or TAA.

Rapid Expansion (1964–1977)

During this stage, Kuwait Airways Corporation achieved remarkable expansion in its fleet, routes, and operations. The government threw its full support behind KAC. It bought out the only competing airline (i.e., Trans Arab Airways) in 1962 and the remaining 50 % of KAC's stock in 1964. KAC had thus become a public corporation reporting to the Minister of Finance and Planning. This gave the company a fresh supply of funds to modernize and expand its fleet and develop a European route network. KAC entered the jet age by purchasing Comet 4-Cs, Tridents, and Boeing 707s, 727s, and 747s. With these fast jets, the company expanded its route network, first to Western European cities (London, Paris, Geneva, Frankfurt), then to Copenhagen, Rome, Istanbul, Amsterdam, Madrid, and Africa (Libya, Tunisia, Morocco, and Sudan).

With the termination of the management contract agreement with BOAC in 1963, KAC became completely independent. It took over all of the administrative responsibilities, even though it was not ready to perform them. It hired two consulting teams from Swissair and from TWA to put the company and its management on the right track. These teams found local management to be thin, inexperienced, confused, disorganized, and highly centralized.

Kuwaiti graduates were hired fresh out of schools to fill in the vacuum created by the departure of the British staff. They were put through extensive training programs both at home and abroad to enable them to acquire the requisite skills for running an airline. Ever since 1963, manpower training and development has been a critical function within KAC's organization, reporting directly to the chief executive officer.

Extensive Growth in Infrastructural Facilities (1978–1983)

This stage in the evolution of KAC's strategy was characterized by four attributes.

First, KAC rounded out its route network to cover destinations in the rapidly growing Asian markets (Bangkok, Seoul, Manila, Colombo) and the glamorous North Atlantic market.

Second, it entered the wide-body age by purchasing four jumbo jets (B-747s) in 1977 and eight Airbuses (A-310s) in 1981.

Third, the company accumulated heavy losses, particularly in the years 1978–1981 when operating costs rose much faster than operating revenues. The government was very generous with its subsidy and refused to raise airfares or cargo tariffs. In addition, the infrastructural projects cost the company a fortune to build and a fat budget to staff and operate.

Fourth, KAC developed in-house capabilities to perform services that once were performed by outside agencies. Today, KAC is almost self-sufficient in the field of maintenance, engine overhaul, crew training, computerized reservations, other computer applications, and catering. In addition, it has its own print shop, technical warehouses, and air-taxi services.

Three strategic questions arose in connection with these costly projects. First, were they economically justifiable? Second, should KAC market its services to other carriers to reduce its unit costs and provide KAC with an additional source of revenue? If so, how?

The company answered the first question in the affirmative. Its planners claimed that in the long run it would be cheaper to provide such services in-house than having to pay outside contractors to perform them. Take training as an example. It would have cost KAC about KD 47,000 to have a deck crew of twelve 727 pilots trained abroad on the Airbus. KAC has done the job in-house for only KD 20,000. Not only is KAC able to control the cost and quality of its in-house services, but it also has generated local jobs and additional revenues. Economics aside, KAC is obligated by its charter to offer a minimum of aviation-related support services to all other carriers passing through Kuwait. KAC is the only agency authorized by the government to provide such services and is also the only agency capable of projecting an honorable image of the country in the process. As for the marketing of these support services, there has been a lot of talk but little action to date.

It is interesting to note that long before the infrastructure projects were built, KAC commissioned a team from the national planning agency to study and audit its operations. A central finding of that team was the absence of a well-conceived strategy that guides KAC's behavior in the marketplace. The study team found neither operational goals nor criteria to measure KAC's achievement against.

The Current Stage: Intensive Development and Retrenchment

Along with other Gulf carriers, KAC is facing severe difficulties in its external environment. The Gulf war is still going on. Political terrorism has led to the tightening of security measures at all airports in the region and excessive delays in the granting of visas. The glut in oil markets and the resulting drop in oil revenues has led to a shrinkage of passenger traffic. The passage of a lot of foreign carriers through Kuwait and other Gulf airports has caused the "dumping" of unoccupied seats at bargain fares. Given its high-cost structure, KAC finds it increasingly difficult to match these heavily discounted fares.

To cope with these adverse environmental conditions, KAC has adopted a number of measures aimed at cutting operating costs and generating instant revenues. It formed three committees: one in charge of disposing of aircraft; a second in charge of cutting fuel costs; and a third one for trimming labor and other operating costs. The third committee recommended a freeze on hiring, a gradual cut in the size of the expatriate labor force, a reduction in flight frequencies, dropping a few unprofitable routes, and better adjusting airplane capacities to specific routes.

The strategic emphasis of the current stage goes beyond retrenchment. For one thing, there is a concern with fine-tuning the present organizational structure to make it leaner and more responsive. There is also concern about manpower development. Management is investing heavily in developing Kuwaiti nationals to assume leadership positions within the organization.

Organization

As a state-owned corporation, KAC is externally controlled by an eight-man board of directors who are appointed by the Minister of Finance. This board is chaired by Mr. Ahmad al-Mishari, who is also KAC's chief executive officer and the chairman of virtually all corporate standing committees.

The present organization structure of KAC is shown in Exhibit 1.
There are five line functions: finance and administration, commercial affairs, engineering, operations, and airline services. Each one is headed by a vice-president. There are also six staff functions: training and development, security, auditing, planning and research, legal affairs, and public relations. Each staff function is headed by a manager.

KAC's management makes heavy use of standing committees. There are at least 15 committees that together form part of KAC's organizational structure. There is a committee in charge of every conceivable aspect of airline operations. Some examples are personnel affairs, scholarships, central planning, budget, aircraft leasing, and purchase and disposal. Each one of these committees is chaired by the chief executive officer (CEO) and composed of the head of the concerned functional areas and other key department heads.

KAC also makes occasional use of ad hoc committees. For instance, in May 1986 it formed five temporary committees to look into ways and means of cutting costs without jeopardizing service levels or safety. Each one of these committees was in charge of a major cost item (e. g., payroll, administrative expenses, flight operation, marketing and sales, engineering maintenance).

Functional Area Strategies

Personnel

KAC is a leading employer in Kuwait. It has more than 6,600 employees on its payroll. Not all of them are Kuwaiti nationals, and not all of them are employed in customer-handling types of activities.

Although the number of employees has stabilized over the last three years, their productivity has improved quite considerably. Available tonne kilometers per employee rose from 106,682 in 1980 to 165,611 in 1985. Revenue per employee – another index of employee productivity – rose from KD 46,049 in 1980 to KD 83,049 in 1985.

As part of its retrenchment strategy, KAC has imposed a freeze on hiring new recruits. It has also implemented a policy of trimming down the size of its labor force.

Training and Development

When the management contract agreement with BOAC was terminated in 1963, training assumed a strategic role in KAC's operations. That role has been recently reinforced by national policy which aims at developing a truly Kuwaiti work force capable of meeting the needs of modern industry and commerce.

All of KAC's training activities are centrally coordinated in one unit headed by a manager who reports directly to the general manager or CED. Whereas in the past technical training was done outside Kuwait at a high cost, it is currently done in KAC's newly established crew training center, which is one of the most advanced in the region. This center consists of the following four sections:

1) B-747 and A 310-600 flight simulators and cockpit procedures trainers. This ultramodern and expensive equipment is used for training pilots and flight engineers;
2) audio visual trainers (AVTs) and route clearance systems (ROCs);

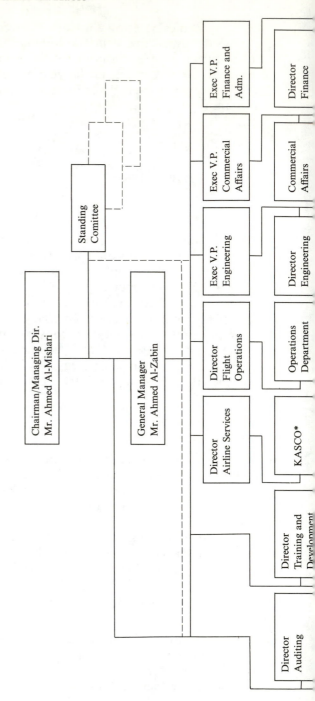

* Kuwait Aviation Service Company

Exhibit 1   1986 Organigram Kuwait Airways Corporation

3) emergency evacuation training, which includes a B-747 and B-727 evacuation trainer, a swimming pool, and various other items used in emergency training;
4) a ground school.

Although the entire management staff is made up of Kuwaiti nationals, a good percentage of technical staff is expatriate. KAC's training objective is to have 25% of its pilots, 100% of the co-pilots, 70% of the flight engineers, and 50% of the ground engineers be Kuwaiti nationals by 1990.

Marketing

KAC is in the business of transporting passengers, cargo, and mail. During 1984 and 1985, passenger service contributed 80% of total revenues, while freight contributed 13%, mail 0.5%, and other operations the remaining 6.5%.

Due to the faltering economy of the Gulf states, the prolonged border war between Iraq and Iran, and the huge excess capacity in the area, intense competition among the region's carriers is the order of the day. Escalating price wars are common throughout the region, particularly in Kuwait.

KAC's traditional response to fare wars was to ignore them. That was in good times, when oil was selling at US $36 a barrel, the economy was booming, and KAC had direct access to the public treasury. But as the economy cooled off and air traffic slowed down, KAC took a more aggressive stance. It broke ranks with its sister Arab carriers and matched competitors' fares in order to maintain its market share. For instance, it offered one of the lowest fares to New York. However, visa restrictions, tight security measures at Kuwait airport, and the resultant flight delays have combined to prevent KAC from attracting sixth-freedom traffic despite its deeply discounted fares. At home, the company uses its own sales offices to distribute its tickets. Abroad, it emphasizes travel agencies, whom it provides with its own computerized reservation system known as SODA.

Unlike other Gulf carriers, the bulk of KAC's passengers (about 53%) are Kuwaiti nationals. The remainder are foreign workers and businessmen who do not pay for their own tickets. This latter passenger group is declining in size with the worsening of the economic situation and the rapid nationalization of critical jobs.

To appeal to its core client group, Kuwaiti nationals, KAC behaves as a responsible corporate citizen. It sponsors educational contests, gives free tickets to outstanding high school and university graduates, and offers training and job opportunities to deserving students. KAC also projects and maintains a positive customer service image. For instance, the company was the first one in the region to offer a business class and long-distance telephone service on its European and North American flights. It offers its business-class travelers roomy space and a selection of foods and inflight entertainment. KAC also provides Arabic-speaking stewardesses tastefully designed uniforms.

Flight Operations

Arab carriers in general and Gulf carriers in particular are in a constant race to enlarge and modernize their fleets. Each one seems to want the biggest and most modern fleet, KAC, being no exception. It has pursued an aggressive and ambitious fleet modernization program. By the end of 1985, it had one of the most modern and uniform fleets in the region. It was the first Arab carrier to use the B-707, the European Airbus, and, more recently, the new B-767. Exhibit 2 shows the size and composition of KAC's fleet.

Exhibit 2   Kuwait Airways Fleet Composition (1986)

Type	No.
B 747–200 B	4
B 727–200	4
B 767	3
A–310–200	5
A–300–600	3
Total	19

Source: Kuwait Airways Corp. (1985) Annual Report: 33.

KAC also had made various attempts to reduce operational costs. It has put a freeze on hiring new employees except as replacements. It consolidated and rationalized its route system to eliminate unprofitable flights and improve the yield on profitable routes. It gradually retired its costly and noisy B-707 fleet and replaced it with B-727s, which have significantly lowered KAC's operating costs. They use less jet fuel per flight hour. KAC also upgraded the technical efficiency of the B-727 and B-747 engines to reduce fuel consumption. It set up a special committee on fuel consumption. And it introduced computerized systems in the operation department for flight programming and fuel consumption calculations. Finally, KAC earmarked two of its newly acquired A-300s for quick sale to generate cash and cut its oversized fleet down to size.

Money Matters at KAC

Exhibits 3–7 provide some recent financial data on Kuwait Airways. In examining this set of financial statements, three observations can be made:

1) Kuwait Aviation Service Company (KASCO) is a wholly-owned subsidiary of KAC that was formed in 1981. KASCO has been making a profit since 1984 at the rate of KD 567,000 and KD 444,000 in 1984 and 1985, respectively.
2) KAC has been making a profit since 1982. However, its profitability has been rather meager, averaging KD 200,000 a year. This profit has not been derived from the core transportation activity (passengers and cargo) of the airline. Still, KAC's profitability is a noteworthy achievement in view of the rapid deterioration of economic conditions in the Gulf region.
3) Whereas operating revenues have stagnated, operating expenses have steadily risen, despite management's efforts to trim them down. Fuel costs and the payroll are the biggest two expense items.

Exhibit 3   Statement of Income (Loss) – Kuwait Airways

	Year ended June 30, 1985 KD	Year ended June 30, 1984 KD
Operating income	128,621,092	126,315,298
Operating expenses	138,725,786	130,534,262
Net operating loss	(10,104,694)	(4,218,964)
Other income (loss):		
Income from deposits and investments	6,309,591	3,249,555
Results of subsidiary company	566,817	443,786
Other items, net.	1,052,629	736,073
	7,929,037	4,429,414
Net (loss) income for the year before extraordinary item	(2,175,657)	210,450
Extraordinary item	2,346,548	
Net income for the year after extraordinary item transferred to due to government	170,891	210,450

Source: 1985 Annual Report

Exhibit 4   Balance Sheet – Kuwait Airways

Assets	June 30, 1985 KD	June 30, 1984 KD
Current assets:		
Cash in hand	208,110	135,101
Cash at banks	24,782,049	30,137,586
Time deposits	80,153,100	57,912,380
Accounts receivable	45,275,228	41,385,176
Prepayments and accrued income	7,645,756	7,101,327
Inventories	870,974	739,450
Total current assets	158,935,217	137,411,020
Other assets	2,217,539	2,243,187
Investments	12,660,516	11,571,822
Fixed assets		
Cost	306,346,608	294,170,444
Less accumulated depreciation	77,555,454	69,532,583
Net fixed assets	228,791,154	224,637,861
Advance against acquisition of aircraft and other fixed assets	14,582,199	20,057,532
Total fixed assets	243,373,353	244,695,393
	417,186,625	395,921,422

Liabilities and Government Equity		
Current liabilities:		
Accounts payable	10,679,600	13,879,040
Accrued expenses	7,721,542	6,278,359
Unearned transportation revenue	31,425,081	31,196,828
Provision for fleet overhaul	2,493,532	2,903,816
Due to government	978,708	807,817
Total current liabilities	53,298,463	55,065,860
Deferred credits	16,595,427	13,534,804
Staff benefit funds:		
Provident Fund	11,058,096	9,544,775
Provision for staff indemnity	10,683,933	9,639,741
Total staff benefit funds	21,742,029	19,184,516
Government equity		
Authorized capital	350,000,000	350,000,000
Paid- up capital	326,052,908	309,383,770
Balance with government	(502,202)	(1,247,528)
Total government equity		308,136,242
	417,186,625	395,921,422

Note: One Kuwaiti Dinar (KD) equals approximately $3.60.
Source: 1985 Annual Report.

Exhibit 5   Statement of Changes in Financial Position

	Year ended June 30, 1985 KD	Year ended June 30, 1984 KD
Funds generated (absorbed) by operations:		
Net income for the year	170,891	210,450
Add (deduct) items not affecting the movement of funds:		
Depreciation of fixed assets	18,067,931	13,112,737
Amortization of key-money	47,553	46,898
Provision for staff benefits	1,300,545	1,627,248
Results of subsidiary company	566,817	(443,786)
Profit on disposal of fixed assets	570,782	(292,549)
	20,724,519	14,260,998
Other sources:		
Advances received from government	17,414,464	108,685,651
Staff contributions and interest on provident funds	1,256,968	1,552,595
Proceeds of fixed assets sales	3,118,318	9,261,041
Deferred credits	3,060,623	13,534,804
	24,850,373	133,034,091
Total funds provided	45,574,892	147,295,089
Applications:		
Capital expenditure	25,939,948	126,641,436
Purchase of bonds and notes	450,910	1,348,640
Increase in other investments		1,405,106
Due to government net income for the year.	170,891	210,450
Increase in other assets	499,526	1,564,571
Total applications	27,060,275	131,170,203
Increase in working capital	18,513,617	16,124,886
Movement in working capital:		
Increase (decrease) in current assets:		
Cash in hand and at banks	(5,282,528)	(9,761,037)
Time deposits	22,240,720	15,167,467
Accounts receivable, prepayments and accrued income	4,434,481	10,292,391
Inventories	131,524	68,430
	21,524,197	15,767,251

Exhibit 5   Statement of Changes in Financial Position (continued)

	Year ended June 30, 1985 KD	Year ended June 30, 1984 KD
Increase (decrease) in current liabilities:		
Accounts payable and accrued expenses	(2,999,440)	(795,744)
Unearned transportation revenue	228,253	2,316,674
Provision for fleet overhaul	(410,284)	(2,089,015)
Due to government	170,891	210,450
	(3,010,580)	(357,635)
Increase in working capital	18,531,617	16,124,886

Source: 1985 Annual Report.

Exhibit 6   Comparative Financial Highlights

Financial Information		Jan. 1980	Dec. 1981	Jan. '82– Jun. '83 (18 mths)	Jul. '83– Jun. '84	Jul. '84– Jun. '85
Passenger revenue	(KD.000)	55,739	70,279	135,133	94,461	94,884
Ex baggage revenue	(KD.000)	3,735	4,130	9,626	7,452	7,305
P.O. Mail revenue	(KD.000)	608	733	1,195	1,006	1,159
Freight revenue	(KD.000)	10,316	12,846	19,952	14,254	16,069
Total traffic revenue	(KD.000)	70,398	87,988	165,870	117,173	119,417
Charter revenue	(KD.000)	936	1,712	2,135	708	505
Handling revenue	(KD.000)	3,443	4,093	8,573	6,983	7,172
Other operating revenue	(KD.000)	1,995	1,434	4,113	5,881	1,527
Total operating revenue	(KD.000)	76,772	95,227	180,727	126,315	128,621
Total operating expense	(KD.000)	88,546	108,462	181,358	130,534	138,726
Operating profit (loss)	(KD.000)	(11,774)	(13,235)	(631)	(4,219)	(10,104)
Other non-operating revenue	(KD.000)	7,645	1,854	1,228	4,429	10,275
Net profit (loss)	(KD.000)	(4,129)	(11,381)	597	210	171
No. of employes		5,920	6,146	6,460	6,685	6,670
Traffic revenue per ATK	(Fils)	111	111	127	115	108
Traffic revenue per PTK	(Fils)	258	232	242	231	216
Unit cost per ATK	(Fils)	140	136	144	128	126
Cost/revenue ratio	(%)	115.3	113.9	102.0	103.3	107.9
Operating Revenue/ Employee	(KD)	12,968	15,494	28,580	18,895	19,284

Source: 1985 Annual Report.

Exhibit 7   Comparative Statistical Highlights

Statistical Information	1980	1981	Jan. 1982– Jun. 1983 (18 mths)	Jul. '83– Jun. '84	Jul. '84– Jun. '85
Revenue hours flown	32,433	37,191	57,188	42,152	42,600
Unduplicated route Kms.	88,503	106,531	100,558	104,500	115,062
Revenue kms flown (000)	19,527	22,851	36,014	26,896	26,861
Available tonne kms (000)	631,557	795,926	1,307,192	1,022,753	1,104,623
Revenue tonne kms (000)	272,608	379,824	686,940	508,239	553,935
Load factor (%)	43.2	47.7	52.6	49.7	50.2
No. of revenue pax	1,076,214	1,252,477	2,165,211	1,493,051	1,512,379
Available seat kms (000)	3,981,343	4,846,841	8,346,801	6,532,102	7,067,311
Pax kms flown (000)	2,113,789	2,880,341	5,325,419	3,683,841	3,863,048
Seat factor (%)	53.1	59.4	63.8	56.4	54.7
Tons of freight	29,062	34,848	58,022	45,720	51,433
Tons of baggage excess	4,421	4,492	9,582	7,254	7,075
Tons of mail	1,527	1,618	2,487	2,181	2,453

Source: 1985 Annual Report.

KAC's Future Direction

KAC continues to serve the needs of its traveling public and fulfill the mission outlined by its owner – the Kuwaiti government. It has offered training and job opportunities to the young generation of Kuwaiti nationals. It has projected a positive image of the country both at home and abroad.

As of late, it has been a victim of a set of environmental conditions which have impacted all of the Gulf carriers negatively: severe economic recession brought about by a glut of oil in world markets, political tension and domestic unrest brought about by the continuation of the Iraq-Iran war and the escalation of international terrorism, and fare wars brought about by excess capacity, deregulation, and currency fluctuations. These have all affected KAC's pattern of growth. In contrast to the rapid expansion of the late 1970s, figures for 1985 show a decline of 3.1% in passenger traffic and 13% in cargo traffic from 1984. KAC is considering the use of various marketing tools (including fare-discounting), cost-cutting measures, and fund-raising tactics (including selling air-craft) to mitigate the negative effects of the slumping economy.

As the recession deepens, the Gulf war continues, and the traffic statistics deteriorate even further; the basic strategy KAC selects will be critical for its survival. The central question facing its top management is how to position the firm in the airline industry? Could KAC share its costly facilities with other carriers in the region through joint operating agreements? Can it better focus on specific segments of its markets? Can it further differentiate itself from competing carriers, and if so, how?

4.4   Gulf Air (GF)

M. Sami Kassem and Ghazi M. Habib

Introduction

Gulf Air (GF) is the second largest, the most profitable, and perhaps the most renowned airline in the Arab world. According to 1984 IATA statistics, it ranked 16th among the 134 IATA members in terms of passengers carried (2.69 million) and 19th in terms of annual growth rate (25 %). It has achieved an unbroken record of profitability among Arab air-carriers since 1980. Its average annual rate of return on shareholders' funds is 18 %. It has been called repeatedly by several specialized international organization the safest and best airline to the Middle East, as well as the region's top cargo carrier.

GF pioneered regional cooperation of air transportation in the Arabian Peninsula. In a real sense, it is the SAS of the Middle East: the only multinational airline in the Arab world. It is jointly owned by the governments of four Gulf states: Bahrain, Oman, Qatar, and Abu Dhabi. It is managed as an economic entity by a team of young Gulf nationals and staffed by people from 40 different countries who work together side-by-side as a single cohesive team.

GF also is one of the first Arab carriers determined to go private. Its board of directors has already approved in principle to sell 49 % of the company's shares to private citizens of the four owner states.

GF is unusual in still another aspect. It is the only Arab airline that has emphasized the role of strategic planning and singled it out for specialized attention by top management. Corporate planning is one of the three basic functional units of the newly organized corporation. It is supervised by an executive vice-president who is in charge of formulating long-term plans in such vital areas as new market entry, airline fleet and facilities, capital structure, human resources, and business diversification. The entire top management groups sits on the planning steering committee, which is headed by the chief executive officer. The theory here is that while planning is made the responsibility of specialized executives, it is at the same time the responsibility of every GF manager. Each one is therefore involved in the strategic planning process and committed to the implementation of the strategic plan itself.

History

On March 24, 1950, the company was founded under the name of Gulf Aviation Ltd. by an ex-British air force officer. This entrepreneur saw a need for fast and reliable air service to link the Gulf countries with one another and with Europe and the Indian subcontinent. The company began its operations by using a modest fleet consisting of an Anson Mark-1, Auster, and De Haviland. It scheduled regular flights between Bahrain, Sharjah, Doha, and Dhahran. Increasing demand for air travel compelled the company to increase the size of its fleet. Lacking the necessary means to finance the purchase of four De Havilands and four DC-3s, the company merged with British Overseas Airways Corporation (BOAC), which became the majority shareholder. More plans were added to the company's fleet. The company purchased one Fokker-27 in 1967, a second one in 1968, and a third one in 1971. It leased and then bought a set of VC 10s for use on its new scheduled service between London and Bahrain, Muscat, Doha, and Abu Dhabi.

In an effort to gain control over a critical national resource, the governments of Bahrain, Qatar, Oman, and the United Arab Emirates decided to purchase all of the company's shares in 1973. In this landmark year, Gulf Air became the national airline of these four states.

The new company started to expand its route network, increase and diversify its fleet, bolster its work force, and develop its organizational structure. In order to expand its international network to cover more cities in Europe, the Middle East, and Far East, the company gradually acquired eight B-737s and nine L-1011s, and slowly phased its VC 10s and BAC 1–11 out of service.

The company suffered heavy financial losses during 1977, 1978, and 1979, totalling 27 million Bahraini dinars (about US $ 70 million). A change in its top management, however, resulted in a spectacular turnaround. Mr. Ali Al-Malki, the present chief executive, was handpicked by the board of directors to engineer and manage that turnaround.

Specifically, the new mangement team put the company on a retrenchment track, improved its productivity, wiped out its accumulated losses, and achieved an impressive return to equity. It expanded the route network by adding 12 destinations, invested in developing the carrier's human resources, diversified its business operations, and, more recently, re-organized the relationships among its key units.

No sooner had the new management put its house in order than it began to face another challenge: the rapid economic contraction in the Gulf region leading to a recession that continues even today. As a result, the airline industry is going through a very difficult period. It is plagued by

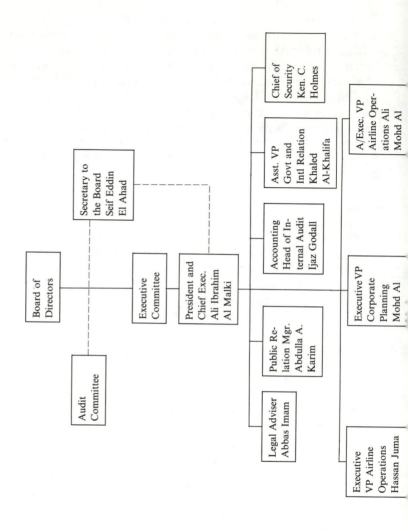

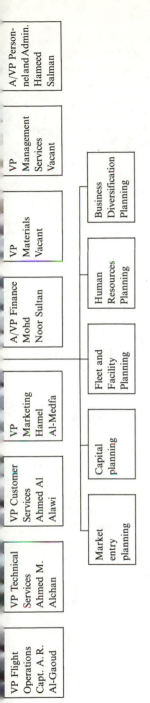

Exhibit 1   Gulf Air Organization Structure

overcapacity and the resultant price wars that go with it. Political uncertainty and stress resulting from the Iran-Iraq war have added to operational pressures and may have affected ticket sales. Finally, improved surface transport systems and the opening of the King Fahd Causeway linking Saudi Arabia to Bahrain are likely to result in reduced air travel, particularly on the profitable Dhahran-Manama route. These factors are likely to work in favor of those foreign carriers passing through the Gulf on a Temporary Operating Permit (TOP), such as Air France, KLM, Lufthansa, Singapore Airlines, Cathay Pacific, and Qantas.

In the face of these environmental challenges, can GF still compete with these big foreign carriers, not only on its own turf but also on theirs? Can Gulf Air still aspire to be a truly global airline?

Gulf Leadership

Gulf Air's management is externally controlled by a 16-man board of directors representing the four shareholding states. Each state selects four prominent public servants drawn from the worlds of finance, civil aviation, and transport. Together, the chosen 16 members and the chief executive elect a chairman, who serves for one year. The chairmanship rotates among the member states in a sequence based on their alphabetical order. Being a multinational public corporation, GF does not report to any national government, thereby guaranteeing that its decisions are not going to be tilted by the political expediencies of any member state.

The board performs three functions. First, it serves as a review organ. Second, it is empowered to remove members of top management who may fail to perform. Third, it represents the interests of the shareholding states.

GF is managed by a team of young, dedicated, and experienced Gulf nationals. The chief executive and his senior staff are all in their mid-thirties, with an average airline experience of 10 years each. The company has a policy of systematically rotating its executive personnel to ensure their cross-fertilization, guard against the tendency toward suboptimization, and engender a feeling of cooperation among them.

The company has been recently reorganized into three functional units: airline operations, airline services, and corporate planning. The new organization is shown in Exhibit 1.

Each of the line units is headed by an executive vice-president. Whereas the first two units focus their activities on the day-to-day operations of the company, the third one – corporate planning – focuses on the long-term process of strategy: adapting GF to environmental Challenges and opportunities and allocating its scarce resources accordingly.

The three major line functions are aided by five staff units. Each one reports directly to the CEO, Al-Malki. These staff functions are:

1) legal affairs;
2) public relations;
3) internal auditing;
4) government and international relations;
5) security.

The following pages detail some functional area strategies and describe the elements of the turnaround strategy implemented in the early 1980s and the new route proposal.

Management and Personnel

GF employs about 4,600 persons. About 25 % of these are flight personnel. About 40 % are Gulf nationals. The remainder have to be imported from other Arab countries, Europe, and the Far East, which puts GF at a competitive disadvantage. The size and composition of the labor force is shown in Exhibit 2. The average wage of its employes, compared with other carriers, is shown in Exhibit 3.

GF invests heavily in training and development. The average annual training bill is US $ 10 million. Comprehensive training programs in Bahrain and elsewhere are available to all employees. Gulf nationals are being trained overseas as pilots and as qualified engineers.

GF considers its employees – foreigners and nationals alike – the essence of its organization. In a service-oriented organization like GF, people

Exhibit 2   Human Resources: Size and Composition

Staff	1984	1983	1982	1981	1980
Gulf nationals:					
Ground personnel	1,689	1,287	1,336	1,319	1,259
Flight personnel	185	159	190	196	180
Expatriates:					
Ground personnel	1,819	1,887	1,854	1,712	1,842
Flight personnel	930	879	627	679	690
Total employee strength	4,623	4,212	4,007	3,906	3,971
Revenue per employee (Barhaini dinars)	51,401	52,789	50,063	47,825	41,635

Exhibit 3   Average Wage (1983) (In U.S. Dollars)

Carrier	Number of Employees	Average Wage
Singapore	9,948	20,121
KLM	19,193	23,298
British Airways	36,096	24,450
SAS	17,710	25,586
Alia	4,760	11,490
Gulf Air	4,623	26,623

Source: GF corporate document.

determine the character and strength of the company. Two people-related policies are key in explaining the success of GF. One is a motivational strategy, which:

1) provides employees with the opportunity to share in the success of the company through high wages and profit-sharing plans;
2) promotes people from within the company on the basis of merit;
3) provides generous fringe benefits including housing loans to Gulf nationals;
4) involves employees in managing the company through an employee suggestion scheme.

The other noticeable feature of GF culture is the unusual team spirit that permeates its work force, particularly the top management staff. Even though the board of directors and the executive vice-presidents come from the four shareholding states, and even though the work force is drawn from over 40 nationalities, all employees seem to work together and pull together in the same direction. Top management obviously sets an example for others to follow. Team efforts are valued dearly. Systematic job rotation and frequent use of committees as decision-making tools combine to promote team spirit and corporate loyalty among GF employees.

Finance

GF recorded its sixth consecutive profitable year in 1984 – a considerable achievement in view of the worsening economic situation in the Gulf region and the increasing competition from international carriers with lower operating costs. The company policy of strenuous cost control which was applied throughout the early 1980s has, in fact, achieved containment of controllable costs.

Exhibit 4   Five Year Financial Record 1980–1984 (in Bahraini Dinars)

	1984 (BD000s)	1983 (BD000s)	1982 (BD000s)	1981 (BD000s)	1980 (BD000s)
Passenger and baggage	208,438	191,297	174,310	158,679	136,930
Freight	17,102	15,668	17,459	18,367	21,110
Mail	1,152	730	723	759	568
Helicopter charters	2,457	2,712	2,719	2,324	2,085
Total traffic revenue	229,149	210,407	195,211	180,129	160,693
Other revenue	8,480	11,940	5,390	6,677	4,640
Total operating revenue	237,629	222,347	200,601	186,806	165,333
Staff costs	46,401	39,711	34,925	33,243	28,969
Fuel	48,769	45,404	45,552	45,489	42,514
Depreciation and amort.	16,368	15,503	14,891	12,561	9,471
Other	99,496	88,495	75,512	80,769	80,043
Total operating expenses	211.034	189,113	170,880	172,062	160,997
Profit operations	26,595	33,234	29,721	14,744	4,336
Net finance charges	(2,184)	(3,670)	(7,351)	(7,568)	(2,570)
Net non-operating expenses	(5,225)	(10,202)	(10.954)	35	1,549
Net profit for the year	19,186	19,544	11,416	7,211	3,315
Shareholder's funds	92,759	79,573	62,377	42,961	36,734
Dividends	6,000	6,000	4,000	1,400	–
Return on shareholders' fund	20.68 %	24.56 %	18.30 %	16,78 %	9.02 %

Source: 1984 Annual Report.

Exhibits 4 through 7 present recent financial data on Gulf Air.

The company has continued to repay its long-term bank loans on schedule. It is in a healthy cash position which enables it to finance aircraft purchases and other capital expenditures (see Exhibit 7). This strong financial performance makes privatization all the more attractive for both the company and the investing public at large.

GF's cost-consciousness is achieving impressive results. Yet, while its cost structure compares favorably with that of Saudia and Kuwait Airways, it compares unfavorably with foreign competitors from outside the region. For example, in a survey of 18 international carriers, GF stood last in the following cost categories:

- general administrative expenses as percentage of total operating expense (7.4%);
- passenger service expense per RPK (US $1.27);
- maintenance expense per aircraft hour (US $1,147);
- total operating expense per RTK (.994);
- seat load factor (54.8%).

Exhibit 5   Gulf Air Company G.S.C. and Subsidiary Consolidated Balance Sheet 31st December 1984 (Currencies in Thousands of Units)

	1983 US$	BD	1984 BD	US$
Assets Employed				
Fixed assets	396,178	149,359	138,127	366,385
Goodwill	30,851	11,631	3,877	10,284
Deposits	6,371	2,402	2,733	7,249
Investments	25,103	9,464	11,779	31,244
Net current assets	36,236	13,661	20,090	53,289
	494,739	186,517	176,606	468,451
Funds Employed				
Shareholder's Funds				
Share capital	106,101	40,000	40,000	106,101
Reserves	97,183	36,638	49,289	130,740
Accumulated profit	7,785	2,925	3,470	9,204
	211,069	79,573	92,759	246,045
Non-current Liabilities				
Term loans	176,318	66,472	51,823	137,462
Lease finance	107,352	40,472	32,024	84,944
	494,739	186,517	176,606	468,451

Source: 1984 Annual Report.

Exhibit 6   Gulf Air Company G.S.C. and Subsidiary Consolidated Statement of
Income and Accumulated Profits – Year Ended 31st December

	1983 US $	BD	1984 BD	US $
Revenue	589,780	222,347	237,629	630,316
Expenditure	501,626	189,113	211,034	559,772
Profit Operations	88,154	33,234	26,595	70,544
Non-operating Income/(Expenses)				
Net finance charges	(9,735)	(3,670)	(2,184)	(5,793)
Amortization of goodwill	(5,143)	(1,939)	(1,939)	(5,143)
Net income from managed funds	–	–	2,215	5,875
Other	1,889	712	478	1,267
	75,165	28,337	25,165	66,750
Profit sharing bonus	(4,775)	(1,800)	(1,700)	(4,509)
Share of profits of associated companies	2,019	761	1,536	4,074
Profit before unusual Items	72,409	27,298	25,001	66,315
Unusual times	(20,568)	(7,754)	(5,815)	(15,424)
Profit for the year	51,841	19,544	19,186	50,891
Statement of Accumulated Profits				
At 31st December 1983	7,037	2,653	2,935	7,785
Profit for the year	51,841	19,544	19,186	50,891
Dividends	(15,915)	(6,000)	(6,000)	(15,915)
Transfer to reserves	(35,178)	(13,262)	(12,651)	(33,557)
At 31st December 1984	7,785	2,935	3,470	9,204
Profits Retained by:				
Parent company	–	–	–	–
Subsidiary company	1,260	475	450	1,194
Associated companies	6,525	2,460	3,020	8,010
	7,785	2,935	3,470	9,204

Source: 1984 Annual Report

Exhibit 7   Statement of Changes in Financial Position (Annual Report 1984)

Source of Funds	1983 US$	BD	1984 BD	US$
From operations:				
Profit before share of profits of associated companies	49,822	18,783	17,650	46,817
Charges not requiring outlay of funds:				
Depreciation and amortization	66,809	25,187	23,609	62,623
Provision for fleet overhaul	1,809	682	576	1,528
Total generated from operations	118,440	44,652	41,835	110,968
Other sources				
Disposal of fixed assets (net book amount)	7,430	2,801	253	671
Surplus on disposal of fixed assets	9,687	3,652	–	–
Unearned revenue	6,435	2,426	1,199	3,180
Other	2,709	1,021	452	1,199
Total sources	144,701	54,552	739	116,018
Application of Funds				
Purchase of fixed assets	9,552	3,601	4,877	12,936
Loans repaid	49,645	18,716	14,327	38,002
Deposits	565	213	331	876
Purchase of investments	–	–	1,231	3,265
Lease finance repaid	8,430	3,178	3,457	9,170
Dividends paid	10,610	4,000	6,000	15,915
Total applications	78,802	29,708	30,223	80,166
Increase in Working Capital				
Current assets:				
Inventories	470	177	73	194
Accounts receivables and prepayments	11,787	4,444	(1,076)	(2,854)
Bank deposits, balances, and cash	62,958	23,735	25,120	66,631
	75,215	28,356	24,117	63,971
Accounts payable and accruals	9,316	3,512	10,601	28,119
	65,899	24,844	13,516	35,852

Operations

GF owns and operates a semi-homogeneous fleet of about 20 aircrafts. The size, composition, and productivity of that fleet are shown in Exhibit 8. The backbone and the GF fleet is the Lockheed L-1011. The company owns 11 of these which have an average daily utilization of 9.5 hours each.

Within the airline operation, there are two units responsible for handling the front office (i.e.; marketing and customer services) and two for handling the back office (i.e.; the technical division and flight operation division). It is within the latter units that the largest concentration of expatriates is found (see Exhibits 2 and 10 A and B). For instance, out of GF's 360 pilots, about two thirds are non-Gulf nationals.

The technical services division is responsible for maintaining the GF fleet, and the flight operation division for the safe and efficient usage of that

Exhibit 8   Fleet Composition

Number of Aircraft	1984	1983	1982	1981	1980
B-747	1	–	–	–	–
B-737	8	8	9	9	9
L-1011	11	9	8	8	6
Bell 212	6	6	6	6	6
Hours Flown:					
B-747	1,120	–	–	–	–
B-737	16,592	19,101	16,784	16,179	16,425
L-1011	34,873	30,543	27,507	25,364	22,288
Bell 212	4,390	4,823	5,094	5,619	4,327

Source: 1984 Annual Report.

fleet. The former unit is proud of its "on-time" departure record, which is the highest (99.5%) of any operator in the world for the B-737 and 1% above the world average for the L-1011 (98.5%). The latter unit – flight operation – is similarly proud of its safety record. GF has received the National Safety Prize from the British Safety Council for the fifth time.

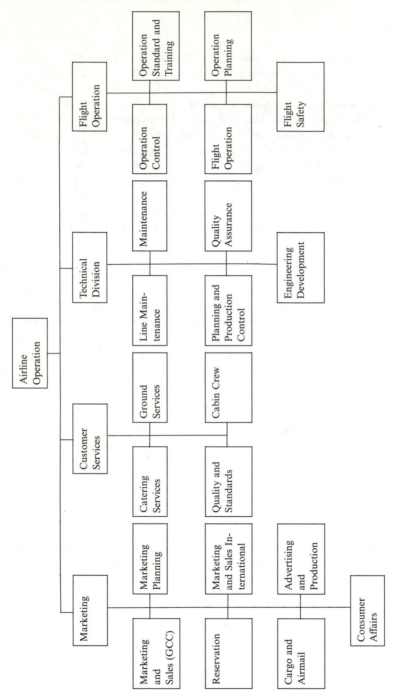

Exhibit 9   Internal Structure of the Operation Division

Marketing

A quick look at the internal structure of GF's operations business line
(Exhibit 9) suggests that marketing is the leading function. This is true not
only on paper but in practice as well. Marketing is internally divided by
function, service, and region. There are managers in charge of cargo and
mail advertising and promotion, reservations, pricing and marketing, and
sales. The latter two functions are geographically subdivided into: (1) Gulf
countries, (2) Middle East, (3) Far East, and (4) Europe.

GF earns about 86 % of its traffic revenues from passenger services and
about 10 % from cargo services (freight and mail).

As is the case with all Arabian Gulf carriers, expatriate labor is the core
passenger segment served by GF. Although statistics are unavailable, it is
estimated that at least two thirds of GF passengers are expatriate

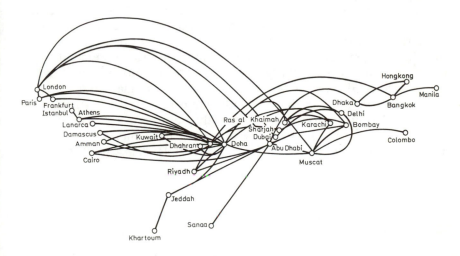

Exhibit 10 A   The Gulf Air International Network

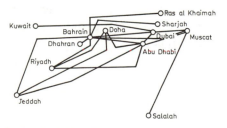

Exhibit 10 B   The Gulf Air GCC Network

employees from Far Eastern or Middle Eastern countries. Business travelers make up the second largest group, followed by vacationers.

About 75 % of GF traffic revenues come from its domestic and regional route network. The remainder comes from its intercontinental network (see Exhibits 10 A and B). The depressed oil economies of the Gulf states are forcing GF to reduce its dependence on intra-Gulf and intra-region routes in favor of more promising growth routes in the Pacific and North Atlantic regions.

Pricing

GF management believes that IATA is dead. The role of this organization in fixing prices has been supplanted by the market place. It is not surprising, then, to find that GF has established a pricing unit within its marketing division, whose job is to survey prices daily to establish the proper fare for each market in its international network. Gulf Air's pricing policy is to match the going market rate, and never allow itself to be undercut by its competitors. This is particularly true with regard to its intercontinental markets, where GF faces stiff competition from the giant international carriers, who capitalize on their cost advantage and global route network to engage in cutthroat price wars. But holding onto one's own clientele at heavily discounted fares is not enough. In order to maintain current levels of profitability in times of price wars, a substantial increase in the seat load factor is necessary.

Passenger Services

GF attracts its guest worker and tourist traffic with reasonable fares and good quality service. It attracts business travelers by offering them everything from an exclusive menu to sprinkling of rose water. There are game sets for the bored and flowers for the sentimental. The carrier also emphasizes the safety and security aspect of its aircraft. More stringent safety and security measures were recently added.

Competitor Profile

GF's competitors are numerous. They vary from one route to another. For example, on its route from Bahrain to Cairo, there are Egypt Air and Alia. On its route from Bahrain to London, there are British Airways, British Caledonian, Qantas, KLM, Alia, Saudia, Lufthansa, and others. Its main competitors are KLM, Singapore Airlines, British Airways, Alia, and Lufthansa.

These five carriers are aggressive on most of GF's main routes. They are, therefore, the ones GF watches most carefully. Virtually all of these carriers thrive on fifth and sixth freedom traffic to keep their planes full and their fares very low. Besides low fares, they offer their customers decent service. In fact, a couple of these carriers are leaders in customer service.

Strategic Planning at Gulf Air

The new GF organization establishing a separate planning function is based on the premise that line executives in charge of sales, operations, and management services are so busy with their day-to-day activities that they would not have enough time and energy to assess alternative strategies.

Therefore, Gulf Air named an executive vice-president to take charge of the strategic planning function. He has a number of specialists reporting to him on market entry, capital budgeting, fleet and facility planning, human resources, and business diversification. In contrast to their counterparts in the line organization whose perspective focusses on the short term, these planning specialists concentrate on the long term. They perform all of the feasibility studies needed to assess the prospect of new market entries and new business ventures. If the study proves promising, a proposal is prepared for the planning steering committee, which is composed of the three executive vice-presidents, the marketing vice-president, and the chief executive officer who serves as chairman.

Opportunities

1) Despite the economic slowdown in the Gulf states, expatriate workers still remain the largest market segment. Traffic from Egypt, the Indian subcontinent, and the Far East to the Gulf states remains healthy and growing – not declining. Improving the services that GF offers to this segment can be a deterrent to aggressive foreign competition.
2) GF might also expand passenger and cargo services to the growing Pacific Basin and Far Eastern markets (Japan, Korea, and China).

3) It could further develop transit traffic for passengers and cargo, and establish or bolster mainline stations in the Gulf states for this purpose.
4) It could further capitalize on its reputation as the most punctual Middle East carrier to expand and improve its cargo business. Perhaps it could offer airport-to-airport delivery of small shipments and parcels.
5) The possibility exists of starting a catering facility to serve other airlines passing through GF's domestic stations.
6) Finally, opportunities may exist for diversifying into airline-related operations such as airport hotels, car rentals, fleet maintenance services, etc.

Threats

The following represent possible threats to Gulf Air:

1) The general economic slowdown brought about by the dependency of the Gulf states on oil.
2) Completion of all major construction projects in the region.
3) Completion of the King Fahd Causeway.
4) The continuation and escalation of the Iran-Iraq war.
5) Intra-Gulf rivalries and sensitivities. The disagreement among Gulf states on free trade and on open skies policy has led Dubai to break ranks and launch its own carrier.
6) Increased competition in GF markets. Competition is getting tougher and stiffer at the area's airports as well as among the 40 or more carriers serving the Gulf. Dubai is becoming a very popular destination for all giant carriers, who use it as a stopover of convenience on their East-West around-the-world trips. Third World carriers, such as Singapore Airline and Cathay Pacific, plus giant European carriers can afford to "dump" their empty seats on most of GF's main routes at a huge discount, thereby making the going rough for the high-cost carriers of the Gulf nations.
7) To compound the problem, GF is denied reciprocity by some Far Eastern nations whose national flag carriers stop at GF's domestic stations using a temporary operating permit (TOP). GF cannot exploit growth opportunities in these markets unless it is granted reciprocal traffic rights.

Facing the Remaining 1980s

In view of the challenges and opportunities cited above, what will it take for GF to grow? Can it compete with the foreign carriers, not only on its own routes, but on theirs as well? What strategic options does it effectively have, and what are the pros and cons of each? What kind of airline does GF want to be by 1990?

The corporate planning division headed by Mr. Al-Masskary is formulating answers to the above questions. Two sets of proposals are being considered simultaneously. The one, by the business diversification unit, outlines a plan to purchase a hotel in London and another one, in Bombay, to cater to GF crews and transit passengers.

The other proposal by the new market entry unit is a plan to start a weekly service to Tokyo via Singapore and to New York, both beginning in 1989. The balance of this report explores the logic underlying this study, and the extent to which GF can operate these routes profitably, either alone or in cooperation with another GCC carrier.

Synopsis From "the New Market Entry" Proposal

The proposed Bahrain-New York and Bahrain-Tokyo routes would:

1) help reduce GF dependency on domestic and regional routes;
2) expedite the transition from a strictly regional carrier into a reputable international carrier;
3) appear to be economically sound:
   a) both satisfy the corporate hurdle rate; each one is expected to generate no less than 15% on invested capital;
   b) both routes satisfy GF's market entry criteria (see Exhibit 11).

Exhibit 11   Gulf Air Corporate Criteria – New Routes Criteria

1) The new route must cover direct costs in the first year of operation for the whole of the first year.
2) The route most cover direct variable costs plus 50% of the direct fixed costs during the second year of operation for the whole of the second year.
3) The route must cover total direct operating costs (variable + direct fixed) during the third year of operation for the whole of the third year.
4) Investment in all new routes (less than three years old) in any year shall not exceed 2% of the net revenue from scheduled services for that year.

Source: GF internal document.

The proposed New York route outranks the Tokyo route in terms of other corporate criteria (see Exhibit 12).

Exhibit 12   The Relative Ranking of New York and Tokyo Market Entry Criteria

	Maximum Score	New York	Tokyo via Singapore
1. Traffic rights			
3rd/4th freedom	200	200	100
5th freedom	100	100	20
2. Marketing			
– General sales administration	15	10	5
– Advertising effort required	15	10	15
– Ground handling	15	10	15
– Reservation infra-structure	15	10	15
– Pricing competitiveness	15	5	10
– Interlining effort	15	15	5
– Sales office/premises acquisition	10	10	5
3. Access in the market (free vs. restricted)	100	100	30
4. Launch effort required	50	15	10
5. Financial problems – if any (e.g., exchange repatriation problems)	25	10	10
6. Technical problems – if any (e.g., overflying, fuel availability, etc.)	25	20	15
7. Political stability	50	50	45
8. Route economics: time it takes to meet commercial objectives	50	10	25
	700	575	335

Notes:
– The less difficult the situation, the higher the score.
– The better the economics, the higher the score.
– Maximum score 700.
– Acceptable minimum score for any proposed route is 500.

Meeting on the New Route Proposal

Airlines' fortunes rise and fall depending on how careful they happen to be in picking the right routes. GF executives are smart enough to know that picking the right route is like picking the right spouse or the right horse: there is a lot of subjectivity involved. One cannot simply look at the numbers alone. They are also aware that there is a strong psychological factor involved in crossing the Atlantic and joining the "major league" of international carriers, and that the North Atlantic route is the graveyard of costly ambition and the historic battleground of "fare wars." They realize that as of 1982, the total number of empty seats on transatlantic routes was equivalent to 18,000 empty 747s crossing the Atlantic, and that this number has increased with the entry to the fray of some powerful American carriers, such as Northwest, American, and Delta. They are also aware of the fact that Pan American discontinued its direct Dhahran-New York flight as of April 1986.

With all these concerns running through his head, Mr. Al-Malki, GF's chief executive officer, has called for a meeting of the planning steering committee. He wants an honest and frank discussion of Mr. Al-Masskary's proposed route to New York. Should GF start a service to New York? If yes, should it be a direct non-stop service or should it be through an intermediate stop in Europe? Should GF offer this service alone or should it be in cooperation with a sister GCC carrier? If GF were to launch a New York service, what capacity should it put on that route, and at what frequency? This set of questions constitutes the agenda for the Steering Committee meeting. The member's decisions may well decide the fate of GF for years to come.

This case was accepted for presentation in the 14th Annual DSI Case Workshop Las Vegas, Nevada, November 21, 1988. An updated version is accepted for publication in a forthcoming issue of the *Case Research Journal*.

References

Gulf Air (1983): Corporate document, unpublished paper.
Gulf Air (1984): *Annual Report*.

4.5 Alia: The Royal Jordanian Airline – The First Twenty Years

M. Sami Kassem

Introduction

Alia, the Royal Jordanian Airline, has been one of the fastest growing airlines in the world. Throughout the 1970s, it recorded an average annual traffic growth of 38 %, against the industry-wide average of 7 %. In a 1981 survey of International Civil Aviation Organization (ICAO) members, Alia ranked fourth in overall traffic growth, showing a 30 % increase over 1980. Today, Alia serves 39 destinations on four continents. It has the most extensive route network among Arab carriers. This network extends from Los Angeles in the west to Singapore in the east.

Alia is one of the leading carriers in the Arab world. It was the first one to operate direct non-stop service to New York and Los Angeles (in 1977 and 1984, respectively), the first one to introduce a business class on its European and North American routes, the first one to introduce low fares, and the first one to champion the cause of regional cooperation in commercial aviation.

Alia also has a history of being one of the best-managed and most profitable carriers in the developing world, though its fortunes have changed somewhat in recent years. Since its inception in 1963, its founding fathers – His Majesty King Hussein of Jordan and Mr. Ali Ghandour, Alia chairman and president – developed the habit of working together as a team: the former as a supreme architect of Alia's mission, the latter as a supreme architect of Alia's strategy and structure. Their love for aviation, careful planning, hard work, imagination, and tenacity are at the heart of Alia's success story.

In contradistinction to its Arab sisters, Alia is not a mere flag carrier. Rather, it is a truly national carrier which operates for profit, and thus makes a positive contribution to Jordan's economy. In 1982, it was the eighth most profitable airline internationally, and the most profitable in the Arab world.

Between 1972 and 1982, it had an unbroken record of increasing profit and decreasing fares. It is the second largest employer in Jordan. Eighty per cent of its employees are Jordanian nationals, the majority trained in Alia's school in Amman. Nearly 20 % of its employees are women, including two pilots and two area managers.

Alia's Mission

Alia is more than just an airline whose principal objective is to move people and cargo for a profit. It is a total public service institution which perceives an obligation to contribute to the economic, social, and cultural development of Jordan.

In a carefully worded, personally prepared document, King Hussein spelled out the charter for Alia's existence and development:

I want our national carrier to be our ambassador of goodwill around the world and the bridge across which we exchange culture, civilization, trade, technology, friendship, and better understanding with the rest of the world. I expect Alia to eventually operate at a profit – to produce revenue for the country as one of its national responsibilities (Alia: Annual Report 1983, inside cover).

Chairman Ali Ghandour explains how these ambitious goals are converted into specific strategies:

Alia is a complete institution. It has a lot to do with transporting people and enhancing tourism and promoting Jordan for the benefit of the economy. It entails co-operating with the private sector, and having offices all over the world acting as tourist offices for the country.

It is not just offering seats to passengers. It is also offering accommodations. We had helped to create hotels – all of them – because we have found it difficult to sell a seat when tourists did not have a bed – and Jordan needed tourism. That is why Alia is participating in ventures like JET transport (Jordan Express Travel) which takes people by coach to different historical sites round the country.

When we talk about cultural exchange, Alia has its own Royal Jordanian Falcons (1977), the only acrobatic flying team sponsored by an airline, and the Royal Jordanian Folklore Troupe (1980). Both are sent all over the world to perform and project an authentic image of Jordan and the Arab world. Other troupes are invited to come to Jordan. Alia is active in helping its mother country – Jordan – organize the Jerash Festival each year. It offers its assistance and lots of money. It invites writers and political figures to come to the country.

In short, although Alia is basically an airline, it offers many public services. That is why it has grown. The policy and goals are set by the state and His Majesty the King. Alia does two things: it sets the strategy which leads to these goals, and finds the executive body which can implement these and execute the strategy towards the goals (Ghandour 1983).

Alia strongly denies that its promotional activities push up costs or eat into profits. Ghandour claims that they produce a net socioeconomic benefit. The coach and hotel operations are profitable. Furthermore, Alia pays no landing fees at the new Queen Alia International Airport. This is a rough compensation for having to fly government employees and military personnel at reduced rates.

Stages of Strategic Development

Alia was not the first airline to be based in Jordan. A series of carriers – including Arab Airways Jerusalem Ltd. (established in 1946), Air Jordan (1950), Air Jordan of the Holy Land, and Jordan Airways (1961) – operated either individually or in combination. They all suffered severe financial deficits due to the lack of management expertise and the shyness of local capital. In 1963, the government decided to step in and provide the needed financial backing and moral support. The new privately-owned Alia was formed, with the government providing almost a quarter of a million dollars or about one half of the initial capital (US $ 460,000).

The history of Alia reflects the political turmoil and economic upheavals the Arab world has experienced over the last 20 years or so. No other airline in the world, except perhaps Middle East Airlines of Lebanon, has experienced as many setbacks and been through as many strategic and operational crises as Alia. Nevertheless, Alia management has been able to answer every environmental challenge with an imaginative strategic response. In this context, Alia's present strategy is a perfect example of logical incrementalism at its best.

Examples of upheavals abound. The 1967 Arab-Israeli war created untold hurdles for Alia. Two of its DC-7s were destroyed by Israeli raids. Israeli occupation of the West Bank put an end to Alia's flights to Jerusalem and deprived it of religious traffic to the Holy Land. The war also prompted a massive influx of Palestinians into Jordan and threatened the internal security of the country. There were many at home and abroad who doubted the ability of Alia to overcome these problems. To make up for the loss of Jerusalem, Alia added Athens to its route network, and to make up for the loss of the DC-7s, it added a few F-27s. Later, the Jordanian government stepped in to save the company by nationalizing it.

Second, Alia experienced a flight of technical manpower to the Gulf states during the economic boom that came in the wake of the 1973 oil price increases. To slow down the brain drain, and to improve the productivity of its work force, Alia spent more on training and fringe benefits than a lot of other Arab carriers. Alia was among the first carriers in the region to set up training schools: the Royal Jordanian Air Academy, the Alia Training

Institute (1972), and the Queen Noor Civil Aviation Training Institute (1979). Together, these schools provide comprehensive aviation-related training to personnel, ranging from ground crews to traffic controllers, cabin attendants, and pilots. Alia also introduced a company-sponsored housing plan, supermarket cooperatives, nursery care for the children of working mothers, a pension plan, and a medical insurance plan to help retain its employees.

Third, when Iraq suspended landing rights in Baghdad for Egypt Air in the wake of President Anwar Sadat's endorsement of the Camp David peace accords, Alia stepped in to fill the vacuum. Its Cairo-Baghdad route became the backbone of its network.

Fourth, after the civil war erupted in Lebanon in 1975 and the Gulf war erupted in 1980, Alia lost three of its most profitable destinations: Beirut, Baghdad, and Teheran. To make up for these losses, the company beefed up its New York service and inaugurated a Chicago service in 1981. It reduced its dependency on airline operations by investing in hotel construction, travel and tourism, and other ancillary activities.

Fifth, the oil glut of 1983 and the sharp decline in revenues of the Gulf states resulted in a shrinkage of the guest worker air traffic. Alia's response was to launch a Los Angeles service in 1984 and service to Moscow in 1985.

Finally, one of Alia's planes, a Boeing 727, was hijacked and destroyed in 1985.

Despite the continued turmoil and political instability in its immediate environment, Alia has managed to thrive, expand, and profit. Its management has gained the reputation for overcoming obstacles by turning adversities into opportunities.

A short chronology of the development of Alia's strategy is given in Exhibit 1.

The Royal Connection

The airline's full title, "Alia, The Royal Jordanian Airline Corporation" underlines its royal connections. The airline was named after the King's daughter Princess Alia. The Arabic "alia" means "high and exalted". King Hussein has continuously taken a very personal interest in the airline's growth and success, as if it were his real daughter. Ever since he signed the Royal decree establishing Alia in December 1963, his active involvement is at the highest level of policy formulation, and his personal support has remained a major influence on the growth of Alia. Like a father, he steps in to help when there is trouble. Thus, when King Hussein saw that the private sector's faith in Alia had waned, due to domestic turmoil brought about by the influx of Palestinians into Jordan, he decided to nationalize the company.

Exhibit 1   Stages in the Evolution of Alia's Strategy

	Strategic Thrust	Destinations Added	Fleet	Market Segment Emphasized
I. The formative Stage: 1963–1967	A) Transporting people and cargo within The Mid-East region	Cairo Beirut Kuwait	2 Handley Pages 2 Super DC-7s 3 Caravelles	Arab business, tourists and expatriate employees
II. The state of vertical growth: 1968–1972	A) The nationalization of the company B) Establishing the airline's infrastructure – Training institute – Maintenance facilities	Munich Copenhagen Madrid Frankfurt Istanbul Teheran Abu Dhabi	2 B-707s 2 B-720s	
III. The stage of Explosive: Growth 1973–1982	A) An aggressive intercontinental sixth freedom carrier B) More infrastructural facilities – Catering – Computerization (1978) C) Horizonzal growth: – Arab Wings (1975) – Arab Air Services (1975) – Arab Air Services (1975) – Royal Jordanian Falcon (1977) – Royal Jordanian Folklore (1980) – Alia Art Gallery (1975) – Other ancillary activities	Amsterdam Vienna Larnaca New York Chicago Arabian Gulf capitals and Far East capitals Belgrade	3 B-747s 5 Tri-Stars 6 B-727s	Chasing the discount passenger: 1) Arab-American travelers: old country express at rock bottom prices 2) Expatriate employees working in Arabian Gulf states: Labor Express 3) European tourists 4) Holy Land American tourists
IV. The stage of intensive growth/ redirection: 1983–present	A) The end of a decade of rising profits Efficiency Comfort Quality service B) Continue as a hub carrier	Los Angeles Moscow	More Tri-Stars	Transit "6th freedom" passengers

The Other Side of Alia

Alia is an institution whose mission goes beyond carrying passengers and cargo. A major component of its mission, which is explicitly stated in its charter, is to serve as an ambassador of goodwill and to project an authentic image of Jordan throughout the world.

To carry out its mission. Alia has been promoting Jordan not only as a desirable tourist destination but also as a gateway to the Holy Land and to Arab business markets. It has used its offices abroad and at home as tourist agencies. It has participated in cultural events taking place inside and outside Jordan, notably the Jerash Annual Festival. It has cooperated with the Ministry of Tourism in producing a documentary film entitled "Bridge to the World" to promote Jordan as a holiday destination.

Alia has also been a major contributor to the promotion of Arab culture. It has sponsored traveling exhibits or shows on Arab fashion, folk dancing, music, and art. As already mentioned, it even has formed its own Alia Royal Jordanian Folk Dance Troupe and the Royal Jordanian Falcons, which it sends to perform abroad. Alia also carries cultural imports from other countries to enrich Jordan's cultural life, particularly in the fine and performing arts. The Alia Art Gallery in Amman has served as a showcase for contemporary art from other countries.

Alia's chief executive, Ali Ghandour, has taken the podium himself at international conferences to speak not only on aviation, but also to address a variety of contemporary issues of concern in East-West relations.

In addition to these activities, Alia has invested in several sectors of Jordan's tourism infrastructure. It is a shareholder of Holiday Inn, the Marriot Hotel, the Jordan Express Tourist Transport Company (JETT), and the Far East Tourism and Travel Company. Alia fully owns a number of other tourism-related businesses, including Royal Tours: the Duty Free Shop at Amman airport; the Cave du Chevalier, a first class restaurant; and the Alia Boutique, a high-fashion shop Amman. For details on Alia's cash investments in these ventures, see Exhibit 4.

Alia's role goes beyond behaving as a leading corporate citizen that stimulates tourism at home and promotes the image of Jordan abroad. It has also been a pioneer in championing the cause of regionalism among its sister Arab carriers. Its chairman Ghandour has been the most energetic advocate of Arab regional cooperation. He has stated:

There are 17 airlines and 300 jet aircraft in the Arab world, which together during 1981 carried 26 million passengers and earned revenues in excess of $ 6.5 billion. If, through cooperative ventures, costs were reduced by 5 % or revenues increased by 5 %, the sums attained would be enormous.

In their race to outshine one another, Ghandour has likened Arab carriers to a group of penguins crowded on the edge of an ice floe wanting to jump into the water where killer whales and tiger seals are waiting. Then one either jumps or is shoved in, and the others immediately follow. Ghandour's idea is to eliminate costly duplication in everything from engineering and maintenance to route networks and training. For instance, there is a great wast of airline resources spent on intercontinental routes between the Middle East, the United States, and Far East. There is also considerable waste in duplicating such facilities as simulation training centers and aircraft maintenance shops. Clearly, cooperation in such activities could result in significant savings for all participating carriers.

Alia has paved the long and slow road of regional cooperation by forming two joint ventures during the past decade. One is Arab Wings, which it jointly owns with the Sultanate of Oman. It is the first executive jet charter service in the Arab world. The other is Arab Air Cargo, which it jointly owns with Iraqi Airways, and which provides its cargo service from Amman and Baghdad to Europe and the Arab Gulf States. The success of the latter experiment is likely to encourage other Arab carriers to join the company, enabling it to enlarge the scope of its service to eventually include five continents.

Organization

Alia is supervised by a seven-man board of directors, chaired by Ali Ghandour, who is also the company's chief executive officer. With the exception of Ghandour, the board is made up of outsiders: two businessmen and five high-level government officials representing the departments of finance, transport, civil aviation and tourism, as well as the Royal Jordanian Air Force.

Alia's organization chart, as of December 1983, is shown in Exhibit 2.

Management Style

As chief architect of Alia's strategy and structure, Ali Ghandour is directly responsible for a great deal of Alia's success. Lebanese by birth, he attended the American University of Beirut, and later received a degree in Aeronautical Engineering from New York University. Prior to forming Alia in 1963, he served as chief engineer and vice-president for technical affairs at Lebanese International Airways. He has been chairman and president of Alia since 1974.

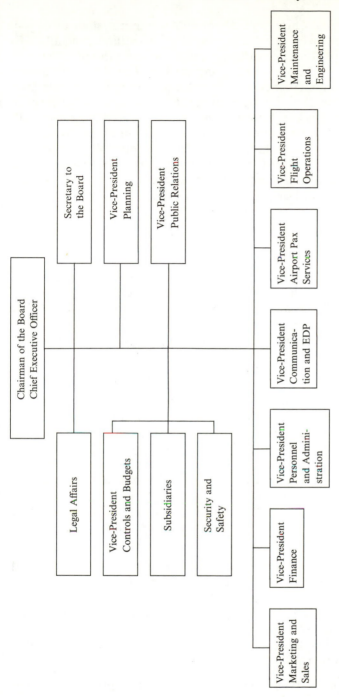

Exhibit 2   Alia Organization Chart – December 1983

Mr. Ghandour uses a highly personal management system to stay in touch with his employees and keep abreast of operational details. His unscheduled tours of Alia's airport facilities to observe the processing of passengers at check-in counters and to inspect the aircraft for cleanliness, safety, security, and punctuality have became part of the corporate lore. Even though he is an engineer by training, Ghandour says his favorite subject is marketing. His knack for recognizing opportunities has paid off. Whereas other Arab airline executives became disoriented and frustrated with the coming of deregulation, Mr. Ghandour adapted his organization to it quite readily. He innovated cheap fares that vary from one market to another, which stimulated demand and helped to keep Alia profitable in the face of declining revenue per passenger kilometer.

Personnel

From the outset, the founding fathers of Alia recognized the importance of training as a critical component of Alia's overall formula for success. They must have sensed that while a developing country's flag carrier might have the requisite traffic rights, the most modern aircraft, and the finest airports, it would be little more than an expensive showcase without highly-trained native professionals on the ground and in the air.

With that realization, Alia has singled out training for special strategic focus since its establishment in 1963. It established the Royal Jordanian Aero Club in 1965 to give Jordanians an incentive to study aviation to make them air-minded. Chairman Ghandour listed himself as the club's first ground instructor, and King Hussein signed up as its first student. Although the king was already an accomplished pilot, he nevertheless attended classes for several weeks. His personal involvement gave the club's student enrollment a healthy boost.

The Aero Club led to the establishment of three fully-equipped training institutions, which together have helped turn Jordan into one of the top aviation centers in the Arab world:

1) Alia Training Institute, which provides technical, commercial, and management training for flight and cabin crew and ground support personnel;
2) the Royal Jordanian Air Academy, which trains both civilian and military pilots;
3) Queen Noor Civil Aviation Training Institute, which trains air traffic controllers and other aeronautical specialists.

Alia views training not only as a strategy for developing a national manpower pool, but also as a strategy to improve the productivity of that pool. Alia's human resource development strategy has worked very well, to the point where Alia has become the second-largest employer in Jordan, with a work force of about 4,800 people. It invests about 1% of its total operating revenue in training. Alia also has created free clinics, cultural and recreational facilities, a commissary, a nursery, and a housing project for its employees. This makes the company a particularly desirable employer in Jordan.

Alia's investment in training and employee benefits has more than repaid itself with a reduced wage bill, improved employee morale, and increased productivity. Alia's labor costs are only 18% of its total operating expenses. This is roughly half of what it costs other carriers. Moreover, Alia has a comparatively high employee productivity rating and the highest among Arab carriers (see Exhibit 3). These factors have helped to make Alia the People Express of the Middle East and a truly developed airline of a developing country.

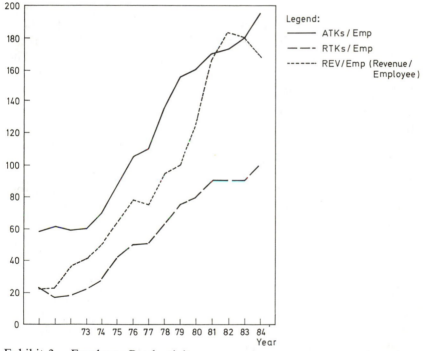

Exhibit 3   Employee Productivity

Source: The Royal Jordanien's Airline Planning and Scheduling Department: *Past, Present, Future,* 13th Ed. (May 1985) p. 41.

Marketing

Core Customer Groups

Alia directs its marketing efforts at five core groups:

1) Arab passengers who live abroad permanently or temporarily as expatriate employees in the Arab states of the Gulf;
2) leisure travelers, usually Western European tourists coming to Jordan to enjoy its recreational facilities on the Red Sea;
3) religious travelers to the Holy Land coming from the Far East and North America;
4) business passengers, whose number is comparatively low, center in the Middle East;
5) cargo shippers, a small and well-defined group of customers that collectively provide 15% of Alia's revenues.

Route Network

Alia's domestic network is rather inconsequential, it provides only 5% of passenger revenues. Since the opening of the new airport in Amman, the number of domestic passengers has been shrinking in number. The international network generates the lion's share of Alia's passenger traffic.
    Basically, the international network consists of:

1) Short-hauls, made up of thin routes carrying intra-Gulf traffic and intra-regional traffic. Travel on this segment is usually restricted by work visa requirements and other limitations imposed on flight frequencies, capacity, and fares.
2) Long-hauls, which are made up of dense routes to North America and the Far East. Alia is gaining a reputation as a sixth freedom carrier able to penetrate these growth markets through cheap, low-yield tickets and reliable service.

Fare Discounting

Alia is an aggressive carrier with a challenging mission. It has to promote tourism for Jordan and improve profitability for itself. In a drive to improve its load factor, particularly on its long-haul routes, Alia has had to lower its fares and improve its services. This has been one of the key components of its success formula for more than a decade.

Creative Marketing

In addition to discounting fares, Alia stresses other competitive marketing devices, such as:
1) the convenience of timely connections and good scheduling;
2) the dependability, appeal, and comfort of a modern fleet manned by experienced staff;
3) traditional Jordanian hospitality extended to all passengers, particularly those traveling in first and business class.

Financial Performance

Exhibits 4 through 7 present recent financial data on Alia.

Alia ended its second consecutive year of losses in 1984, after more than a decade of profits. Passenger counts fell by 12.5% in 1982 and 8.9% in 1984. Yet, there has been an increase in the average passenger distance flown from 653 kilometers in 1964 to 2,349 in 1983 and 2,719 in 1984 due to increased long-haul operations.

As for the sources of revenue, it is worth noting that passengers provide 70% of Alia's earnings, down from 80% in 1965 and 73% in 1976. By contrast, cargo has provided an increasing percentage: 3.5% in 1965 against 14% in 1983. Similarly, the percentage of revenue from ancillary activities (e. g., charter service, mail, hotel operation) has risen from 3.3% in 1965 to 13.3% in 1983.

Despite its cost-control policy, Alia's expenditures have been increasing steadily at an annual rate of 3.3% due primarily to increasing costs of fuel, aircraft handling, and borrowing money. Although Alia has no trouble borrowing from banks to finance new equipment, its small equity base and high interest payments combine to block its progress and dampen its initiative.

Exhibit 4   Consolidated Balance Sheet and accompanying notes

Assets	1984* JD	1983* JD	1982* JD	1981* JD	1980* JD
Current Assets:					
Cash on hand and at banks	18,965,089	18,253,543	21,205,752	7,241,496	2,045,53
Receivables (Note 1) less allowance for doubtful receivables of JD'	1,015,829	30,229,484	26,088,812	22,879,800	15,569,519
Spare parts, materials, and supplies	13,318,140	12,672,370	11,342,344	9,420,554	6,343,858
Total current assets	62,512,713	57,014,725	55,427,896	39,656,541	23,958,927

Exhibit 4 (continued)

Assets	1984* JD	1983* JD	1982* JD	1981* JD	1980* JD
Investments and other assets (Note 2)	23,179,058	16,799,981	4,098,763	3,526,560	3,919,564
fixed assets:					
Flight equipment	211,486,462	201,718,613	206,349,757	141,204,431	61,561,061
Ground equipment	11,522,147	10,398,197	7,726,356	5,684,475	4,567,534
Land and buildings	2,156,887	1,523,066	1,501,770	1,330,945	1,290,204
	225,165,496	213,639,876	215,577,883	148,219,851	67,418,799
Less: Accumulated depreciation	57,864,633	46,441,490	35,356,703	25,213,156	18,671,671
Net book value of fixed assets	167,300,863	167,198,386	180,221,180	123,006,695	48,747,128
Advance payments on aircraft and equipment purchase contracts	4,671,652	1,361,430	–	18,117,190	24,160,351
Total fixed assets	171,972,515	168,559,816	180,221,180	141,123,885	72,907,479
total assets	257,664,286	242,374,522	239,747,839	184,306,986	100,785,970

Liabilities	1984* JD	1983* JD	1982* JD	1981* JD	1980* JD
Current Liabilities:					
Due to banks	21,186,093	7,201,765	–	–	–
Current portion long-term loans	20,938,643	14,790,953	18,400,000	14,926,928	5,857,793
Accounts payable	8,181,550	6,235,447	7,548,059	6,907,344	4,129,122
Accrued charges	8,658,097	5,909,350	7,192,445	6,951,466	1,748,258
Unearned revenue	12,353,155	12,420,341	12,039,079	8,004,471	6,493,044
Total Current liabilities	71,317,538	46,557,856	45,179,583	36,790,209	18,228,217
Long-Term Liabilities					
Loans-foreign	132,870,500	128,172,704	133,788,097	104,839,509	45,755,190
Loans-local	25,795,919	25,185,237	20,980,887	13,015,443	4,457,520
Bonds payable	16,000,000	16,000,000	16,000,000	10,000,000	5,000,000
	174,666,419	169,358,031	154,768,984	127,854,952	55,212,710
Current portion of long-term debt	(20,938,643)	(14,790,953)	18,400,000	14,926,928	5,857,793
Total long-term debt	153,727,776	154,567,078	152,368,984	112,928,024	49,354,917
Provision for staff indemnities	2,812,797	2,720,842	4,742,624	2,571,434	2,099,386
Provision for fleet overhaul	8,993,453	8,011,706	6,104,222	2,104,858	3,083,976
Total long-term liabilities	163,534,026	165,299,626	163,215,830	117,604,316	54,538,279
	Equity of the government of jordan				
Authorized capital	21,000,000	21,000,000	21,000,000	21,000,000	21,000,000

* Year ended December 31

Note: One Jordanian Dinar (JD) equals approximately $ 3.00.
Source: Annual Reports.

Exhibit 4 (continued)

Assets	1984* JD	1983* JD	1982* JD	1981* JD	1980* JD
Paid-up capital	21,000,000	21,000,000	21,000,000	21,000,000	21,000,000
general reserve	9,517,040	10,244,393	8,912,461	7,014,474	5,769,352
Net loss for the year	(9,704,318)	(727,353)	1,439,965	1,892,987	1,250,122
Total government equity	20,812,722	30,517,040	31,352,426	29,912,461	28,019,474
Total liabilities and equity of the government of Jordan	257,664,286	242,374,522	239,747,839	184,306,986	100,785,970

Note (1) Receivables

	1984* JD	1983* JD
Government departments and public organizations	7,974,690	7,884,899
Head office receivables	7,156,730	3,918,681
Station receivables	10,481,316	7,745,922
General sales agents	2,588,633	1,838,898
Other carriers and other accounts	2,761,828	4,648,822
Advances and deposits under letters of credit	282,116	1,067,419
	31,245,313	27,104,641
Less: Allowances for doubtful receivables	(1,015,829)	(1,015,829)
	30,229,484	26,088,812

Note (2) Investments And Other Assets

	Alia Ownership 1984* %	1984* JD	1983* JD
Arab Wings Co., Ltd.	64	1,554,990	1,554,990
Jordan Holiday Inn Co., Ltd.	5.6	133,330	133,330
Arab International Hotels Co.	3.3	100,000	100,000
Duty Free Shop	100	500,000	500,000
Arab Air Cargo	50	1,087,200	1,087,200
Jordan Express Tourist Transport Co. Ltd.	6.6	15,000	15,000
Simulator Project	100	1,500,000	1,500,000
Arab Air Services	100	83,603	83,603
Jordan T.V., Cinema, and Radio Co.	5	125,000	101,400
Royal Tours	100	37,000	37,000
Alia Boutique	100	30,000	30,000
Sierra Leone Airline	20	56,738	56,738
Aircraft maintenance facility (a)	100	10,215,644	6,381,170
Alia Hotel-Amman (b)	100	7,582,546	5,076,175
Other investments	–	158,007	143,375
		23,179,058	16,799,981

Exhibit 5   Statement of Income

	1984* JD	1983* JD	1982* JD	1981* JD	1980* JD
Operating Revenues					
Scheduled services					
Passenger	82,793,887	87,419,163	92,421,166	77,332,190	59,964,595
Cargo	17,473,604	14,723,971	19,640,826	17,263,863	11,496,781
Excess baggage	1,981,529	2,848,631	4,180,799	3,174,532	1,882,473
Mail	302,816	276,375	400,847	328,793	204,771
Total scheduled revenues	102,551,836	105,268,140	116,643,638	98,099,378	73,548,623
Nonscheduled services:					
chartered flights	3,002,802	2,168,984	5,480,179	3,136,558	1,407,312
Total operating revenues	105,554,638	107,437,124	122,123,936	101,235,936	74,955,935
Operating Expenses:					
Flying operations	38,378,816	36,834,807	38,145,032	36,883,175	26,486,898
Maintenance	10,177,969	11,821,204	13,571,571	8,876,516	6,779,878
Depreciation of flight equipment	12,054,929	11,884,486	9,624,563	6,593,380	5,434,771
Sation and ground	12,349,118	10,912,067	10,358,085	8,821,493	6,581,077
Passenger services	10,226,315	10,401,234	9,922,909	8,979,091	7,225,837
Sales and promotion	21,758,862	18,555,794	18,932,632	18,185,900	13,936,750
General and administrative	4,203,052	3,581,367	3,735,991	3,307,137	3,195,701
Total operating expenses	109,149,061	103,990,959	104,290,783	91,646,692	69,640,912
Operating income (loss)	(3,594,423)	3,446,165	17,833,034	9,589,244	5,315,023
Non-Operating Income (Expenses)					
Other income (Note 9)	13,499,959	16,438,816	7,423,294	7,785,506	5,181,913
Interest and other expenses (Note 10)	(19,609,854)	(20,612,334)	(23,816,363)	(15,484,763)	(9,246,814)
Non-operating expenses-net	(6,109,895)	(4,173,518)	(16,393,069)	(7,696,257)	(4,064,901)
Net loss for the year – Exhibit (A)	(9,704,318)	(727,353)	(1,439,965)	(1,892,987)	(1,250,122)

* Year ended December 31

Source: Annual Reports.

Exhibit 6   Statement of Changes in Financial Position

	1984* JD	1983* JD
Sources of Funds:		
Net loss for the year	(9,704,318)	(727,353)
Expenses not requiring current outlay:		
Depreciation of fixed assets	13,335,947	12,938,925
Increase (decrease) in long-term provisions	1,073,702	(114,298)
Difference from translation of long-term borrowing in foreign currencies	–	5,345,232
Gain on the sale of aircraft	(2,341,688)	–
Total funds from operations	2,363,643	17,442,506
Proceeds from new borrowings	20,768,698	7,921,871
Proceeds from disposition of fixed assets	3,512,134	703,461
Total sources of funds	26,644,475	26,067,838
Application of Funds:		
Additions to fixed assets	17,919,092	1,981,022
Repayments and current position of long-term debt	21,608,000	11,069,009
Reduction in general reserve	–	108,033
Increase in investments and other assets	6,379,077	25,701,218
Total applications of funds	45,906,169	25,859,282
Increase (decrease) in working capital	(19,261,694)	208,556
Increase (Decrease) in Working Capital Components:		
Cash	711,546	(2,952,209)
Receivables	4,140,672	3,209,012
Spare parts, materials, and supplies	645,770	1,330,026
Due to banks	(13,984,328)	(7,201,765)
Current portion of long term loans	(6,147,690)	3,609,047
Accounts payable	(1,946,103)	1,312,612
Accrued charges	(2,748,747)	1,283,095
Unearned revenue	67,186	381,262)
	(19,261,694)	(208,556)

* Year ended December 31.

Source: Annual Reports.

Exhibit 7   Alia Fiscal and Traffic Highlights: Two Decades' Review

	1963/64	1973	1982	1983	82/83 ± %	73/83 ± %	63/83 ± %
						(Average Annual Growth)	
Capital (JD)							
Authorized capital	150,000	6,000,000	21,000,000	21,000,000	–	+ 15.0	+ 29.7
Paid-up capital		5,231,573	21,000,000	21,000,000	–	+ 16.7	–
Equity		5,411,829	31,352,426	30,517,040	– 2.6	+ 21.2	–
Long-term loans		4,009,198	152,368,984	154,567,078	+ 1.4	+ 50.0	–
Working capital			10,248,313	10,456,869	+ 2.0	–	–
Economics (JD)							
Operating revenue		7,382,987	122,123,817	107,437,124	– 12.0	+ 34.6	–
Other revenue		693,922	7,423,294	16,438,816	+ 121.4	+ 42.1	–
Total revenue	1,119,614	8,076,909	129,547,111	123,875,940	– 4.3	+ 35.3	+ 28.1
Operating expenditure			104,290,783	103,990,959	– 0.2	–	–
Non-operating expenditure			23,816,363	20,612,334	– 13.4	–	–
Total expenditure	1,086,905	7,896,653	128,107,146	124,603,293	– 2.7	+ 35.8	+ 28.4
Operating profit			17,833,034	3,446,165	– 80.6	–	–
Net profit (loss)	32,709	180,256	1,439,965	(727,353)	– 49.4	–	–
Capacity							
Number of aircraft	4	5	18	17	– 5.6	+ 14.6	+ 7.9
Available seat-kms (000)	132,416	656,436	5,538,036	5,949,710	+ 7.4	+ 27.7	+ 22.1
Available tonne-kms (000)	11,510	76,822	801,090	837,747	+ 4.5	+ 30.4	+ 25.3
	1963/64	1973	1982	1983	82/83 ± %	73/83 ± %	63/83 ± %
Traffic (Scheduled Services)							
Revenue passengers carried	86,877	162,327	1,667,273	1,457,334	– 12.6	+ 27.6	+ 16.0
Excess baggage carried (tonnes)	105	156	4,047	2,432	– 39.9	+ 35.6	+ 18.0
Cargo carried in tonnes	630	2,110	38,223	33,866(B)	– 11.4	+ 36.1	+ 23.3
Mail carried in tonnes	85	85	1,063	704	– 33.8	+ 26.5	+ 11.8
Total freight carried (tonnes)	820	2,351	43,333	37,002	– 14.6	+ 35.8	+ 22.2
Passenger kms flown (000)	56,760	289,303	3,286,995	3,423,147	+ 4.1	+ 31.6	+ 24.1
Pax tonne kms flown (000)	4,257	26,037	295,828	308,079	+ 4.1	+ 31.6	+ 25.3
Cargo tonne kms flown (000)	391	5,371	129,496	119,264(C)	– 8.0	+ 41.1	+ 35.1
Mail tonne kms flown (000)	40	147	1,927	1,442	– 25.2	+ 28.9	+ 20.8

Overall load factor %	41.4	41.5	55.5	51.2	– 2.1p	+ 7.1p	+ 5.0p
Passenger load factor %	42.9	44.1	59.4	57.5	– 1.9p	+ 13.4p	+ 14.6p
Employment and Productivity (E)							
Number of employees	250	1,277	4,627	4,662	+ 0.8	+ 15.6	+ 16.6
ATKs per employees	46,040	60,158	175,178	184,363	+ 5.2	+ 13.2	+ 7.6
RTKs per employee	18,752	24,710	93,429	94,361	+ 1.0	+ 16.1	+ 8.9
Operating revenue per employee (JD)	4,478	5,782	26,705	23,644	– 11.5	+ 16.9	+ 9.1

Notes:

– Economic figures this column cover the period December 15, 1963 – March 31, 1965.

– Excluding all-cargo services turned over to Arab Air Cargo in May, 1983. Total cargo tonnes growth was + 4.7%.

– Excluding all-cargo services, per above. Total cargo tonne-kms growth was + 3.8%.

– Excluding excess baggage RTKs.

– "Number of employees" reflects all staff. Productivity has been computed after deducting subsidiary and seconded staff not on Alia operations.

Source: Annual Report 1983.

Facing Turbulent Times

After more than a decade of profits, the 1983 and 1984 results came as a surprise to Alia's management. But Alia had simply been postponing the inevitable. The entire Arab airline industry was going through hard times. Political turmoil, the continuation of the Gulf war, a severe economic recession in the oil-producing countries, unpredictable traffic restrictions, and stiff competition have all adversely affected traffic movement in and out of Arab airports. For instance, whereas the annual rate of growth in passenger traffic at Amman Airport was 24 % and 27 % in 1980 and 1981, respectively, it was − 12 % and − 22 % in 1983 and 1984, respectively.

Alia's deteriorating performance can be explained not only in terms of the aforementioned exogenous factors but also in terms of endogenous factors. One such factor is the introduction and heavy promotion of services that have comparatively lower revenue yields than the average system yield. But the most important endogenous factor is unusually high debt-equity ratios and the resulting high interest payments. Thus, whereas the debt to equity ratio was 4 : 3 for Alia in 1973, it became 5 : 1 in 1983, a fact which prompted Ghandour, Alia's chairman, to say:

Quite frankly, I find myself working for the banks. All the operating profits go to the banks to pay off loans and interest.

Another factor is that Alia's tickets are not widely distributed through travel agents in key markets, such as Cairo, Alexandria, Detroit, and Dammam. Furthermore, while Alia has priced its tickets low to stimulate sales and market share, sometimes it has done so even at the expense of profits.

To reverse the current losses, and to cope with the hard times, Alia's management is contemplating major changes in corporate structure, strategy, and tactics.

As far as strategic changes are concerned, Alia's management is seriously considering a number of options:

1) It may enter new markets to round its route network. Alia is interested in Miami, Houston, Rio de Janeiro, and Santiago via Abidjan and Lagos in West Africa. It is also interested in Manila, Seoul, Colombo, and Tokyo in the Far East. Gaining traffic rights from other nations who see Alia as a threat to their national carriers is the most difficult problem facing Alia in this connection.
2) It may provide more capacity for existing points in an effort to expand its market share.
3) It may further control costs by reducing frequencies on thin and less

profitable routes, reducing involvement in non-profitable activities, and putting a freeze on hiring and overtime.
4) It may strive to improve profit margins by emphasizing full-fare passengers and deemphasizing discount passengers.
5) It may try to manage assets more wisely by selling some planes to reduce debt, eliminating non-profitable routes, and divesting non-profitable business ventures (e. g., Arab Wings).

Alia's caretakers are also considering revising the company organization structure to enable top management to spend more time on strategic planning and less on managing the day-to-day operations of the company. More specifically, they are considering injecting a fresh supply of outside executive talent into Alia's top command to facilitate a smooth turnaround.

The question facing Alia's top management is which of the above-listed changes, or a combination thereof, needs to be implemented now, which ones later, and in what sequence in order to get the company back on the course of profitability and growth.

References

Ghandour, A. (1983): The role of air carriers in developing air transport in the Arab world, A paper presented at the Civil Aviation Forum sponsored by the Arab League's Civil Aviation Council, Al Rabat, July 7–11, 1983, Amman: Alia's Public Relations Department.

Chapter 5
Banking Industry

5.1 A Note on the Banking Industry

Ghazi M. Habib

Introduction

With the exception of Saudi Arabia, the Arab Gulf States were historically subject to similar political and economic circumstances. The Gulf region fell under the British mandate, which was managed by the British administration of India. The Indian rupee was the currency used in the Gulf states of Bahrain, Kuwait, Qatar, Oman, and the U.A.E. for a long time. This situation lasted until 1959, when the government of India decided to replace the Indian rupee with a paper currency called the Gulf Rupee, which was exchangeable with the Indian Rupee and British Sterling (Al-Masaref Al-Arabia 1985).

In 1950, Saudi Arabia became the first of these states to establish its own paper currency, followed by Kuwait in 1961, Bahrain in 1965, Qatar and Dubai in 1966, and Oman and U.A.E. in 1973. Bahrain introduced banking activities in 1920, when the Eastern Bank Limited was established. Bahrain was also the first Gulf state to discover oil in 1930. Today it has the lowest oil producing capacity and the second highest refining capacity in the region. In 1941, the British Bank of the Middle East (BBME) was the first bank to be established in Kuwait. The bank was granted a 30-year license which expired in 1971. The BBME was then replaced by the Bank of Kuwait and the Middle East. The Kuwaiti economy used to rely basically on trade, particularly of pearl, and navigation. Kuwait started to produce oil in 1946. Currently oil represents about 86 % of Kuwait's GNP. There was a bank in Dubai in 1946 and a bank in Abu Dhabi by 1958, before the establishment of the U.A.E. confederation. Qatar's first national bank, Qatar National Bank, was established in 1965. Oman had a bank in 1948, but the first national bank was not established until 1973, when the National Bank of Oman was launched.

The development of commercial banking in Saudi Arabia passed through two main stages. The first stage started with the opening of the first branch of a foreign bank, Netherlands Trading Society, in 1927. The period lasted until July 1976, the start of the Saudization program promulgated by a Royal decree.

The pace of banking activity and the size of bank holdings were low during most of the initial stage. Combined assets of the commercial banks did not reach SR 4 billion until 1973 (Abdeen and Shook 1984). It was only in the early 1950s that the first local commercial bank, National Commercial Bank (NCB), was set up. NCB's establishment was followed by the formation of another local bank, Riyadh Bank, in 1958. By 1976, 12 commercial banks were operating in Saudi Arabia. These banks had a total of 98 branches, and, with the exception of United Bank Limited, they were all based in Jeddah. The move of the Saudi Arabian Monetary Agency (SAMA) headquarters from Jeddah to Riyadh in 1978 signaled the shift of the traditional banking center in the Kingdom (Habib et al. 1987) to the capital.

Exhibit 1 is a consolidated balance sheet for all commercial banks in the Gulf Cooperation Council (GCC) countries. Total assets of these banks reached US $ 105.85 billion in 1984.

Present Status of the Gulf Banking Industry

The oil boom witnessed by the Arab Gulf States in the early 1970s was unprecedented on a global scale. The Gulf banking system grew at an exponential rate. New domestic banks were established, and international banks moved in to capitalize on the new opportunity.

By the end of the 1970s, there were 250 banks in the Arab Gulf States (Stutely 1986). Kuwait and Saudi Arabia pursued prudent policies that limited the number of banks to 6 and 11, respectively. Qatar has 15 banks serving a population of about 300,000 inhabitants. The U.A.E. has 50 banks with 300 branches. In its pursuit to succeed Beirut as the new financial center in the Middle East, Bahrain has a staggering 180 financial institutions. Oman has 11 banks serving a population of less than 1.25 million. During the period 1973 through 1981, the number of bank branches in Saudi Arabia grew from 70 to 375.

Government expenditure has been the prime stimulus of economic activity in the Gulf states. However, because of the declining demand for OPEC oil and excess supplies in the international oil market, the economic boom has ended in the Arab Gulf States. The decline in the monetary value of oil revenues accruing to the Arab Gulf States, from a peak of US $ 165 billion in 1981 to an estimated US $ 46 billion in 1986 (Field 1986), led to substantial reductions in government expenditures, which created a mild

Exhibit 1   G.C.C. – Locally Incorporated Commercial Banks' Consolidated Balance Sheet (in Billion of US $)

	Bahrain 1983	Bahrain 1984	Kuwait 1983	Kuwait 1984	Oman 1983	Oman 1984	Qatar 1983	Qatar 1984	Saudi Arabia 1983	Saudi Arabia 1984	U.A.E. 1983	U.A.E. 1984	G.C.C. 1983	G.C.C. 1984
Assets														
Liquid assets	1.59	1.64	17.83	14.52	0.78	1.07	1.12	1.64	19.86	23.25	10.01	11.85	51.19	53.97
Loans and discounts	2.09	2.32	15.32	16.15	1.01	1.21	0.94	0.77	17.28	17.92	7.42	5.83	44.06	44.20
Other assets	0.07	0.10	0.62	0.71	0.01	0.04	0.03	0.04	1.86	2.10	0.24	0.36	2.83	3.35
Permanent assets	0.40	0.35	0.56	0.67	0.03	0.04	0.05	0.04	1.80	2.03	0.93	1.20	3.77	4.33
Total assets	4.15	4.41	34.33	32.05	1.83	2.36	2.14	2.49	40.80	45.30	18.60	19.24	101.85	105.85
Liabilities and share-holder' equity														
Bank deposits	0.51	0.68	–	–	–	–	0.39	0.33	2.87	3.62	5.42	3.97	9.19	8.60
Customers' deposits	3.04	3.12	32.00	29.34	1.63	2.10	1.49	1.83	31.50	35.61	10.66	12.70	80.32	84.70
Other liabilities	0.14	0.15	0.10	0.04	0.06	0.07	0.05	0.08	3.28	2.54	0.65	0.60	4.28	3.48
Shareholders' equity	0.46	0.46	2.23	2.67	0.14	0.19	0.21	0.25	3.15	3.53	1.87	1.97	8.06	9.07
Total liabilities share-holders' equity	4.15	4.41	34.33	32.05	1.83	2.36	2.14	2.49	40.80	45.30	18.60	19.24	101.85	105.85
Contra accounts	0.49	0.63	7.12	6.51	1.03	1.22	0.76	0.97	25.12	26.02	4.59	3.89	39.11	39.24
In percentage of G.C.C. total:														
Assets														
Liquid assets	3.1	3.0	34.8	26.9	1.5	2.0	2.2	3.0	38.8	43.2	19.6	21.9	100.0	100.0
Loans and discounts	4.7	5.2	34.8	36.5	2.3	2.7	2.1	1.8	39.3	40.6	16.8	13.2	100.0	100.0
Other assets	2.5	2.9	21.9	21.2	0.3	1.2	1.1	1.2	65.7	62.8	8.5	10.7	100.0	100.0
Permanent assets	10.6	8.1	14.8	15.5	0.8	0.9	1.3	0.9	47.8	46.9	24.7	27.7	100.0	100.0
Total assets	4.1	4.2	33.7	30.3	1.7	2.1	2.1	2.4	40.1	42.8	18.3	18.2	100.0	100.0
Liabilities and share-holder's equity														
Banks' deposits	5.5	7.9	–	–	–	–	4.2	3.8	31.3	42.1	59.0	46.2	100.0	100.0
Customers' deposits	3.8	3.7	39.8	34.6	2.0	2.5	1.9	2.2	39.2	42.0	13.3	15.0	100.0	100.0
Other liabilities	3.3	4.3	2.3	1.1	1.4	2.0	1.2	2.3	76.6	73.0	15.2	17.3	100.0	100.0
Shareholders' equity	5.7	5.1	27.7	29.4	1.7	2.1	2.6	2.8	39.1	38.9	23.2	21.7	100.0	100.0
Shareholders' equity	4.1	4.2	33.7	30.3	1.7	2.1	2.1	2.4	40.1	42.8	18.3	18.2	100.0	100.0
Contra accounts	1.3	1.6	18.3	16.6	2.6	3.1	1.9	2.5	64.2	66.3	11.7	9.9	100.0	100.0

Source: Arab Banks 1985.

recession in the Gulf region. Field (1986) reported that because of recession, trading companies in the Arab Gulf States, particularly those involved in supplying construction contractors, experienced drops in turnover of up to 80%. Furthermore, about two million expatriate workers, out of a peak of about five million, have left; the real estate market collapsed; and rents have fallen 50% to 80%. Field also reported that foreign investment by Arabian Gulf businessmen looking for profitable investments abroad has been conspicuous.

The slowdown in Gulf economic activity has made domestic banking a very competitive industry in an already over-banked Gulf environment. This has given Arab Gulf banks new impetus to further internationalize their operations.

The involvement of Gulf banks in the international financial market started with the creation of the European Arab consortium of banks in the late 1960s on a very limited scale. These banks were based in Paris and Brussels and dealt in trade financing and Euro-deposit activities. In 1973–1974, three Kuwaiti investment companies participated in the international financial markets mostly through the underwriting and management of Eurobonds. In 1977, other Gulf banks such as the National Commercial Bank entered the international financial market and became aggressive participants in Euro-credits and in lending to developing countries (Al-Masaref Al-Arabia 1985).

Bank analysts argue that Gulf banks abroad should expand their service portfolio beyond the Euro-loan market and diversify into Eurobond underwriting and investment banking (Al-Masaref Al-Arabia 1985). Furthermore, they identified the key factors for the success of international Gulf banking as follows:

1) Long-term strategic planning should be the result of proactive planning rather than a reaction to a changing environment.
2) In order to achieve growth in a steady and consistent style, Arab banks should endeavor to train a new generation of international banking professionals, to reduce the high turnover of senior-level staff abroad.
3) Internal reorganization and improved efficiency and cost-control are necessary.
4) The banks should carve out a niche on the basis of comparative advantage by establishing an overseas presence to cater to their customers' needs abroad (Al-Masaref Al-Arabia 1985).

Industry Analysis

Commercial banking is based on the process of borrowing money from the masses at low or no interest, and lending this money to individuals, corporations, or governmental agencies at higher interest.

In general, commercial banks have the following objectives:

1) to attract customers' current and deposit accounts;
2) to increase deposit accounts, thereby increasing the bank's share of savings;
3) to lower the cost of acquiring new deposits by avoiding direct competition with other commercial banks;
4) to provide new services not available in other banks.

The banking industry structure in the Arab Gulf States is made up of five components (see Exhibit 2):

1) key players;
2) key buyers;
3) key suppliers;
4) exit and entry barriers;
5) substitutes.

Key Players

During the British mandate in the Gulf region, British banks such as the British Bank of the Middle East, Chartered Bank, and Grendlines were the only players in the Gulf banking industry. The duration of this era varied from one Gulf state to another; in Kuwait it lasted from 1941 to 1971; in Abu Dhabi from 1958 to 1968; in Dubai from 1946 to 1963; in Oman from 1948 to 1973; and in Qatar from 1950 to 1957 (Al-Masaref Al-Arabia 1983). The first foreign bank in Saudi Arabia was the Netherland Trading Society, established there in 1927. The first national bank, National Commercial Bank, was set up in the early 1950s.

Currently, the key players in the Gulf banking industry can be segmented into three groups:

1) banks of Gulf origin;
2) nationalized banks;
3) Islamic banks.

Exhibits 4 through 10 show the financial results of Arab banks in each GCC state. These exhibits show both banks of Gulf origin as well as foreign banks that were nationalized. Currently, Bahrain has two Islamic banks: one onshore, Bahrain Islamic Bank, and one offshore, Faisal Islamic Bank.

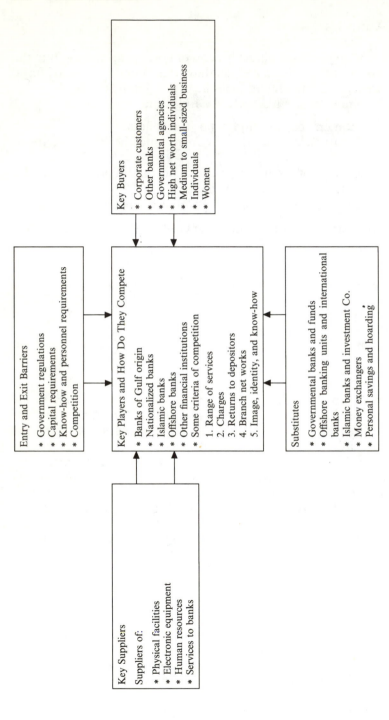

Exhibit 2   Competitive Forces in the Banking Industry.

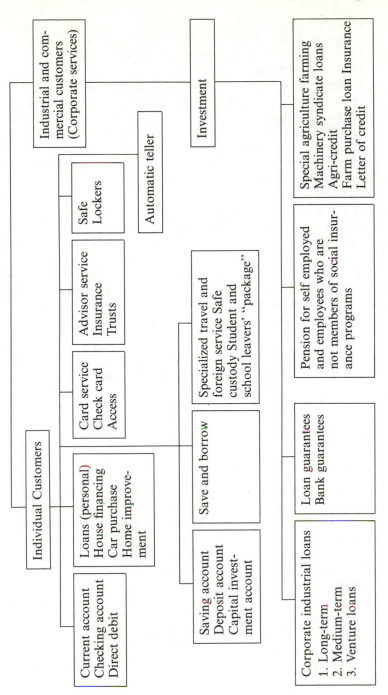

Exhibit 3   Banking Services in the Arab Gulf States (comments on page 171)

Kuwait has one Islamic bank, Kuwait Finance House. Saudi Arabia has the Islamic Development Bank and the newly authorized Al-Rajhi banking network, and U.A.E. has Dubai Islamic Bank. For a breakdown of Islamic banks by country, see Exhibit 12, p. 173.

The Arab Gulf States have different policies regulating the presence of foreign banks in their markets. Bahrain has about 180 financial institutions: 19 commercial banks, 1 housing bank, 75 offshore banks, 63 representative offices, 16 investment banks, and 6 money exchangers (see Exhibits 4, 5). Recently, the Bahraini government announced that it will not allow new foreign banks into its domestic market except offshore banking units that add new factors to the market.

Exhibit 6 shows that Kuwait has 6 banks.

Oman has not allowed foreign banks into its domestic market for some years, and is unlikely to relax this policy (see Exhibit 7).

The Qatari government enacted legislation that limits the equity share in banks to a maximum of 49% by foreign partners (see Exhibit 8).

Saudi Arabia's Council of Ministers enacted legislation to Saudize (nationalize) foreign banks (see Exhibit 9). Foreign banks operating in Saudi Arabia were asked to become 60% Saudi-owned joint stock companies. The following were the primary motives behind the government's decision (Habib et al. 1987):

1) Foreign banks formulated strategies, set by parent banks abroad, targeting their services to financing foreign contractors and foreign trade. They overlooked local financing of medium- to long-term projects necessary for economic development.
2) Foreign banks concentrated their branches in the large cities of Jeddah and Riyadh at the expense of other cities.
3) SAMA had little control over foreign banks' activities, especially with regard to the transfer of funds abroad.

The foreign partner in the joint venture was given the right to manage the bank for the first five to eight years on a renewable basis. The banks were also required to train and develop Saudi nationals for eventual promotion to all management levels.

In the United Arab Emirates, there have been withdrawals and mergers of banks. The governor of the central bank expressed a desire to see the number of local banks reduced further through voluntary of forced mergers. There have been hints that the government may soon require major equity shares in foreign banks operating there (see Exhibit 10).

The banks of Gulf origin are characterized by experience in the market, sensitivity toward the local culture, relatively large branch networks, and to some degree less state of the art banking know-how. They perform both wholesale and retail banking activities.

Exhibit 4 Bahrain's major offshore banks – 1985 (US $ Million)

	Assets	%Change on 1984	Loans	%Change on 1984	Provisions	%Change on 1984	Net Profit	%Change on 1984	% return on asset
Arab Banking Corporation	13,066.0	+18.2	5,095.0	+9.6	61.0	+35.6	-109.0	-0.9	0.83
Gulf International Bank	7,781.6	+4.9	4,150.3	-0.1	na	-	67.0	+4.9	0.90
Arlabank International	1,699.6	-8.3	1,184.3	-2.1	5.8	+3.6	13.3	-33.5	0.80
Al-Bahrain Arab African Bank	1,113.5	-28.6	611.8	-25.3	na	-	0.4	-97.8	0.03
Gulf Riyadh Bank	1,070.4	-9.7	466.0	-10.7	na	-	5.3	+4.0	0.50
Al UBAF Arab International Bank	718.8	+17.3	231.5	+12.5	3.5	+75.0	3.4	+5.6	0.50
Kuwait Asia Bank	649.1	+13.1	241.8	+17.2	3.6	+44.0	5.0	-6.7	0.80
Bahrain Middle East Bank	558.0	+25.0	327.3	+25.0	8.0	+166.0	0.3	-50.0	0.05
United Gulf Bank	502.7	-55.4	224.7	-48.1	9.2	+39.4	-10.1	-87.0	-
Nomura Investment Banking (M.E.)	356.1	+16.9	na	-	na	-	3.0	+5.1	0.80
Bahrain International Bank	316.0	+7.3	33.1	+5.4	na	-	14.1	+27.8	4.50
Trans-Arabian Investment Bank	307.9	+12.9	98.7	+12.4	2.0	+17.6	6.2	-13.9	2.00
Arabian Investment Banking Corporation (Investcorp)	259.5	+10.0	na	-	na	-	12.1	+9.0	4.70

Note: Exchange Rate: US $ 1 = Bahraini Dinar (BD) 0.379 (Nov. 11, 1987)
Source: MEED October, 1986

Exhibit 5   Bahrain: Local Banks – 1985 (BD Million)

	Assets	%Change on 1984	Loans	%Change on 1984	Provisions	%Change on 1984	Net Profit	%Change on 1984	% return on assets
Bank of Bahrain and Kuwait	772.0	– 6.9	516.0	+ 1.4	na	–	7.8	– 31.0	1.0
National Bank of Bahrain	533.0	– 16.6	197.0	– 20.6	4.3	+ 85.0	8.0	– 25.0	1.5
Al-Ahli Commercial Bank	167.3	+ 5.3	96.7	– 4.6	na	–	2.3	– 1.7	1.4

Source: MEED October 1986.

Exhibit 6   Kuwait: Local Banks – 1985 (KD Million)

	Assets	%Change on 1984	Loans	%Change on 1984	Provisions	%Change on 1984	Net Profit	%Change on 1984	% return on assets
National Bank of Kuwait	2,589.9	– 2.4	1,149.9	– 5.9	na	–	23.0	+ 11.1	0.89
The Gulf Bank	1,820.8	– 3.2	997.6	+ 5.7	18.1	+ 69.2	0.0	– 100.0	0.00
Commercial Bank of Kuwait	1,635.7	– 9.8	970.3	0.0	9.4	+ 84.3	0.0	– 100.0	0.00
Al-Ahli Bank of Kuwait	1,511.8	– 5.1	778.2	– 1.4	na	–	3.9	– 60.6	0.26
Burgan Bank	999.2	+ 5.8	543.9	+ 13.0	na	–	0.0	– 100.0	0.00
Bank of Kuwait and the Middle East	874.8	– 4.3	544/4	+ 5.1	na	–	1.5	– 77.6	0.17

Note: Exchange Rate: US $ 1 = KD 0.293 (Nov. 11, 1987)
Source: MEED 1982.

Exhibit 7 Oman: Local Banks – 1985 (RO Million)

	Assets	% Change on 1984	Loans	% Change on 1984
National Bank of Oman	373.3	+3.8	180.7	+18.7
Oman International Bank	124.6	+29.8	87.2	+64.2
Bank of Oman, Bahrain and Kuwait	89.4	+13.6	66.4	−23.2
Oman Arab Bank	88.2	+43.2	52.3	+81.0
Commercial Bank of Oman	69.0	+16.2	47.5	+34.5
Al-Bank Al-Ahli Al-Omani	52.9	+7.7	38.4	+39.6
Bank of Muscat	39.6	+8.5	25.7	+2.8
Union Bank of Oman	33.5	−29.9	23.3	−16.0
Bank of Oman and the Gulf	24.0	−0.8	17.1	+6.2

Note: Exchange Rate: US $1 = Oman Dinar (RO) 0.385 (Nov. 11, 1987)
Source: MEED September 1986.

Exhibit 8 Qatar: Local Banks – 1985 (QR Million)

	Assets	% Change on 1984	Loans	% Change on 1984	Provisions	% Change on 1984	Net Profit	% Change on 1984	% return on asset
Qatar National Bank	8,141.3	+18.4	3,666.6	+28.2	na	–	90.4	+2.5	1.1
Doha Bank	1,511.9	+10.3	393.0	+9.1	na	–	31.7	−5.9	2.0
Commercial Bank of Qatar	724.0	−1.3	221.0	−21.2	na	–	19.4	−25.1	2.7
Al-Ahli Bank of Qatar[1]	179.6	–	57.0	–	na	–	3.3	–	1.8

[1] 1985 was the first full year of operation.
Note: Exchange Rate: US $1 = Rialys Qatari (QR) 3.64 (Nov. 11, 1987)
Source: MEED Special Report, October, 1986.

Exhibit 9   Saudi Arabia: Local Banks – 1985 (SR Million)

	Assets	%Change on 1984	Loans	%Change on 1984	Provisions	%Change on 1984	Net Profit	%Change on 1984	% return on assets
The National Commercial Bank	55,473	– 3.7	20,970	+ 4.7	691.0	+ 62.5	99.6	– 80.1	0.18
Riyadh Bank	32,824	+ 7.4	10,856	– 4.8	333.1	+ 10.9	189.3	– 63.0	0.58
Saudi American Bank	14,444	+ 2.5	5,263	– 12.0	103.9	+ 75.2	174.4	– 37.8	1.20
Al-Bank Al-Saudi Al-Fransi	13,725	+ 5.8	6,842	+ 10.1	75.5	+ 53.8	110.4	– 35.2	0.80
Arab National Bank	10,411	+ 14.3	2,602	– 4.7	na	–	185.1	– 23.4	1.80
Albank Alsaudi AlHollandi	9,383	+ 12.2	4,173	+ 3.1	70.0	+ 100.0	19.0	– 81.9	0.20
Saudi British Bank	8,186	+ 12.9	3,306	– 3.3	95.9	+ 47.3	9.1	– 90.9	0.10
Saudi Cairo Bank	7,180	– 0.3	3,920	– 1.0	91.1	– 15.7	0.0	– 100.0	0.00
Bank al-Jazira	5,600	+ 7.1	1,900	–	45.0	+ 28.6	45.3	– 35.5	0.80
Saudi Investment Bank (Saib)	4,567	1.1	1,182	– 10.8	40.0	+ 13.6	– 15.4	–	–
United Saudi Commercial Bank	3,290	+ 33.5	696	+ 17.3	22.0	+ 340.0	– 17.0	–	–

Note: Exchange Rate: US $ 1 = Saudi Riyals (SR) 3.645 (Nov. 11, 1987)
Source: MEED Special Report, October 1986.

Exhibit 10   U.A.E.: Top 12 Local Banks – 1985 (DH Million)

	Assets	% Change on 1984	Loans	% Change on 1984	Provisions	% Change on 1984	Net Profit	% Change on 1984	% return on assets
National Bank of Abu Dhabi	20,737.2	− 5.0	10,488.2	+ 77.0	206.4	+ 56.0	12.7	− 66.0	0.06
National Bank of Dubai	18,844.6	+ 12.2	1,238.1	− 14.8	33.6	+ 5.3	374.9	+ 7.4	2.00
Bank of Oman	8,907.4	–	3,087.1	− 3.5	47.6	− 34.2	40.3	− 7.8	0.50
Bank of Credit and Commerce (Emirates)	4,193.1	+ 13.0	2,018.8	+ 45.1	11.0	− 64.3	47.0	+ 91.1	1.10
Abu Dhabi Commercial Bank	5,364.8	− 16.4	3,833.5	+ 3.9	na	–	− 176.7	–	–
Arab Bank for Investment and Foreign Trade	3,759.9	− 7.4	1,779.0	− 18.6	41.2	+ 19.1	3.1	− 83.1	0.08
National Bank of Sharjah	2,335.6	− 9.1	1,585.5	+ 18.7	24.3	+ 24.6	29.0	− 3.3	1.20
Investment Bank for Trade and Finance	1,811.2	+ 9.7	1,005.2	+ 12.9	4.0	− 13.0	26.1	− 14.4	1.40
The Commercial Bank of Dubai	1,163.0	− 6.9	596.7	− 1.3	4.1	− 4.7	20.6	− 29.7	1.80
United Arab Bank	812.3	− 0.1	652.2	− 4.5	18.4	− 25.8	5.2	+ 92.6	0.60
Bank of Sharjah	644.5	+ 9.6	359.5	− 5.7	9.7	+ 110.9	13.8	− 11.0	2.10
First Gulf Bank	623.2	+ 2.3	183.8	− 4.6	7.7	− 10.5	11.1	− 26.0	1.80

Note: Exchange Rate: US $ 1 = U.A.E. Dirham (DH) 3.673 (Nov. 11, 1987)
Source: MEED Special Report, October 1986

Nationalized banks tend to be of a medium to small size. They are characterized as having affiliations with foreign international banking firms, smaller branch networks, and less sensitivity to cultural needs. They place differing emphasis on wholesale, private, and retail banking.

Key Buyers

Users of banking services are generally grouped into the following categories:

1) corporate customers;
2) other banks;
3) government agencies;
4) high net-worth individuals;
5) medium- to small-sized businesses;
6) individuals;
7) women.

There is some overlap between these segments, but these are the areas of distinction in terms of both deposits and services required.

The first two segments constitute the area where wholesale banking is specialized, covering tailor-made loan facilities, syndications, yield plans for customers, and financial advisory services. These segments were relatively more important during the boom period.

Government agencies mainly require payroll services. However, other services may be performed that banks may not be willing to admit.

Segments four and five are in the area of private banking, and required services range from investment plans to more standardized loan facilities.

Segments six and seven involve retail banking. These segments now receive more attention, in order to absorb extant cash in circulation in the Gulf economies.

Whereas the customers of the 1970s were more affluent and highly liquid, less sophisticated, less sensitive to interest rates, and more loyal to specific institutions, those of the 1980s are quite the opposite: less affluent, less liquid, better informed, more sophisticated, more sensitive to interest rates, and less loyal to specific institutions. This is certainly a sign of the changing times.

Key Suppliers

Key Suppliers may be grouped according to the following resources they supply:

1) physical facilities;

2) electronic equipment;
3) human resources;
4) services to banks.

Worldwide, banks first started to install computers in the 1950s and 1960s. From 1970 onward, with the development of micro-electronics and cheap computing power, it became possible to provide automated machinery at a reasonable cost for staff in the branches and even for the customers to operate themselves.

All around the world, banks use technology for five main reasons (Economist 1986: 15):

1) Simplifying their bookkeeping by transferring their accounting activities from hand-written branch ledgers to central mainframe computers;
2) automating the processing of payments;
3) freeing customers from the need to go into their banks (cash dispenser);
4) making possible new product and services;
5) managing the business better and market selectivity on profitability.

The new economies of scale in computing power made possible the development of extensive networks of Automatic Teller Machines (ATM), high speed cash dispensers, and counter terminals to help the cashier and branch processing systems to provide customers' information swiftly for managers. On the wholesale side, it made possible aid for the banks' foreign exchange and market dealers, electronic cash management systems, and inter-bank messaging and communications (MEB & F, February 1986, p. 15).

Technology is also being used increasingly to gain a competitive edge in business development, since the catch up time needed to emulate systems-based products is longer than more traditional banking products (The Banker, March, 1986).

The main supply constraint is that of human resources, especially under the requirement of hiring Gulf nationals, where a considerable expense must be incurred in training. Also, larger salaries must be awarded compared to other industries due to: the cultural aversion toward banking, the scarcity of Gulf nationals with banking experience, and the problem of high turnover.

Entry and Exit Barriers

These include:

1) approval by the Council of Ministers and Royal decree, such as in Saudi Arabia;
2) government regulations by monetary agencies;
3) capital requirements;
4) know-how and personnel requirements;
5) heated competition.

The first three are barriers to both entry and exit, while the fourth and fifth are entry barriers only.

The most important entry barrier is securing approval by the Council of Ministers and the recommendation of the monetary agencies. At present, governmental approval of new banks in the Gulf is highly unlikely, due to the government's belief that the banking market is saturated and further competition will lead to bank failures. Even though it is not mentioned in the banking control law of Saudi Arabia, a Royal decree is also required to establish a bank.

Saudi Arabian Monetary Agency (SAMA) regulations stipulate that a new bank must be a joint stock company with a minimum capital of Saudi Riyals (SR) 1.5 million. Also, an account must be opened at SAMA, and reserves withheld at SAMA as well as at the bank. There are additional requirements mentioned in the banking control law and stipulated by SAMA. For exit, certain requirements must be met, such as the clearance of all liabilities, in addition to SAMA approval.

In addition to governmental requirements, large capital costs must be incurred to vie with the competition, unless a totally different market niche is found. This could pose an exit barrier, especially in the case of purchase of specialized electronic equipment, which is difficult to sell off.

Banking know-how and skilled personnel are required for successful entry into the banking business, which poses a formidable barrier due to the high cost of personnel.

At the moment, the banking industry in the Gulf states is in heated competition for deposits, and the competitive reaction to a new entrant will be strong, especially if the entrant is big and has found an important new market niche.

Substitutes

In the Arab Gulf States, commercial banks compete for business by offering a wide variety of banking services (see Exhibit 3 on page 161). They can be distinguished by several salient attributes:
1) location and branch network;
2) type, range, and quality of services;
3) charges on loans and services;
4) return to depositors;
5) image – social attitude toward the bank;
6) cultural sensitivity;
7) sophistication of know-how and facilities;
8) promotion and advertising;
9) appearance of facilities, personnel, and customer treatment;
10) long-term commitment to local economy.

Competition with commercial banks in the Arab Gulf States is primarily posed by the following substitutes:
1) governmental banks;
2) Islamic banks
3) offshore banks;
4) money exchangers;
5) personal saving and hoarding.

Governmental Banks and Funding Agencies

Governmental banks proliferate all over the Gulf states and concentrate on providing medium to long-term loans. For example, in Saudi Arabia there is the Real Estate Development Fund (REDF) for setting up real estate projects for private and commercial use, the Saudi Industrial Development Fund (SIDF) for providing medium or long-term loans to new or existing industrial establishments, the Public Investment Fund (PIF) for financing and taking equity shares in large-scale public projects in commerce and industry and the Saudi Arabian Agricultural Bank (SAAB) for providing loans and credit facilities required for the development of agriculture and related activities.

There are two other small agencies for special funding requirements. The Credit Fund for Contractors grants loans to Saudi contractors for financing the direct purchase of the basic materials they need. The Saudi Credit Bank provides loans to low-income Saudis for such personal needs as getting married or carrying out home repairs (Habib et al. 1987).

These government loans are interest-free. Hence, for parties that can come up with the required seed money, government funds become much more attractive relative to funds supplied by commercial banks.

172   Ghazi M. Habib

Islamic Banks

Islamic banking has its underpinnings in Islamic law (Shariah). As can be inferred from Exhibit 11, presenting the major financial instruments of Islamic banking, interest (riba) is prohibited under this system.

Exhibit   11   Financial Instruments of Islamic Banking[1]

Mudaraba: A unit trust agreement between a lender (the bank) and an entrepreneur (the mudarib) whereby the lender agrees to finance the entrepreneur's project on a profit-or-loss (PLS) sharing basis. The *mudarib* undertakes to pay back the capital invested and a share of the profits. He acts as the manager, while the bank plays the role of capital provider.

Musharaka: A partnership for a specific business activity in which the bank and the partner (e.g. a contractor) create joint venture projects with the aim of making a profit, whereby there is a participation in the management.

Murabaha: A resale contract where the client requests the bank to buy a specific commodity or goods. The bank resells the goods at a price which covers the purchase price plus the profit margin agreed upon by both parties, which transforms traditional lending into a sale and purchase agreement, under which the bank buys the goods wanted by the client for resale to the client at a higher price agreed upon by both parties.

Qard Hasan: A loan without interest. Literally a "good loan." This is a loan by which a borrower is obliged to repay the lender the principal sum borrowed on the loan. It is left to the discretion of the borrower to reward the lender for his loan by paying any sum over and above the amount of the principal. Usually this instrument is used in a transaction between the state and a less wealthy member of society.

Ijara: Renting, a contract of lease or hire.

Wadia: An agreemen to deposit an asset (excluding land) in the custody of another party who is not the owner (e.g. a bank).

Takafol: Mutual support which is the basis of the concept of solidarity among Muslims – an alternative to western insurance. The idea is that the various participants agree to pay installments to a *takafol* fund managed by the Islamic bank. The Islamic bank acts as management company – thus it admits participants, collects installments, provides management service, invests the funds in *halal* projects, and pays *takafol* benefits – all to achieve solidarity and cooperation under the conditions of contract.

---

[1] For a balanced treatment of Islamic banking see Sezneck (1987) Ch. 5, and Ahmad (1985).

Source: Abdullah (1984).

The objectives of Islamic banks are:

1) to attract funds and employ these resources in Islamic countries;
2) to develop the saving habit among Muslim individuals;
3) to offer interest-free bank services according to Islamic Shariah.

Islamic banking in the 1950s was considered unworkable. During the 1960s, the status of Islamic banking improved marginally, but was still thought of as an unworkable system by some Muslim and many Western bankers. In the past 10 years, however, the Islamic banking system has made tremendous strides and is now represented on five continents (see Exhibits 12 through 14).

Exhibit 12   Islamic Banks in Arab Countries

Name of Bank	Year of Establishment	Paid Up Capital US $ (1,000,000)	Country
Bahrain Islamic Bank	1979	15	Bahrain
Masaraf Faisal Al-Islami (Bahrain)	1980	20	Bahrain
Banque Mier	1980	–	Egypt
Faisal Islamic Bank	1977	21	Egypt
Islamic International Bank for Investment and Development	1981	12	Egypt
Jordan Islam Bank for Finance	1978	9	Jordan
Kuwait Finance House	1977	30	Kuwait
Islamic Development Bank	1975	–	Saudi Arabia
Faisal Islamic Bank (Sudan)	1978	9	Sudan
Tadamon Islamic Bank	1983	–	Sudan
Sudanese Islamic Bank	1983	–	Sudan
Dubai Islamic Bank	1973	14	U.A.E.

Sources: 1. MEED 1980: 35.
2. Arab Banking and Finance Magazine 1985.

Offshore Banking Units

In 1975, Bahrain, which is now connected to Saudi Arabia by a causeway, initiated a policy of licensing offshore banking units (OBUs). Since then a good portion of the revenues from offshore banks has come from dealing in the Saudi riyal – giving Saudi riyal-nominated loans to foreign companies operating in Saudi Arabia. According to one estimate, 70% of offshore loans are made to Saudi Arabians (Al-Iktissad Wal Naft 1985).

Exhibit 13   Islamic Banking Institutions in Non-Arab Countries

Name of Bank	Year of Establish- ment	Paid Up Capital in US $	Country
Dar Al-Mal Al-Islamia Trust	1982	1 bn.	Bahamas
Kibris Islamic Bank	1982	1 m.	Cyprus
Islamic Bank International	1982	Kr 25 m.	Denmark
Masaraf Faisal Islami (DMI)	1982	20 m.	Guinea
Iranian Banking System	1982	20 m.	Iran
Islamic Banking System International Holding S.A. (27 Countries)	1982	20 m.	Luxemburg
Bank Islami Malaysia	1983 DMI	100 m.	Malaysia
Masaraf Faisal Islami	1983	20 m.	Niger
Pakistani Banking System	1983	20 m.	Pakistan
Masaraf Faisal (DMI)	1983	20 m.	Senegal
Dar-al-Maal (DMI)	Subsidies	–	Switzerland
Masaraf Faisal Islami	1982	20 m.	Turkey
Kuwait Finance House	1978	10 m.	Turkey
Masaraf Faisal Islami	1982	.6 m.	U.K.
Al-Raijhi Company for Islamic Investment	1981		U.K.

Source: 1. MEED 1980: 35.
       2. Arab Banking and Finance Magazine 1985.

Exhibit 14   Islamic Banks in Gulf States – Total Assets From 1981–1985

Name of Bank	1981	1982	1983	1984	1985
Islamic Devel. Bank	1,270,825	1,474,988	1,800,690	1,980,000	2,143,300
Kuwait Finance House	108,233	177,648	279,193	373,275	488,238
Bahrain Isl. Bank	6,547.5	10,778.3	13,447.5	14,666.6	23,568.5
Faisal Isl. Bank	–	21,122	23,125	30,845	45,292
Qatar Isl. Bank	–	–	–	101,631	166,255
Dubai Isl. Bank	112,750	138,528	214,025	311,112	268,364
Al-Barka Isl. Bank	–	–	–	125,112	268,364

Source: Abdul-hammid (1987).

Money Exchangers

Most of the money exchangers' business is in foreign exchange and travelers checks, but the bigger exchangers have been taking short-term deposits and arranging short-term finance for customers. Dubbed as "people's banks," money exchangers have hundreds of branches throughout the Gulf region. In several Gulf states, money exchangers started to lose the important role they used to play, due to limitations placed on their activities by the local monetary agencies.

Personal Savings and Hoarding

Paying and receiving interest are considered immoral in some Gulf states such as Saudi Arabia. Many Saudis refuse to deposit their money even in non-interest-bearing accounts in commercial banks and continue to view banks with distrust. Estimates indicate that more than 50% of all Saudis still do not have an account in any of the commercial banks (Wilson 1983). These people think that mixing their money with a bank's money may make them sinful.

Our observations and interviews indicate that resentment of interest is common among many Gulf nationals. One such example is the experience of a bank manager who paid a visit to a wealthy Saudi businessman to invite him to deposit some of his money in a new branch. He was flatly told that if it were not for the traditional Arabian hospitality, he would have been thrown out immediately. Similar anecdotes are widespread, especially in rural areas. As a result, a large amount of money in the Saudi economy goes untapped and underutilized. Some estimates place the amount at more than one billion Saudi riyals.

References

Abdeen, A.M. and Shook, D. (1984): *The Saudi financial system*, New York: John Wiley and Sons, p. 60.
Abdul-hammid, M.J. (1987): *Financial analysis of Islamic banks vs. traditional banks*, Working Paper, College of Industrial Management, KFUPM.
Abdullah, II. (1984): Islamic banking: Consolidating the vision, *Ahlan Wasahlan*, (June); published by Saudi Arabian Airlines.
Ahmad, Z. (1985): The present state of the Islamic finance movement in the impact and role of Islamic banking in international finance: A conference of the US Arab Chamber of Commerce, New York: June 28, 1985.

Al-Iktissad Wal Naft (1985): Banks in Bahrain, (September): 24–43.

Al Masaref Al-Arabia (1983): Banking and financial development in the Arab Gulf States, 3, 25 (January): 27–42.

Al-Masaref Al-Arabia (1985): Volume 5, Number 49: 63.

Arab Banking and Finance (1985): *Survey of Islamic Banking*, London.

Arab Banks (1985): Financial structure of local commercial banks in GCC countries in 1984, (June): 56–63.

The Banker (1986):... (March):

The Economist (1980): The Gulf Cooperation Council countries: A survey, (8 February).

The Economist (1986): Survey... (March 22).

Field, M. (1986): Weathering the storm, *The Arab Banker*, (December): 75.

Habib, G., U. Yavas, S. Kassem, and K. Al-Modaifer 1987): The bank marketing scene in Saudi Arabia, *The International Journal of Bank Marketing*, 5, 2: 20–32.

MEB & F (1986):... (February): 15.

Middle East Economic Digest:

MEED (1979): Special report on Qatar, (November).

MEED (1980): Special report, (May): 35.

MEED (1982): Special report on Kuwait, (May).

MEED (1985): Special report on Saudi Arabia, (July).

MEED (1986): Special report on Oman, (September).

MEED (1986): Special report... (October):

The Middle East (1984): Banking in hard times.

Seznec, J. (1987): *The financial markets of the Arabian Gulf*. Kent, U.K., Croom Helm.

Stutely, R. (1986): The Middle East banks – Crisis compounded, *Accountancy*, (August): 18.

Wilson, R. (1983): *Banking and finance in the Middle East*, London: Macmillan.

Wilson, R. (1983): Arab banking in the Gulf: Trends and prospects, in: *Arab banking and finance handbook*, Manama, Bahrain: Falcon Publisher.

5.2 National Commercial Bank (NCB)

Ghazi M. Habib

Introduction

The National Commercial Bank (NCB) is Saudi Arabia's oldest and biggest bank. It was formed in 1951 by the present general manager, Salim Ahmed Bin Mahfouz, and his partners, Abdel-Aziz Al-Kaaki and Salah and Abdullah Mousa Kaaki.

NCB is unusual in several aspects. It has over a million clients nationwide, and it is more than twice the size of its nearest rival. NCB is the biggest private bank in the Middle East and the second biggest one, after the Hong Kong Bank, in the entire developing world.

NCB has 169 branches, eight of which are seasonal. It has three foreign branches – in Beirut, Bahrain, and New York; and it has representative offices in London, Frankfurt, Singapore, Tokyo, and Seoul. NCB has a branch in Jeddah and another one in Riyadh, that are designed exclusively for women who prefer to carry out their banking transactions without any men around in accordance with Islamic teachings.

The size and financial strength of NCB is well reflected in its prestigious new headquarters in Jeddah. Twenty-six stories high, the headquarters dominates Jeddah skyline and houses the bank's central and regional operations apart from the computer and training center. As the tallest building in Saudi Arabia, it is an architectural statement of NCB's strength and security and of its status both in the banking industry and in the Saudi business community.

NCB is unusual in another respect. It is the only private joint liability bank among the 11 banks operating in Saudi Arabia. While Riyadh Bank and NCB are 100 % Saudi-owned, the 9 remaining banks are joint stock banks with at least 60 % of their equity owned by the Saudi public.

Finally, NCB and Riyadh Bank have been successful in capitalizing on their status as the only banks in the Kingdom that are wholly owned and managed by Saudis. This advantage has enabled them to attract 60 to 70 % of government deposits.

Some banking industry analysts argue that some of the major comparative advantages that NCB has been enjoying may soon become less favorable due to several reasons. First, many have been questioning the prudence of maintaining NCB as the only private bank, which deprives the bank of the benefits derived from broader stock ownership and broader participation on the board of directors. Second, NCB has kept its headquarters in the city of Jeddah and away from the capital where government ministries are located, and where the Saudi Arabian Monetary Agency (SAMA) would prefer them to be. Third, NCB has been accused of not being "really" 100% Saudi, a charge which Ben Mahfouz detests and strongly denies. Finally, NCB succeeded in getting SAMA's approval to venture outside the Saudi market, and this decision has serious national and strategic implications for both the Saudi economy and NCB.

Objectives/Mission

NCB has multiple objectives that include:

- contributing to the development and well-being of the Saudi Arabian economy;
- generating a stable level of profit performance;
- establishing excellent relationships with the business community, particularly small businesses; and
- developing and maintaining a well-trained cadre of efficient and satisfied bank personnel.

History

The banking industry in Saudi Arabia has seen unparalleled growth in the last 15 years. Before that time, the structure of the banking industry in the Kingdom was traditional and lacked the modern and sophisticated technologies that are proliferating in the Saudi market today. Banking was mostly confined to currency exchange and financing of import trade by prominent Saudi trading families.

Bin Mahfouz and the Al-Kaaki partners were among the few pioneer money exchangers before the discovery of oil on a commercial scale in Saudi Arabia in 1938. At that time, there was one branch office of the Netherlands Trading Society conducting limited financial services in the country.

In 1948, Bin Mahfouz persuaded King 'Abd al-'Aziz Al Sa'ud of the importance of starting a national financial company as a sign of national financial independence. The King gave his blessing. Then, one year after the establishment of SAMA in 1952, Bin Mahfouz managed to convert the status of his financial company to a full-fledged banking institution under the name of the National Commercial Bank. NCB was the first commercial banking institution to be recognized officially in Saudi Arabia.

Organization

In the past, there was no board of directors or an executive committee. The general manager used to meet periodically with his deputy general managers. However, the diversity and rate of growth of NCB's portfolio of services rendered the old structure ineffective and inefficient. Thus, the planning and business development division was delegated the responsibility of designing an appropriate organizational structure (see Exhibit 1).

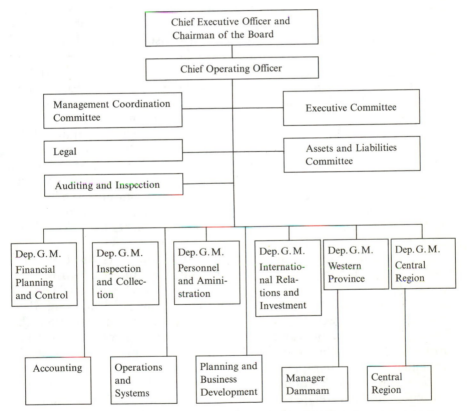

Exhibit 1   National Commercial Bank Organization Chart
Source: NCB Plannung and Business Development Department

In the new structure, a number of committees and deputy general managers report directly to the chief operating officer (C.O.O.). The executive committee is chaired by the C.O.O., Mr. Mohammed Bin Mahfouz, and plays the role of the board of directors. It formulates the long-term strategic plans of the bank. It is comprised of Khalid Bin Mahfouz, vice chairman, and all deputy general managers.

The management coordination committee is in charge of communicating and executing the plans and policies formulated by the executive committee.

The assets and liabilities committee is chaired by the C.O.O. Its in charge of evaluating the financial position of the bank and directing the divisions responsible for operating the funds and investments, lending monies to the various economic sectors, and overseeing loans and deposits. The assets and liabilities committee reports its recommendations to the executive committee. If approved, a recommendation is then referred to the management coordination committee for implementation and communication to the divisions concerned.

The planning and business development division has dual functions. Some relate to policy, and others are line functions. The division formulates strategies and is involved in such areas as new product development, choosing new branch locations, economic forecasting, marketing, and market research.

The international relations and investment division deals with international markets. It has responsibility for investing the excess equity of the bank in money markets. The division has a foreign exchange room which is the largest in the country and deals daily in hundreds of millions of riyals.

Cash management looks after lending capabilities and ensures the liquidity of 25% of the bank's deposit liability which amounts to billions of Saudi riyals that should be readily and prudently invested to earn a return. Typically, these monies are invested in local instruments like SAMA's or placed in the interbank market.

The financial planning and control division supports the asset and liability committee by collecting and reporting all the figures from the accounting division. It is in charge of the budget and the financial control functions. All branches develop their own budgets, which are then consolidated at the regional level. There are two regions, one comprises the Western and Eastern provinces, while the other comprises the South and North. Each region then submits its budget to the central region which in turn submits it to general management in a consolidated budget forecast.

The credit and collections division is responsible for credit policies. Collection functions relate to bad or problematic loans. The division tries to work out settlements through rescheduling. It also tries to help customers by advising them about how to meet their obligations.

The accounting department is responsible for the consolidation of all bank accounting functions. It also issues accounting policies to branches and departments, prepares settlement letters between branches through central accounting, and supports two external auditors who work for the bank.

Personnel is responsible for training. Each employee must receive at least one training course a year. Manpower development encompasses introductory courses, on-the-job training job rotation to explore employees' aptitudes and potentialities, and more intensified training once an employee has settled into a certain field. Personnel is also responsible for planning employee replacements and successions, and for charting employees career paths. The personnel and administration Division also evaluates salary levels against market norms, as well as incentive compensation or bonuses to management. It also handles executive recruitment and such personnel services as payroll, benefits, administrative services, contracts, and insurance.

Operations and systems division is responsible for bank-wide automation, upgrades and expansions, security, data processing, choosing vendors, evaluating, operations systems and procedures, and improved efficiency to speed transaction and reduce their costs.

Audit and inspection division ensures that bank operations are carried out in an efficient manner, and all branches and divisions are abiding by the policies issued by the senior management of the bank. It also receives loan portfolio of the bank. It monitors problematic loans and brings them to the attention of branch management, region management, and the executive committee.

Services Portfolio

The core of NCB business consists of three activities: deposits, trade financing, and industrial financing. NCB renders a wide variety of services, including maintaining current accounts and time deposits; issuing loans, remittances, and letters of credit; dealing in collections, foreign exchange, mutual funds; and processing equity shares in Saudi companies and trading in these shares.

NCB innovated the service for buying, processing, and following-up on shares bought in corporations, for a fee of a quarter of a percent of the annual value of the share. The service starts when a customer subscribes to a share issued by a company. NCB secures the authority to act on behalf of the customer, submits his subscription, and then waits for the allocation of shares when there are more subscriptions than shares. The bank then follows up on the share offer, receives the original share certificate, and stores it in safe custody. It also monitors dividends and capital appreciation and prepares a quarterly printout for the customer, showing the nominal and market value of the share as well as the dividends. In brief, the bank represents the customer in his stock. NCB now manages about 600 millions worth of shares.

NCB is known in the Saudi banking scene as the master of syndicated loans. NCB has more than 13 billion riyals of loans given to firms in the private and semi-private sectors.

Personnel

To enhance the productivity and loyalty of its personnel, NCB tries to treat its personnel fairly and compensate them well. Compensation benefits are reviewed regularly to make sure that they remain competitive with the market.

NCB prides itself on the prevailing openness and friendliness between top executives and all bank employees. This informal, paternalistic family type of relationship seems to pay off in terms of employee loyalty and low employee turnover and absenteeism. It is not uncommon for NCB employees to continue working for the bank for a lifetime. Most of those who quit the bank do so to start their own businesses.

It has been the policy of the bank since its inception to nationalize its key positions. Members of top management are all Saudis, except in certain specialized areas such as loan syndication, bonds trading, or security trading. However, even in these areas Saudi substitutes are under training. In other areas, too, training is under way. However, Saudization lagged, especially during the period of economic boom, when not many suitable candidates were available. Moreover, many fundamentalist Saudis still believe that it is sinful to work for banks, because they are usurious. Despite NCB's efforts to Saudize, the bank has been accused of not being truly Saudi in either the composition of its work force or in its corporate culture. Some teasingly comment that NCB is really a "Hadrami" bank, people originally from South Yemen. NCB has more than 6,154 employees. About 34% of them are Saudis. NCB is planning to increase its Saudi work force to 75%.

Marketing

At NCB, marketing activities are performed at the branches level as well as at the headquarter. The marketing budget varies from 5 to 7 million annually and is allocated to advertising, personal selling, media publicity, and sales promotion in terms of gifts and publications.

Finance

In 1986, total assets of the bank stood at SR 91.4 billion; loans and advances SR 24.4 billion, leaving a net profit of SR 80 million, after substantial general contingency and loan provisions had been set aside in conformity with the bank's policy (see Exhibits 2 and 3).

New Challenges

NCB is faced with new challenges requiring serious consideration:

First, NCB considers Riyadh Bank and Saudi American Bank (SAMBA) as its major competitors. Both NCB and Riyadh Bank are 100% Saudi-owned. However, NCB is a joint liability partner-ship between Ben Mahfouz and al-Kaaki, while Riyadh Bank is partially owned by the Saudi government and partially by the Saudi public, which may enable Riyadh Bank to receive more government deposits than NCB. Furthermore, Riyadh Bank maintains its headquarters in Riyadh, while NCB is based in Jeddah, far from the capital.

NCB competes with SAMBA for corporate business. SAMBA has a management contract with Citibank, while NCB is basically managed by the sons of Ben Mahfouz and their Saudi deputies. The state of technology employed by SAMBA is more advanced than that of NCB, which has a lot of catching up to do.

Finally, NCB received the approval of SAMA to branch out into the international market. Given the tough competition in international markets, the prudence of this strategic move by NCB remains to be seen.

Exhibit 2 Balance Sheet

Assets	1986 SR	1985 SR	1984 SR	1983 SR
Cash Funds				
1. Cash in hand	598,195,402	858,674,608	2,520,892,994	2,503,956,386
2. Statutory deposits with SAMA	1,812,474,750	1,676,425,411	1,757,096,616	1,679,472,654
3. Other deposits with SAMA	1,717,286,197	1,769,541,146	2,091,740,435	2,850,195,674
	4,127,956,349	4,304,641,165	6,369,730,045	7,033,624,714
Deposits with banks				
1. Saudi Arabia	345,575,017	1,068,629,744	397,331,829	107,927,949
2. Abroad	23,804,574,518	23,760,885,576	25,293,258,011	18,410,475,742
	24,150,149,535	24,829,515,320	25,690,589,840	18,818,403,691
Investments (Not exceeding lower of cost or market value)				
1. Shares and securities:				
a) In Saudi Arabia	414,323,481	411,286,918	402,337,815	380,243,880
b) Abroad	7,116,674,898	1,952,461,728	1,584,911,918	1,112,669,717
2. Other investments	—	—	—	—
	7,530,998,379	2,363,748,646	1,987,249,733	1,492,913,597
Loans and advances etc. (Less provision for bad and doubtful debts)				
1. To:				
a) Private sector	21,710,528,103	19,183,554,291	18,323,387,825	19,914,457,969
b) Banks	1,579,885,918	560,878,602	490,336,785	109,766,802
c) Others	1,012,403,267	870,349,030	903,570,909	901,913,561

estate (at cost or revaluation)	2,020,896,200	1,549,438,188	1,511,728,030	1,328,328,173
2. Furniture, fixtures, and equipment (less depreciation)	116,432,317	132,333,114	144,789,172	122,153,517
	2,137,328,517	1,681,771,302	1,656,517,202	1,450,481,690
Other Assets				
1. Customers' liabilities for outstanding acceptances	421,653,366	352,466,663	556,103,771	428,176,567
2. Other assets	888,562,240	970,793,375	1,324,622,280	971,966,595
	1,310,215,606	1,323,260,038	1,880,763,051	1,450,481,690
Subtotal	63,702,444,734	55,472,904,532	57,615,325,597	51,111,822,076
Contra accounts				
Customers' liabilities under guarantees, letters of credit, and other obligations	27,755,918,594	29,901,312,020	33,018,000,200	31,777,164,885
Grand total	91,458,363,328	85,374,216,020	90,633,325,797	82,888,986,961
Liabilities				
Capital	30,225,133	30,225,133	30,225,133	20,225,133
Statutory reserve	32,774,867	32,774,867	32,774,867	32,774,867
Other revenue reserves	3,059,027,254	3,059,027,254	3,059,027,254	2,659,027,254
Surplus of revaluation of properties	45,095,605	46,095,605	46,095,605	46,095,605
Surplus on revaluation of investments	31,877,141	31,877,141	31,877,141	31,877,141
Total capital and reserves	3,200,000,000	3,200,000,000	3,200,000,000	2,800,000,000
Deposits				
1. Customers' deposits (Note: covers total current, time, and saving deposits	46,039,182,513	43,612,431,242	44,833,669,152	37,859,397,240
2. Deposits from banks				
a) In Saudi Arabia	2,623,850,640	1,951,879,799	1,313,078,774	1,289,846,904
b) Abroad	8,136,148,356	12,379,839,449	3,977,710,461	2,803,816,850
3. Sundry deposits (Note: includes margins for letters of credit, guarantees, drafts, and other transfers)	1,437,357,393	1,379,839,449	1,475,107,788	2,039,595,489
	58,236,538,902	49,961,663,916	51,619,566,175	43,992,656,483

Exhibit 2   Balance Sheet (continued)

Assets	1986 SR	1985 SR	1984 SR	1983 SR
Borrowings				
1. From banks:				
a) In Saudi Arabia	—	—	—	—
b) Abroad	—	—	—	—
2. From others	—	—	—	—
3. Notes issued	750,000,000	730,000,000	—	—
	750,000,000	730,000,000	—	—
Profit and loss account				
Balance brought forward from last year	377,678	733,635	1,283,421	17,261,990
Add: Net profit for the year 1986 as per profit and loss account annexed	75,977,217	99,644,043	99,450,214	144,342,691
	80,354,895	100,377,678	100,733,635	161,604,681
Other liabilities				
1. Acceptances outstanding on behalf of customers	421,653,366	352,466,663	556,130,771	428,176,567
2. Other liabilities	1,013,897,571	1,128,396,275	2,138,895,016	3,729,384,345
	1,435,550,937	1,480,862,938	2,695,025,787	4,157,560,912
Sub-total	63,702,444,734	55,472,904,532	57,615,325,597	51,111,822,076
Contra accounts				
Guarantees, letters of credit, and other obligations	27,755,918,594	29,901,312,020	33,018,000,200	31,777,164,885
Grand total	91,458,363,328	85,374,216,552	90,633,325,797	82,888,986,961

Source: NCB's Annual Report 1986.

Exhibit 3   Profit and Loss For the Year Ended 4th September

Expenses	1986 SR	1985 SR
Salaries and other staff expenses	656,787,850	689,106,831
Director's fees, remuneration, etc.	–	–
Service charges	2,557,603,136	3,023,481,401
Provision for depreciation, etc.		
a) Depreciation on buildings, furniture, etc.	81,499,995	83,806,927
b) Other provisions	835,885,438	691,000,000
Other expenses	306,250,007	266,424,713
Donations	51,237,105	48,074,365
Net profit for the year	79,977,217	99,644,043
Carried to balance sheet	4,569,240,748	4,901,538,280
Income		
Net income from foreign exchange trans-actions and other services	4,187,905,249	4,673,631,868
Net income from investment and real estate	381,335,499	227,906,412
Total income	4,569,240,748	4,901,538,280

Source: NCB's Annual Report 1986.

5.3 Saudi American Bank (SAMBA)

Ghazi M. Habib

Introduction

Mr. Shawkat Aziz has been recently appointed as the managing director to succeed Mr. Robert Botjer who has been in charge of SAMBA since 1981. Mr. Aziz is the first Third World national to represent Citibank in its history.

The new managing director is deeply concerned about the budget reported for 1986 which shows that the net profit has declined by 53.8 %. Mr. Aziz has requested a thorough evaluation of the thrust of SAMBA's banking strategy and its fitness to the prevailing market conditions.

SAMBA is an unusual bank in several aspects. SAMBA is a pioneer in introducing technological banking innovations. It is the first one to introduce voice banking, which allows customers to receive banking services from home and in either Arabic or English. A person can use voice banking to check the balance of his account, order a check book, or a statement of his account. SAMBA was also a pioneer in electronic banking for corporate clients, both inside Saudi Arabia and in nearby states such as Bahrain. SAMBA has a centralized computer network that links all its branches to the headquarters in Riyadh. Thus, customers can go to any SAMBA branch and get banking services.

SAMBA is still unusual in another aspect. Its foreign joint-venture partner is Citibank with which it has an eight year management contract giving it access to the global communication network of the giant American banking corporation.

SAMBA claims to be a pioneer in introducing automatic teller machines (ATM) in the Saudi market. SAMBA is trying to introduce ATMs in all airports and major shopping centers all over the country.

SAMBA was the first to start an investment division catering to Muslims who feel that accepting interest for their deposits violates Islamic strictures.

Finally, SAMBA is known for its aggressive marketing. At SAMBA, marketing officers are typically credit officers. They are responsible for marketing a wide range of products. Each economic segment in the Kingdom is covered by an account management team. There is a bank officer specializing in each banking relationship.

Corporate Mission

SAMBA's corporate mission is to:

- be the strongest, most profitable, and most professionally managed of all Saudized financial institutions;
- manage the profitable delivery of a full product range to principal markets, so that return on total assets and return on equity are higher than that of any other financial institution in the Kingdom;
- maximize its contribution to the development of the Saudi economy through professional management, innovation, branch expansion, service quality, and staff development.

Strategy

Since its inception in 1980, SAMBA has opted to make corporate banking the thrust of its business. This strategy translated into a selective branch policy which focuses on maintaining an adequate number of branches in major cities. SAMBA has 30 branches all over the Kingdom. The choice of a branch location is subject to thorough research and analysis of such factors as population, banking concentration, growth trends, and prospects of profitability.

SAMBA lately has been reevaluating the prudence of its strategy, since corporate business has been declining, not only in Saudi Arabia, but all over the globe. SAMBA's competitors, such as National Commercial Bank and Arab Bank, have not limited their customer base to corporate business and have been expanding aggressively to reach retail customers wherever they are.

History

Saudi American Bank (SAMBA) was formed pursuant to Royal Decree No. M/3 dated 26/3/1400 (February 12, 1980) to take over the then existing branches of Citibank, N. A. in Riyadh and Jeddah. Citibank had a presence in Jeddah since 1955 and in Riyadh since 1966.

SAMBA was formed in accordance with a program adopted by the Kingdom in the mid-1980s, under which all foreign banks were required to sell majority equity interests to Saudi nationals. SAMBA was the next to the last foreign bank to be Saudized. The principal terms and conditions for

Saudization were:

- 44.5% of the equity was sold to the Saudi public for cash, under rules which favored the allocation of shares to small subscribers. Share allocations were made to nearly 166,000 individual subscribers.
- An additional 15.5% of the equity was sold for cash to a selected group of 60 Saudi founders, including the original Saudi members of the board of directors. Thus, 60% of the total share capital was held by Saudi nationals.
- The remaining 40% of the equiy was acquired by Citibank in exchange for the assets of its Riyadh and Jeddah branches.
- Citibank entered into a technical management agreement under which it was to run the new bank for eight years. This agreement provided that Citibank would train the staff of the new bank, provide technical support, and would not receive compensation for these services other than reimbursement of actual expenses. As a share-holder, it would, of course, also receive a share of dividends paid.
- SAMBA was to open for business on July 12, 1980.

Organizational Structure

The board of directors (see Exhibit 1) is composed of 11 Saudi members, elected by Saudi stockholders, and 4 representatives of Citibank, nominated by Citibank. It is interesting to notice that the number of Citibank representatives is less than the proportionate representation of stockholder's interest. Exhibit 2 shows senior management of SAMBA. Nine department heads report to the managing director, Mr. Shawkat Aziz (see Exhibit 3, p. 193).

The investment banking department was launched in early 1985 to manage investment in securities, money markets, foreign exchange, and other products. The group's objectives are:

- improve SAMBA's profitability by increasing the client base;
- achieve higher returns to customers through expert portfolio management locally and abroad;
- introduce new products and services for the domestic market; and
- entrench SAMBA as the leading investment bank in the Kingdom.

The treasury department deals in foreign exchange, money markets, swaps, transfers, and collection services.

The retail banking department is in charge of attracting consumer accounts and managing branches.

Exhibit 1   SAMBA's Board of Directors

Abdul Aziz Al-Gosaibi	(Chairman)
Abdullah A. Sudairy	
Shawkat Aziz	(Managing Director)
William P. Sutton	
Mohamed S. Joukhdar	
Khalid Al-Turki	
Husein Alireza	
Khalid A. Al-Zamil	
Abdulaziz Al-Nowaiser	
Glen R. Moreno	
Usama R. Mikdashi	
Mohammed Al-Ohali	
Khalil Kordi	
Rashid Al-Romaizan	
Peter S. Fudge	(Corporate Secretary)

Policy Committee

Shawkat Aziz	Managing Director
William P. Sutton	Corporate Banking
Peter S. Fudge	Corporate Secretary and Chief of Staff
Moinuddin Khan	Operations
Carlos Palomares	Saudi Commercial Business
Donald P. Hill	Treasury
Thomas A. F. Moss	Credit Policy
William Barnes	Western Province
James C. Higgins	Eastern Province
J. N. Kudwah	Senior Credit Officer
John Bouckley	Corporate Banking

The corporate banking department provides large businesses with loans and advances, bid and performance bonds and advance payment guarantees, current and call deposit accounts, time deposits, foreign exchange and money market services, and syndication services. This group maintains three regional offices in the Kingdom, each of which is organized on industry sector lines. There are specialized lending and service units for the contracting, trading, manufacturing, agri-business, and public sectors of the Kingdom's economy, as well as a private banking division which deals with individuals who have substantial personal wealth as part of their business interests. The corporate banking group targets its services at big clients with sales of at least SR 20 million per year.

The merchant banking group is in charge of syndicating large loans and offering various corporate finance services.

Exhibit 2   Senior Management

Saad S. Balhonaim	Banking Head
William Barnes	Regional Corporate Banking Head
Robert Eichfeld	Corporate Banking Head
Eisa M. Al-Eisa	Banking Head
Dalip Gambir	Banking Head
Kane Gong	Banking Head
Stephen Graham	Senior Country Operations Officer
John Hill	Training Center Director
Mohmoud S. Jawdat	Corporate Secretary
Zakaria Ibrahim Kaabaa	Senior Branch Operations Officer
Daniel Li	Banking Group Head
Mustafa I. Malaika	Western Region Personnel Head
Farooq Maroof	Treasury Group Head
Mishari I. Al-Mishari	Retail Banking Relationship Division Head
Rashid H. Mohsin	Retail Banking Group Services Division Head
Thomas A. F. Moss	Country Credit Supervisor
Mohammad A. Al-Muhanna	Public Affairs Director
Ali Munir	Accounting, Planning and Control Head
Mike Pettitt	Senior Branch Operations Officer (Eastern Province)
Steve Reece	Regional Corporate Banking Head (Eastern Province)
Saud S. Sabban	Western Region, Deputy Head
Deepak Sharma	Senior Branch, Operations Officer (Western Province)
Amr H. Al-Taher	Central and Eastern Region Personnel Head
Tarek M. Tamimi	Country Personnel Head
Adom Tenjoukian	Private Banking and Investment Head

The operations group is responsible for high quality service and the control of day-to-day operations of the bank in three key areas: branch operations, systems, and physical premises.

The branch operations division within this group looks after the large volume of branch transactions, such as deposits, check cashing, letters of credit, letters of guarantee, loans, money transfers, etc., and ensures that the bank's policies and procedures are properly adhered to, and that the services offered meet an acceptable standard.

The systems divisions provides the day-to-day crucial computer support and data center equipment needed, updates the bank's records, generates and analyzes important management reports, and develops new systems or enhances existing systems of operations to continually support an upgrading of service to the bank's customers.

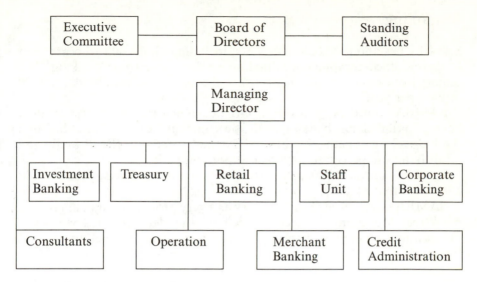

Exhibit 3   Samba Organization Chart

The premises division looks after all of the bank's properties and is responsible for the design, construction, and maintenance of new branches around the Kingdom.

The credit group is responsible for the management and control of facilities portfolio and monitoring problematic accounts.

The staff unit is in charge of personnel, public affairs, financial control, a training center, and administration of resident inspectors (auditors).

Personnel

SAMBA is not having much difficulty in recruiting new personnel. On the average, the bank receives about 10–15 applications a day. Applicants come from high schools, commercial training schools, and universities. Recruiting takes place in all of the SAMBA offices and usually is conducted by two or three officers who look into applicants' credentials in mathematics, accounting, and experience.

SAMBA prides itself on the quality and professional training of its personnel. Training is conducted at its center of banking and finance in Riyadh.

SAMBA currently has 1,284 employees, about 40 % of them are Saudis who have assumed responsibilities at various levels of the organization.

Marketing

SAMBA has about 70,000 customers, including about 300 who use their home or office computer terminal to perform electronic banking. The majority of its customers are corporate clients with sales of at least SR 20 million per year.

SAMBA considers Al-Rajhi, a large currency trading house recently licensed as an Islamic banking institution, and all the other banks in Saudi Arabia, as its competitors. National Commercial Bank, Riyad Bank, and Arab Bank are perceived as direct major competitors.

Exhibit 4 contrasts the small portfolio of services rendered by SAMBA in 1980 with that of 1987.

SAMBA is perceived in the industry as a very progressive and aggressive marketer. Marketing is decentralized at the department head level. Duplication is eliminated through planning, market segmentation, and targeting.

Exhibit 4   Samba's Service Portfolio

1980	1987
General Ledger	General Ledger
Current Accounts	Current Accounts
	Saving Accounts
	Foreign Exchange
	Fixed Assets
	Automated Money Transfers
	Automated Drafts
	Deposits/Placements
	Shares Transfer/Dividends
	Electronic Banking
	Voice Banking
	Central Liability
	Letters of Guarantee
	Letters of Credit
	APR (Account Profitability Reports)
	MIS (Management Information System)
	ATMs (Automated Teller Machines)
	Message Switching
	Word Processing
	Loans
	Automated Clearing House
	Check Book Ordering
	Travellers' Checks

   SAMBA maintains daily contact and visits with its core customers and assigns an account manager for each of them. American firms and individuals as well as many Saudi technocrats, educated in America, tend to prefer banking with SAMBA.

Exhibit 5   Comparative Balance Sheet as of December 31

Sharehoulders' Funds and Liabilities	1986 SR '000	1985 SR '000	1984 SR '000
Shareholders' Funds:			
Share capital [1986]	300,000	300,000	300,000
Reserves			
Statutory reserve	300,047	300,000	300,000
General reserve	860,000	850,000	763,000
Retained earnings	1,658	1,000	549
Total shareholders' funds	1,461,705	1,451,000	1,363,549
Deposits:			
Customers' deposits including			
current savings and time deposits	11,557,737	10,881,747	10,709,211
Other deposits	812,576	716,109	859,278
	12,370,313	11,597,856	11,568,489
Due to banks:			
Current			
Inside Saudi Arabia	16,600	27,975	26,608
Abroad	239,820	98,685	222,936
Deposits			
Inside Saudi Arabia	832,813	595,608	231,301
Abroad	64,452	13,415	3,036
	1,153,685	735,683	483,881
Other liabilities:			
Proposed dividend	70,000	87,000	82,500
Acceptances outstanding	141,333	148,660	173,348
Other liabilities	126,185	124,066	129,531
	337,518	359,726	385,379
Total shareholders' funds and liabilities:	15,323,221	14,144,265	13,801,298
Contra Accounts			
Customers' guarantee, letters of credit, and other obligations	13,533,199	11,340,627	10,234,586

Source: SAMBA-Annual Report 1986.

Finance

Exhibits 5, 6 and 7 show the balance sheet and income statements, respectively.

Exhibit 6   Statement of Income and Retained Earnings for the Year Ending
            December 31

	1986 SR '000	1985 SR '000	1984 SR '000
Income:			
Loans, advances, and placements	900,000	1,015,826	1,093,210
Commissions and foreign exchange	143,358	125,757	143,926
Bonds and securities	136,078	116,293	124,377
Total income	1,179,673	1,257,876	1,361,513
Less: Cost of funds	506,068	533,070	578,290
Reserve for possible loan losses	–	103,863	59,344
Income before operating expenses	673,605	620,943	723,879
Operating Expenses:			
Salaries and related expenses	268,739	294,635	286,033
Director's fees and remuneration	909	599	675
Bank premises expenses	51,526	52,936	57,241
Depreciation and amortization of premises and equipment	41,132	38,330	33,556
Other operating expenses	50,334	59,992	65,772
	412,640	446,492	443,227
Net Income for the year	260,965	174,451	280,602
Earnings per share	26.90	58.15	93.53
Statement of Retained Earnings:			
Balance at beginning of the year	1,000	549	447
Net Income for the year	80,705	174,451	280,602
	81,705	175,000	281,049
Transfer to general reserve	(47)	(87,000)	(198,000)
Proposed dividend	(10,000) (70,000)	(87,000)	(82,000)
Balance at the end of the year	1,658	1,000	549

Source: SAMBA Annual Report 1986.

Exhibit 7   Comparative Statement of Funds for the Year Ending December 31

	1986 SR '000	1985 SR '000	1984 SR '000
Funds provided			
Operations:			
Net income for the year	80,705	174,451	280,602
Charges not requiring current outlay of funds:			
Depreciation and loss on disposal of fixed assets	50,738	58,155	36,183
Funds generated from operations	131,443	232,606	316,785
Disposal of fixed assets	562	332	177
Increase in:			
Deposits	772,457	29,367	1,668,759
Due to banks	418,002	251,802	
Decrease in:			
Other deposits with SAMA	80,702	134,802	–
Investment portfolio	485,423	11,887	98,006
Loans and advances	1,341,068	716,784	253,699
Other assets	136	–	99,034
Cash	6,234	6,837	–
Total funds provided	3,326,027	1,384,417	2,436,460
Funds utilized:			
Dividend paid	87,000	82,500	76,500
Decrease in:			
Due to banks	22,548	–	422,430
Other liabilities	5,208	30,153	47,444
Increase in:			
Cash	14,861	–	25,031
Statutory deposits with SAMA	2,626,012	26,539	35,640
Other deposits with SAMA	480,398	–	604,971
Due from banks	–	651,422	1,082,044
Trading portfolio	–	551,534	60,868
Additions to fixed assets	–	41,715	81,532
Other assets	–	554	–
Total funds utilized	3,236,027	1,384,417	2,436,460

Source: SAMBA Annual Report 1986.

New Challenges

SAMBA and other members of the banking industry in Saudi Arabia are faced with the following threats and challenges. The recessionary economic period being experienced by Saudi Arabia and other Gulf states, triggered by the decline in oil revenues, has led to fewer investments and fewer opportunities for financial institutions and increased competition among them.

The legal system has not kept pace with the development of sophisticated banking activities achieved in the Kingdom over the last 15 years. Banking agreements are not enforceable by Saudi courts – a fact which has led to closer scrutiny and more conservatism by the banks.

The cost of funds to banks has been increasing over time, due to the rising competition between banks to attract deposits and the increasing sophistication of the Saudi business community who have learned how to shop for the best banking deal in town.

In addition to the challenges facing the banking industry as a whole in Saudi Arabia, SAMBA is facing the following specific challenges:

- SAMBA is still perceived as the bank of the rich and of the foreign contractors.
- SAMBA has a limited number of branches, given its market share of deposits compared to its major competitors.
- In its drive for efficiency, SAMBA has been accused of using Western impersonal professional norms and ignoring the more personal Arab style of transacting business.
- The Saudi Arabian Monetary Agency (SAMBA) has restrained SAMBA from introducing technological innovation at the rate it wants.
- In its drive to maintain and strengthen the relationship between its clients and the bank as a whole, rather than between clients and particular account officers, SAMBA has upset some traditional customers who prefer to conduct all their banking transactions with a single account officer whom they trust.

5.4 Saudi French Bank (BSF)

Mohamed S. Al Madhi and M. Sami Kassem*

Introduction

In early 1985, the managing director of the Saudi French Bank (BSF), Yves Max, had to face great changes in the Saudi banking scene in recent years and to decide whether long-range planning was really worth the effort. Accelerating rates of technical change, increased competition, and economic recession have made long-range planning and strategic decision-making increasingly complex. Max, therefore, decided that improvements were needed in strategy, structure, and tactics.

History

Saudi French Bank (also referred to as Al-Bank Al-Saudi Al-Fransi, or BSF) is a commercial bank organized under Saudi Arabian law. Its capital is held by Saudi nationals (60%) and by Banque Indo-Suez (40%). Its first branch was opened in Jeddah in 1948 under the name of Banque de L'Indochine. A second branch was established later at Al-Khobar. In December 1977, with the Saudization of the two offices of Banque de L'Indochine et de Suez, BSF was created with an authorized capital of Saudi Riyals (SR) 100 million (US $ 30 million), which was later increased to SR 200 million. Bank Indo-Suez was contracted to manage BSF and to train its employees for eight years. A composite picture of the growth in the bank's operations is provided in Exhibit 1.

Mission

The BSF has only recently (early in 1986) decided on its mission statement. It states that the bank's aim is:

---

* This case is prepared by Mr. Mohamed S. Al Madhi under the direction of Professor Sami Kassem.

Evolution

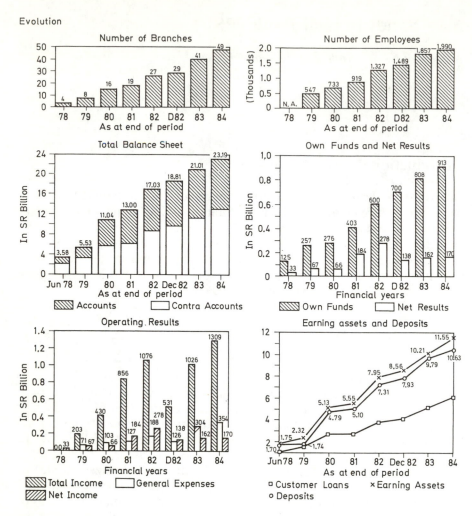

Exhibit 1   Evolution of BSF's Operations

(To efficiently provide, using the most effective technology, a wide range of high quality financial services adapted to its targeted customers, and to contribute to the continuing development of the Saudi financial and capital markets, while maximizing the returns of our shareholders within the framework of the applicable laws and banking regulations of the Kingdom of Saudi Arabia, progressively Saudizing positions at all levels, and keeping all our work force productive and highly motivated.)

Management and Board of Directors

The management and board of directors of BSF believe that they have been operating a successful organization ever since the bank was launched in 1977. The board is composed of 10 members, 6 of whom are elected by Saudi stockholders and usually are prominent members of the business community. The remaining board members are Frenchmen appointed by Banque Indo-Suez; they are no strangers to the banking industry. The majority of the board members are 48 years or older, with only one being under 40 at the time this case study was prepared. By virtue of their positions as full-time banking executives, these latter board members control the strategic decision-making process.

With 40% of the stock, Bank Indo-Suez owns a sizeable share of the bank, although 4 other shareholders, including the chairman of the board, hold large stock positions.

Mr. Max served first as general manager of the Eastern Province. He was then promoted by the board of directors to the position of managing director about four years ago. He had been employed by Indo-Suez, Paris, before joining BSF.

The board's committees include the executive committee, the general management loan committee, and 4 regional loan committees. These committees meet at least once every other week. Other special committees are formed as needed to handle matters of an exceptional nature. The executive committee is composed of most of the board directors. The general management loan committee is composed of the chairman of the board, managing director or deputy managing director, and officers responsible for larger loans. Each regional management loan committee is composed of the regional manager, his assistant, and the manager and deputy manager of each of the main branches in the region. Each regional management loan committee reviews all loans exceeding SR 2 million. These committees meet at least once a month.

Bank Organization

There are 52 branches supervised by 4 regional offices (see Exhibit 2).

Each branch is linked to its regional management office, which, in turn, is linked to central management in Jeddah. Branches are uniform with few minor differences distinguishing them.

The Dammam branch is divided into five functional departments, namely operations, foreign exchange, marketing, bill collection, and letters of credit, and the risk or credit department (see Exhibit 3). The operations

Exhibit 2   BSF's Four Regional Offices

Region	Based in	Regional Manager
Central Region	Riyadh	Mr. Abdul Rahman Jawa (Saudi)
Eastern Region	Al-Khobar	Mr. P. Chavanon (French)
Western Region	Jeddah	Mr. A. Monclaire (French)
Dapo-Western (Remote Area Branches)	Jeddah	Mr. Garcia (Spanish)

department cashes and clears checks and handles transfers, including discounting of checks, wire transfers, and issuance of demand drafts, cashier orders, and certified checks. The department's cash section consists of a cash manager along with several tellers and clerks to handle the clearance of checks. The transfer section consists of a transfer manager and clerks.

The foreign exchange department consists of a dealing room and back office. Dealers handle the actual transactions. In simple terms, foreign exchange consists of the exchange of foreign currencies to Saudi riyals, and treasury functions that involve the conversion of Saudi riyals to foreign currencies.

The marketing department focuses on attracting new customers. It is headed by a marketing manager, who oversees marketing officers, and a back office staffed by clerks. The functions of this department include allocating interest on fixed deposits, selling and buying shares, and opening and closing accounts.

The fourth department consists of an account receivable section and a letter of credit section. The section supervisors report to the head of the department. This department issues letters of credit (i.e. a written undertaking by a bank given to the seller, and, in accordance with the instructions of the buyer or customer of the issuing bank, to effect payment up to a stated sum of money within a time limit against stipulated documents).

The last and most important department is the risk or credit department, which consits of a senior credit officer, several credit officers, and a back office staffed by clerks. The back office is divided into four sections which respectively handle local bills, letters of guarantee, credit information or correspondence, and credit administration.

When this case study was prepared, there were serious difficulties in the working relationships amongst the staff at the Dammam branch of BSF, and top management believed those difficulties had roots in the organizational structure.

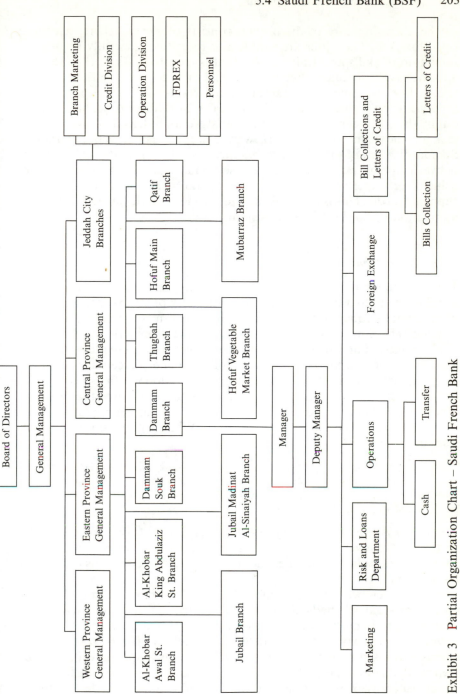

Exhibit 3   Partial Organization Chart – Saudi French Bank

The operating core of the branch consists of clerks, tellers, telephone operators, etc. Their jobs are simple and repetitive, generally requiring a minimum of skills and training. All that is required of a clerk is to fill in a form, have it signed by two officers, and then deliver it to the computer room. For example, a marketing clerk responsible for opening new accounts is only required to pull out a card for that purpose, have it filled out by the customer, and secure the signatures of at least two officers. The task of the teller is even narrower, since he usually counts money. Standardization of the work process means that coordination is necessary between operators; sometimes you see middle-line managers intervene using direct supervision to ensure that operators are doing what they are supposed to do. This is primarily due to the fact that the operators lack the motivation to do their jobs consistently well.

Turnover Problem at BSF

The dysfunctional consequences of such highly repetitive, formalized, and specialized (both vertically and horizontally) work took various forms: impersonal treatment of clients, heavy absenteeism, and frequent turnover of personnel. Some Saudi-dominated departments experienced high rates of absenteeism and turnover. Usually, turnover rates were more prevalent among middle-line managers because of the higher percentage of Saudis working there than in the operating core. This is noteworthy since the jobs of the middle managers are less repetitive and less structured than those of operators, and one would suspect higher turnover among operators. In an illuminating article, "Al-Bank Al-Fransi...What is going on inside?," Al Yamamah Magazine reported:

"It looks like that what is happening inside Al-Bank Al-Fransi, an increasing number of resignations by experienced Saudis, is not a special case but one that all banks in general face... However, this problem is becoming highly visible and more pronounced in Al-Bank Al-Fransi..."

The Saudi Arabian Monetary Agency (SAMA) is trying to reduce this increasing turnover by requiring that an officer who resigns from his bank cannot join another bank unless he spends at least two months outside the banking industry.

An interview with a few former officers of the bank (all of whom are college graduates) sheds light on the sources of their dissatisfaction. According to them, a Saudi bank officer is expected to walk a tightrope. Internally, he is expected to compete with his fellow officers to satisfy both clients and his superiors, a situation which he finds alien and distasteful. Externally, he may be ostracized by some members of the Saudi culture, which generally frowns upon working for and dealing with an institution deemed usurious and therefore sinful. Some Saudi families considered respectable in certain large circles refuse to do business with or to allow their daughters to marry a Saudi banker. These BSF ex-officers felt that although they were relatively well-paid, they were not treated properly by their French superiors. They said their talents and skills were not properly utilized. Their rewards were not related to performance, and opportunities for innovation and promotion were non-existent, according to them.

Functional Area Strategies

Personnel and Human Resources

A quick glance back at Exhibit 1 shows that the size of BSF's work force increased steadily through 1984. The work force then declined to 1,910 by the end of 1985 and to 1,698 in 1986. Since employee costs represent a significant portion of BSF's operating expenses, and since the bank management is under pressure to combat a worsening financial position, it instituted some staff reductions, salary cuts, wage freezes, and other measures.

The bank has consistently pursued its mission of Saudizing positions at all levels. Exhibit 4 indicates that the percentage of Saudis in the work force is on average 40.8 %.

The bank has its own training facilities at the three main regional centers. It subscribes to some of the national training programs provided by SAMA. It sends some of its trainees to the Indo-Suez Training Center in London. On-the-job training does take place, but the constant demands of work render this practice inefficient.

Exhibit 4   Manpower Distribution by Level and nationality

Level	Grades	# Employees	% Saudis
Top management	19,20	2	50 %
Executives	16,17,18	23	9 %
Mid. mgt.	13,14,15	50	44 %
Junior mgt.	10,11,12	180	36 %
Supervisors	7,8,9	210	37 %
Clerical	4,5,6	868	37 %
Non-clerical	1,2,3	365	56 %
Total manpower		1698	
Average			40.8 %

Source: Primary.

Operations Accounting

Saudi banks have computerized and automated their back office operations quite extensively. BSF is no exception. It is slightly behind the leader
in this field − the Saudi American Bank − but far ahead of other
competitors. The bank pursues computerization vigorously and uses it as a
means of combating boredom and cutting down clerical tasks. It also uses it
as a competitive weapon when applied to such new products as ATM
(Automatic Teller Machines) and home banking systems.

Marketing

BSF was formed in the midst of an economic boom. Without having to be
attracted, customers sought out the bank to finance their trade and massive
construction projects. The bank's strategy was to gain market share by
attracting corporate clients as both depositors and borrowers. According
to Exhibit 5, the bank's loan/deposit ratio by mid-1982 was almost 106 −
meaning it borrowed money from other banks to finance clients. This
aggressive loan policy has enabled the bank to earn the goodwill of its
customers and reflected its long-term commitment to the Saudi economy.
However, as of late, the bank has followed a more conservative loan policy.
It cut back lending, and the loan/deposit ratio stood at about 64 % by the
end of 1986.

BSF advertises its corporate image through the mass media. It projects
the image of being friendly, innovative, and efficient.

Exhibit 5   Selected Performance Indicators (million SR)

	1979	1980	1981	1982	1983	1984	1985
Loans	1,587	3,897	5,365	7,716	10,005	11,553	11,695
Deposits	2,146	4,790	5,102	7,312	9,790	10,627	10,907
Loans deposit ratio	74%	81%	105%	106%	102%	109%	107%
Revenues	−	429	856	1,076	1,026	1,299	1,203
Profits	43	66	184	278	162	170	110
Total assets	3,271	5,686	6,282	8,725	11,348	12,978	13,824
Return on assets	1.3%	1.16%	2.93%	3.19%	1.43%	1.31%	0.8%
Equity	259	276	403	600	808	915	955
Return on equity	16.6%	23.9%	46%	46%	20%	19%	12%
Debt	2,146	4,790	5,102	7,312	9,790	10,360	10,907
Equity/debt ratio	12%	6%	8%	8%	8%	9%	9%

Source: Primary; based on analysis of annual reports.

BSF has the fourth largest branch network in the Kingdom with 52 branches. It has a policy of training and hiring a well-known Saudi figure in the locality as branch manager who assumes a marketing role. His assistant, preferably a Lebanese who speaks Arabic and French, is put in charge of operations. The physical appearance of BSF's branch personnel and facilities are both very attractive.

Financial Profile

BSF's revenues increased from SR 430 million in 1980 to SR 1,299 million in 1984 and then fell back somewhat to SR 1,203 million in 1985. The bank's net income rose from SR 66 million in 1980 to SR 278 million by 1982 and then dropped dramatically in 1985 to SR 110 million (see Exhibit 5 and Exhibits 6–8). An aggressive loan policy, an unforeseen drop in oil revenues, the completion of the Kingdom's infrastructure projects, high interest rates, and an unsympathetic public attitude toward interest have all combined to produce an unusual amount of bad loans and to sharply curtail the bank's profitability.

Problems and Opportunities Facing the Banking Industry

A revival of Islamic fundamentalism has hardened certain Arab attitudes toward the concept of interest, but also has paved the way for more acceptable alternatives to traditional interest-bearing banking instruments. Islamic banking is gaining momentum throughout the Muslim World. In Saudi Arabia, the recent entry of Al-Rajhi Company as an officially recognized Islamic banking institution with its 180 branch network is expected to shake up the Saudi conventional banking system.

Another challenge facing the banking industry is the continuation of the business recession and the failure of corporate clients to meet their obligations to their employees, suppliers, and creditors.

At the same time, potential depositors are becoming more knowledgeable about alternative investment vehicles.

Despite these challenges, there is some cause for optimism among Saudi bankers. A steady growth in multinational business should expand the market. Technological improvements in data-processing and the execution of fund transfers show promise of continued product innovations and cost reduction. The presence of large amounts of still undeposited money in circulation in rural areas of the Kingdom also presents opportunities. The

Exhibit 6   BSF Balance Sheet as of 31st December

Assets	1985 SR '000	1984 SR '000
Cash funds		
Cash in hand	68,083	97,407
Balances with SAMA		
Statutory deposit	324,437	313,772
Current accounts	18,928	12,539
Bankers' security deposits	535,000	235,000
Due from banks		
Current-in Saudi Arabia	722	8,525
Current abroad	84,457	266,390
Deposit-in Saudi Arabia	327,675	179,130
Deposits abroad	4,440,832	4,887,687
Bonds and securities	227,734	9,267
Loan and advances (net of provisions)		
To (a) Private sectors	5,926,102	5,298,547
(b) Banks	60,011	10,000
Bills purchased and discounted	856,216	903,754
Fixed assets		
Bank premises and other real estate	50,263	43,156
Furniture, fixtures, and equipment	103,603	94,760
	153,866	137,916
Other assets		
Customers' liabilities for outstanding acceptances	266,661	260,879
Other assets	433,994	357,544
	700,655	618,423
Total assets	13,724,718	12,978,357
Contra accounts		
Customers' liabilities under guarantees, letters of credit and other obligations	9,071,342	10,209,397
	22,796,060	23,187,754

Exhibit 6   (continued)

Assets	1985 SR '000	1984 SR '000
Sharehoulders' Equity and Liabilities		
Share capital		
Authorized 2,000,000 shares of SR 100 each		
fully paid	200,000	200,000
Reserves		
Statutory reserve	200,000	200,000
General reserve	555,000	513,000
Retained earnings	451	278
Total shareholders' equity	955,451	913,278
Deposits		
Customer deposits		
(Total current, time and savings deposits)	8,888,782	8,244,366
Other deposits	1,797,769	2,223,105
	10,686,551	10,467,471
Due to banks		
Current-in Saudi Arabia	1,132	2,548
Current abroad	220,557	156,664
Deposits-in Saudi Arabia	924,293	490,749
Deposits abroad	49,556	61,398
	1,195,538	711,359
Other liabilities		
Acceptance outstanding on behalf of customers	266,661	260,879
Other liabilities	581,422	586,865
Proposed dividend	39,095	38,505
	887,178	886,249
Total shareholders' equity and liabilities	13,724,718	12,978,357
Contra accounts		
Bank's liabilities under guarantees, letters		
of credit, other obligations	9,071,342	10,209,397
	22,796,060	23,187,754

Source: 1985 Annual Report.

Exhibit 7   BSF Statement of Income for the Years Ended 31 December

	1985 SR '000	1984 SR '000
Revenue		
Revenue from foreign exchange transactions		
and other services	1,191,449	1,297,907
Other revenue	12,191	593
Total revenue	1,203,640	1,298,500
Expenses		
Salaries and employees' benefits	257,472	243,432
Board of directors remuneration and fees	660	712
Cost of services paid	626,498	705,760
Depreciation of premises and equipment	21,841	20,832
Other provisions	75,467	49,126
Other operating expenses	111,303	108,214
	1,093,241	1,128,706
Net income for the year (note 2)	110,399	170,424
Net income per share	SR 55	SR 85

Source: 1985 Annual Report.

growing tendency of some corporations, private businesses, and citizens to take advantage of interest-bearing accounts despite Islamic strictures against them also offers opportunities for banks to widen their client base. The potential for women's banking and Islamic banking products still remains largely unexploited by modern banks in Saudi Arabia.

Competition and Competitor Profiles

Saudi banks offer quite similar services and rates to their customers. They all maintain comparable hours of operation, and all are closed on Friday. None offer absolutely "free" checking accounts, and all of them require some minimum deposit level for the depositor to avoid monthly services charges. All Saudi banks offer the usual variety of savings and time deposits, checking accounts, and other bank services. All of them pay the maximum rates on time deposits allowed under SAMA regulations.

Among the Saudized banks, the Saudi American Bank (SAMBA) is perhaps the one most similar to BSF in terms of size, foreign connection, technological sophistication, profitability, and market share, though

Exhibit 8   Statement of Source and Application of Funds for the Years Ended 31st December

	1985 SR '000	1984 SR '000
Sources		
Net income for the year	110,399	170,424
Non-cash items depreciation	21,574	20,870
Increase in:		
Deposits	219,080	1,064,485
Amounts due to banks	484,179	69,796
Other liabilities	–	281,434
Decrease in:		
Amounts due from banks	438,035	–
Bills purchased and discounted	47,538	–
Cash in hand	29,324	–
Other assets	–	16,336
Total sources	1,350,129	1,623,345
Applications:		
Dividends paid	36,381	37,685
Purchase of fixed assets	37,791	42,269
Purchase of bonds and securities	218,200	1,000
Increase In:		
Balance at SAMA	317,054	183,709
Loans and advances to private sector	627,555	924,187
Amounts due from banks	–	399,399
Bills purchased and discounted	–	22,830
Cash in hand	–	12,266
Other assets	76,450	–
Decrease in:		
Other liabilities	36,698	–
Total applications	1,350,129	1,623,345

Source: 1985 Annual Report.

SAMBA outshines BSF in all these respects. Arab National Bank comes right after SAMBA as a direct competitor of BSF. As the oldest bank in the Arab world, its strong traits include sensitivity to local culture, contacts with government officials, and an extensive network of 79 branches.

Adapting Strategy and Structure to Changing Times

The following list briefly describes major changes which top management of BSF has recently instituted with respect to strategy and structure:

1) Reduce dependence on wholesale banking and diversify into retail banking;
2) Follow a more conservative loan policy and broaden the portfolio to include loans to overseas customers;
3) Consolidate the corporate planning function at the HQ level (see Exhibit 9);
4) Establish Private & Retail Banking as a division whose function is to develop and introduce retail products and services;
5) Move away from product-based organization toward a client-based organization:
   a. Decentralize marketing at the branch management level to retain a "local touch."
   b. Centralize loan approval decisions, foreign exchange functions and letter of credit functions at the regional management level.

Issues and Problems

BSF is a strong player on the Saudi banking scene. It has a long-term commitment to the Saudi economy. Given that it wants to diversify its sources of income and service portfolio by concentrating on retail as well as corporate banking, it has to develop answers for the following set of issues and problems:

1) How will it recoup loans already extended, particularly to firms hit hard by the current recession? Should it renegotiate them out of court or arbitration boards? Should it write off some loans?
2) How will it maintain its local presence and commitment to the Saudi economy without accumulating even more bad loans?
3) How will it position itself to take advantage of opportunities in the retail banking field? How will it reach the female sector? Will it be able to reach the conservative Muslim with suitably designed monetary instruments?
4) Another threat, facing all Saudi banks, is the turnover of large numbers of Saudi middle managers. BSF may be suffering more from this problem than its competitors. It has to be aggressive in practicing

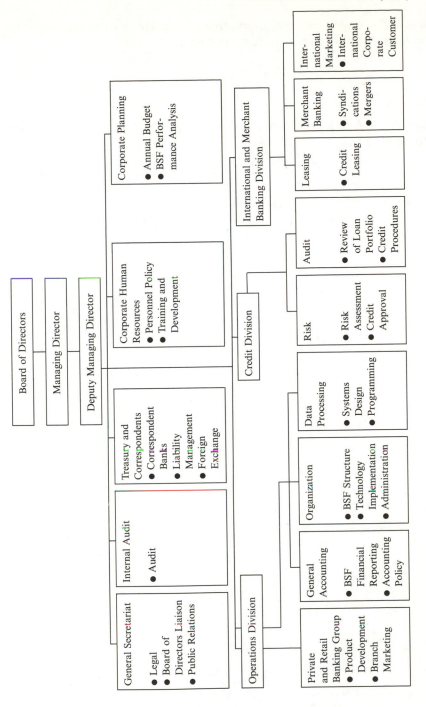

Exhibit 9   BSF Present Organization Chart
Source: Internal Document, 1986.

internal as well as external marketing, if it is going to be successful in pursuing retail banking strategy and its Saudization policy.

References

Al-Yamamah: Al-Bank Al-Fransi... What is going on inside? *Al-Yamamah Magazine*.

5.5   Gulf International Bank (GIB)

*Anwar Yousif Abdulrahman**

Introduction

Gulf International Bank (GIB) is an offshore wholesale commercial and investment bank incorporated in Bahrain. It was formed by six Gulf Cooperation Council (GCC) states and Iraq to serve the banking interests of the shareholding states. The seven states hold equal shares in the bank.

GIB was formed shortly after the first oil price adjustment by OPEC in 1974. The most famous Arab bank at that time was the Paris-based UBAF (Union de Banques Arabes et Françaises). The GIB shareholders realized that UBAF was not adequately capitalizing on the new petrodollar wealth. Furthermore, when GIB's originators realized that their own local banks were too unsophisticated to play a major role in recycling new income, the governments decided to launch a banking institution of their own.

GIB is unusual in many respects. First, it is supported by government shareholders, and thus receives preferential access to major government business in the Gulf states. Second, it has a strong top management team of experienced expatriate bankers. Third, its assets portfolio is characterized by very low risk. Fourth, GIB is considered the most efficient offshore bank in the Gulf region. In 1985, it was ranked fourth in performance, measured by net profit per employee. Finally, GIB was the first wholly-owned Arab bank to establish presence in New York (1980) and the first one to join the CHIPS Clearing System in New York (1983).

Corporate Mission

GIB's mission is to:

1) remain one of the most professional international merchant and wholesale commercial banks, head-quartered in Bahrain but with a physical presence elsewhere when justified;

---

* Mr. Anwar Yousif Abdulrahman is MBA student at KFUPM.

2) service the needs of the Gulf states and other Middle Eastern governments, agencies, and business institutions through expertise in merchant and investment banking, portfolio management, and industries most closely associated with the area; and
3) maintain a commitment to technological advancement and the training of an increasing pool of Gulf nationals in banking skills.

From the start, two strategic principles have guided the bank: rendering quality financial services and spreading the risk geographically, both by industry and borrower. Careful emphasis was placed upon developing "human resources" before piling new assets on the books. The objective has been to deliver one of the best customer service facilities in the Gulf, through highly qualified personnel and computerized accounting and information systems. Most of GIB's early involvement was in the syndication of loans to sovereign borrowers. It was not until around 1980 that GIB turned significantly towards the corporate sector. The early avoidance of non-sovereign credits was simply due to insufficient corporate credit expertise within the bank.

History

The bank was founded on Nov. 13, 1975 by an international treaty between the governments of Saudi Arabia, Kuwait, United Arab Emirates, Qatar, Oman, and Bahrain – which later formed as the Gulf Cooperation Council (GCC) – and Iraq. GIB became fully operational in late 1976.

GIB has established a presence in the major financial centers of the world. It opened a representative office in London in 1978, New York in 1980, Singapore in 1982, and Tokyo in 1986. Some of these offices were later converted into full branches.

During 1980, the bank's emphasis on marketable securities was confirmed with the establishment of the bond and new issues department to handle the management and underwriting of new issues. This department has been very aggressive in obtaining business, offering attractive and confidential portfolio management services to both Gulf institutions and individuals.

The bank plans to open offices in Frankfurt and Geneva. The new offices are part of GIB's strategy of serving the needs of prime customers of the shareholding states.

GIB's Organization

Board of Directors

Each shareholding state provides two directors, one of whom serves on the executive committee. The composition of the board of directors is shown in Exhibit 1.

Senior Management

Ghazi M. Abdul-Jawad
General Manager

John S. Porter
Assistant General Manager

Costi F. Chehlaoui
Executive Vice-President, Banking Group Head

Stuart Westwater
Executive Vice-President, Assets and Liabilities Group Head

Adrian Van Buren
Senior Vice-President, Merchant Banking Group

Jürgen Klimm
Senior Vice-President, Operations Group

Exhibit 1 shows that the general manager as well as the executive committee, audit committee, and the assets and liabilities committee report to the board of directors. The general manager heads two assistant general managers as well as the human resources division and the audit division.

Services Portfolio

In the past, syndicated loans were dominant among all other services, due to the region's need for financing huge infrastructure projects. Now that most of the infrastructure has been built, syndicated loans have diminished and merchant banking is coming to the fore. Also, investors have found that syndicated loans are more expensive than the introduced Euronote source. Merchant banking (marketable securities) has therefore become more dominant. Further, the economic slowdown and the many defaults on large pooled loans has made the bank more conservative in entering into syndications.

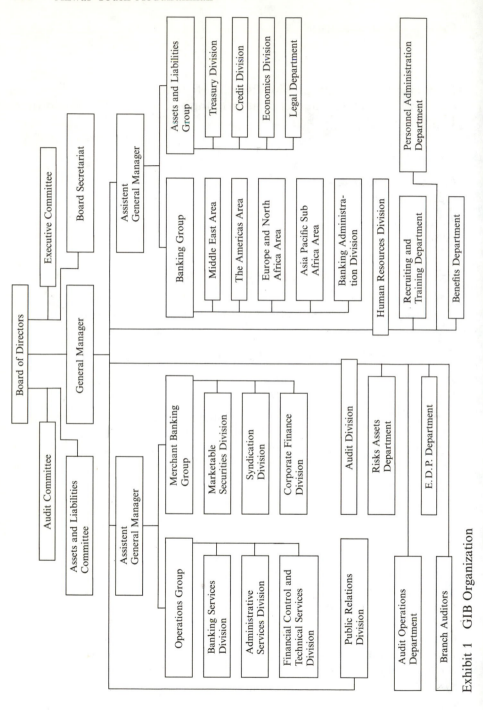

Exhibit 1   GIB Organization

GIB is also shifting into investment banking, centralized away from Bahrain. The bank's overseas operations reflect its dedication to the Gulf. GIB's branches in London, New York, and Singapore and its representative office in Tokyo are but marketing and executing arms of the Bahrain headquarters.

GIB's future in investment banking appears to lie in portfolio management, unit trusts, corporate finance, and underwriting Eurobonds and Euronotes; especially issues of Arab states, corporations, and banks. GIB recently introduced two new financial instruments: the first unit trust by an Arab bank, introduced in February 1986, which was designed to provide Arab investors with higher returns on their investments than what they were getting on bank deposits; and the first uncommitted Euro-commercial paper issued by a Middle East bank. The latter financial instrument provides institutional investors in the region with an attractive investment vehicle characterized by high liquidity and low risk.

Although forming only a small part of its staff, the marketable securities group has been a fair contributor to GIB's profitability. In late February 1986, GIB unveiled its new dollar money market fund designed to offer Gulf investors an opportunity to put their money to work in the international capital and money markets. With a minimum investment of US $ 5,000, GIB targeted the small investor, having already announced the fund to private clients.

In summary, GIB offers the following financial services (see Appendices A, B, and C):

- A. Commercial Banking
  - Term loans: short-term; medium; long-term.
  - Deposits: Demand; Call; Time.
  - Acceptances: Import/Export bills; discounted.
  - Letters of credit: opening and confirming.
  - Guarantees.
  - Bonds: Bid; Performance; Advance payment.
  - Fund transfers.
- B. Money Market: placements; deposits; foreign exchange.
- C. Merchant Banking: Syndication of loans; Management and underwriting of bonds and new issues; Financial packaging for projects; Corporate finance services.

Marketing

GIB realizes the importance of marketing personnel for the success of the bank. The bank has provided its marketing employees with many facilities:

free overseas calls, free transportation costs, free accommodations abroad, any publication that seems necessary, and even a full-time tea and coffee service in the office, something the other employees do not have.

Account officers are directly responsible to the customer. They are divided on a geographical basis. Within each geographic area, some are responsible for specific industry segments. The marketing function is done on a client basis, which personally serves both the client and the bank. The client knows to whom he should refer, and the corresponding account officer knows the client's up-to-date financial state.

All new customers who need loans facilities are referred to an account officer. The analysis of the customer's financial statement is carried out by personnel in the analysis department. Both the marketing officers and the analysts make recommendations on the proposed facility. A board committee then discusses the proposed facility. Upon preliminary agreement they announce their decision to the customer, who in turn gives it to his own analysts to study. If there is disagreement, the proposal goes back to the bank and so on, until either a deal is struck or dropped. The costs associated with market research and financial analysis conducted by the bank on behalf of a client are charged to the customer.

The credit analysis section determines the limit of risk for each country. An exposure limit for each sector within that country is also specified. So each country and each customer will have a credit line. If, however, a promising opportunity presents itself that exceeds these limits, an exception can be made. The bank ranks potential customers as the top 10 or 20 in a country or a sector. Moreover, GIB works internationally in a highly competitive market. Low margins are the main competitive tool. These differ from one client to another and from one deal to another. Usually it is a long process that leads to the final agreement on credit terms.

Clientele

A GIB official commented that it was getting more difficult to trace the financial activities of customers, since clients are increasingly dealing with more than just one financial institution, including, perhaps, the other competitors. Individual customers have gained some experience over the last decade. Now, they are more apt to bargain for the lowest rates possible, since they know about any rate differentials in the marketplace. If a bank does not give them a good rate, they will soon turn to another bank. Some customers even subscribe to financial wire services to keep themselves apprised of the market fluctuations.

Contractors were potential customers to the bank some years ago, but less so today. Governments or government agencies are still potential customers. Well managed businesses are also considered potential customers. In brief, a significant portion of GIB's business comes from private and public institutions as well as corporate clients from the GCC region.

Competition

Headquartered in Bahrain, GIB can be considered an offshore facility. However, like the Arab Banking Corporation, GIB distinguishes itself from other Bahrain offshore banking units (OBUs) by its size and its sovereign shareholders. Its most important customers reside in the shareholding states but, because the Gulf region requires relatively little financing, 83% of loans are to borrowers outside the shareholding states. The rapid fall in oil prices and the long Iraq-Iran war have greatly depressed the level of business activity in the region. There is still some volume of prime quality business available from government entities, but there is also major competition for that business from local banks. The partial or complete withdrawal of many foreign banks from Bahrain present further marketing opportunities, and GIB is able to present itself as the most sophisticated Arab bank. Management recognizes that the future for commercial banking is not bright and, therefore, wants its merchant banking activities to increase as a percentage of the bank's income flow, with commercial banking and trading each providing a quarter of total revenues. GIB is likely to move ahead of other leading Arab banks by building up teams of traders in marketable securities in its branches located in major capital markets.

Bahrain's two biggest offshore banks, Arab Banking Corporation (ABC) and GIB, have been building up their capacities in the field of investment banking and portfolio management. Both have a presence in the major financial markets of the world. They are taking advantage of their presence in these markets and of their staff's expertise to design sophisticated lending packages and financial transactions for Arab customers. Both are trying to develop into full-line global banks. The traditional commercial banking activities (large syndications, project finance, trade financing, etc.) will be complemented by specialized financial products (options, swaps, futures, arbitrage, ferns, Euronotes, etc.) which most other banks in the region are not yet capable of providing. The decline of the syndicated loan markets, on which both banks were dependent, has led the banks to reassess their operations.

ABC and GIB differ somewhat in their overall development strategy. ABC has a global network and a commitment to worldwide expansion. GIB places far greater emphasis on the Gulf region; and the purpose of its presence in the international market centers is to facilitate Gulf-related business.

The two banks were affected by the decline in the interbank market worldwide. The fact that both ABC und GIB are offshore wholesale banks and do not have a dependable customer deposit base to draw upon has left them over-exposed to the changing winds of the highly unreliable interbank markets. The two banks are working hard on diversifying their funding sources. ABC looked outside its shareholding states (Kuwait, Libya, and UAE) to establish its funding base through the acquisition of subsidiaries in countries such as Spain and Hong Kong. GIB, on the other hand, wants to establish a customer base in seven Gulf states.

In the business of arranging project-related funding, both GIB and ABC are front runners. At the other end are the specialized firms with particular regional market or product niches; Kuwait Asia Bank, for instance, has been successful in penetrating the Pacific Basin. Similarly, Investcorp has found a niche as a deal-cutting investment bank, and the Al-Mal Group as a Eurobond underwriter.

Many of the financial institutions in between are either collapsing or rapidly becoming "end users" of the investment products and loans carried out by Western banks.

Personnel

GIB employs a wide range of qualified professionals at all its locations and, in adapting to changes in the world's financial markets, the bank is committed to continual development of the staff's banking skills. GIB continues to emphasize its commitment to the nationals of its shareholder states through training programs. However, as an international bank, GIB continues to rely heavily on expatriate expertise. A GIB official stated that: "It is a fact and we've got to accept it – our experience is still far behind what we would like it to be." Expatriates are present in almost every unit in the bank, and without their experience the institution would suffer. Other international banks face the same problem. The Algemene Bank Neder-land manager in Bahrain said:

Without professional expatriates in this highly competitive environment, we won't be in business for long. We still need their depth of knowledge from time to time (personal interview by the case develops).

Moreover, it may be interesting to note that some Arab customers hold expatriate banking knowledge in higher regard than that of the nationals. Some banks capitalize on this perception for promoting their business and building their images.

GIB seeks the highest-skilled personnel available to compete efficiently in the marketplace. At the same time, one of the GIB's main objectives is to localize its staff as much as possible. However, a strong need for expatriates still exists and probably will continue at least for another decade.

Accounting

Branch and department auditors report through the audit division directly to the general manager. The audit division is directly responsible for the electronic data processing facilities. The bank has a computerized accounting system. Almost all of the bank's routine jobs have been computerized.

Finance

Exhibits 2, 3, and 4 provide financial data about GIB.

Challenges

Gulf banks are facing the following challenges:

1) lack of qualified and sophisticated Gulf nationals to manage highly competitive financial institutions;
2) diversion of Arab clientele and wealth from Arab banks to more competitive foreign banks;
3) lack of innovation in creating new business opportunities, and inability to identify niches where foreign banks are neither competitive nor interested;
4) isolation from the major capital markets. Gulf banks lack a market base equal to the huge amount of capital available;
5) difficulty in recruiting well-experienced expatriates because of two reasons:
    a) experienced Westerners do not like to work in relatively underdeveloped financial markets;
    b) due to the economic recession in the Gulf, those people can not be as highly paid as if they were in strong financial centers such as New York and London.

Exhibit 2   Statement of Condition as of December 31

	1986		1985	
	BD. 000	US $ 000	BD. 000	US $ 000
Assets				
Cash and due from banks	6,603	17,515	15,123	40,116
Money market instruments	39,313	104,278	42,601	113,000
Placements	1,030,377	2,733,095	1,109,464	2,942,875
Marketable securities	209,739	556,337	119,331	316,528
Loans	1,681,119	4,459,201	1,564,650	4,150,266
Customers' liability on acceptances	16,111	42,735	15,347	40,709
Fixed assets	9,527	25,269	10,639	28,219
Other assets	47,676	126,464	56,499	149,866
Total assets	3,040,465	8,064,894	2,933,655	7,781,579
Liabilities				
Deposits at call and due to banks	171,982	456,185	128,349	340,448
Time deposits	2,510,527	6,659,222	2,455,908	6,514,345
Acceptances outstanding	16,111	42,735	19,306	51,209
Other liablities	45,921	121,804	49,137	130,334
Proposed dividend	14,000	37,135	11,410	30,265
Total liabilities	2,758,541	7,317,081	2,664,110	7,066,601
Shareholders' equity				
Issued share capital	200,000	530,504	200,000	530,504
Compulsory and volunary reserves	27,898	74,004	22,622	60,010
Undivided profits	54,026	143,305	46,923	124,464
Total liabilities and shareholders' equity	3,040,465	8,064,894	2,933,655	7,781,579

Source: GIB's Annual Report 1986.

Exhibit 3   Statement of income, expenses, and appropriations

	For the Year Ended 31.12.86		For the Year Ended 31.12.85	
	BD. 000	US$ 000	BD. 000	US$ 000
Interest revenue:				
Interest and fees on loans	130,274	345,553	146,430	388,409
Interest on placements	72,713	192,873	79,193	210,060
Interest and fees on marketable securities	14,720	39,047	10,520	27,904
Interest on money market instruments	4,487	11,902	5,598	14,850
	22,194	589,375	241,741	641,223
Interest expense:				
Interest on deposits	187,159	496,444	205,482	545,045
Net interest and fee revenue	35,035	92,931	36,259	96,178
Other net operating income	9,896	26,250	5,732	15,207
Net interest, fees, and other operating income	44,931	119,181	41,991	111,385
Other operating expenses:				
Staff	10,359	27,478	9,334	24,760
Premises	2,880	7,640	2,770	7,348
Other expenses	5,028	13,336	4,302	11,409
	18,267	48,454	16,406	43,517
Net income before tax	26,664	70,727	25,585	67,868
Overseas tax	(285)	(757)	(313)	(831)
Net income after tax	26,379	69,970	25,272	67,037
Appropriations:				
Compulsory reserve	2,638	6,997	2,527	6,704
Voluntary reserve	2,638	6,997	2,527	6,704
Proposed dividend	14,000	37,135	11,410	30,265
	19,276	51,129	16,464	43,673
Transfer of balance to undivided profits	7,103	18,841	8,808	23,364

Source: GIB's Annual Report 1986.

Exhibit 4   Statement of Changes in Financial Position

	For the Year Ended 31.12.86		For the Year Ended 31.12.85	
	BD. 000	US $ 000	BD. 000	US $ 000
Source of funds				
Operations:				
Net income after tax	26,379	69,970	25,272	67,037
Items not involving the movement of funds:				
Depreciation	2,425	6,432	2,491	6,609
	28,804	76,402	27,763	73,646
Other:				
Increase/(decrease) in:				
Share capital	–	–	37,000	98,143
Deposits at call and due to banks	43,633	115,737	52,402	138,996
Time deposits	54,619	144,877	66,117	175,377
Other liabilities	(3,216)	(8,530)	(6,471)	(17,165)
Acceptances outstanding	(3,195)	(8,474)	(28,817)	(76,438)
	120,645	320,012	147,994	392,559
Use of funds:				
Dividends paid	11,410	30,265	8,960	23,767
Increase/(decrease) in:				
Cash and due from banks	(8,521)	(22,601)	10,714	28,417
Money market instruments	(3,228)	(8,722)	(36,638)	(97,183)
Placements	(79,087)	(209,780)	192,577	510,813
Marketable securities	90,408	239,809	31,959	84,773
Loans	116,469	308,935	(7,454)	(19,772)
Other assets	(8,823)	(23,402)	(41,712)	(110,641)
Additions to fixed assets-(net)	1,313	3,482	913	2,423
Customers' liability on acceptances	764	2,026	(11,325)	(30,038)
	120,645	320,012	147,994	392,559

Source: GIB's Annual Report 1986.

GIB is facing several additional challenges:

1) Competition in the Gulf banking industry is intensifying from offshore banks, onshore banks, Gulf national banks, and international banks.
2) Revenues of GCC states declined precipitously with the worldwide drop in oil prices.
3) Big business opportunities in the Gulf have declined due to completion of infrastructure projects, economic recession, diversion of private capital into investments in international markets, and the war between Iraq and Iran.
4) Despite its current strategic emphasis on low-risk assets, GIB has its share of risks in Latin America and Iraq.
5) Rising competition makes it more difficult to replace experienced expatriates with inexperienced Gulf nationals.

Executive management at GIB is contemplating some strategic options:

1) Should they open branches in GCC states?
2) Should they enter the more highly competitive international markets?
3) Should they change their low-risk strategy and pursue high-risk, high-yield ventures?
4) Should GIB pursue the strategy of some international banks in shifting its emphasis from extending commercial credit to becoming an underwriter, investor, security trader, funds manager, broker, and advisor?
5) Given their limited experience in managing marketable securities, the difficulty of recruiting well-experienced marketable security personnel, the long lead time required for training Gulf nationals, and the dynamic nature of this financial instrument, is GIP up to this challenge?
6) GIB has recently reduced its training budget by about 40 %. Given that the new average training cost per employee is still higher than their counterpart in the West, and some Arab banks, is this a prudent tactical move to reduce costs?

5.6 "Bank Arabia" Computer Services

*M. Sami Kassem and Yousef Dashkouni**

This case study has been arranged in a sequential fashion in order to parcel out information as the situation develops. The purpose of this exercise is to give the reader the opportunity to analyze a series of real events and to test his analysis and predictions against the situation as it unfolds, much the way a business consultant would.

The case study is divided into five parts. Following each of the first four parts are questions asking the reader to make predictions about the results of management actions described in the case study. In making predictions, take the point of view of a consultant who has been called in from the outside and is learning about the company.

Suggestions for Group Participation

1) Divide the class into groups. Prior to a group meeting, each individual should read the case, and make his or her own predictions, and carefully list the steps of reasoning that led him or her to those predictions.
2) Through group discussion, arrive at a group consensus and a rationale.
3) Each group should then designate a spokesperson who will present its predictions and analysis to the class.

Part One

"Bank Arabia" is one of the largest banks in Saudi Arabia with over 140 branches throughout the Kingdom. A key element of its competitive strategy is to computerize its operations and link its branches with each other and with the main office. Presently, the bulk of its banking activities is controlled and computerized using two main-frame systems, each fitted in a

---

* This case was prepared by Professor M. Sami Kassem with the assistance of Mr. Yousef Dashkouni of King Fahd University of Petroleum and Minerals. The name of the bank and its employees have been disguised.

computer data center, one located in Jeddah, feeding branches in the Western region and the other in Dammam, feeding branches in the Easter region of the Kingdom.

As Exhibit 1 shows, each of the two data centers consists of five sections, as follows:

1) a communication section maintaining hardware equipment and insuring communication between the branches and the mainframe;
2) a branch support section detecting problems that might occur in branches, and initial installation of the computer system in new branches;
3) a customer services section performing data entry for new branches;
4) an operation section operating the mainframe, storing data, printing reports and customer statements;
5) a programming section which consists of seven programmers with relatively different experiences distributed in the following areas:
   two in the one-line area responsible for maintaining the programs that handles all the on activities of the mainframe;
   two in the batch area in charge of all necessary amendments in some of the programs in order to run specific requests;
   two in the direct control line area maintaining programs for customers information accounts establishment and amendments; and
   one programmer maintaining the file that controls the whole system.

On-line programming is a very critical and complex area, especially for a newcomer to such a job. During early days in the Dammam Data Center, only one person, Mr. Adel Khorshed, was in charge of this job. Mr. Dabbousi, the other person in the on-line area, was given one month's training by Mr. Khorshed. Upon completion of this training, Mr. Khorshed went on vacation, and Mr. Dabbousi found himself facing this huge task alone. To him, the job was challenging, and he felt that the Dammam Data Center was counting on him. Some problems occured while he was in charge, and he managed to solve them.

Four months later, the Bank decided to buy a Microfiche System. The Bank bought two systems: one for the Dammam Data Center (DDC) and the other for Jeddah Data Center (JDC) with a cost of approximately SR 2.25 M. Staffers were selected to operate and program the system at each center. A training progam was conducted in Jeddah which lasted for two weeks. The training instructor then went to Dammam to train the other selected staff. Unfortunately, the training period allocated for the Dammam Data Center was only five days. Everyone in the group of selected personnel tried to understand and grasp the operation but then started backing out at the last moment. Mr. Dabbousi, who was one of those selected, found himself doing the job alone. He buried himself in the

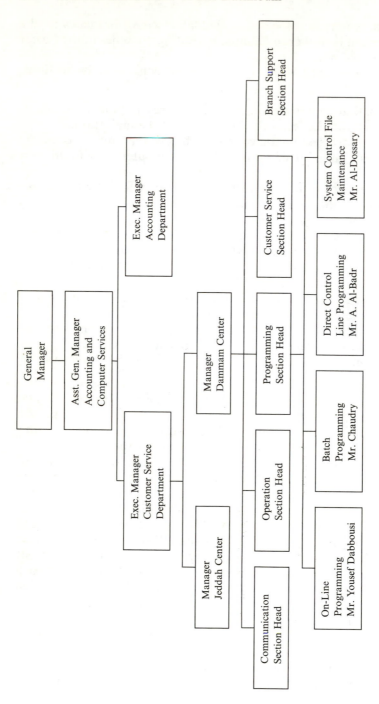

Exhibit 1   Computer Services Organizational Structure

manuals of the system for almost ten days and then started programming the system. He got excellent results. The Assistant General Manager asked the Dammam Data Center Manager to instruct Mr. Dabbousi to make a copy of his program and send it to Jeddah in order for them to work on.

Questions for Part One

1) a) How was the Data Center structured?
   b) What are the pros and cons of such a structure?
2) What recommendations (if any) do you suggest to improve the structure?
3) What will be the effect of the request made by the assistant general manager on the morale of:
   a) Mr. Dabbousi
   b) The Jeddah programmers
   c) The Dammam programmers

Part Two

In September 1985, the bank decided to build its own system internally. This decision was made due to the deficiencies that appeared in the old system. The old system was only capable of computerizing 30% of the bank's branches. Its maintenance was very expensive, and the software used by that system could not cope with the increasing demand for modern banking applications.

The bank decided to switch to micro-computers which would be more reliable and relatively cheaper, with the software to be developed in-house by the bank programmers. Six persons were selected from both centers to do the job. They were Messrs. Badr (Saudi), Osman and Khorshed (Egyptians), and Dabbousi (Bahraini) from the the Dammam Data Center and Messrs. Bakr (Saudi) and Butcher (English) from the Jeddah Data Center. Mr. Butcher was selected to be the project leader and to report directly to the executive manager. The project was named the Universal Work Station (UWS). The first phase was to be conducted in Jeddah for a duration of three months.

Mr. Dabbousi was requested to go there to start on the project. However, he was preparing for his MBA degree, and going to Jeddah for this project would have meant dropping the semester. But management insisted, telling him that he would gain very good experience and the

Jeddah project represented an opportunity for him to prove himself to the bank. Mr. Dabbousi decided to join the team.

The team was composed from the remaining bank staff. The bank rented a villa in Jeddah and requested the team to work there. The villa also served as living quarters for the four Dammam programmers. The team members were told that the project was highly confidential, due to the bank's competitive position vis-à-vis other major banks in Saudi Arabia and the fact that the bank had not yet selected bidders offering micro-computers. The bank prepared the necessary equipment for the staff, and the project started.

The project was divided into a set of interrelated tasks which were distributed among the team members by a project leader, who also assigned some of the tasks to himself.

In the first week of the project, problems arose. First, it was not clear who was to do what. Second, some of the team members were not very familiar with the programming language and, thirdly, due to the nature of their tasks, some programmers had to wait for others to finish their part of the project, before testing could begin. The effort required a great deal of informal communication, facilitated by management's decision that the team was to work and live all on the same premises.

By the end of the first month, almost all of the problems had disappeared. A friendly atmosphere pervaded the team. It became easy for them to coordinate their work and assist each other, with minimal guidance form the project leader. His role then became one of just collecting the weekly activity report and submitting it to the executive manager. He also did his project tasks, but his performance was low.

By the end of the third month the team had successfully completed the project. It developed an interactive system that could handle a major amount of bank activities. This allowed in-house maintenance which was relatively cheaper than maintenance of the old system. In fact, the new system was much easier to maintain.

A dinner party on behalf of the staff was prepared by the executive manager, who promised that the group would be given training programs in the United Kingdom and the United States. He also promised that each one of the staff who worked on this program would be given his own micro-computer and that his job status would be reevaluated in light of the outstanding success of the project. However, these promises were not fulfilled quickly.

Questions for Part Two

1) Evaluate the group's performance at each of the following stages:

	High	Moderate	Low
a) First week of the project	[ ]	[ ]	[ ]
b) End of the first month	[ ]	[ ]	[ ]
c) By the end of the project	[ ]	[ ]	[ ]

2) The interdependence of the team members in performing their tasks was of what type?
   [ ] pooled   [ ] sequential   [ ] reciprocal.
3) What role did the project leader perform?
   [ ] conductor   [ ] developer   [ ] master technician.
4) How fitting was the management style of the team leader to the task at hand and to the needs of his subordinates?
   [ ] good fit   [ ] adequate fit   [ ] poor fit.
5) Do you agree with the motivational strategy used by the executive manager? State reasons.
   [ ] Yes   [ ] No.

Part Three

Upon the successful completion of the first phase of the UWS, the system was installed in 25 branches, and work on the next phase began. Each phase was designed to be a project by itself. The old team was divided into two new teams: one located in Dammam and the other in Jeddah. New members joined the teams.

From the old team, Mr. Osman was selected to be the project manager in Dammam and Mr. Bakr to be the project manager for the Jeddah team. The new Dammam team consisted of four programmers, namely Mr. Badr and Mr. Dabbousi from the old team along with two new Saudi members. The Jeddah team consisted of five new members: one Canadian, two Egyptians, and two Saudis. It was not easy for the old team members to accept the fact that a fellow member became their manager.

Initially, the Data Center manager said that the new arrangement would be temporary, with the Dammam team reporting to two bosses: their project manager and a programming manager.

The Dammam team was assigned a new task: Arabize the whole system built in the initial project team, in a period of only one month. The project consisted of translating and validating more than 100 screens into Arabic. Mr. Badr and Mr. Dabbousi had to educate the new team members about the system, while at the same time performing their own tasks. Aside from that, they had to trace any malfunction that appeared in the first phase of the UWS. The project duration was so short that problems started to crop up. Mr. Dabbousi even found himself at one time tracing faults for 15 branches alone, because Mr. Badr was on vacation. On top of that, he was trying to prepare for final exams at his school. Frustration and depression crept in, as he was not able to do all these tasks simultaneously. He barely made it, but the project did manage to reach a successful conclusion. However, he paid a heavy price: his academic grades took a dive.

Questions for Part Three

1) Was it a good decision to include Mr. Badr and Mr. Dabbousi in the new Dammam team? Give your reasoning.
   [ ] Yes   [ ] Undecided   [ ] No.
2) How will the reorganization of the programming department affect the job satisfaction of:
   a) the programmers?
      [ ] Positively   [ ] Marginally   [ ] Negatively.
   b) their functional manager?
      [ ] Positively   [ ] Marginally   [ ] Negatively.
3) How will the reorganization of the programming department affect the performance of:
   a) the programmers?
      [ ] Positively   [ ] Marginally   [ ] Negatively.
   b) their functional manager?
      [ ] Positively   [ ] Marginally   [ ] Negatively.

Part Four

Projects continued one after the other, with both Mr. Badr and Mr. Dabbousi still reporting to the same bossess. More organizational problems were encountered which needed resolution. Reporting to two bosses was really a strain. One case arose when Mr. Dabbousi needed a day off. He was confused as to whom he should approach – the project manager or the programming manager, who was a newcomer to "Bank Arabia."He thought of asking the project manager about it but the manager was somewhat busy, so he decided to ask permission from the programming manager with a written request, which was approved. After coming back from his day off, he was called to the office of the Data Center manager who berated him for not telling his project manager about his leave. Mr. Dabbousi replied that he had secured the approval of his programming manager. The Data Center manager accused him of exploiting the unfamiliarity of the programming manager with the details of the bank's regulations. Mr. Dabbousi felt irritated and told the Data Center manager that there were no rules that require an employee to ask permission from the project manager and not from the programming manager. He said that the bank must spell out all the rules for him in order to know what to do when such a case occurs. The Data Center manager agreed, and a new procedure was decided: Dabbousi's monthly overtime and activity reports go to the programming manager, and the remaining activities and actions would have to be approved by the project manager. It was clear that the programming manager was not happy about this new arrangement, since the project manager has been a subordinate who was initially a programmer reporting his monthly activities to the programming manager.

The situation became more uncertain, until the Data Center manager stated formally that the project manager would be reporting directly to him and that the project team would report all activities directly to the project manager and not to the programming manager.

Questions for Part Four

1) What sort of structure did the Data Center have as initially described in Part Four?
   [ ] Functional   [ ] Matrix   [ ] Product.
2) What do you think of the approach of Mr. Dabbousi when he requested a day off?
   [ ] Sound   [ ] Unsound.
   Why?
3) What was the main reason for a problem to occur when he asked for a day off?
   a) Lack of formalization
   b) Role ambiguity
   c) Role conflict.
4) The Data Center manager decided to cut off the project programmers from their permanent functional home. How do you feel about this decision?

	Agree	Undecided	Disagree
a) as a programmer	[ ]	[ ]	[ ]
b) as the head of the programming section	[ ]	[ ]	[ ]
c) as the manager of XYZ project	[ ]	[ ]	[ ]

5) What were the objectives of the Data Center manager?
6) Could he have achieved these objectives differently and painlessly? How?
7) What sort of structure did the Data Center have as described at the end of Part Four?
   [ ] Functional   [ ] Matrix   [ ] Project.

Part Five

The Dammam team continued working on the projects, while becoming more proficient. The project manager delegated every task to the team members informally and coordinated the work with them.

To speed up completion of projects, the Data Center manager provided each one of the team members with a micro-computer to work on at home. This gave the members more freedom and flexibility. All projects given to the team were completed on time, sometimes even before the target dates.

Many projects were added later on, such as ATMs (Automatic Teller Machines), and DBM (Data Base Management). Mr. Dabbousi was selected to be the project manager for the DBM. As of today, 80 branches are fully computerized using the UWS – a fact which gives "Bank Arabia" a definite competitive advantage.

Chapter 6
Lodging Industry

6.1   A Note on the Lodging Industry

Ghazi M. Habib

Introduction

Hotels represent an important segment of the hospitality industry, which includes travel, lodging, food, entertainment, and recreation provided to consumers away from home.

The hotel industry enjoyed sizable growth in the Arab Gulf States since the start of the oil boom in 1973. At that time, the hotel industry was not developed enough to meet the requirements of the impending massive influx of customers attracted by Gulf governments investing huge sums in infrastructure development. Realizing the shortage of hotel accommodations, Gulf governments started a system of financial support and incentives aimed at enticing the private sector to invest in hotel development. The private sector accepted the challenge, and the number of hotels increased tremendously. For example, in 1975, Saudi Arabia had only 64 hotels with just over 5,000 rooms. Exhibit 1 shows that within 10 years the total number of hotels has more than tripled to 245 and the number of rooms more than quadrupled to 21,510.

Exhibit 1   Hotels in Saudi Arabia (1985)

Rank	No. of Hotels	%	No. of Rooms	%
Deluxe	14	5.7	3,672	17.0
First Class	40	16.3	7,005	32.0
Second Class	99	40.4	7,415	34.5
Third Class	92	37.6	3,418	15.9
Total	245	100.0	21,510	100.0

Source: Al-Iktissad 1986: 28.

The two objectives of an industry analysis are to determine the attractiveness of an industry and to identify its key success factors. A key success factor is a competitive skill or asset that is particularly relevant to the industry. To "play the game," a competitor usually needs to possess some minimum assets or level of skills with respect to each of the industry's key success factors.

Industry Structure

The attractiveness of the hotel industry depends largely on its structure, which is made up of the following five components (see Exhibit 2):

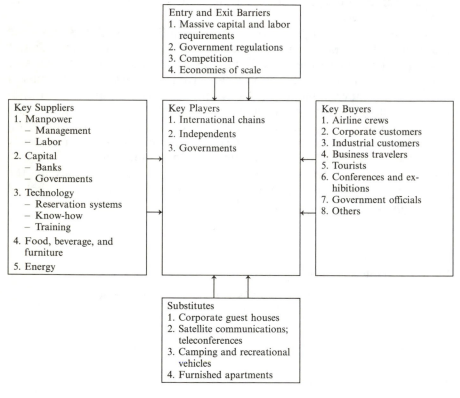

Exhibit 2   Competitive Forces in the Lodging Industry

1) key players;
2) key buyers;
3) key suppliers;
4) exit and entry barriers; and
5) substitutes.

The intensity of competition in an industry depends largely on the number of players or competitors, their commitment to the industry, product differentiation, the amount of the fixed costs, and the strength of the exit barriers.

Key Players

The key players in the hotel industry can be divided into three main types: international chains, independents, and governments.

International Chains

These hotels are usually operated by internationally known hotel chains, where each hotel carries the corporate name. The Meridien and Sheraton chains are prime examples of such players. The usual set-up is that the international chain will handle management of a local hotel for a fee or a percentage of the profits. The involvement of the local owner with the managing firm will be mainly financial. These players are mostly found in the luxury segment and tend to have a high fixed-cost structure. This is mainly due to the high standards that have to be met before carrying the chain name. Exhibit 3 provides some of the advantages and disadvantages of the hotel chain arrangement.

Exhibit 3   Advantates and Disadvantages – Hotel Chains

Advantages	Disadvantages
– Name, known worldwide	– Paying some amount for holding the name as percentage of sales/profit
– Improves marketability	
– Job security (for the employees)	– Inflexibility in reacting to changes in the market (must consult headquarters)
– International reservation system	
	– No local image

Independents

This type of hotel is not associated with any international chain and is usually operated by the individual owners, who tend to be involved in all aspects of the hotel's management. Examples of such players are Al-Gosaibi Hotel (luxury class) and Al-Hamra Hotel (budget class). These players are not required to meet any specific outside standards. Most of the hotels in the Gulf area, especially in the non-luxury class, are of this type.

Government Hotels

GCC governments partially or totally own a number of hotels, such as the Riyadh Intercontinental; the Gulf Hotels in Bahrain, Qatar, and Oman; and the Abu Dhabi Intercontinental.

Key Buyers

Exhibit 4 shows Middle East market data for 1984. Three major types of buyers from the core of hotel customers in the Gulf states are identified. Exhibit 5 shows the breakdown of guest nationalities at hotels in the Middle East.

Exhibit 4   Middle East Market Data – 1984 (in %)

Source of business:	
Domestic	43.9
Foreign	56.1
Percentage of repeat business	41.4
Composition of market:	
Government officials	9.2
Businessmen	49.9
Tourists	12.9
Conference participants	4.6
Other	23.4
Percentage of advance reservations	63.4
Composition of advance reservations:	
Direct	52.0
Reservation systems	27.5
Travel agents and tour operators	15.4
Other	5.1
Ratio of travel agent commissions to room sales	0.5

Source: Lamanno and Evans 1985.

Exhibit 5   Nationality of Guests in the Middle East Hotels

	Rank 1986	1985	1983	Total Region 1986
Middle Eastern	1	1	1	25.4%
American	5	2	2	8.9%
French	2	3	4	13.5%
British	4	4	3	10.7%
German	7	5	5	5.0%
Other European	6	6	7	8.6%
Other African	3	7	6	11.9%
Other Asian	8	8	8	4.1%
Italian	10	9	9	3.0%
Japanese	9	10	10	3.4%
Scandinavian	13	11	13	1.2%
Canadian	12	12	12	1.3%
North African	11	13	14	1.5%
Australian	14	14	11	0.6%
South American	15	15	15	0.5%
Central American	17	16	16	0.3%
Mexican	18	17	17	–

Source: Horwath & Horwath 1987, p. 47.

Airline Crews

This type consists of pilots, flight attendants, and stewards of international airlines, which tend to have strong bargaining power, since they bring significant and consistent business volume to the hotel. Discounts of up to 50% and special business contacts are common tactics used by hoteliers these days to attract those important buyers.

Corporate Customers

These are mainly company employees on a business assignment. This segment accounts for about 50% of hotel business in the area (see Exhibit 4). However, this segment has declined markedly in size, due chiefly to the completion of the infrastructure projects and the decline in oil revenues. Moreover, local companies, as part of cost-saving measures, are reducing the number of their business travel assignments and limiting allowable travel expenses.

The resultant bedding crisis has intensified competition among hotels to attract business customers, since hotel profitability is highly dependent on its ability to attract this rapidly declining market segment.

Individual Customers

This segment represents mainly the walk-in type of customer. It is generally small and seasonal. The hotel business generated from this segment usually picks up during school vacations (especially the spring vacation) and the Eid holidays. This trend of internal tourism is becoming more important, since the business volume brought by those buyers during the seasonal peak is quite high. This segment could represent a valuable substitute for the declining business traveler segment.

In addition, hotel services are also attracting the following business:

1) local customers eating out;
2) catering for institutions and airlines;
3) catering for private and public banquets;
4) hosting international and local exhibitions;
5) lodging conference and seminar participants.

Key Suppliers

The key suppliers to the hotel industry tend to have little bargaining power, since they are large in number, selling undifferentiated products that have a number of potential substitutes. However, a few suppliers, mainly of capital, energy, and communications, tend to have significant bargaining power. Government financing of hotels has virtually stopped, and new investors must turn now to the commercial banks. Bank loans are very expensive compared to government loans and are difficult to obtain, since the current room capacity in the area far exceeds demand. Energy and communication suppliers are monopolies in the Gulf states. Electricity bills for hotels have increased dramatically because of the recent increase in electricity rates, which has further dampened hotel profitability.

Suppliers of hotel management training services have gained more importance because of government policies requiring the hiring of local nationals. The Bahrain Institute for Hotel Management is an important supplier of such services. Currently, most major hotels in the region have employees studying at this institute.

Entry and Exit Barriers

Entry and exit barriers affect both the ability of potential competitors to enter the industry and the ability of current competitors to exit from it. One of the major entry and exit barriers is the need for capital. The cost of building a first-class or luxury hotel can range between US $ 5 million and

US $ 50 million. The massive amounts of capital needed to enter the hotel industry also acts as an exit barrier, since hotel buildings have few alternative usages. Hotel construction costs in the Gulf states have been very high. Cunningham et al. (1980) reported that while a cost of US $ 100,000–US $ 150,000 per room is the international norm, a cost of US $ 500,000 per hotel room is not uncommon in the Arab Gulf States.

The labor intensity of hotel operations is another entry barrier.

Government regulations represent the most formidable entry barrier, since investors are required by law to obtain a license from the government before they can build a new hotel. Currently, most Gulf governments have stopped issuing new licenses because of the excess capacity in the market. Government regulations also cover many operational aspects of the hotel industry. In most Gulf states, the government issues regulations that direct the hotel industry to operate within the strictures of Islam, hire more local nationals, and use local suppliers whenever possible.

Volume is a crucial factor in determining a hotel's profitability due to the economies of scale that are involved. The volume of business required for a hotel to break even is quite high. One manager of a Gulf luxury hotel reported that his hotel needs an occupancy rate of about 56 % to break even (see Exhibits 6 and 7).

A final barrier to entry is location, a key factor in hotel profitability. The ability to secure a good location can significantly affect the ultimate success or failure of a hotel. The availability of high-quality staff is another powerful entry barrier, which works in favor of the big chains.

Prevailing market conditions, characterized by excess supply of hotel capacity and declining demand, have intensified the ferocity of competition, which in turn constitutes a formidable entry barrier. The few hotels that are relatively insulated from this competition are those owned by Gulf governments. They enjoy a captive market of government officials and government guests.

Factors that differentiate hotels in this highly competitive environment seem to be:
1) location;
2) service quality and room amenities;
3) physical appearance and architecture;
4) price;
5) business service facilities;
6) recreation facilities;
7) conference facilities; and
8) exhibition space and facilities.

Despite the belief by some Gulf hoteliers that price-cutting is "economic suicide," the majority are engaged in pricing wars triggered by low occupancy rates.

Exhibit 6   Shows that occupancy rates in the Middle East slid from a peak of 115% in 1977 to 66% in 1981).

Projected Opening of New Hotels

Year	# of new hotels	%	# of Rooms	%
1978	62	37	10,250	25
1979	59	35	14,750	37
1980	24	14	7,250	18
1981	23	14	7,950	20
Total	168	100	40,200	100

Room Supply and Demand

End Year	Demand	Supply	Occupancy
1977	15,000	14,000	115%
1978	20,000	24,250	83%
1979	25,000	39,000	64%
1980	31,250	48,250	57%
1981	36,000	54,200	66%

Classification

Class	New hotel	%	# of Rooms	%
5-Star	62	37	18,980	47
4-Star	77	46	18,535	46
3-Star	29	17	2,685	7
Total	168	100	40,200	100

Source: Cunningham et al. (1980).

Exhibit 7   Room Rates in the Middle East Hotels

	1986	1985	1984	1983
Annual room occupancy	49.6%	57%	53.3%	62.0%
Number of guests per room	1.18	1.19	1.22	1.21
Average daily rate:				
Per room (U.S. Dollars) $	63.8	64.3	68.92	68.84
Per guest (U.S. Dollars)	51.4	52.0	49.14	55.14

Source: Lamanno and Evans 1985 and; Horwath & Horwath (1987), p. 48.

Substitutes

There are several potential substitutes for hotel services. However, only one substitute can cause any real threat to the hotel industry: some companies, in their attempt to control costs, have their own guest houses to accommodate their visitors. Large firms in the area have started to use their own guest houses as a substitute for hotels. However, using such a substitute depends mainly on the number of company visitors. Tele-conferences and camping vehicles do not exert any noticeable threat to the hotel industry in the Gulf. – Furnished apartments are gainning in popularity, particularly for large traveling families.

Cost and Revenue Structure

An understanding of the cost and revenue structure of the industry can provide insight into the possible key success factors that differentiate successful from unsuccessful hotels.

Our research of the luxury hotels and budget hotels (see Exhibit 8 for a sample questionnaire) has shown that the major cost components for the luxury and budget hotel segments are the following:

1) Employees' salaries constitute about one-third of the total operating costs.
2) Food and beverages represents the second major cost component and constitutes 23% of the operating cost in the luxury segment and about 25% in the budget segment.
3) Other costs include mainly maintenance, electricity, and communications. This component constitutes about 22% of the total operating costs in the luxury segment and 21% in the budget segment (see Exhibit 9).
4) Administration and marketing costs include mainly the general operating expenses not traceable to any operating division plus marketing costs.

Our own research[1] has shown that the major sources of revenues for both the luxury and budget segments are the following (see Exhibits 10 and 11):

---

[1] A group of our MBA students at the College of Industrial Management at King Fahd University of Petroleum and Minerals conducted a field survey to find the cost and revenue structure of the industry in the area.

Exhibit 8   Sample Questionnaire Luxury and Budget Hotels

---

1. Hotel name: ....
2. Hotel capacity:..................
   a. No. of single rooms: ....
   b. No. of double rooms: ....
   c. No. of deluxe rooms:..........
3. Date of operations: .../.../19
4. Hotel customers: Please indicate
   the percentage of each of the
   following types:
   a. Saudi businessmen:............
   b. Foreign businessman: ....
   c. Tourist: ....
   d. Others (indicate): ....
   Total: 100%
5. Hotel annual revenues: Please
   indicate in percentage form the
   revenues from each of the following services:
   a. Lodging services (rooms):......
   b. Room services: ....

c. Restaurants:..................
d. Laundry services: ....
e. Outside catering:.............
f. Other services:...............
Total: 100%

6. Occupancy rate: Please indicate the
   occupancy rate of the hotel for the
   following years:

   (   )%   (   )%   (   )%
   1983   1984   1985

7. Annual expenses: Please indicate in
   percentage form the annual expenses of the following:
   a. Administration
      (except salaries): ....
   b. Employees' salaries:...........
   c. Marketing: ....
   d. Food and beverages: ....
   e. Taxes:........................
   f. Others:.......................
   Total: 100%

Exhibit 9   Energy Costs per Occupied Room per Day in the Middle East – 1984
             (in US $)

	1986	1984
Fuel	$ .80	$ 0.98
Electricity	3.82	2.59
Water	1.02	0.77
Steam	.42	0.36
Credit for sale of energy	.23	0.53
Net energy cost – 1986	6.33	4.71
Net energy cost – 1984	4.50	4.50
Increase (decrease)	1.83	4.7

Source: Lamanno and Evans 1985, and Horwath & Horwath (1987), p. 55.

Exhibit 10   Composition of Sales in the Middle East Hotels

	1986	1984
Rooms	51.1%	44.0%
Food	24.9	29.6
Beverage	8.8	10.4
Telephone	7.1	6.6
Minor departments	3.6	4.1
Rentals and other income	4.5	5.3
Total	100.0%	100.0%

Source: Lammano and Evans 1985, and Horwath & Horwath (1987), p. 49.

1) Rooms: this is the major revenue source for both segments. It accounts for 45% of the total revenues in the luxury segment and about 51% in the budget segment.
2) Food and beverage: this second major source of revenues consists of restaurants, room services, and outside catering. For the luxury segment, these three sources account for about 40% of the total revenues, while in the budget segment they account for about 37%.
3) Other services: revenues from other services constitute the third major source of revenues. These services include telephone and telex, secretarial services, and the membership in hotel health clubs. This category accounts for 11% of total revenues in the luxury class segment and about 10% in the budget class segment.
4) Outside catering: this provides a valuable revenue source for the luxury class segment. Outside catering accounts for 11% to 18% of total revenues for this class of hotel.

Exhibit 12   Method of Payment for Hotel Services in the Middle East Hotels

	1986	1984
Cash	35.4%	33.3%
Credit card	21.5	21.5
Travel agents and tour operators	–	9.4
All other credit	43.1	35.8

Source: Lammano and Evans 1985, and Horwath & Horwath (1987), p. 55.

Exhibit 11   Ratio to Total Sales in the Middle East – 1984*

Rooms	
Sales	100.0%
Departmental expenses:	
Payroll and related expenses	15.0
Other	8.7
Total	25.0
Departmental income	75.0
Ratio to total sales	31.8
Food and beverages Sales:	
Food	72.4
Beverage	30.5
Total	100.0
Cost of sales:	
Food	32.9
Beverage	21.0
Total	29.0
Gross profit	70.6
Public room sales	0.4
Other income	2.6
Gross profit and other income	73.6
Departmental expenses:	
Payroll and related expenses	37.7
Other	12.3
Total	49.1
Departmental income	22.3
Ratio to total sales	8.4
Telephone profit	1.4
Net income from minor departments	1.4
Rentals and other income	2.1
Gross income	50.3
Undistributed operating expenses:	
Administrative and General Payroll and related expenses	6.2
Other	4.3
Total	10.8
Marketing	3.6
Energy costs	3.4
Property operation and maintenance	7.5
Total undistributed expenses	25.9
Income before management fees	25.2
Management fees	11.7
Income before fixed charges	19.4
Property and insurance	1.2
Income before interest and depreciation	17.1%

* Note: All figures are medians and do not necessarily add up to 100%.

Source: Lamanno and Evans 1985. For an update see Horwath and Horwath (1987), p. 58.

References

Al-Bilad (1982): An account on the hotels of the Kingdom, *Al-Bilad Newspaper*, Jan. 6; 2.

Creel, R. (1984): Assessing the Kingdom's hotel industry, *Saudi Business*, (May 7): 12–13.

Cunningham et al. (1980): *Middle East travel*, (quoted in newspaper article).

Editorial Report on new grading system for the hotels, (1981): *Al-Iktissad Magazine*, (13 Shaaban 1981) (Arabic).

Horwath & Horwath (1987): *Worldwide Hotel Industry*: 17th Annual Report on International Hotel Operations, New York: Horwath & Horwath Int'l.

Kenny, A., Abbas, M., and Javid, H. (1983): Owners take plea to Riyadh, *Saudi Business*, (Jan. 7): 16–19.

Khusro, A. (1981): Vacancies plague Jeddah hoteliers, *Saudi Business*, 30; 15–16.

Lamanno, M. and W. Evans (1985): *Worldwide lodging industry*, Laventhol and Horwath Corp. New York.

Orakzai, S. (1984): Hotels – Special report, *Saudi Business*, VIII, 30, (November 26); 32–37.

Rahman, H. (1984): Hotels – Special report, *Saudi Business*, VIII, 30, (Nov. 26): 22–31.

Saudi Business (1983): Making room for hotels, Cover Story, *Saudi Business*, VI, 7, (June 4): 30–51.

Thomas, D. (1978): Strategy is different in service business, *Harvard Business Review*, (July-August): 158–165.

6.2 The Gulf Meridien (GM)

Prince Abdulaziz bin Salman Al-Saud*

Introduction

In 1978, a group of highly influential Saudi investors perceived the need for a first-class (five-star) hotel which would cater primarily to businessmen in the Dhahran – Al Khobar – Damman area. These gentlemen approached the Meridien Hotel chain in France and asked them to develop the design, supervise the construction, and manage the day-to-day operations of the hotel. The GM opened in 1981.

Out of the four luxury hotels operating in the Eastern Province, GM is blessed with the finest location and enjoys the highest occupancy ratio. It is situated in the most prestigious area in the Khobar, 10 minutes away from the Dhahran airport and 15 minutes from the Dammam Seaport. It is located on the beach and overlooks the blue expanse of the Arabian Gulf. The hotel has 18 suites, 14 villas, and 327 rooms. Even with the reduction in international business travel, the GM boasts an average occupancy rate of about 80%.

Regardless of its cause, this unusual success has put the hotel management in a tough decision situation. On the one hand, it is seriously petitioning the Commerce Department for approval of an increase in room rental. On the other hand, it fears the on-going price war waged by the Meridien's competitors and the opening of both the Bahrain-Khobar Causeway in 1987 and the new King Fahd International Airport in 1989 may adversely affect the occupancy rate and negatively reflect on the competency of its French management.

---

* This case is prepared by HRH Prince Abdulaziz bin Salman Al-Saud of the Ministry of Petroleum.

The Hotel Industry in Saudi Arabia

During the early 1970s, the Ministry of Finance invested in the first government-owned hotel. At that time an agreement was reached with the Intercontinental Hotel chain to design, build, and manage the Intercontinental Hotel in Riyadh. Through this move, the Saudi government signaled to the private sector that the domestic hotel industry was an untapped market where there were high demands and high profits.

Three factors contributed to this high demand. The first and main factor was the unexpected, huge revenue increases in late 1973 and early 1974 due to the rise in crude oil prices. These revenue increases were reflected in the first five-year plan where spending was above initial proposals. During this time, emphasis was placed upon building the Kingdom's infrastructure and, as a consequence, there was an influx of foreign businessmen and experts to help with this building. Saudi Arabian business personnel also increased in number at this time. As a result, a huge surge in the demand for hotel facilities occurred.

The second factor that increased demand for hotel facilities during this period was the sudden rise in per capita income which gave the average Saudi more money to spend and allowed him to be more mobile. This stimulated domestic travel and increased the demand for hotel facilities.

The third factor was the development of a network of first-class international airports. This increased the demand for hotel facilities by airline crews and transit passengers.

The above factors, at first, led the government to invest public funds directly by owning hotels and indirectly by giving incentives to the private sector to stimulate further building of hotels. These incentives included a soft loan of 50 % of the projected cost up to SR 50 million and no customs or tariff duties on hotel furniture and other supplies (the furniture tariff is 20 %). Such lucrative incentives along with the prospect of a high growth industry attracted international hotel chains such as Intercontinental, Sheraton, Meridien, Oberoi, Marriott, Ramada, and others. In the 1970s, these hotel chains developed designs, supervised the construction of their respective hotels, and supplied the entire management staff of the hotel for a fee and/or a share of the profits.

The hotel market in the 1970s in Saudi Arabia was characterized by high growth, low supply, high demand, little to no competition, and no price control. Today, the hotel industry is completely different: supply exceeds demand, competition is very stiff, services are being upgraded to attract customers, prices cannot go above ceilings set by responsible government agencies, and in some cases, the industry is declining due to competition. Services are also expected to conform to the norms and ethics of Islam and Arab society. For instance, there are strict regulations banning the mixing of single people and the serving of alcoholic beverages and pork meat. The Department of Hotels within the Ministry of Commerce inspects all hotels, classifies them, prices their services, polices their hospitality standards (room, food, beverages, and recreational facilities), and issues licences for the construction and operation of hotels.

The hotel industry in the Kingdom is seasonal. Hotels in Jeddah, Mecca, and Madina have a high occupancy rate during the Hajj and Ramadan; Eastern Province hotels have a low occupancy rate at this time. The hotel industry is both capital-intensive and labor-intensive. An emphasis on high-quality construction, facilities, services, location, etc., make some hotels more capital and labor intensive than others. Due to the lack of trained Saudi personnel, hotel management and staff are made up of expatriates from many parts of the world, most of whom do not speak Arabic.

Competitive Analysis

In the Eastern Province, the hotel industry is taking the brunt of the slow-down in the oil industry. Since the Province is not a haven for tourists, its hotels are directly dependent on the pace of the oil industry. When the oil pipelines reduce production, the international business traffic, the back-bone of the hotel industry, virtually becomes non-existent. This pheno-menon means that major hotel operations and airlines serving the area are forced to operate below the break-even point; hence they are condemned to engage in price wars to remain competitive. Discounts of up to 50 % of the published fares are the rule, not the exception. Additionally, many major airlines have been forced to stop their services to Dhahran.

Not only did the Eastern Province loose its appeal to the international business traveler, but has lost it to the local traveler as well. With the opening of the Bahrain-Khobar Causeway in 1987, many Saudi business-men and tourists will prefer to conduct their meetings and spend their weekends in Bahrain.

An analysis of customer mix for the Eastern Province hotels shows that Saudis are the largest group of customers (36 %), followed by Europeans (20 %) and Far Easterners (17 %). The total number of rooms available in 1985 were about 2,339, registering an average overall occupancy rate of about 43 %. About 68 % of the customers' nights were spent in luxury hotels, registering an overall occupancy rate of 46 %. The remaining 32 % of customer nights were spent in budget hotels, registering an occupancy rate of 38 %. Not only do the two segments reflect different occupancy rates, but also a different customer mix. Anglo-Saxons patronize luxury

Exhibit 1   Size, Occupancy Rate and Market Share of Luxury Class Hotels in the
Eastern Province of Saudi Arabia

Name of hotel	Size: number of rooms	Occupancy rate 1984	1985	Market Share % 1984	1985
Gulf Meridien	327	81	70	34	35
Al Gosaibi	349	48	36	27	25
Dhahran Int'l	191	62	56	17	15
Dammam Oberoi	272	65	49	22	25

Source: Primary; based on field data compiled by the case writer.

hotels, while Arab and Far Easterners patronize budget hotels. Exhibit 1
provides data relating to market share, number of rooms, and occupancy
rates for each of the luxury class hotels.

The Meridien competes with three other five-star hotels in the Eastern
Province, the Oberoi, the Al Gosaibi, and the Dhahran International. Each
competitor has a distinctive capability profile and strategy for maintaining
and gaining market share in the now mature market for luxury lodging.

Al Gosaibi Hotel was the first five-star hotel in the Eastern Province. It
was built in the early 1970's at the beginning of the boom period. It boasts
the largest banquet and exhibition facilities. Its excellent location,
ownership, and management by the well-known Al Gosaibi family are its
major strengths. However, the hotel is threatened both from within and
from without by an image problem. First, the owners view it as a cash cow
and second, the customers do not consider it as attractive as its next-door
competitor, The Meridien.

The Dhahran International Hotel is an airport hotel which seeks to
attract the airline crews and associated airline business (e. g., catering
transit and layover passengers). Its location, its excellent banquet and
catering facilities, and its aggressive and innovative sales organization are
among its noted assets. Its major weaknesses include the fact that it is not
managed by a famous international chain and that its facilities are getting
old.

The Dammam Oberoi, handicapped by its location, about 15 minutes
away from the Dhahran airport, and by its affiliation with a Third World
multinational chain, is condemned to be the most aggressive one of all the
luxury class hotels in the Eastern Province. It seeks to maintain its market
share by engaging in price wars and by diversifying its service portfolio into
catering and dry cleaning. Its target customers are airline crews and large
corporate accounts. Its in-room services are second to none.

Internal Analysis

Management and Organization

Why French?

The prominent group of Saudi investors chose the Meridien Hotel Chain to manage their property for several reasons. First, the Meridien Corporation is a sister company of Air France which spends millions of dollars promoting the 55 member hotel chain on all of its flights, in airports, and travel agencies.

Second, the Meridien Corporation has a well-developed technostructure and support staff. Both consist of specialists in operational management, purchasing, marketing, training, and auditing. These specialists standardize and monitor the work of the field units from their headquarter in Paris and the regional office in Jeddah. They also offer support services such as a computerized reservation system (ALPHA-3), quality control, and management development.

Third, the Meridien is a young organization. It has been allowed the opportunity to learn from the mistakes of its predecessors (Hilton and Sheraton).

Finally, the Meridien Corporation specializes in the Middle East market. It has a better feel for the service requirements of this market than do its American or European competitors. To insure the French accent in its service delivery system, the Meridien Corporation employs numerous French people (1,400 out of 12,000) and puts them in executive positions (225 out of 640)

Organization and Management

The management hierarchy of the Gulf Meridien consists of three levels: the home office, the regional office in Jeddah, and the local hotel level. As already mentioned, the head office supplies its purchasing, personnel, promotional, and operational expertise to field units. It also designs service standards and monitors their application through a system of unannounced spot inspections. Senior headquarter executives in charge of food and beverage, room division, sales and marketing, and auditings make periodic inspection of the Gulf Meridien facilities and services. Regional office staff, based in Jeddah and Cairo, visit the Gulf Meridien and make similar and more frequent inspections. For instance, the regional chief engineer checks the functioning of equipment and installations at the Gulf Meridien three or four times a year. Similarly, the regional sales and marketing executive checks the activities of the marketing and sales department, while the regional controller audits the Gulf Meridien's books and quarterly financial statements. These regional and head office executives are typically housed in the best empty villas or rooms at GM.

Exhibit 2 contains synopses from the personnel files of the management team. The hotel is managed by a French general manager – Mr. Michael Sabot – who presides over an executive committee made up of an assistant G. M., a financial controller, a food and beverage manager, a sales manager, a chief engineer, a personnel manager, and a room division manager. Together, these managers have about 55 years of experience with the Meridien Corporation. There is a high rate of turnover among them. In only a few years, the general manager position has changed three times, and the assistant G. M. has changed twice. The average age of the management staff is thirty-four years. About one half of the management staff speaks Arabic. Recruitment is done primarily through inter-unit transfers; about one third of the Gulf managers have served at another Meridien hotel.

Exhibit 2   Men at the Helm

Michel Sabot – General Manager
Mr. Sabot, 41, started his career as a trainee in food and beverage departments in France before going abroad. Initially he worked for Intercontinental before joining Trusthouse Forte Hotels which posted him as food and beverage manager in Australia, Tahiti, and Fiji Islands. After seven years with Trusthouse Forte, Mr. Sabot joined Meridien Hotels 11 years ago and had the pleasure to be posted to Bahia (Brazil) and the French West Indies (Martinique) as executive assistant manager. Then his job brought him to the Middle East: Cairo and Damascus as manager, and now as head of the Gulf Meridien Hotel, Al Khobar.

Michel Darcy – Food and Beverage Manager
Mr. Darcy joined the Meridien chain in 1982. He was restaurant manager in Al Salam Meridien, Jeddah, and was promoted as assistant food and beverage manager in Meridien Damascus in 1984. In October 1986, he became a member of the Gulf Meridien Hotel Al Khobar family as food and beverage manager.

Andre Papillon – Chief Engineer
Mr. Papillon started his career in the construction business in 1970 in Guinea where he participated in building a palace and two banks. Then he moved to Senegal and to Mauritania for the construction of hotels, lagoons, and a residental complex of 800 villas. In 1980, Mr. Papillon joined the Gulf Meridien Hotel and is now the longest serving employee of the hotel. He was present at the handover stages of the hotel from the constructors.

Abdel Kader Muhtadie – Rooms Division Manager
Mr. Muhtadie started his career in 1971 with the Intercontinental Hotels wherein he held the positions of assistant front office manager, front office manager, and as assistant manager in charge of IHC villas in Riyadh. After two years, he was transferred to Riyadh Conference Palace as rooms division manager, and was consequently promoted as conference centre manager to prepare and organize for the 13th Annual Arab Summit Conference scheduled in December 1973, he joined the Gulf Meridien Al Khobar in March 1984.

Naceur Mechmoum – Director of Sales & Marketing
Mr. Mechmoum graduated in 1979 from a hotel school in Britain. During that time, he was trained by Trusthouse Forte Hotels in England and joined them for the opening of the Hannibal Palace Tunisia, where he spent four years in the positions of reservations manager, front office manager, assistant sales manager, and then rooms division manager. From there, he moved to Bahrain with the Holiday Inn as rooms division manager. In September 1985, he joined the Gulf Meridien Al Kohbar in the position of director of sales and marketing.

Fathi Kchaou – Financial Controller
Mr. Kchaou, 37, started his career in 1968 at the Hilton Tunis where he went through various positions in the accounting department. In July 1971, he joined the Meridien Tunis and in February 1972, he was promoted to assistant financial controller, a job he held during the 10 years he spent in that hotel. In January 1981, he joined the Gulf Meridien Hotel Al Khobar as financial controller. During the 1986 Meridien Worldwide Financial Controllers' Meeting in Singapore, Mr. Kchaou received first prize for excellence on overall performance.

Management Training

a) On-site training – Rank and file training is a continuous process performed in the hotel itself by the executive of each department and includes: on the job training; audio-visual; language (done by outside teachers).
b) Inter-hotel training – Specially selected personnel are transferred from hotel one Meridien to another ensuring a high quality of expertise and professional excellence. This training and transfer ensures a continuity of Meridien standards from hotel to hotel.
c) Outside training – The Meridien International Institute is a training school for Meridien Hotel personnel (management and suervisory) in Tours, France. Selected personnel are taught the latest ideas and methods of hotel management. The institute uses state of the art teaching methods and materials. The institute also offers advanced training programs in the hotel environment or at an interprofessional

training center for senior managers with high potential. This is a very select program; tuition and fees are paid by the head office.

d) Compensation Policy – The Meridien Hotel chain has a compensation plan adapted to the French social security program for its executives. It includes: medical care; death/disability/daily indemnity; and a pension fund. G.M. offers its executives the added protection of an unemployment fund.

Marketing

A. Segmentation

The Gulf Meridien serves three markets: the accommodation market, the food services market, and the entertainment and sports facilities market. The segmentation of the customer target groups are local and foreign corporations, individuals with high incomes, and airline crews (see Exhibits 3 and 4). Several ethnic groups patronize GM: Middle Eastern – 52 %; non-French European – 15 %; French – 14 %; Japanese – 9.1 %; Americans – 8 %; Asians – 2 %. Interestingly enough, the sales department, headed by a French-speaking Mauritius, is internally differentiated by nationality: there is a Japanese sales executive to work on Japanese accounts, a Sudanese to work on government accounts, and a Lebanese on Saudi accounts.

GM's current market share of the four leading hotels in the Eastern Province is almost 35 %. Potential customers are reached by applying a

Exhibit 3   Customers Mix of Luxury Class Hotels in the Eastern Province, Saudi Arabia – 1985

Market Mix	Dhahran Int'l	Oberoi	Al Gosaibi	Meridien
Corporate accounts	43	65	60	26
Airline crew	19	20	15	33
Long term	–	–	–	–
Walk-ins	12	10	20	10
Government	–	5	5	19
Lay-over	17	–	–	–
Others	9	–	–	12
Total	100 %	100 %	100 %	100 %

Source: Primary, based on field data compiled by the case writer.

Exhibit 4   Company Production Report I for the Month of March, 1985

Gulf Meridien Hotel		Top 10		General	
Grade	Company Name	Month	%	Cumul.	%
1	Saudia "Saudi Arabian Airlines"	2,647	30,79%	7,651	31.53%
2	Full Rate	2,397	27.88%	6,516	26.85%
3	Walk in	788	9.16%	2,298	9.47%
4	Air France	697	8.11%	1.963	8.09%
5	Alpha 3: AF/Meridien computerized reservation network	461	5.36%	1,201	4.95%
6	W/W Corporate	332	3.86%	867	3.57%
7	Travel agents	262	3.05%	786	3.24%
8	Mitsubishi Corporation	234	2.72%	516	2.13%
9	Olayan Group of co.	145	1.69%	404	1.66%
10	Ernst Basler	135	1.57%	371	1.53%
Total		8,098		24,269	

Source: Meridien Hotel, Internal Document.

worldwide corporate rate, a Saudi Arabian corporate rate, promotion that includes invitations to lunch or dinner, gadgets given to distributors, and complimentary club memberships given to persons designated "decision makers." High level personal contact is used to promote the Gulf Meridien in each of the above ways. In order to serve the particular needs of each customer segment group, particularly businessmen and airline crews, efficiency is stressed in checking in and out and making up rooms as quickly as possible. A quick-dial telephone service, telex services, telephone books, and a business center are provided. Telephone messages are delivered, wake-up calls are done promptly, and the rooms are well laid out. The bathroom is completely equipped, including a telephone and hairdryer, and a TV video is provided for entertainment. Room service, a coffee shop, and a cafeteria are available twenty-four hours a day. Segregated facilities for sports and leisure are provided, including tennis, pool, sauna, and gymnasium facilities.

Airline crews enjoy all of the above and are welcomed by a refreshment upon arrival. Extra care is taken to ensure that their visit is leisurely and relaxed. Exhibit 5 provide further insight into how to serve hotel guests better.

The Gulf Meridien management claims that its systematic preparation and anticipation of guests' needs are the reasons for the above average occupancy rate of about 80%.

Exhibit 5   How to Better Serve Airline Crews

A Much Sought After Clientele Segment: Airline Crews
The "12 Key Points" concerning the crew clientele, more specifically how crews are to be welcomed, are more than ever before a major topic of discussion. Only five minutes are needed to break a contract which takes at least three years to re-establish. This clientele segment long remembers unfortunate experiences in a hotel. Let us make sure that this hotel is not one of ours. Aside from the fact that the airlines, which act both as ambassadors for our hotels to their passengers and as our main business partners, must never be neglected, crew clientele should be pampered, as it is a true source of steady revenue, and a good one.

One Basic Question: What Do Crews Expect When They Come to Our Hotel?
Services identical to those provided to businessmen. The rate paid for crews is almost identical to the corporate rate (see insert below). A smiling welcome, rapid delivery of baggage to the rooms, and the availability of a meal at any time, those are all highly appreciated by airline crews who spend long hours at high altitudes in a pressurized atmosphere. Crew members spend about half of their time in hotels, a fact worthy of serious consideration. What can the hotel offer? Welcome drinks. Little attentions, simple, but graciously proffered, are often preferable to expensive ones which may be somewhat less gracious in style. The products of the country are the best solution. Fresh orange or pineapple juice, for example, provide the guest with the feeling that he is indeed a well-appreciated guest. The hotel will know through the local airline agencies if any flights are late or if any have been added. It can also obtain a list of the names of the crew members. The reception attendant will, therefore, be able to assign the rooms in advance of arrival, prepare the keys, welcome cards and welcome drinks, and warn the porters to be ready. Finally, there are the meals at all hours. There is no question of presenting the full menu of the gastronomic restaurant. A choice of two or three cold platters is sufficient, but the possibility of choice is of the utmost importance. Assigning rooms: the rooms assigned must respect the terms of the contract as initially signed for crews. They must be far from any source of noise such as elevators, ice distributors, frequently used passageways, etc. Crew members must retain the right to request a change. Why not, if at all possible?

Period of High Occupancy
One precaution is to be taken by the hotel manager and his collaborators. Managers should maintain constant relations with the destination manager, greet the captain (who also may be area manager), and thus create a climate of confidence. Why not approach the airline heads concerning possible problems before they arise. Airlines are our business partners, and are themselves used to offering services to their clientele in often difficult circumstances. By describing the situation in a clear manner, the problem may be solved to the satisfaction of both parties (for example, lodgings provided in a different hotel but arranged by Meridien, with a letter of apology).

Enticing Food and Beverage Service
A specially adapted menu can be offered, but, above all, not a "crew menu" which can be considered discriminating and not very attractive. It is better to offer crews the regular guest's menu to which an insert has been added, listing dishes which are more adapted to the needs of crew members.

Special Services
Whenever the layout and operations of the hotel permit, it is good to be able to set aside a small lounge just for airline crews. Other types of extra attention, such as birthday cakes or Yule log cakes, should also be provided.

Representing 15% of our global volume of clientele (with Air France alone accounting for half of this), crews are a segment which are much sought after by all of our competitors (and by us, too of course!). But we cannot hope to expand on crew business if we do not, at the same time, develop adequate services which aim to satisfy the crew member. Airlines are also tour operators, often fulfilling a 110% commitment with extra flights.

(Interview of Jean Sarrazin, September 1984, C.C.)

B. Products, Services, and Facilities

It also claims that the hotel's location, structure, and design have all been well thought out in terms of volume, decor, furnishings and maintenance. After seven years, the hotel is in almost as good a shape as when it opened; this is supposedly due to quality construction and an excellent maintenance program.

Kitchen and dining facilities are adequate. Functional rooms (rooms for weddings, banquets, and exhibitions) are too small for large local gatherings. This is not considered a problem at present due to a decrease in the number of local people requesting such facilities.

Rate Description
Rate 40% lower than a moderate single rate. However, there is no payment of a commission to travel agencies. There is no credit card payment. Payment is regular at the end of each month. All of the above accounts for 20%, that is, in the vicinity of the corporate rate.

Public areas are well designed and built of quality materials. Recreational facilities were adequate when the pool first opened, but a second indoor swimming pool for women is being contemplated in order to better serve families while meeting the regulations of the Kingdom. A complete gymnasium is being contemplated in order to complement the present facilities. The hotel provides a video channel which operates almost twenty-four hours a day and also provides seven TV channels that receive programs from the Arabian Gulf area. A study is presently being made as to the feasibility of providing laundry facilities.

Food and Beverage

In addition to the cafeteria,which offers a variety of menus from Arabian to French, an international buffet is offered nightly. Another restaurant serves mostly European food. For banquets, weddings, etc., the menu is organized as requested by the guests. The Gulf Meridien dabbles in outside catering but is not as aggressive in this regard as other competing hotels.

The restaurant that presently serves mostly European food is being converted into an Asian style restaurant that will serve dishes from many different Asian countries. A Japanese restaurant management firm has been contacted about the possibility of opening and operating a Japanese restaurant. A carry-out pastry shop overlooking the main hall is being contemplated. Friday barbecue for families has been a success and will continue to be modified and expanded.

Meridien hotel management claims its room service is excellent (guest opinion is unknown). During this study, room service was personally tested. The order was delivered reasonably fast and the order was understood. The reliability of the study may be questionable, since the bulk of the staff are expatriates. There is potential for misunderstanding, due to the existence of language barriers.

The idea of private, separate dining areas for families is being studied. Also, separate dining areas for newly married couples and the younger generation are being considered. These dining alterations reflect changes in government regulations regarding the segregation of sexes in public areas.

Pricing

The Gulf Meridien has a different pricing strategy than the other hotels in the Eastern Province. The Gulf Meridien believes that its quality accommodations and service are under priced, and that higher rates are necessary. Present rates are SR 330 (US $ 100) + 15 % (service charge) for a single room, SR 430 + 15 % for a double room, and SR 700 + 15 % for an executive suite. The Meridien management says it would like a 10 % rate increase; however, the Ministry of Commerce froze all hotel room prices at a certain ceiling, and they are not allowed to go above this ceiling. Rate reductions are allowed. In a personal interview with the Meridien management, contradictory claims were made. It was said that the Meridien had applied to the Ministry of Commerce for a room price increase. Later, it was said the hotel may participate in a price war by lowering its room rates.

Pricing for food and beverages is considered adequate by management. Banquets are considered underpriced (reflecting competition), and meeting rooms are provided without charge for conferences if participants agree to purchase other hotel services (i.e. rooms and food).

Pricing reflects customer segmentation as follows:

- worldwide corporate rate – SR 280 + 15 % (service charge) for a single room;
- Saudi Arabian corporate rate – SR 265 + 15% each room for a minimum of 400 rooms per night, SR 250 + 15% each room for a minimum of 600 rooms per night, SR 235 + 15% each room for a minimum of 1,000 rooms per night;
- transit/layover passengers – SR 250 + 15% for a single room;
- package deals – rates adjusted per agreement based upon volume and length of stay.

Financial Matters

Although GM lost money in 1981 and 1982, it made up for the losses in subsequent years. The company is financially sound and compares favorably with its local competitors. It has experienced the highest occupancy rate for the last four years (1983–1986), which has made it the most profitable.

Since the company is privately-held, detailed financial statements are not readily available. However, selected ratios are used to portray its comparative financial health. Different sources are used to compute these ratios, and a few gaps are inevitable. Exhibits 6 and 7 provide the comparative costs and revenue structure of the luxury-class hotels in the Eastern-Province for the years 1982 through 1985. Several observations can be made:

a) The percentage of the management fee is significantly higher for GM than its immediate competitors.
b) The percentage of cost of food and beverage sold is lower for GM than its competitors.
c) GM is top on room sales and bottom on food sales.

Finally, GM enjoys good liquidity and an acceptable debt ratio. The liquidity ratio was 2.19, 2.40, 2.06 for 1981, 1982, 1983, respectively. The debt ratio increased significantly for the same years from 2.54 to 21.93 and 20.7.

Exhibit 6   Revenues Structure for First Class Hotels for 1982, 1983, 1984, and 1985. Al Gosaibi Hotel is excluded because it didn't provide the needed information.

Items	Hotels				
	Carlton	Meridien	DIH	Oberoi	Intl. Average
1982:					
Room sales	52	58.7	30	37.33	44.50
Food sales	34	22.6	23	46.99	31.64
Beverage sales	04	02	03		02.25
Other op. depts.	10	16.7	16	15.68	14.59
Airline catering	–	–	28	–	07
Total	100%	100%	100%	100%	100%
1983:					
Room Sales	55	57.4	33.6	38.72	46.18
Food Sales	33	23.4	26	45.76	32.04
Beverage Sales	3	2.3	–	–	1.32
Other op. depts.	9	16.9	17.6	15.52	14.75
Airline catering	–	00.0	22.8	–	05.7
Total	100%	100%	100%	100%	100%
1984:					
Room sales	50	57.5	33.7	40.04	45.3
Food sales	35	22.5	26.1	44.71	32.0
Beverage sales	4	2.3	–	–	1.6
Other op. depts.	11	17.9	17.4	15.25	15.4
Airline catering	–	00.0	22.8	–	05.7
Total	100%	100%	100%	100%	100%
1985:					
Room sales	54	57	43.7	44.39	47.26
Food sales	34	22	28.7	41.58	34.85
Beverage sales	03	3	–	–	01.00
Other op. depts.	09	18	18.2	14.03	13.77
Airline catering	–	00	9.4	–	3.12
Total	100%	100%	100%	100%	100%

Source: Primary, data compiled from different sources.

Exhibit 7   Costs Structure for First Class Hotels for 1982, 1983, 1984, and 1985. Al
Gosaibi, Meridien, and DIH hotels are partly excluded because they
didn't provide the needed information.

Items	Hotels				
	Carlton	Meridien	DIH	Oberoi	Intl. Average
1982:					
Salaries and Benefits	34	–	–	27.56	30.78
F and B Cost	11	–	–	14.19	12.59
Operating Expenses	26	–	–	30.25	28.12
Balance					
Depreciation, Interest and Others	29	–	–	28.00	28.50
Total	100	–	–	100	100 %
1983:					
Salaries and Benefits	35	–	–	27.23	31.11
F and B Cost	10	–	–	15.03	12.51
Operating Expenses	27	–	–	32.94	29.97
Balance					
Depreciation, Interest and Others	28	–	–	24.80	26.40
Total	100	–	–	100	100 %
1984:					
Salaries and Benefits	37	24	–	29.15	30.07
F and B Cost	09	8	–	13.83	11.41
Management fees					
Operating expenses	28	28	–	20.42	28.71
Balance					
Depreciation, Interest and Others	26	34	–	24.60	26.80
Management fees	–	6	–	3.50	3.20
Total	100	100	–	100	100 %
1985:					
Salaries and Benefits	34	25	–	26.55	30.27
F and B Cost	10	8	–	12.81	11.40
Operating Expenses	28	29	–	28.84	28.24
Balance					
Depreciation, Interest and Others	28	33	–	28.80	29.9
Management Fees	–	6	–	3.30	
Total	100	100	–	100	100 %

Source: Primary, data compiled from different sources.

Challenges Ahead

Excellent location is absolutely necessary for a successful hotel business. As mentioned above, the Gulf Meridien enjoys an excellent location because:

1) it is ten minutes from the Dhahran airport;
2) it is located on the beach and all rooms have a fine view;
3) it is located near the business center of Al-Khobar, and local and visiting businessmen find the location convenient;
4) it is only ten to fifteen minutes away from Dammam;
5) it has easy access to Mosques;
6) it is the center of new development projects; and
7) it is located near the most fashionable part of Al-Khobar.

Prior to 1984, the Meridien was somewhat isolated, but new roads have put an end to this problem. Since then, a number of exogenous variables are threatening the long-term survival of the hotel. First, with the reduced number of the international business travelers, a number of foreign-flag carriers, including Air France, have stopped their service or reduced their frequencies to Dhahran Airport. Second, with the opening of the Khobar-Bahrain Causeway, many Saudi businessmen and tourists prefer to "get away from it all" and spend their nights in Bahrain rather than Al-Khobar. Finally, the construction of the King Fahd International Airport is currently under way and expected to be completed by the end of 1989. It is an hour drive from the Meridien. Management believes that the new highway network will make the relocation of the Dhahran airport less of a headache. Such a change will only add fifteen to twenty minutes to the present travel time to the hotel. However, the hotel owners believe that something needs to be done to maintain the current occupancy rate and profitability level. They have contracted the services of a strategic planning consultant who specializes in hotels.

6.3   Al Gosaibi Hotel

M. Sami Kassem

Introduction

Recently, Mr. Mounir Tadros received word of his reappointment as general manager of the Al Gosaibi Hotel, a wholly-owned unit of the Al Gosaibi Group. The hotel is located in Al-Khobar in the Eastern Province of Saudi Arabia. Tadros is not a newcomer to this position; he occupied it previously in 1979–82, when he was working for the Grand Metropolitan Hotel chain. Thus, he knew the business, its owners, and the home office executives when he accepted his reappointment. However, while he was gone, the situation at the hotel had changed for the worse. A severe business contraction had hit the greater Dammam area in the center of the oil-rich Eastern Province. Among major hotels in the area, the Al Gosaibi was hit hardest (see Exhibits 1 and 2 for a comparative analysis of occupancy rates). Mr. Tadros was expected to bring about the strategic and operational turnaround needed to save the hotel and the jobs of its employees.

Both Mr. Tadros and the home office executives realized there were several unique features of this challenging assignment. As a self-motivated achiever, Mr. Tadros decided to diagnose the patient and assess its changes for recovery before accepting the assignment. As he reviewed the case history of the hotel since 1982, when, he left as general manager, the following picture emerged.

Exhibit 1   Al Gosaibi Hotel vs. its Competitors: Capacity Share and Market Share

Hotel	Capacity Share %	Market Share 1985	% 1986
Al Gosaibi	29.4	22	20
Gulf Meridien	28.8	37	39
Dhahran International	16	17	16
Oberoi	25	25	24

Source: Primary, based on field data and secondary information provided by the Hotel Division of the Saudi Department of Commerce.

Exhibit 2   Occupancy Rate (in %)

	1980	1981	1982	1983	1984	1985	1986
Al Gosaibi	49	58	57	55	48	36	35
Gulf Meridien	–	–	60	80	81	70	70
Dhahran International	44	71	73	68	63	56	50
Oberoi	–	–	–	60	65	55	50

Source: Primary, based on field data and checked against information provided by the Hotel Division of the Saudi Department of Commerce.

Overview

Al Gosaibi is the oldest luxury hotel in the Eastern Province and the second oldest one in the Kingdom, right after the Riyadh Intercontinental.

It is conveniently located in Al-Khobar – off the Dammam-Khobar coast highway, not far from Dhahran International Airport. The four-story hotel has 300 rooms, 37 suites, and 25 villas. It also has an Olympic-size swimming pool, a recreational center, a conference hall, three rooms for banquets or weddings, and the largest exhibition hall in the Eastern Province.

When it opened for business in June 1973, its occupancy rate was a phenomenal 150 %. Some guests slept on lobby couches or in the corridor. Single rooms operated in two shifts. Daily rates were sky-high: 550 Saudi riyals a night (US $ 160). The Al Gosaibi family ran the hotel during these formative years with the help of few foreign managers.

However, the seller's market did not last for long. Other hotels soon mushroomed in response to high demand and lucrative government incentives. In the Dammam metropolitan area, which includes Dhahran and Al-Khobar, five big new hotels were built: the Dhahran International in 1978, Carlton Al Moaibed in 1978, the Dhahran Marriott in 1979, the Gulf Meridien in 1982, and the Dammam Oberoi in 1983. One of these, the Gulf Meridien, was built within a few hundred meters of the Al Gosaibi Hotel. All but one – the Carlton – are luxury class hotels. This huge new bedding capacity threatened to depress occupancy rates. Under pressure from hotel owners, the government stopped issuing licenses to build new hotels. It further regulated the industry by fixing a ceiling for room rates and by requiring Saudization of critical jobs and conformity to the Islamic code of behavior.

A couple of demand-related events led to the eventual collapse of the market for luxury hotels in the Eastern Province. First, an oil-induced business recession hit the area very hard. Incoming passenger traffic at

Dhahran International Airport was drying up. A number of giant airlines stopped their service to Dhahran, including Pan American, Swissair, and Lufthansa. A number of joint ventures dissolved. Several business firms cancelled their permanent block room reservations in major area hotels and started accommodating their visitors in their own guest houses. The Marriott Hotel was converted into a hospital.

Furthermore, in 1986 the opening of the King Fahd Causeway linking Al-Khobar to Bahrain lured the Saudi leisure traveler to Bahrain hotels.

While all luxury hotels suffered, Al Gosaibi suffered the most. Whereas the luxury hotel market declined 24% over the 1983–86 period. Al Gosaibi's business declined by 45%. Its full-paying clients were going to the competition.

Previously, to cope with declining occupancy rates, the Al Gosaibi family contracted the Grand Metropolitan Hotel (GMH) to manage the hotel on their behalf for SR 700,000 per year. The owners thought that the GMH name, reservation system, superior recruitment, training programs, and purchasing expertise would help improve the deteriorating situation. Responding to pressure from the next management contract firm – the Forum Hotels – the Al Gosaibi family launched a SR 20 million renovation program geared to improve the hotel's interiors and exteriors and upgrade the amenities of the guest rooms.

Despite some handicaps, the Al Gosaibi Hotel is a substantial investment property that has a historic presence in the area.

Personnel

The size and composition of the hotel labor force is changing. There are 280 employees now compared with 380 five years ago. Highly-paid staffers are being replaced by lower-paid employees from the Middle East and Far East. Job security is an issue on the minds of present employees. Few of the present staff are European-trained. Saudi employees are virtually missing from the payroll.

Financial Position

The hotel is meeting its obligation on time. Its receivables are collected on time, but were it not for the tight austerity program, the hotel would be in the red. Rather, it is doing a bit better than breaking even, generating a net profit of 6% for its owners. The food and beverage category of service is not pulling its weight. Fewer funds are being directed to operations and maintenance (see Exhibit 3 for a comparative analysis of sources and uses of funds).

Marketing

Exhibit 4 clearly shows that the Al Gosaibi focuses on large corporate accounts (airline crews, traveling businessmen, exhibitors). These accounts are heavily discounted. One has to sell more of these accounts simply to break even. They are very difficult to attract and retain and, because they involve multiple bookings, the loss of just one account can hurt the hotel's profitability. Such was the case, for instance, when Thai International Airlines cancelled its contract with Al Gosaibi in December 1986, presumably because its crews were not getting the personalized attention they sought. This narrow focus on the discounted corporate account diverts management attention from the walk-in customer – traditionally the most profitable type of account for luxury hotels. About two-thirds of the hotel's customers are non-Arabs and 15 % are Arabs (see Exhibit 4) for details of client mix).

Two future events worry Mr. Tadros. Their likely effect on the hotel's occupancy rates and profitability remains to be seen. First is the upcoming relocation of Dhahran International Airport, possibly by 1990. The new airport – renamed King Fahd International – is about 75 kilometers away from the Al Gosaibi Hotel and only 18 kilometers from the new Holiday Inn at Jubail.

The second worrisome event is the planned opening of the Dhahran EXPO Center late in 1988. This is a permanent large-scale exhibition facility.

Home Office – Hotel Management Relation

Historically, the owners of the Al Gosaibi Hotel have run the business themselves on and off. Despite the fact that they are primarily traders rather than hoteliers and have about 20 different businesses to run, they seem to have been ambivalent about subcontracting the management of the hotel to specialized agencies.

The home office of the Al Gosaibi Group performs the following functions:

– plan the strategic portfolio;

Exhibit 3   Composition of Revenues and Expenses, Luxury Hotels, 1985

| Revenues = 100% | | | | | | Hotel Name | Expenses = 100% | | | | |
Room	Food and beverages	Banquets and wedding	Business services	Catering	Laundry		Payroll	Food and beverages	Operation and maintenance	Management fee	Marketing costs
40	22	9	8	3	7	Al Gosaibi	40	30	9	–	21
58	25	3	10	2	2	Gulf Meridien	34	31	27	5	3
36	27	0	10	24	3	Oberoi	26	38	18	4	14
44	29	5	4	10	8	Dhahran Int'l	46	28	22	2	2

Source: Primary, data compiled from different sources.

Exhibit 4   Core Clients and Client Mix of Luxury Hotels, 1985

| Core Client Group % | | | | Hotel Name | Client Mix % | | | | |
Airline crews	Buisnessmen	Pleasure traveller	Exhibition guests		Saudis	Arabs	Westerners	Far Easterners	Others
63	27	–	10	Al Gosaibi	6	9	31	28	26
30	70	–	–	Gulf Meridien	60	6	27	7	–
42	58	–	–	Oberoi	40	12	32	13	3
36	58	6	–	Dhahran Int'l	16	22	29	13	20

Source: Primary, data compiled from different sources.

- design, implement, and monitor the budgetary control system;
- select and decide the replacement of the general manager of each subsidiary;
- manage each business on a personal basis, particularly when its performance is judged to be unsatisfactory;
- perform some support functions on a pooled basis, such as purchasing, government relations, and internal auditing.

All imported items the hotel intends to purchase from abroad and all purchase orders in excess of 25,000 riyals have to be authorized by the central purchasing division. Internal auditors are expected to drop in unannounced to check the hotel's books. In addition to normal transactions, they audit operations, personnel, and purchasing. The general manager is expected to report to Dr. Hussein Al-Samadi, assistant vice-president for operations (see Exhibit 5 for details).

The New General Manager

Mr. Tadros is not sure whether he can turn the hotel around. One thing he can be sure of, however, is himself. Though born and educated in Egypt, he is a European-trained hotelier. He is a 1968 graduate of the Swiss Hotel School and a member of the Hotel Catering and Institutional Management Association (HCIMA). He is multi-lingual. He has managed a number of luxury and first-class hotels throughout Europe and the Middle East and has worked for a leading international hotel consulting firm. Based on independent sources, Mr. Tadros is generally well-liked and respected by people inside the hotel and around the home office. However, he is aware of the fact that his immediate superiors, both of whom are Palestinians, may not wish him well. Mr. Tadros summarized his position as follows:

"I'm offered a challenging assignment involving a larger number of changes – a renovated facility, a reduced and scared staff, and a buyer's market. But most of all I will be dealing with a set of changed relationships."

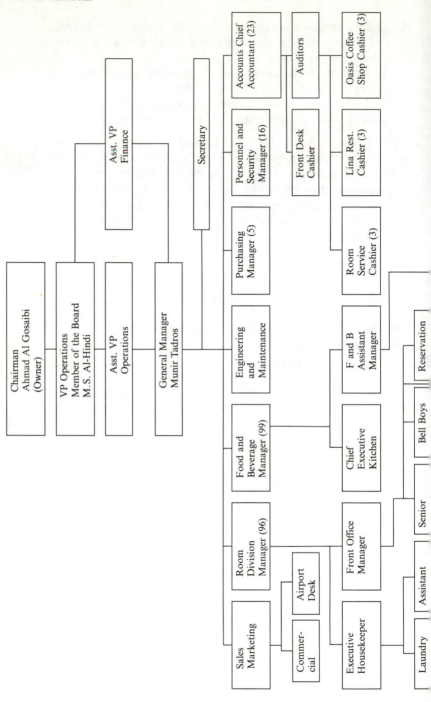

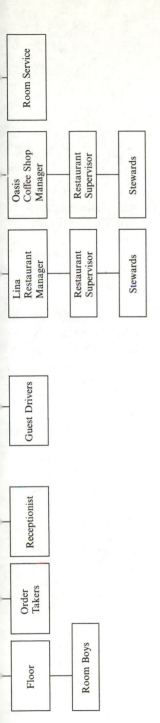

Exhibit 5   Partial Organization Chart

6.4 Al-Hamra Hotel

Eman Al Betairi and Ghazi M. Habib

Introduction

In the early 1980s, Mr. Abdulaziz Al-Shiha, a Saudi businessman, established Al-Hamra Hotel through a governmenal loan of SR 15 million secured from the Ministry of Finance and National Economy.

Al-Hamra is a budget hotel and is unique in several aspects. It has a room capacity of 36 single bedrooms, 74 double bedrooms, and 14 deluxe rooms. Each room has its own bathroom, TV set, an international telephone dial, two in-house video channels, and six musical channels.

Al-Hamra Hotel is located on King Khalid Street right in the middle of Dammam's busy business center. The hotel is managed by Mr. Hans, a very experienced Swiss hotelier. His career in the hotel business started when he joined a Swiss hotel as a chef. Later, after reaching the position of chief chef, he quit his job to study hotel management in England. He has been working as a general manager of Al-Hamra Hotel for about six years, when this case study was written. The business connections that he established with the local business community as well as with hotels in his own country and most other European countries have helped to attract business to Al-Hamra. The hotel offers services to local businessmen and those traveling from Europe. His association with the Swiss hotel management company "COMANA AG" and Swissair have enabled the hotel to attract Western businessmen looking for clean, goods, and reasonably priced accommodations. Western customers feel at home in the atmosphere created in Al-Hamra Hotel.

Capitalizing on his strong background in food and beverage business, the hotel has been able to offer excellent food services through its restaurants and catering activities. The food and beverage revenues provide a valuable substitute for room revenues, which have declined. Al-Hamra Hotel is also unique in having a budget rent-a-car as well as an overnight dining service, SNASS, located in the hotel lobby.

The owner of the hotel and its management have been concerned about the continuous decline in room occupancy. They scheduled a number of sessions to analyze the changes that have been taking place in the internal and external environment affecting the hotel industry in Saudi Arabia in general and Al-Hamra Hotel in particular.

Hotel Organization

Exhibit 1 shows that the hotel is organized into five main divisions:

Food and Beverage Division

This division is headed by an Indian manager personally supervised by the general manager. It runs three restaurants: the grill room, Chinese restaurant, and recently opened Mamma Mia restaurant. It also provides outside catering for banquets and runs a coffee shop, tea lounge, mini-bar, and room service.

Exhibit 2 shows the breakdown of food and beverage sales by type of function in 1985. About 76% of food and beverage revenues come from the grill room, Chinese restaurant, and the coffee shop.

Rooms Division

This division is in charge of room cleaning and preparation for occupancy.

Accounting Division

This division handles and maintains general ledger, and prepares budgets, balance sheets, and income statements. It also handles all billing and invoicing activities.

Maintenance Division

This division performs the maintenance work of the hotel and is headed by a chief engineer, who supervises the work of the mechanical and electrical crews.

Marketing Division

The marketing division consists of two groups: the front-office, which handles customer reservations and inquiries, safety boxes, cashier functions, and customer relations; and the sales and marketing group. The latter contacts current and potential customers, visits companies, and explains to them the features of the hotel. It also contacts local promotion and advertising agencies for designing and printing hotel pamphlets, brochures, business cards, and promotional gifts.

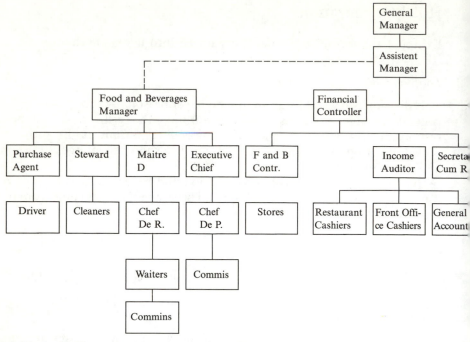

Exhibit 1   Al-Hamra Hotel Organizational Structure

Exhibit 2   Al-Hamra Hotel – Dammam, Food and Beverage Sales (1985)

Type	%
Banquet	11.1
Tea lounge and minibar	6.2
Chinese restaurant	26.7
Grill room	27.5
Coffee shop	21.5
Room services	7.0
Total	100.0

Source: Al-Hamra Hotel.

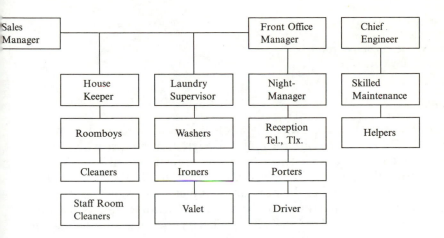

Pricing

The surplus of room capacity and the declining number of foreign businessmen visiting the Gulf region have triggered a price war within the lodging industry. At Al-Hamra Hotel, the prices of the rooms fluctuate between an upper and lower limit depending on demand and the importance of the customer to the hotel. The following prices were quoted by the general manager and are subject to further discounts (Exhibit 3).

Price discounts are mainly given on single bedrooms frequently used by business travelers. Discounts on other accommodations are limited and depend on the type of customer (single or with family) and the number of nights the customer stays. Special discounts are given to newcomers and loyal customers who repeat their visits.

Exhibit 3   Prices at Al-Hamra Hotel

Room Type	Price/Night (SR)
Single bedroom	185–230
Double bedroom	276
Junior suite (one bedroom and one sitting room)	400
Senior suite (one master bedroom, one single bedroom, and one sitting room)	518

Customer Mix

Foreign businessmen represent 67% of the hotel's total customers. Europeans and Americans are the major foreign nationalities who use the hotel. Exhibit 4 shows a comparison between the customer mix of 1984 and 1985. It shows that the hotel has successfully adapted to the new trend in economic conditions and to the declining number of foreign businessmen by targeting Gulf nationals and Saudi customers. Customer nights declined slightly in 1985 compared to 1984 (13%). The average customer stay in Al-Hamra Hotel ranges from two to three nights.

Exhibit 4   Al-Hamra Hotel – Dammam

Customer Mix	Saudi (%)	Arab (%)	European (%)	American (%)	Far East (%)	Others (%)	Customers Nights
(1985)	31.21	18.11	31.1	4.1	15.42	0.13	22,723
(1984)	18.0	15.2	44.0	4.5	18.3	0.10	26,150

Source: Data compiled by the authors.

Exhibit 5   Al-Hamra Hotel – Dammam, Types of Customers

Customer Type	1984	1985	1986 January	February
Direct reservations (%)	40.5	32.6	19	39
Airport shuttle (%)	1.1	1.0	1.6	3.0
Walk in (%)	41.2	47.6	65	37.3
UTELL reservation system HORIS reservation system (%)	0.7	0.36	0.4	0.4
House guests (%)	16.4	18.5	14.0	20.3
Airlines (%)	0.1	–	–	–
Total	100	100	100	100

Source: Al-Hamra Hotel.

Exhibit 6 Customer Mix for Budget Class Segment – 1985 "Dammam – Khobar Area"

Hotel Name (City)	Saudi (%)	Arab (%)	European (%)	American (%)	Far East (%)	Others (%)	Total Customer Nights	Market Share (%)
Al Hamra (Dammam)	31.21	18.11	31.1	4.1	15.42	0.13	22.723	19.60
Dammam (Dammam)	28.46	10.52	31.39	6.03	6.60	17.00	7.665	6.60
Al-Nemer (Dammam)	65.6	22.6	6.05	0.53	5.20	–	5.324	4.60
Al Arifi (Dammam)	52.8	23.5	11.6	0.83	10.50	0.80	5,265	4.50
Balhamer (Dammam)	56.6	17.64	1.95	2.70	20.11	1.0	6,277	5.40
Al-Nimran (Al-Khobar)	53.75	20.62	11.13	1.25	5.0	8.25	9,319	8.02
Al-Nasr Royal (Al-Khobar)	3.25	8.88	5.38	0.83	81.0	0.68	35,307	30.40
Al-Khobar Palace (Al-Khobar)	46.2	21.94	18.60	3.56	6.24	2.5	7,473	6.43
Al-Hammad (Al-Khobar)	64.0	19.0	3.25	2.0	10.75	1.0	11,752	10.10
Al-Kadisiyah (Al-Khobar)	66.13	22.18	1.33	0.40	4.40	4.90	5,081	4.35

Source: Field data compiled by the authors.

Exhibit 5 shows the hotel major types of customers during the 1984–85 period. Direct reservations, walk-ins, and house guests represent over 98 % of the hotel's customers. There is some seasonableness in the arrival pattern of this type of customer. During summer (June, July, August, and September), the walk-in segment accounts for more than 62 % of the hotel's customers. Direct reservation customers are mainly corporate customers who stay on their company's account and are mainly of Western nationalities. House guests are customers staying more than one night and account for about 20 % of the total customers at the hotel.

Exhibit 6 shows the customer mix for the budget hotel class in the Dammam – Al-Khobar area during 1985. Al-Nasr Royal customers are mainly Korean Airline crews (81 % of its customers), with Saudi customers representing only 3 % of the hotel's customers. Al-Hamra and Dammam Hotel customers seem to be spread among different nationalities. Al-Hamra Hotel attracts about 46 % of the European and 36 % of the American customers staying in budget hotels. Al-Nasr Royal, the market leader, had registered the highest occupancy rate in 1985 (69 %), followed by the Dammam Hotel (57 %) and Al-Hamra (47 %).

Competition

In the budget class segment, the major competitors are listed in Exhibit 7.

Exhibit 8 shows the occupancy rate for the competing hotels in the budget class in the Dammam–Al-Khobar area.

Exhibit 7   Major Competitors

Hotel Name	Market Share
Al-Nasr Royal	30.4%
Al-Hamra	19.6%
Al-Hammad	10.1%
Al-Nimran	8.0%
Dammam	6.6%
Al-Khobar Palace	6.4%

Exhibit 9 shows the core clients, major sources of revenue, and the relative strengths and weaknesses of each competitor in the local budget class hotel market.

Exhibit 8 Occupancy Rate for Budget Class Segment

Hotel Name (City)	1983 Avg.	1984					1985				
		Q1	Q2	Q3	Q4	Avg.	Q1	Q2	Q3	Q4	Avg.
Al-Hamra (Dammam)	65.5	75.0	57.1	50.2	62.4	61.18	58.1	47.8	42.0	40.3	47.0
Dammam (Dammam)	62.2	58.7	57.7	56.7	49.7	55.7	63.3	62.7	53.0	49.3	57.1
Al-Nemer (Dammam)	24.8	25.7	20.0	20.3	24.7	22.7	28.7	25.3	32.0	35.0	30.3
Al-Arifi (Dammam)	55.0	55.7	44.0	41.6	50.2	47.9	49.4	40.0	33.5	33.7	39.2
Balhamer (Dammam)	NA	46.7	37.3	42.3	37.2	40.9	41.0	34.0	34.6	25.3	33.7
Al-Nimran (Al-Khobar)	45.0	52.0	41.0	40.0	36.0	42.0	41.0	38.0	42.0	37.0	39.5
Al-Nasr Royal (Al-Khobar)	85.0	76.0	67.0	60.0	72.0	68.8	78.0	73.0	64.0	61.0	69.0
Al-Khobar Palace (Al-Khobar)	NA	44.0	41.0	35.7	53.0	43.4	41.8	37.0	40.3	43.7	40.7
Al-Hammad (Al-Khobar)	NA	24.0	22.0	35.0	30.0	27.8	34.0	26.0	33.0	27.0	30.0
Al-Kadisiyah (Al-Khobar)	NA	26.0	20.3	20.3	18.2	21.2	15.7	18.4	22.2	18.2	18.6

Source: Field data compiled by the authors.

Exhibit 9   Competition in the Budget Class

Hotel	Core Clients	Major Revenue Sources	Strengths	Weaknesses
1. Al-Nasr Royal (Al-Khobar)	Korean Airline crews	F & B – 50 % Rooms – 39 %	– Excellent Lebanese food – Business connections with Korean Airlines – Location in Al-Khobar residential area – Price	– Customer mix not strategically distributed – Less emphasis on Saudi customers and culture
2. Al-Hamra (Damman)	Western and Saudi businessmen	Rooms 43.5 % F & B 32.5 % Room services 13 %	– Excellent connection with local businessmen – The Swiss identity and strong association with Swissair – Western and Chinese foods – Customer mix is strategically distributed – Location is in the heart of Dammam business area	– The outside look of the hotel – Future expansion is limited – Lack of Arabic food in the menu
3. Al-Hammad (Al-Khobar)	Saudi businessmen families	Rooms 69 % F & B 16 %	– Business connection of the owner – Location is near Al-Khobar shopping area (Al-Suwaiket) – Price	– Old building and outdated facilities – Heavily dependent on rooms as a prime source of revenues – Poor management
4. Al-Nimran (Al-Khobar)	Saudi and Arab, businessmen	Rooms 65 % Rest. 18 % Room services 11 %	– Excellent location in Khobar residental area – Price – Large parking area	– The F & B cost is significantly high (38 % of total costs) – Highly dependent on rooms as a prime source of revenues
5. Dammam (Damman)	Indian and Western businessmen	Rooms 52 % Rest. 24 %	– Its association with Dammam Oberoi – Price	– Location behind Dammam Oberoi – The building is of portabletype – Less emphasis on Saudi customers

Personnel

Al-Hamra Hotel has employees representing eight different countries. Exhibit 10 shows that about 93 % of the manpower employed in the hotel comes from the developing countries of India, Thailand, the Philippines, and Pakistan due to the low wages employees from these countries can demand. Saudi nationals account for a small number, because only few Saudis have degrees in hotel management.

Exhibit 10   Al-Hamra Hotel – Dammam, Manpower – 1985

Nationality	Number
Indian	35
Thai	40
Filipino	23
Pakistan	14
Swiss	3
Saudi	2
Egyptian	2
Moroccan	1
Total	120

Source: Al-Hamra Hotel.

Finance

Revenue from rooms has been the most vulnerable to economic fluctuations in the region. However, at Al-Hamra, it only represents 43 % of total revenue, compared with an average of 51 % for all budget hotels in the Eastern Province of Saudi Arabia. Al-Hamra Hotel managed to shift its strategic emphasis from rooms as a major source of revenue to food and beverages, which accounted for 46 % of the hotel's total revenues in 1985 (see Exhibit 11). The shift was in response to the decline in the business travel market that had seriously affected budget hotels. Al-Hamra and Al-Nasr Royal were the least affected by this trend. Al-Hamra Hotel has continued its efforts in promoting food and beverages as a major source of revenue by opening the Mamma Mia restaurant near the hotel in Dammam. However, the hotel profitability has suffered a continuous decline during the past few years. The peak profitable years were in 1983 and 1984, and since then the hotel's profitability has declined at the rate of 10– % per year. Exhibit 12 shows a summarized income statement of the hotel for 1984. It shows that the hotel realized a net profit of SR 1,259,000 in 1984, or 9.19% of total operating revenues. The loan repayment of SR 1.5 million represents the yearly installment owed to the Ministry of Finance as part of a payback schedule which will end in 1990.

Exhibits 13, 14, and 15 give a breakdown of annual revenues and expenses in the budget hotel class by type of service.

Exhibit 11   Al-Hamra Hotel – Dammam Annual Sales Break Down

Type	1985	1984
Rooms	43.5	44.3
Food and beverages	45.5	43.9
Telephone/telex	9.1	9.8
Dry laundry cleaning	1.0	0.8
Miscellaneous	0.9	1.2
Total	100.0	100.0

Source: Al-Hamra Hotel.

Exhibit 12   Al-Hamra Hotel – Dammam, Income Statement (SR 000)

	1984
A. Operating revenues:	
– Department revenues	13,407
– Other revenues	291
Total operating revenues	13,698
B. Operating expenses:	
– Cost of sales	5,958
– Depreciation	2,500
– Marketing	875
– Maintenance	210
– General and administration	1,381
Total operating expenses	10,924
Operating income (loss)	2,774
C. Non-operating expenses:	
– Loan repayment	1,500
D. Net income (loss)	1,274

Source: Al-Hamra Hotel.

Exhibit 13   Annual Revenues Break Down by Type of Services Budget Class 1985

Hotel Name (City)	Rooms (%)	Room services (%)	Restau- rants (%)	Laundry services (%)	Outside catering (%)	Other services (%)
Al-Hamra (Dammam)	43.5	13.0	27.5	1.0	5.0	10.0
Dammam (Dammam)	51.8	4.2	24.0	3.7	–	16.3
Al-Nemer (Dammam)	73.0	4.0	7.0	1.0	6.0	9.0
Al-Arifi (Dammam)	70.0	5.0	20.0	3.0	2.0	–
Al-Nimran (Al-Khobar)	65.0	11.0	18.0	–	0.5	5.5
Al-Nasr Royal (Al-Khobar)	39.0	5.0	40.0	1.0	5.0	10.0
Al-Khobar Palace (Al-Khobar)	55.0	8.0	17.0	4.0	2.0	14.0
Al-Hammad (Al-Khobar)	68.5	3.5	16.0	–	–	12.0

Source: Data compiled by the authors.

Challenges

Al-Hamra's owner and managers are contemplating the appropriate strategic response to the changes affecting the lodging industry in the Eastern Province of Saudi Arabia. In the Eastern Province, the hotel industry is bearing the brunt of the slowdown in the oil industry. Hotels there do not benefit from Hajj customers, as hotels in the Western Province do. Nor do they benefit from customers calling on the government or foreign embassies, as hotels in the capital of Riyadh do. Rather, Eastern Province hotels are highly dependent on the oil industry. For example, Aramco, a major driving force for the hotel business in the Eastern Province, shook the industry when it cancelled its permanent hotel reservations – a total of 120 rooms booked year round for visiting consultants and businessmen who are now accommodated in the company's guest houses as part of Aramco's cost-saving measures. Unofficial industry statistics show that in 1983, the total demand for room accommodations was at 60% of the available capacity in the Eastern

Exhibit 14   Annual Expenses Break Down, Budget Class – 1985

Hotel name (City)	Adminis-tration (%)	Employees-salaries (%)	Marketing (%)	Food and beverages (%)	Taxes (%)	Others (%)
Al-Hamra (Dammam)	15.0	30.0	10.0	29.0	2.0	14.0
Dammam (Dammam)	18.0	31.5	4.0	18.0	2.0	26.5
Al-Nemer (Dammam)	13.0	50.0	2.0	16.0	1.0	18.0
Al-Arifi (Dammam)	22.0	27.0	5.0	30.0	3.0	13.0
Al-Nimran (Al-Khobar)	18.0	31.0	5.0	38.0	1.0	7.0
Al-Nasr Royal (Al-Khobar)	15.0	35.0	5.0	30.0	1.0	14.0
Al-Khobar Palace (Al-Khobar)	18.0	32.0	5.0	18.0	3.0	24.0
Al-Hammad (Al-Khobar)	27.5	36.5	2.5	17.0	1.0	15.5

Source: Data compiled by the authors.

Exhibit 15   Weighted – Average Revenues and Expenses Break Down Budget Class Segment – 1985

Annual Revenues	Rooms (%)	Room services (%)	Restau-rants (%)	Laundry services (%)	Outside catering (%)	Other services (%)
Break down	51.1	7.2	26.9	1.3	3.3	10.2

Annual Expenses	Adminis-tration (%)	Employees salaries (%)	Market-ing (%)	Food and Beverages (%)	Taxes (%)	Others (%)
Break down	17.3	33.6	5.6	26.6	1.5	15.4

Source: Data compiled by the authors.

Province, due primarily to the sudden oil slump. The reduction in volume of business had, therefore, prompted an undeclared price war between the major hotels in the area. Discounts of up to 30 % of posted prices was the rule, not the exception. The major hotels also started to upgrade their facilities to attract more customers. For example, Al-Gosaibi Hotel launched a three-year renovation program at an estimated cost of about SR 20 million. The Gulf Meridien opened in September 1984, while the Dammam Oberoi expanded its banquet and exhibition facilities.

Al-Hamra Hotel management is concerned about the impact of the King Fahd Causeway, connecting Saudi Arabia and the state of Bahrain, on its business. Western customers, who are eligible for a 72-hour visa to Bahrain, may find the Bahraini hotel atmosphere more like home.

Generally, customers observed that the outside physical appearance of Al-Hamra Hotel was not very attractive. Furthermore, room for future expansion of the hotel is limited. The hotel's newly opened Mamma Mia restaurant is in a separate location a few blocks from the hotel.

Management is considering catering some of its services to Saudis and Gulf nationals. This would require adding an Arabic meal to its menu and perhaps hiring more Saudi or Gulf nationals.

Chapter 7
Health Care Industry

7.1 A Note on the Health Care Industry

M. Sami Kassem

Introduction and Overview

Health care is one of the services which GCC planners have singled out for special attention. Together with education, their government policies have always been to provide these essential services to their citizens free of charge. This commitment has resulted in a phenomenal growth in the number of hospitals and hospital beds, as well as a growth in medical, technical, and administrative personnel.

Exhibit 1 provides a statistical portrait of the outstanding achievements attained by the GCC states regarding health care policies.

The GCC's achievement in the health care field cannot be measured in numbers alone. Quality is important as well. A qualitative index of achievement is the change in the citizens' attitude regarding health care. In the past, the average citizen did not have faith in the quality of medical care he was getting locally. Experience taught him that he had to go out of the GCC states to get quality care. Now this attitude is rapidly disappearing. Patients are patronizing local hospitals in increasing numbers and for every conceivable ailment.

The Quality of Care: The Case of Kuwait

The quality of medical care can be evaluated by such measures as availability and accessibility of medical services, the level of medical technology (science of medicine), the therapist-patient relationship (art of medicine), and the outcome of medical practice. Availability of and accessibility to medical care is high in Kuwait. For one thing, Kuwait compares favorably well on the population per doctor ratio. There is one doctor for every 570 persons in Kuwait, against 553 elsewhere in the developed world. For another, everyone is assigned to a clinic where an attending physician is available at all times. In less than one generation,

Exhibit 1   Statistical Profile of Health Care Services in the GCC States (1980–1984)

Country	No. of Government Hospitals					No. of Private Hospitals and Private Clinics					No. of Physicians					No. of Beds in Government Hospitals				
	'80	'81	'82	'83	'84	'80	'81	'82	'83	'84	'80	'81	'82	'83	'84	'80	'81	'82	'83	'84
United Arab Emirates	20	25	25	27	28	76	90	96	114	119	1,244	1,682	1,676	1,742	1,840	2,972	4,148	3,919	4,125	4,853
Bahrain	6	9	9	8	8	38	37	36	40	40	–	403	432	455	459	–	1,071	1,056	1,036	1,093
Saudi Arabia	69	70	72	78	93	911	1,454	1,549	1,755	1,879	6,536	7,680	9,663	11,443	14,267	17,547*	18,849*	20,777*	24,047*	26,410*
Oman	14	14	14	15	15	108	126	265	410	555	543	632	668	831	1,021	1,784	1,866	2,041	2,133	2,587
Qatar	4	4	5	4	4	127	161	162	188	197	297	336	530	497	539	713	747	872	891	900
Kuwait	11	14	15	15	17	673	708	731	782	820	2,441	2,580	2,726	2,834	2,983	5,148	5,036	5,471	5,479	5,522
Total for GCC	123	133	137	145	165	1,923	2,579	2,841	3,292	3,618	11,061	12,312	15,715	17,802	21,10	28,164	31,717	24,134	27,711	41,366

Source: Gulf Council of Cooperation 1987: 258.

usership of modern health service has been extended from a tiny minority to the great majority of residents in Kuwait. Per capita medical utilization rates are higher in Kuwait than in the United States. For example, according to Nagi (1983), the per capita utilization rate is 8 to 9 visits per year in Kuwait against 4 to 8 in the U.S.

Kuwait has at present the lowest levels of mortality and the highest expectancy of life at birth. In 1981, for example, the infant mortality rate was approximately 39 per 1,000, and life expectancy at birth was 70 years. By contrast, Yemen has an infant mortality rate of approximately 162 and a life expectancy of about 41 years.

During its twenty-year development, the health care system in Kuwait has managed admirable accomplishments. These include:

1) eliminating financial barriers to access;
2) making the system more rational and equitable;
3) providing care on a community level with community-based primary physicians; and
4) maintaining a high level of medical care quality. The Kuwait health care system is by no means a medical utopia. Because it is a public welfare service, it must compete with other services, such as education, housing, and income maintenance, for funding; therefore, by some accounts it is perceptibly underfinanced. Although inequities of services have lessened, they have not totally disappeared.

Health Care Expansion in GCC States

The expansion of health care in the GCC states has been rapid, as well as uncoordinated (see Exhibit 2). In virtually all of the Gulf states, the Ministry of Health (MOH) provides about two-thirds of the hospital beds. Many government agencies and private firms offer first-class service to their employees through their own network of clinics and hospitals.

Exhibit 2   Growth of Health-Care in Private Sector in Saudi Arabia (1981–1985)

Service	1981	1982	1983	1984	1985	% of Change
Clinics	491	545	639	729	771	+ 57%
Hospitals	28	31	32	31	37	+ 24%
Beds	2,685	3,264	3,440	3,412	3,993	+ 48%
Physicians	1,436	1,966	2,634	3,024	2,942	+ 104%
Nurses	2,062	3,422	4,548	4,722	5,257	+ 157%

Source: Saudi Arabia's Ministry of Health 1985.

The financing of health care comes from two primary sources: (1) the government through government agencies, and (2) the private sector which has resulted in "for profit" or "proprietary" hospitals and health care centers. Just as in other capital-intensive service industries, the private sector is a newcomer to the hospital industry. GCC businessmen were not attracted to the industry until the mid-1970's when a seductive public policy coupled with a healthy business environment made their entry less difficult. However, for reasons that will be pointed out later, their successful stay in that business is uncertain – given its prohibitive economics.

Health Care Providers: The Case of Saudi Arabia

The growth of medical care in Saudi Arabia has proven contagious. As Exhibit 2 indicates, the growth in health care has had a tremendous impact on the availability of clinics and hospitals as well as medical personnel. At first, hospitals were built in Jeddah, Riyadh, and the Dammam area. Private medicine coupled with the incentives to establish hospitals in the Kingdom are beginning to make significant contributions in creating available hospitals.

The Ministry of Health has been assisted by the Saudi Arabian National Guard (SANG), and the Ministry of Defense and Aviation (MODA), both of which maintain large, well-equipped hospitals throughout the Kingdom. In addition, the Ministry of Education is working with the Ministry of Health to provide medical schools to produce a new generation of Saudi doctors. This cooperation of ministries enabled the Kingdom by 1985 to maintain 180 hospitals which provided 30,959 beds. The bed/population ratio had reached 2.95/1000, while the doctor/population ratio was 1/705.

The largest organization in Saudi Arabia health care is the Ministry of Health, which is responsible for 62 % of the nation's hospital bed capacity. The ministry operates approximately 105 hospitals with close to 20,800 beds, and has planned 67 new hospitals which would add another 13,845 beds. The Ministry of Defense and Aviation (MODA) is number two in the Kingdom's health care field, operating 21 hospitals with 3,954 beds. MODA tends to hire foreign management firms such as Whittaker and HCA to manage its hospitals.

SANG is an essential provider of imported health care through its 500-bed hospitals in Jeddah and Riyadh. Four more hospitals with a total 600-bed capacity have been planned. SANG also uses foreign management firms, such as International Hospitals Groups (IHG) of Great Britain, to manage its hospitals.

The Government Organization for Social Insurance (GOSI), the

Ministry of Labor and Social Affairs, and the Public Security Organization of the Ministry of Interior have three cooperative health care projects.

As Exhibit 3 indicates, the private and semiprivate sector is also expanding. There are currently 37 hospitals with a 3,400-bed capacity. New projects have been planned. In Jeddah, which houses the majority of private hospitals, 13 new projects are planned. Riyadh, which has 2 functioning private hospitals, is expecting 9 more by 1990.

The Kingdom's hospital construction program is costly. Experts say a hospital may cost US $ 300,000 per bed in the remote regions of the country.

Exhibit 3   Hospitals and Beds in Saudi Arabia

Ope-rator	Operational Hospital/Beds			Hospitals/Beds to Be Completed			Total
	Feb. 1985	1985	1986	1987	1988	1989	
MOH	97/19,624	36/5,348	7/1,079	29/4,134	8/4,125	5/1,000	182/35,310
MODA	13/2,422	2/1,020	–	1/125	2/850	–	18/4,417
SANG	2/1,000	–	–	–	1/500	–	3/1,500
PSC	1/135	–	0/379	–	1/250	1/250	3/1,014
GOSI	1/90	–	0/35	1/250	1/250	1/250	4/875
MOHE	4/1,654	–	0/90	1/50	2/180	3/2,000	10/3,974
RCJY	2/268	1/200	–	1/342	1/200	–	5/1,010
Prvt.	37/3,995	3/910	8/1,513	7/769	3/485	–	58/7,497
Total	157/29,013	42/7,478	15/3,096	40/5,670	19/5,670	10/3,500	283/55,597

MOH : Ministry of Health
MODA: Ministry of Defence and Aviation
SANG: Saudi Arabian National Guard
PSC : Public Services Commission (Interior Ministry)
GOSI: General Organization for Social Insurance (Labor and Social Affairs Ministry)
MOHE: Ministry of Higher Education
RCJY: Royal Commission for Jubail and Yanbu

Source: Saudi Arabia's Ministry of Health 1985.

Health Care Development in Kuwait

The evolution of modern health care in Kuwait can be focused upon in phases. The first phase (1911–1949) consisted of the establishment of the American hospital which was the only one in Kuwait. The population then was much smaller than it is today, and most of it relied on folk medicine, a knowledge of which was passed down through the generations. The second phase (1949–1962) witnessed the development of several general hospitals. The third phase (1962 to the present) is characterized by the introduction of the medical registration system which is based on territorial principles. Additional general and specialized hospitals were built, as well as clinics and health care facilities.

In 1981, there were 20 modern hospitals and over 500 clinics and other health care centers throughout the country. These include dental clinics, mother and child care centers, and preventive health centers. The country had over 1,400 fully qualified medical doctors drawn from a variety of countries. This number of physicians gave Kuwait one of the highest ratios of doctors to population in the world. Kuwait had become so attuned to health care that in the rare event of specialist treatment not being available, patients were flown to appropriate overseas centers at no cost to themselves. In addition to these state-run facilities, there was a private medical sector which conducted services at several private clinics and held a substantial technical staff and 326 doctors/dentists.

Health Care Development in the Emirates (U.A.E.)

The U.A.E. has emerged as the Gulf's big spender on health. In 1984, an estimated US $ 350 million was channeled into medical services throughout the seven Emirates. This represents almost 9% of the country's total budget and the highest percentage of public spending on health anywhere in the region.

But big public health budgets do not necessarily mean better health care for the public – particularly if, as in the U.A.E., too much of that money goes towards hospital-based curative care. The Emirates' health authorities now realize this, and after years of heavy expenditure on free hospital care, the U.A.E. has begun to reshape its health service along markedly different lines.

In the past six years, almost all of the money spent on health in the U.A.E. has gone into hospital care and its development. In order to meet its planned target of a network of top flight hospitals strung across the Emirates, the government launched an ambitious construction program. The results, both in terms of the quantity and quality of services created, have been dramatic. Since 1979, the country has increased its available hospital beds from 1,700 to just under 5,000. This decreased the Emirates' hospital bed to population ratio to 1/200. In the past three years alone, 10 new hospitals totalling some 2,000 beds have been built.

High Costs

Like most Gulf countries, the U.A.E. suffers from a chronic shortage of local manpower and services. The answer has been to import them from abroad. Almost 90 % of the doctors working in the country are expatriates, and a number of key hospitals throughout the Emirates are managed, staffed, and serviced by private foreign companies. The cost of paying for these imported skills is estimated to be one third of the country's health budget – a source of growing concern for the country's health authorities.

The heavy concentration on secondary and tertiary care has also created problems. The health system is top-heavy with hospitals at the expense of an adequate referral network, and the results are misuse and inefficiency. The public has come to associate health care with hospital care, and with no gatekeepers built into the system, out-patient departments are often clogged with self-referrals seeking treatment inappropriately. Also the neglect of adequate patient records has lead to multiple patient visits and higher maintenance costs.

Changing Directions

The U.A.E. is the first state in the Gulf to introduce health fees (previously all public health services were free). All U.A.E. residents must now pay for individual health cards and for medical treatment with the exception of emergency and preventive services.

Health officials admit the new charges will recoup a welcome 10 % of the health budget, and may cut hospital visits by as much as 30%. As one health care official said, "The aim of introducing charges is not to save money but to encourage better use of our facilities."

Health cards have also been introduced to streamline the system. By linking the cards to computerized record systems currently being installed throughout the country, physicians will have easy access to patient files. This will ensure continuity of treatment and make available a ready check on patient visits. The new drug controls will give a better indication of prescribing patterns and ensure regulation of unnecessary formulations.

Primary Care

To back these moves aimed at ensuring proper use of institutional care, the authorities are also upgrading the country's front line health services. The ministry has had a special department with responsibility for preventive and primary care for some years, but it has long been under-funded and over-shadowed by the attention paid to the curative sector. Health planners now hope to reverse this situation.

The new targets will boost the number of local health centers throughout the Emirates. Dubai, for example, now has 9 health clinics, but plans to more than double this number in the next few years. Similar expansion is set for all the urban districts as well as increased mobile teams to serve isolated communities in the rural regions. Each new health center is to be equipped with basic laboratory, X-ray, and pharmaceutical facilities so as to act as an effective first-entry point for the public health system.

The country's school health service is also undergoing reorganization. Initially set up in 1975, it now covers about 150,000 students and teachers. However, in recent years it has veered away from its original role as a screening and immunization service towards that of a curative health system for students. The aim is to redirect its facilities towards preventive activities and transfer all other work to either the new primary care centers or the hospital services.

Competitive Structure of the Industry

This section examines the five key factors which individually and collectively determine the competitiveness and profitability of an industry. As Exhibit 4 indicates, these forces are:

1) competitors;
2) key client groups;
3) entry and exiting barriers;
4) health care substitutes;
5) suppliers.

While all these factors are important, the third one is the most critical one in shaping overall industry competition.

Key Competitors

As pointed out earlier, the health care industry in GCC states is made up of numerous players. Government is the most dominant of these. It owns 3 out of every 4 hospitals. The remainder is owned and managed by private players who differ in location, size, power, strategies, origins, and personalities.

The "concentration of the industry" in the hands of the government has its roots in the prohibitive economics of entry and in the ideology of the welfare states referred to earlier. Although slow in its growth, the health care industry in GCC states offers ample room for differentiation and segmentation.

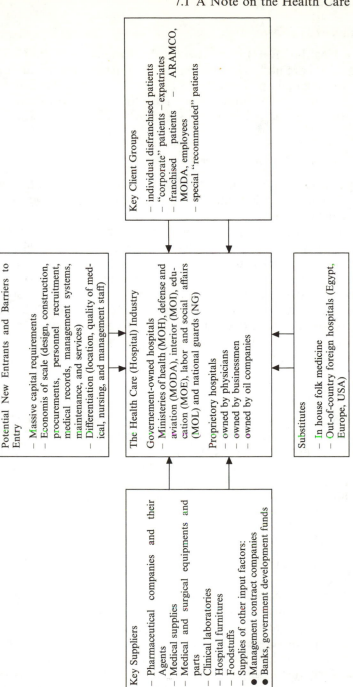

Potential New Entrants and Barriers to Entry

- Massive capital requirements
- Economis of scale (design, construction, procurements, personnel recruitment, medical records, management systems, maintenance, and services)
- Differentiation (location, quality of medical, nursing, and management staff)

The Health Care (Hospital) Industry

Government-owned hospitals
- Ministeries of health (MOH), defense and aviation (MODA), interior (MOI), education (MOE), labor and social affairs (MOL) and national guards (NG)

Proprietory hospitals
- owned by physicians
- owned by businessmen
- owned by oil companies

Key Client Groups

- individual disfranchised patients
- "corporate" patients – expatriates
- franchised patients – ARAMCO, MODA, employees
- special "recommended" patients

Key Suppliers

- Pharmaceutical companies and their Agents
- Medical supplies
- Medical and surgical equipments and parts
- Clinical laboratories
- Hospital furnitures
- Foodstuffs
- Supplies of other input factors:
● Management contract companies
● Banks, government development funds

Substitutes

- In house folk medicine
- Out-of-country foreign hospitals (Egypt, Europe, USA)

Exhibit 4   Competitive Forces in the Arab Health-Care Industry

Existence of Numerous Providers

The Ministry of Health (MOH) owns two-thirds of the hospitals in GCC states. These facilities are no longer concentrated in urban centers but are now spread all over the regions. The result is increased intense competition, particularly when growth in demand is limited due to the massive exodus of the foreign workers and the rising health standards of GCC citizens.

Competitors of Varying Size and Power

There are two giant operators in this industry – the Ministry of Health and the Ministry of Defense. The first ministry specializes in providing acute, routine, and ancillary medical services – usually free of charge to civilian personnel. The Ministry of Defense, by contrast, offers an upscale version of the above-cited services, also free of charge, to military personnel and their dependents, and to some acute-care civilian patients who are referred to military hospitals. The private sector owns and runs about one-fourth of the total number of hospitals. Finally, health care is a service industry, which means the service is typically rendered as close to the patient's home as possible. Thus, competition, particularly for emergency patients, takes place in great part on a location-by-location basis – a factor which tends to offset the balance of size and power.

Diverse Rivals in Strategies

Competition among private hospitals is intense. Some competitors (44%) run their hospitals as a business to be milked in the interest of high profits. Others (56%) run them as if they were non-profit oranizations. Each camp uses different strategies which vary from limited, no-frill services to full service, well-staffed, elegant facilities. In addition, some are managed by their owners while others are run by foreign management companies.

Ample Room for Differentiation

Hospitals do differ among themselves not only in their location but also in the type and range of services they offer. First, there are general hospitals which offer the full range of medical service to all kinds of patients. Secondly, there are specialty hospitals which focus on particular medical areas, such as maternity, eye, children, and emergency care. In addition to differences in the type of service portfolio offered, extensive efforts have been made to increase the level of differentiation among hospitals. Some hospitals, particularly the private ones, compete on the basis of quality of service offered. They promote their use and knowledge of the latest technology, their well-credentialed Arabic-speaking staff, and famous visiting physicians, as well as their luxury-hotel-style accommodation and dining. Some hospitals compete on pricing; others on availability of easy credit terms. Although all government hospitals offer their services "for free,"private hospitals offer theirs "for fee." In comparison to any other service industry, there is no limit on imagination when it comes to differentiation.

Slow Industry Growth

The market for health care services is not growing as fast as expected. This is apparent by the surplus in the number of hospital beds. It is estimated that the overall health care system operates at about 55% occupancy. Some hospitals run higher; others run lower. There are three factors which contribute to this overbedding crisis.

First, the sudden and sharp reduction in oil prices led to massive cuts in government spending on both the physical and social infrastructure and in payment slowdowns. It also led to an exodus of massive numbers of foreign workers – traditionally the key client group of private hospitals.

Second, the rise in the educational levels and health care awareness of the GCC states population, as evidenced by declining infant mortality rates and increasing life expectancy rates, has caused hospital occupancy rates to decrease.

The third factor is the negative public attitude toward staying in a hospital. Culturally, there is a feeling of being abandoned by one's family and friends, which accompanies an extended stay in the hospital. Financially, private hospital administrators believe that they make the highest return on their investment during the first few days of hospitalization. Afterwards, marginal revenues decline with each passing day. The average length of hospitalization in private hospitals tends to be comparatively short. In the Kingdom, the hospital stay is 3 to 4 days, compared to 7 in the U.S. and 9 in Japan.

In the light of the above-mentioned factors, keeping the occupancy rate up in the face of a deteriorating environmental scenario is one of the toughest strategic challenges facing government hospitals in general and private ones in particular.

Perishability of the Product

The services a hospital offers are very perishable: around-the-clock medical and nursing staff, costly medical and diagnostic equipment, and a room to use for 24 hours or more. If these costly services are not "consumed" today, they cannot be "stored" until tomorrow.

Segmentation of the Industry

The health care industry in GCC states is segmented by price/service/location characteristics. Using price as a key parameter, the industry is segmented into two camps: "for free" and "for fee."

The "For Free" Segment

The "for free" segment is exemplified by MOH and oil companies' hospitals and clinics. This segment is the one that has expanded the most over the last 10 years due to their response to public sentiment to offer high quality medical care free of charge to all GCC citizens, military personnel and their dependents, and employees of oil companies. Free medical care is viewed by public policy makers as an essential commodity – a commodity which is available to all citizens at home and abroad. With the exception of military hospitals, most public hospitals offer basic services. Most of their nursing staff is from Korea and Taiwan. Most of their physicians are from India, Pakistan, and Egypt. The hospitals are usually not as clean, not as responsive to patients' needs, and not as well-managed as their private or military counterparts. Patient waiting lines are long. Delivery systems are cumbersome and inefficient. These are some of the reasons which are behind the poor performance of, and lack of confidence in, public hospitals.

An additional reason for the poor performance of public hospitals is that their administrators seldom have the right to hire or fire any employee, except for the housekeeping staff. Civil service rules and regulations infringe upon their organizations.

The "For Fee" Segment

The "for fee" segment is exemplified by the network of private hospitals and is basically found in major metropolitan areas. All private hospitals offer high quality services for the well-to-do, highly educated, and status-conscious patients. They enjoy a better image than public hospitals. Citizens and expatriates alike have great confidence in them. They employ male and female Arabic-speaking physicians. A few attract and employ noted visiting British and American physicians. Most of their nursing staff comes from the Philippines. Critical care nursing personnel – if and when used – come from the UK, USA, and Sweden. Most private hospitals are well-equipped and offer much of the same technology as American hospitals. Most employ a business manager to oversee daily operations. Virtually all of them are managed on a personal basis by their owners who are zealous of protecting the patients' goodwill and promoting their image.

It is not surprising, therefore, to find that management contracts have not made an inroad in this segment of the industry.

Location is a competitive weapon and a key factor in market segmentation. As discussed above, due to the emergency nature of health care services, they must be rendered locally. This has given rise to the development of a huge network of hospitals and primary care clinics throughout the Gulf states. Major hospitals and medical centers are located in large urban communities where there are high population densities. These metropolitan multi-specialty units attract physicians and patients from all over the world. The new Jeddah Clinic and King Fahd Specialty Hospital in Riyadh are cases in point.

Key Patient Groups

Another factor which influences the competititve structure of the health care industry is the patient groups, or the buyers, of health care services. Patients typically fall into one of the four following categories.

Individual Disfranchised Patients

This group is fragmented and has no concentrated bargaining power. They include the economically deprived, the nonsponsored foreign workers, and traveling pilgrims who get sick during their religious holiday. This crowd reluctantly patronizes public hospitals and clinics.

Corporate Patients

Some forms of insurance appear to exist in the GCC states, particularly contractual relationships between private hospitals and corporations. Corporations have to provide health care services to their employees in general, and expatriates in particular. It is the latter group of employees who provide the patient market for private hospitals. Hospitals are paid a negotiated daily (per diem) rate. However, a company may contract with one hospital for its management staff and with another one for its hourly employees.

Franchised Patients

These are the very fortunate patients who work for a prominent military or civilian organization (such as the armed forces, national guard, or oil companies). These organizations consider their employees as assets and shower them and their families with high quality medical services – free of charge.

Special Recommended Patients

Well-informed and well-connected patients, and those patients with difficult cases can be referred to a military or to a foreign hospital for treatment – at the expense of the government.

Entry and Exit Barriers

Health care is both a capital- and labor-intensive industry. To successfully
compete in it, one has to possess four ingredients:

1) financial muscle;
2) access to highly qualified medical and nursing personnel;
3) economies of scale; and
4) professional management.

Financial Support

Financial muscle is needed to support the initial investment in building
hospitals, in the acquisition of equipment, in the acquisition of auxiliary
power-generating units and laboratories, as well as the acquisition of
furniture, laundry and kitchen appliances. It can cost as much as US
$ 200,000 per room to build a complete modern hospital with supporting
facilities. This room would have to be priced at a daily rate of US $ 200.
Clearly, old hospitals will have a competitive advantage over newly
constructed properties.

There is more to a hospital than a building. The building has to be
equipped with new state of the art medical equipment and systems, (such as
digital radiography, nuclear medicine, ultrasound scanners, sterilization
units, and digital angiography systems), computerized patient record
systems, and laundry and kitchen equipment. Diagnostic equipment is
expensive. For example, the cheapest GE CAT scanner costs US $ 500,000.
To cover its cost, this machine must be utilized 24 hours a day for five years!

Both buildings and equipment depreciate fast and have to be maintained
continuously and/or replaced periodically. Air condition units break down.
Diagnostic equipment becomes obsolete fast. Nowhere is technological obsolescence more visible and pronounced than in the field of
diagnostic imaging. For instance, conventional X-rays locate areas of
altered anatomy and produce a flat, two-dimensional image of a three-
dimensional object. By contrast, the CT scanner locates areas of altered
functions, and with the aid of computer technology produces a three
dimensional image. The CT scanner also provides better pictures of soft
tissues, as in the case of the brain or the liver. Therefore, the competitive
advantage of a hospital may be wiped out if it does not acquire the latest CT

scanner in the market. In this respect, a hospital is no different from a commercial airliner which must modernize its fleet periodically or lose its market share to a more aggressive competitor with an ultra-modern fleet.

Attainment of Medical Personnel

There is more to a modern hospital than physical plant, state of the art equipment, stylish furniture, appliances, and computers. These physical entities, no matter how modern, cannot comfort a patient, diagnose his ailment, or prescribe his treatment. Only medical personnel can. Their availability in the right number and right quality is what decides the competitive fate of a given hospital.

Arabs do not trust their lives or those of their beloved ones in the hands of freshly trained medical graduates. They prefer to be seen by a famous local or foreign medical specialist. The former one for his language and technical skills, the latter for his presumably superior technical competence. Since these talents are in short supply, they have to be imported – and at a premium. Cardiologists, orthopedic surgeons, and urologists are highly trained specialists and must be well paid for their services. Often, when relocating, these specialists bring families and preferred staff. The employing hospital has to provide for their orientation, housing, transportation, and schooling for their children. It is not surprising then to find that salaries and fringe benefits deplete a hospital's operating budget.

The combination of fixed costs (represented by buildings and equipment and the activities needed to maintain both) and payroll expenses make it exceedingly difficult for a private investor to develop his own hospital and earn an honest and sustainable profit from it. The initial costs of getting established and the concomitant risks are simply too prohibitive.

Economies of Scale

Economies of scale are the third entry barrier. In order to compete successfully, a hospital has to operate at a given capacity to meet its fixed and operating expenses. Only then can the per patient fee be kept at an affordable level. This is the level which an average patient can tolerate without having to switch his business to a local or foreign competing hospital.

Two examples are in order. First, it would be costly to support a night shift outpatient clinic if it only serves 3 to 5 patients per night. On the other hand, if the patient number jumps to 12 or 15, the night outpatient clinic would pay for its operating expenses. Secondly, a burn center or a cardiac intensive care unit that serves only 1 to 3 patients a month could not pay for its operating expenses and would be an economically, although not socially, unwise investment.

If an entrant seeks to build a strong market position, it has to build capacity ahead of demand to reduce its fixed and operating costs and make it difficult for a newcomer to compete. The Dr. Fakhry Hospital in Khobar, Saudi Arabia, is a case in point. If the hospital's projected capacity is not reached, the hospital will struggle to spread its cost over the available heads. These patients would have to cover the operating costs of the hospital during their stay. There could be no fixed per daily dollar amount. Their hospital costs would be determined by the number of occupied beds. This could result in incredibly high hospital bills. This is precisely what recently happened to one of the noted investment hospitals in Cairo. The hospital targeted the rich Arab patients as its desirable market segment. When that core client base failed to turn up in sufficient number, the hospital found it difficult to compete. Its fees skyrocketed, which further scared the Arab patients away.

Management

Management is the fourth entry barrier to the health care industry. Our analysis thus far has suggested that there is more to a modern hospital than a well-equipped building, well-trained medical personnel, and a sizeable client-base. This facility has to be managed efficiently to function like a well-oiled machine. Just as a machine has a variety of parts which must function simultaneously, a hospital has a variety of components which must function in unison in order to ensure efficiency and effectiveness within the hospital. These components are administrative duties which must be performed by a management team. Such duties as patient communications and scheduling, employee hiring and scheduling, equipment acquisition and maintenance, quality control and accounting procedures must be fulfilled by a competent staff. The function of the management staff is to ensure the efficiency of the ongoing activities within a hospital and to maintain a comfortable climate for the physicians, technical staff, and, in turn, the patients. The management staff is the most evident cause for the performance and image gap between private and public hospitals.

Just as it is difficult to get into the health care industry, it is equally difficult to get out of it. After all, there are few alternative uses for an existing hospital building. It cannot be easily converted into a hotel, apartment or condominium without major renovation. Nor can its laundry, food processing, laboratories, and diagnostic equipment be dislodged and converted into cash. In other words, the bulk of the costs of getting started are "sunk costs" making it exceedingly difficult to withdraw from the industry.

The combination of high entry and exit barriers explains the reluctance of the private sector to invest heavily in the hospital industry. It is not suprising then that governments step in and correct the situation in two ways. First, government directly owns and runs the largest network of hospitals and clinics in the GCC states. Second, it encourages the private sector to play an active role in this industry. For instance, the Saudi government offers direct subsidies together with an assortment of incentives (such as free land, interest free loans, duty free imported equipment) to ease entry barriers and enhance the level of competition within the hospital industry. It has developed a system through which participating hospitals are guaranteed 15% occupancy rates. This system of subsidies reduces the break-even bed factor and enables some hospitals to continue operation.

So much for the government's facilitating role. In addition to offering incentives, the government regulates the industry. Through the Ministry of Health, the government licenses private hospitals and medical personnel and inspects the quality of their infrastructure. It fixes the fee to be charged for every item and every class of service offered by private hospitals, including the time limits needed to qualify for a free return consultation. Governments also approve the dispensing of restricted medicine and medical supplies to patients.

Substitutes for Health Care Services

According to conventional economic theory, the availability of substitutes enhances the competitiveness of an industry. Currently, there is no substitute that represents a major threat to the modern hospital industry in the GCC states. However, two sources of minor threat do exist: folk and foreign medicine.

Throughout the developing world, folk and spiritual medicine are still viewed as an efficacious and inexpensive substitute for modern medicine. Most pregnant women do not deliver their babies in a hospital – but at home with the help of a mid-wife. Arthritic and chronic back problem patients are advised to take Turkish baths, bury their bodies in mineral springs or sunny sands, or use Egyptian "hot lamp" treatments. In addition to this, there are plenty of recipes for every conceivable ailment and for every member of the familiy: the infertile wife, the impotent husband, the less productive grand-father, and the teething infant. Not all of these treatments are risk-free. Moreover, some can be bought from the drug stores or traditional herb stores. All too often, patients consult their favorite pharmacist or religious leader for treatment without ever having seen a physician.

Traditional medicine is not upheld only by the poor and illiterate villagers. Well-to-do, urban professionals and artisans develop their own version of folk medicine. They get on "heavy drugs" to relieve the stress and strain of their jobs, or go and visit their favorite witch doctor.

As for the ultra sophisticated, well-to-do, status-conscious, and critically ill patients, the preference is to seek help abroad – usually in first-class medical centers in Europe, the United States, or Egypt. These choosy patients are sold on "foreign medicine," even when local and inexpensive substitutes are available.

Key Suppliers

Suppliers to the hospital industry offer a large array of diverse products and services. The suppliers of most of these items are a rather fragmented group, and generally compete only on a local or regional basis. However, the suppliers of drugs, medical and surgical equipment, maintenance parts, and management knowledge are a concentrated group of international firms that operate locally through GCC agents. These elite groups of suppliers do have some power relative to the hospitals and patients. They can and do manipulate the arrival time of critical parts and supplies (such as films) to render costly equipment useless. Excessive delays are common. Idle equipment is not the exception. In the absence of a centrally coordinated purchasing system, public and private hospitals are so numerous and fragmented that they cannot bargain successfully over prices or delivery terms. To cope with this situation, some private hospitals, such as Al-Mana Medical Services in Saudi Arabia, set up their own medical supply subsidiaries to serve their own needs as well as the needs of others in their league.

The Hospital Management Contract Segments

The Case of Saudi Arabia

The capacity of the Gulf states to build and equip fine health care facilities has been outdistanced by their ability to staff and manage them. The gap exists because an effective health care system and the requisite effective educational system are both only one generation old.

The fact that local managers are in short supply, coupled with the fact that they do make a difference in a hospital's performance, compelled the government of the Gulf states to trust their hospitals (civilian and military alike) to foreign companies specializing in hospital management. It is within this context, that the large-scale entry of international hospital management firms has to be seen as one of the most notable developments in the hospital industry in the Kingdom of Saudi Arabia.

Leaders in this field are American hospital management companies, such as Hospital Corporation of America, National Medical Enterprise, Amercian Medical International, American Medicorp, and Humana. As of late, competitors in this field are becoming more numerous with the entrance of a new generation of low-cost European, Korean, and Saudi management companies into the industry, such as Allied Medical Group, General Arabian Medical Allied Services, Saudi Medical Services, First-Saudi Medics, and Al-Muttabbaggani. American standards, including American personnel and physicians, are perceived to be too expensive in today's market. With the exception of critical care nurses, who come from the USA and the U.K., most of the nursing personnel are from Korea, Taiwan, and the Philippines.

Hospital management companies follow different strategies in the Gulf market. As a general rule, they do not own hospitals. They manage them on behalf of their clients who are most often composed of government agencies and private investors. Briefly, this means that they render their cost-saving, revenue-producing, and purchasing expertise to these in-experienced entities in exchange for a management fee.

A management firm could achieve economies of scale in at least three areas:

1) personnel recruitment and selection (including physicians, nurses, technicians, administrators);
2) procurement (group purchasing of drugs, medical and surgical supplies and equipment) and
3) maintenance (keeping the equipment in a state of operational read-iness).

Once a management contract company bids for a contract and wins, it does not utilize its own personnel to staff the entire hospital, but installs a team of turnaround managers to the project. This team usually includes the chief administrator who manages the hospital, the director of nursing, and the financial officer. This team works together for the first year of the contract, getting a feel for the hospital, reviewing its operation, diagnosing its problems, restructuring its departments, training its personnel, and streamlining its service delivery system. This intensive effort to turn around the client hospital is a time-consuming, money-losing activity. As a result, the management company typically breaks even on the fees charged during the first year. Thereafter, as much as one third to one half of the annual fee is profit.

The hospital management business is getting fiercely competitive in the GCC states. Multiple bidding is now common. Fees are steadily falling. Payments are becoming slow. Liquidity is becoming a real problem. Some companies like Fairview are reportedly having trouble breaking even in their hard won contracts. Military hospitals are moving towards a "man/month" method of contract management. This method of contract management is a total contract management which includes all personnel. Payment is based on staffing levels. The staffing requirements are listed by category and number of personnel.

To succeed in this market, a hospital management company must possess the following critical success factors:

1) excellent marketing capabilities – to scan the environment, know about a potential contract situation, and cultivate good relations with local health care officials;
2) financial muscle – to qualify to bid for the contract and provide for short-term finance in periods of payment slowdowns;
3) access to medical and management personnel – to staff the contract hospital;
4) access to medical supplies – to ensure timely shipment of necessary medical supplies and equipment.

By 1983, Saudi businessmen were encouraged, once again, by their government to get into the management contract market, as they were earlier encouraged to establish hospitals of their own. Only those people with proven track records were urged to bid for hospital management contracts. Some Saudi businessmen responded positively to this opportunity and engaged in operations of staffing, purchasing, and maintenance. Their ultimate success will be gauged in terms of how long it takes them to train local hospital talents to engage in self-management.

The Market of Private Hospitals

The private hospitals in GCC states are part of a mature industry. They usually cater to the small market of upper-class private and corporate "citizens." The decline in oil revenues, and the subsequent economic downturn in GCC states, and the exodus of the expatriates have reduced the demand for their services to attract the local citizens. Their operations are closely monitored by the health authorities through licensing, quality control, and fee restrictions.

The future of private hospitals in the Gulf states is highly uncertain. For one thing, their customers are becoming dissatisfied with their inability to retain competent medical personnel and to acquire the latest medical equipment. They also complain about inflated hospitalization bills. For another, private hospitals are facing a number of environmental challenges. First, they cannot compete with the public treasury of their countries and offer their customers high quality care at a nominal fee. Nor can they do much to prevent the decline in patient load. Corporate buyers are getting stingy and have begun telling hospital officials what costs are reimbursable and what are not. As a consequence, most private hospitals are running in the red.

Sixty percent of private hospital revenues come from the corporate and walk-in patients as well as government subsidies. The hospital business is both capital and labor intensive. Employee salaries consume between 60 and 80 percent of a hospital's operating budget. Depreciation, medical supplies, rent and maintenance consume 15, 12, and 10 percent respectively. These figures do not reflect any miscellaneous expenses which may come into play.

Trends in the Health Care Industry

The following trends characterize the health care industry as of 1988. Their underlying causes have been hinted at throughout the preceding analysis:

1) a shift of emphasis from curative to preventive health care;
2) substitution of:
   a) modern for folk medicine;
   b) public (for-free) for private (for-fee) hospital services: less patients go to private hospitals these days;
   c) local for foreign hospitals (services): in hard times, patients do not seek medical care abroad, except for high-risk cases;
   d) endogenous for foreign hospital management companies: the GCC's governments, as a matter of national policy, want to offer more contracts to GCC's companies which employ GCC nationals;
   e) Asian (Filipinos, Koreans) for American/British nurses;
   f) Arabic speaking for non-Arabic speaking physicians;
3) a sharp decline in the number of expatriates (traditionally the core client group of the private hospital), and the subsequent rediscovery of native patients by these hospitals;
4) voluntary price cuts are becoming common among private hospitals. Some hospitals are discounting their rooms and medical services by 40%. Others are topping this percentage, but simultaneously require patients to pay for unnecessary diagnostic tests and prolonged stays in their facilities;

5) hospitals – like all other GCC's employers – are required by Labor Office to cut the size of their foreign manpower pool. This will undoubtedly affect the level and quality of their services. The drive is certainly to produce more home-grown physicians, nurses, and technicians;
6) the emergence of regional cooperative ventures among private hospitals, such as the blood bank scheme in Dammam/Khobar/Dhahran area, and the sharing of the Green Crescent diagnostic equipments by some neighboring clinics in Riyadh;
7) the market for equipment maintenance, although uncoordinated, is rapidly growing. The average hospital deals with a large number of service organizations to provide for its total service needs. It purchases a lot of sophisticated equipment whose average downtime is higher than its counterpart in any other foreign hospital;
8) the trend in the field of hospital construction is now toward erecting small hospitals and clinics, as opposed to the past trend of constructing very large and lavish ones;
9) although manpower nationalization policies require the reduction of foreign medical manpower, it will remain a key trend in the health care field in the Gulf states.

References

Al Aamal (1987): (Unsigned editiorial), Continuing possibilities of Saudi health care market, *Al Aamal*, 63, (September 15): 5.
Al-Madina Moharam (1985): Saudi medicine: Yesterday & today: A special issue on the evolution of health care in Saudi Arabia, *Al-Madina Moharam*, October 14, 1985: 18.
Cunington and Associates. *Hospitals in Saudi Arabia project and contract opportunities.*
Gulf Council of Cooperation (1987): *Economic bulletin.*
Health services in Saudi Arabia (1974): A study conducted by the University Associates for International Health Inc., Boston, Mass.
High technology service and training international (1983): *Feasibility study for a high technology service and training organization* in the Kingdom of Saudi Arabia, Unpublished report (December).
Middle East Health (1985): Health care in the Emirates: A special report, *Middle East Health*, (June, July): 29–32.
Middle East Health (1987): A time of change for Saudi health care, *Middle East Health*, (February): 13–15.
Ministry of Health (1985): *Annual statistics review.*

Nagi, M. (1983): The health care system in Kuwait: A welfare perspective, in: *Third World medicine and social change*, E. Morgan (ed.), Washington: The University Press.

Projects and Opportunities for Medical Equipments, Hospital Supplies, and Health Care Services in Saudi Arabia, World Wide Medical Markets, Sussex, England 1984.

Regina, E.H. and William, S.E. (1987): Who profits from non-profit? *Harvard Business Review*, (January-February).

Saudi Business (1983): Hospital growth enters new phase, *Saudi Business*, (June 18): 21–26.

Saudi Business (1984): Hospitals' growth, *Saudi Business*, February 6: 12–16.

Wren, G. (1976): The hospitals of Saudi Arabia, *World Hospitals*, 12, (2).

7.2 Al-Mana General Hospital

M. Sami Kassem

History

Sheikh Muhammad Al-Mana – interpreter at the court of King Abd Al-Aziz al Sa'ud and a noted businessman and historian – is now in his eighties. He is the founder of Al-Mana Hospital. When he was 10, his father took him from his birthplace, Zubair, Iraq, to live with him in Bombay, India. He was sent to study in Jesuit schools. He quickly picked up Hindustani, Urdu, and English and found himself sought out as an interpreter and translator by many of the Arabs who came to Bombay in great numbers for medical treatment. As a teenager, he came to know all of the Bombay physicians. This childhood experience led him to wonder: "You Arabs, why do you come here? Why don't you get treated in your own countries?" The standard answer was, "We don't have any doctors." Sheikh Muhammad Al-Mana has said,

"I decided then and there that, given the opportunity, if I am going to touch the lives of my people and be remembered, I'd start a hospital or a medical college if possible."

In 1957, at the age of 54, his dream was fulfilled. Al-Mana opened a clinic, with a capital of Saudi Riyals (SR) 50,000. It was a small-size institution specializing in providing dental and eye care. Interviewed in his office at the hospital, Sheikh Muhammad was asked to recount how it all happened. This is what he said:

After a short stint as a translator, first at the court of King 'Abd Al-'Aziz and later at Aramco, I decided to go into business for myself. I got into contracting, building the Ras Tanura and Dhahran airstrips, and I owned an ice-making plant.

One day I went to see Amir bin Jiluwi in Dammam to ask for an operator for the ice-making plant. I spoke to an adviser to the Amir who had been impressed by the medical treatment he had received from the Germans. He asked me "Muhammad, why do you bring an operator for a plant? Why not bring doctors?" So I called my brother Abd Al-Aziz who was in Germany at that time and told him to advertise for a dentist and ophthalmologist for me. In response to my ad, a dentist volunteered with his car and dental unit. He packed his equipment and clothes into the car and set off on the long voyage across Turkey, Lebanon, and on the Tapline

Road. After the dentist got his practice established in Al-Khobar, the townspeople came to me and said, "Why have you brought us a dentist? It is not our teeth, but our eyes that need help the most."

So I went to Germany hunting for an eye doctor. I approached the Academy of Medicine in Stuttgart. It was a mission impossible in post-World War II Germany to find a physician willing to exchange the familiar and lucrative life for the unknown and austere. Luckily, I found my man in the person of Dr. Dieter Herman. He wanted to become my partner in the hospital project, but did not have the requisite capital. This, however, proved to be only a temporary setback. Herman married a Chinese girl and with her dowry of 30,000 German marks, he formed a joint venture with me. I chipped in SR 50,000 which I saved from my other business ventures. Together, we started a small-size hospital in 1957, specializing in dental and eye care. The hospital had two German doctors and 6–8 beds. Its mission then was to provide the best dental and eye care to the population of the Eastern Province."

The Business of Al-Mana

When people think of Al-Mana, they generally think only of the hospital. However, Al-Mana is a diversified establishment with a focus on the health care field in general. In fact, about 70–80 % of the total corporate revenues result from the hospital operation itself. The firm has structured itself into five divisions (see Exhibit 1):

1) Al-Mana General Hospital;
2) health care management division;
3) construction division;
4) distribution division; and
5) medical services division.

In the mid-seventies, top management – made up of the young, ambitious, college-educated sons of Sheikh Muhammad – sought to respond to market opportunities and broadened the firm's earnings base. Under the leadership of Sheikh Muhammad, the mission was broadened from providing only dental and eye care to providing general medical services. This led to the formation of the above five business groups.

Each division is organized and managed as a semi-autonomous business unit. Each one is headed by a manager who is responsible for its operation and reports all its activities to the board of directors. Division managers hold weekly, monthly, and emergency meetings with members of the board to study areas that need improvement, detect problems, and find solutions.

As a family firm, the board is made up of three sons of Sheikh Muhammad: Ibrahim, Mansoor, and Nagib. Both Ibrahim and Mansoor

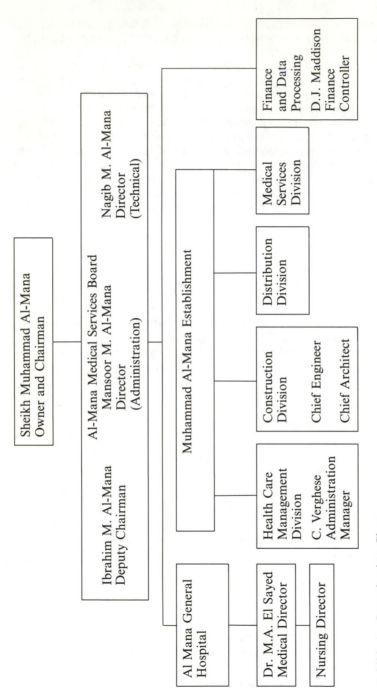

Exhibit 1   Organization Chart

have been educated in the United States, while Nagib is a 1976 graduate of the University of Petroleum and Minerals, with a B.S. in civil engineering.

A re-examination and possible restructuring of the establishment's operations are being considered, as top management devises a strategy for the rest of the 1980s. The focus of the re-examination involves both the basic mission of the establishment and the appropriateness of each of the five business units. Exhibits 4 and 5 provide some insight into financial operations at Al-Mana Establishment through 1984. The remainder of this report describes in some detail the operation of the hospital division.

Service/Market Development

One can distinguish three stages in the development of Al-Mana General Hospital's strategy.

The Missionary Stage, 1955–1975 (Eye and Dental Clinic)

The original idea was to concentrate on doing a few things well rather than many things poorly. As already mentioned, Sheikh Muhammad originally limited his service portfolio to dental and eye care. His idea was to provide Eastern Province residents with the best and least expensive dental and eye treatment possible.

He knew that his countrymen were afflicted by severe eye diseases, particularly trachoma and cataracts, and that their teeth suffered for lack of proper care. There was no other facility to meet these needs. Sheikh Muhammad's response was to combine German medicine with Eastern altruism in a pleasant two-story building. Patients flocked into his clinic not only from the remote towns and villages of the Eastern Province, such as Al-Hasa and Qatif, but also from all over the Kingdom. Many of these patients were poor and could not afford to pay even five riyals for the office visit. They were treated for free. Word of mouth and patient goodwill spread like fire. The result: daily out-patient traffic soared. More doctors and more equipment were needed to cope with the demand. Not surprisingly, Sheikh Muhammad soon faced a deficit. To counteract it, he liquidated part of the assets he had accumulated before he founded the clinic.

Becoming a General Hospital, 1976–1984

The massive transformation of the Saudi landscape that took place during the boom years of the 1970s and early 1980s brought a large expatriate work force to the Kingdom. To attract manpower, foreign and local organizations had to offer their employees a range of benefits, including free health care that extended to their dependents to entice them to come to Saudi Arabia and participate in its development. The massive influx of foreign workers put heavy pressure on all service organizations, including hospitals, but also offered them unique opportunities. The expatriates had to be given pre-employment medical examinations, as well as eye examinations to get a driver's license; they also had to be examined and treated when injured or sick. Moreover, their children required medical exams for school, and their expectant wives needed care. These employees and their dependents could not use the facilities of public hospitals by law, their employers had to make an arrangement on their behalf with a private hospital.

Eastern Province employers – foreign and local alike – approached Al-Mana's management with an offer: to become a general hospital to service the new arrivals on a contractual basis. The new management at Al-Mana – made up of the young, aggressive, business-minded sons of the retired owner – could not afford to back away from such an opportunity. They agreed to expand the clinic and broaden its service portfolio to include other branches of medicine such as gynaecology, obstetrics, pediatrics, surgery, orthopedics, radiology, pathology, ENT (ear, nose and throat), dermatology, and physiotherapy.

To facilitate the conversion into a general hospital, a new six-story edifice was added to the old-two-story building. Each floor was designed to modern medical specifications. Both the old and new buildings were fully air-conditioned and fully equipped with elevators and state of the art operating rooms, medical and dental laboratories, X-ray, ultra-sound, and other diagnostic equipments.

Today, Al-Mana General Hospital offers a full range of medical services, including:

- acute medical care;
- routine in-patient care;
- ancillary services (such as respiratory and physical therapy, clinical lab testing, electrocardiography, ambulance and emergency room serivce available 24 hours a day, medical interpreting and translation services, pre-employment medical examinations for prospective corporate employees, and routine checkups for present corporate employees);
- periodic special clinics by visiting consultants from prominent teaching hospitals in the U.K. and Egypt.

Focussing on Maternity, 1984 —

As the Kingdom completed its infrastructure projects and as the demand for oil suddenly dropped and oil revenues plummeted, Saudi Arabia found itself on a retrenchment track. Foreigners and their dependents, who once provided the raison d'être for private hospitals, were sent home in droves. Many of those remaining had to pay for their own medical bills, at least in part, if not in full. Hence, the customer base upon which private hospitals thrived quickly shrank. Virtually all private hospitals, including Al-Mana, responded by rediscovering the Saudi patient. Each one has selected a special niche within this customer base. For Al-Mana, it is obstetrics and pediatrics. Upon surveying their own patient records, segmented income statements, population statistics, and competitors's strengths and weaknesses, Al-Mana's management decided to concentrate on Saudi expectant mothers and their babies. Their rationale was as follows:

1) Saudi women tend to have large families. Their fertility rate is comparatively high.
2) More and more Saudi mothers deliver their babies at hospitals, not at home.
3) More and more young Saudi families prefer to have the wife deliver her baby painlessly in the comfort of a private hospital, where visiting hours are flexible, rooms are private and cheerful, and meals are plentiful and tasty.

In contrast to their close competitors, Al-Mana executives decided to target their maternity services to the upper middle-class segment of Saudi mothers. These executives cite superior "British" operating standards, intensive nursing, highly trained anesthesiologists and gynaecologists, continuous monitoring of cases from pregnancy to delivery, responsive housekeeping, and cheerful and luxurious accommodation as key elements of their new success formula. Al-Mana's high rate of repeat customers suggests that its formula is working.

To implement this strategic move, and to conform to cultural sensitivities, Al-Mana hired four English-speaking gynaecologists, two of whom are female. It also has two competent anesthesiologists who are skilled in administering epidural shots commonly used to anesthetize women during child labor.

In focusing on maternity cases, Al-Mana executives went through a process of elimination. They weeded out the traditional focus on eye and dental care, since eye diseases have become almost a thing of the past and plenty of eye and dental clinics have sprung up all over the Kingdom, including government clinics which render their services free of charge. They rejected general and orthopedic surgery, despite growing demand in these segments (see Apendices A and B). They reasoned that growth in these areas would not continue, since the case load depended to a considerable extent on job-related injuries among expatriate employees. Finally, management rejected specializing in emergency medicine despite the fact that the demand for it is growing and the attention it has received from hospital authorities has been scanty. Although Al-Mana has emergency room facilities and staff, it does not consider this service a crucial part of its income-producing portfolio of services.

Mr. Mansoor Al-Mana sums up the hospital's current strategic posture as follows:

"We cannot be good in treating all kinds of patients. We have to specialize and focus on doing just a few things better than any of our competitors can. Maternity and babies go together, and they suit us fine."

Management Philosophy

The success of Al-Mana is due to the continuous effort and commitment of Sheikh Muhammad Al-Mana, who is a great believer in Islam and its values, and who perceives it as his Islamic duty to help his people.

Sheikh Muhammad believes in the right of all people to receive medical treatment, whether they are rich or poor, natives or foreigners. He also believes that a reasonable minimum profit is the just reward for delivering compassionate and personalized care. In all the meetings of the board, he always reminds his sons to give people the best service possible, not to overcharge or pressure them to pay, and accept whatever they can afford to pay.

When his sons once objected to such a philosophy of running a business, he is reported to have said: "My sons, no one is going to have more than his preordained lot in life. This is what God has already planned for him, no more or less."

Al-Mana's philosophy manifests itself in different forms. It goes beyond the mere reluctance to accept fees from disadvantaged patients (see Exhibit 2). It involves doing other things as well without regard to their economic payoffs. Sheikh Muhammad is not a sentimental fool, however. He emphasizes growth through long-term patient satisfaction not through short-term profit maximization. Moreover, in his eyes, it is impossible to place a monetary value on the saved life of a poor patient. For him, economic imperatives sometimes yield to humanitarian considerations.

With the opening of public clinics throughout the Kingdom as part of the expanding social welfare system, the number of welfare cases at Al-Mana sharply dropped from 50 % to 5 % of the daily out-patient load. This is a very affordable ratio, even in highly developed countries. In light of this trend, it is believed that Al-Mana's sons will be able to continue the philanthropic tradition that their father championed over a generation ago.

Exhibit 2   Discounted Free Treatments (in Saudi Riyals)

Type of Donation	1984	1983	1982
Discount allowed	2,138,729	1,984,692	2,048,318
Free Treatment	343,762	420,583	340,552
Total	2,484,491	2,405,275	2,388,870

Source: Al-Mana General Hospital's records.

Human Resources

The management of Al-Mana Hospital considers the employee the "heart" of the operation. It is he or she who provides the care, operates the systems, runs the equipment, and thereby achieves the hospital's objectives and shapes Al-Mana's image in the Eastern Province. The staffing profile by specialty, nationality, and sex of the employee is shown in Exhibit 3.

Recruitment and Selection Policy

Manpower represents the most critical areas of any hospital operation. And if and when found, qualified personnel can dictate salary and working conditions. In Saudi Arabia, the availability of well-trained medical personnel constitutes a critical success variable in the hospital industry.

For example, an Arabic-speaking female gynaecologist who is certified by an American or British medical boards is rare. Even more critical in the Kingdom is the availability of well-trained nursing staffs. Al-Mana General Hospital has a very well-planned, highly organized recruiting program. It has managed to establish a strong relationship with reliable recruiting agents and with some of the best hospitals in the countries it recruits from. It considers this relationship the key to its success in staffing the hospital with qualified personnel. It has selected personnel for the hospital and for several other projects from the following countries: Ireland, the Philippines, India, Egypt, Yemen, Pakistan, Sri Lanka, and Saudi Arabia. The recruiting agents advertise in the local papers of their respective countries and conduct preliminary interviews and selections. Then an expert team

Exhibit 3   Summary of Current Staffing Profile

I. By Profession Specialists	30	
General practitioners	15	
Dentists	12	
Nurses and paramedics	155	
Medical technicians	84	
Dental technicians	20	
Support services	115	
Total	431	
II. By Country		
Saudi Arabia	8	
U.S.A.	1	
U.K.	8	
Arab countries	76	
India	99	
Philippines	153	
Pakistan	39	
Korea	2	
Others	45	
Total	431	
III. By Sex		
Male	323	
Female	108	
Total	431	

Source: Al-Mana General Hospital's records.

from Al-Mana goes to that country to make the final selection. They carefully screen the candidates by examining their credentials and professional experience and evaluate whether they will fit in with the expectations of Al-Mana and its Saudi Arabian operating milieu.

Training and Development Policy

Al-Mana General Hospital invests handsomely in developing its human resources. It offers on-the-job training to all of its employees, particularly medical personnel. These programs are conducted periodically to update personnel on the latest methods and techniques. It also maintains a well-established medical library consisting of the latest medical books, journals, and magazines which give health professionals much of the current information they need to practice modern medicine.

Compensation Policy

There is no indication of job dissatisfaction among the hospital staff. To the contrary, employees seem reasonably satisfied. Whenever a new employee is hired, a mutual employment contract is made, and management has always lived up to the terms and conditions of the contract. Additionally, Al-Mana provides fringe benefits for all its employees, including fully-furnished housing, free medical treatment, transportation, and annual repatriation tickets.

Employees seem satisfied not only with their compensation but also with the work environment. Small groups of staff members meet regularly to analyze mutual problems and submit possible solutions to the administration for a final decision. The emphasis throughout is on effective communication and teamwork. Management considers every employee, no matter what his specialty or nationality may be, an important part of the Al-Mana organization.

Marketing

Al-Mana is an established and respected name in the health care industry of the Eastern Province of Saudi Arabia. Commitment to service quality is the single most important element affecting the future of this hospital.

Al-Mana mainly serves the outpatient market. The average inpatient population housed at the hospital at any given time is 200–225. Around 200 of the daily outpatient load at Al-Mana are Saudis. Another 100 are from other Arab countries. The remainder are mostly Indians and Pakistanis. Management is proud of the fact that despite its location in Al-Khobar – a district which is heavily populated by foreigners – and despite the availability of free, high-quality public hospitals in the area, Al-Mana has managed to attract a sizeable number of Saudi patients.

Competition

The management of Al-Mana General Hospital perceives Dr. Fakhry Hospital and Abdulla Fouad Hospital as major competitors. Minor competitors are Al-Salama and Al-Dossary Hospitals.

Abdulla Fouad Hospital is centrally located in Dammam, and most of its patients come from that area or areas north of Dammam, such as Qatif and Safwa. The hospital employs a sizeable number of British physicians and nurses, who adhere to British medical standards and procedures.

King Fahd Specialty Hospital is a showcase of modern technology and medicine. Located in Al-Khobar, this leading medical center receives its patients (Saudis and non-Saudis) by referral from the general practitioner or specialist. Since it is a teaching hospital, they attracts doctors and students from all over the world. Treatment is given free of charge.

Dr. Fakhry Hospital is the oldest and best-known one in Al-Khobar, particularly among middle-class Saudi patients. It competes in terms of location and the quality of its medical and nursing staff – all of whom are Egyptians who speak Arabic and earn the confidence and trust of their Saudi patients. Egyptian standards of medical care prevail at Fakhry Hospital, since the owner-founder, Dr. Fakhry, is a Saudi national who was born and educated in Egypt.

Customers and Market Share

Al-Mana customers are members of the general public as well as employees of government agencies and business firms. Al-Mana has a 60% share of the institutional "third party" market.

Pricing Policy

The Ministry of Health establishes and enforces a fee for every conceivable service offered by private hospitals. This fee schedule is intentionally low to make health care affordable by middle- and low-income patients. Al-Mana Hospital adheres to the government fee schedule, except when it discounts rates for needy patients.

Advertising and Promotion

Al-Mana does not have a promotion budget as such, but it does promote its service through:

1) distribution of pamphlets;
2) classified advertisements in local papers;
3) visits to companies and other organizations;
4) word-of-mouth communication by satisfied customers recommending the hospital to their friends and relatives.

Marketing Research

Al-Mana's management has conducted several market studies in the Eastern Province on pricing systems, quality of care, occupational health, and community health. Recommendations based on the findings are being applied. The general result has been an improvement in the system of levying charges for medical treatment, and an improved quality of service.

Finance

Exhibits 4 and 5 provide financial statements for the period 1982–1984. A quick look at Exhibit 5 suggests that the Al-Mana Hospital is in excellent financial shape. Partly because of the diversity of its business portfolio and partly because of its preference for internal financing, Al-Mana has stayed healthy. Unlike its competitors, it has never failed to pay its wage bill or

Exhibit 4   Al-Mana General Hospital – Consolidated Balance Sheet for the years ended December 31, 1982–1984 (in thousands of Saudi Riyals)

	1984	1983	1982
Current Assets			
Cash	15,672	11,590	8,796
Accounts receivable	11,367	5,560	3,337
Inventories	2,270	1,355	1,298
Notes receivable	3,160	3,821	4,056
Total current assets	32,469	22,326	17,487
Current Liabilities			
Accounts payable	4,482	2,929	2,300
Other liabilities	8,065	4,874	3,534
Total current liabilities	12,347	7,803	5,834
Net current assets (1)	20,122	14,523	11,653
Fixed Assets	59,239	50,381	34,730
Less: Accumulated depreciation	15,706	11,068	6,370
Net fixed assets (2)	43,533	39,313	28,360
Investments			
Investment for trade division		801	
Building under construction	10,330	8,769	5,072
Total investments (3)	73,985	63,406	45,085
Financed By:			
Capital	55,584	42,007	13,856
Government loans	9,483	11,625	11,886
Net profit for the year	8,908	9,774	19,343
Total financing	73,985	63,406	45,085

Source: Hospital records.

loan installments on time. It has enough cash to enable it to exploit opportunities as they develop.

One of management's most difficult tasks is to collect receivables. They offer credit terms of one month, sometimes more, but many customers, including companies, delay payments even longer. Of Al-Mana's total revenue, 40% is received in cash.

Exhibit 5   Al-Mana General Hospital – Consolidated Profit and Loss Account for the Years Ended December 31, 1982–84 (in thousands of Saudi Riyals)

	1984	1983	1982
Revenue			
Hospital	44,706	48,480	46,621
Public Health Project			
Jubail	6,954	7,402	4,540
Al Hadid Project	1,578	2,019	–
Methanol Project	306	132	–
Yanbu Project	3,016	–	–
Muhammad Al-Mana Establishment			
Clinics	–	2,988	4,142
Miscellaneous	1,951	371	35
Total revenue	61,239	61,762	55,338
Less			
(1) Direct expenses			
– Hospital	18,172	20,443	15,171
– Public Health Project	5,364	5,901	1,764
– Al Hadid Project	1,390	1,604	–
– Methanol Project	157	99	–
– Yanbu Project	2,633	–	–
– Al-Mana Establishment	2,826	343	2,280
– Clinics and other projects	–	2,385	–
(2) Indirect expenses	12,621	21,213	16,730
(3) Operating expenses including depreciation			
(4) Other expenses	786	–	50
Total Expenses	52,330	51,988	35,995
Net Surplus (Deficit)	8,909	9,774	19,343

Source: Hospital records.

Facilities and Equipment

Today, Al-Mana General Hospital owns and operates 12 operating rooms, an intensive and coronary care unit, a radiology unit, a well-stocked pharmacy, a physiotherapy unit, and a well-equipped medical laboratory. The hospital has its own kitchen facility which prepares meals that suit every palate. It also has an around-the-clock maintenance unit to service its buildings and medical equipment.

The Future

Al-Mana's strategy of offering low-cost, high-quality medical care worked well, when times were good and expatriate employees were present in large numbers. The post-oil-boom era has posed these new challenges:

1) Competition has arisen from newly-established public hospitals and from aggressive private sisters in the greater Dhahran-Dammam-Al-Khobar metropolitan area.
2) Massive cuts in the number of expatriates undermined a key source of revenue for the hospital.
3) Al-Mana's compliance with the Labor Office mandate to cut down on the number of expatriate employees on its payroll is likely to affect the quality of patient care.
4) Some organizations are cutting down their medical expenses. Others have slowed payments. These factors have negatively affected Al-Mana's cash flow.

In an effort to cope with the above-cited changes, the management of Al-Mana General Hospital has contemplated the following set of measures:

1) Reposition the hospital to appeal more to Saudi patients in general and Saudi women and children in particular. Gaining the trust and confidence of this often-ignored market segment is a challenge facing private hospitals throughout the Kingdom.
2) Complete the physical expansion of the hospital which will add 135 beds. This addition will be used to separate female from male patients in an effort to adapt the facility to the local culture.
3) Adopt the suite concept in all its inpatient accommodation facilities. Each suite consists of a separate room with a bathroom and visitors' room. Saudis demand and are willing to pay for such hotelstyle accommodation.
4) Provide restaurant services 24 hours a day for all patients, with a wide selection of menu items.

5) Improve the collection of bad debts and reduce outstanding receivables.
6) Emphasize the hospital as the prime strategic business unit, while de-emphasizing or holding steady other activities.
7) Reorganize the company so that each of the founder's sons gets a share which is agreed upon by all. This plan would provide for a smooth and orderly transition upon the eventual death of the founder.

Appendix A

Al-Mana General Hospital Segmented Income Statement by Type of Medical Service Rendered For the Years Ended Dec. 31, 1984–85 (in Thousands of Saudi Riyals)

Service Center	Revenues		Expenses		Surplus/(Deficit)	
	1984	1985	1984	1985	1984	1985
Ophthalmology (Eye)	5,131		1,450		3,681	
Dental	4,919		1,582		3,336	
Surgery	4,615		1,925		2,689	
General laboratory	4,109		1,421		2,687	
Medicine	3,524		1,651		1,873	
Orthopaedics	3,264		1,706		1,557	
Dental lab	3,210		485		2,725	
Obstetrics & Gyn	3,050		1,081		1,969	
Pharmacy	2,991		189		2,802	
Radiology	2,002		722		1,280	
Ear, Nose & Throat	2,000		745		1,255	
Pediatrics	1,384		1,126		258	
Visiting professors	1,240		743		496	
Pre-employment	1,045		–		494	
Contact lens	697		203		494	
General practice	578		602		(24)	
Dermatology	532		187		344	
Physiotheraphy	399		–		5	
Outpatient's dept	5		–		5	
Total:	44,706		15,945		28,760	

Source: Hospital's records.

Appendix B

Department Contribution – May 1986

Department	Inpatient		Outpatient	
	Patient Days for the month	Percentage shared	Total Patients for the month	Percentage shared*
Pre-employment exam	–	–	96	.7
Physiotherapy	–	–	101	.8
Surgical	681	22.1	648	5.1
Orthopedic	550	17.8	853	6.7
Medical	520	16.9	670	5.3
E.N.T.	148	4.8	984	7.8
Gynaecology	105	3.4	–	–
Obstetrics-Ante	85	2.7	1,361	10.8
Obstetrics-Post	211	6.8	–	–
Ophthalmic	302	9.8	2,386	18.9
Dental	–	.0	1,906	15.1
Psychiatry	–	–	–	–
Dermatology	16	.5	564	4.4
New-born-nursery	190	6.1	–	–
New-born-incub.	4	.1	–	–
Pediatrics-normal	247	8.0	1,018	8.0
Pediatrics.-Incub.	17	.5		
Visiting professors	–	–	321	2.5
Laboratory	–	–	272	2.1
Radiology	–	–	47	.3
Internal medicine	–	–	1,384	10.9
	3,076	100	12,613	100

* Percentages do not add up to 100

Source: Hospital's records.

7.3   Abdulla Fouad Hospital (AFH)

Haman Al Otaibi and M. Sami Kassem

Introduction

One day, in the early seventies, while Sheikh Abdulla Fouad was drinking his Arabian coffee after he performed Asr Prayer in the yard of his palace in Dammam City, his son came to inform him that his mother, the Sheikh's wife, had suddenly gone into labor and needed to go to a hospital. The wealthy businessman immediately drove his wife to Dr. Fakhri Hospital in Al-Khobar city, one of the best private hospitals in the Eastern Province at that time. When the Sheikh reached the hospital he was told by the hospital receptionist that all beds were occupied. He was advised to go to Al-Salama Hospital which was not far. The Sheikh had no choice except to go as told. But, the administrators at Al-Salama would not admit her either. So he went immediately to Al-Sharq Hospital. After a great effort, his wife was admitted.

Out of this experience, the idea of building a hospital was born. It found enormous support among Sheikh Abdulla's friends and technical advisors. A seductive public policy and a healthy business environment made this business proposition very appealing. The government had been offering interest-free, long-term loans to Saudi entrepreneurs who whished to build hospitals. Moreover, it enacted a policy which requires every business establishment and government agency to have a valid contract with a health care provider in the private sector.

Sheikh Abdulla was not a dreamer. He realized that building and operating a private hospital was a completely different proposition than contracting and trading which was where he had made his fortune. He understood that hospitals are complex labor and capital intensive businesses, which require massive investment of funds to keep them operating profitably. But Sheikh Abdulla decided to go ahead with the idea of constructing a private hospital, mainly to improve the health care in the community and to capitalize on the opportunity he discovered.

Development of the Hospital

Abdulla Fouad Hospital (AFH) is considered one of the best hospitals in the Kingdom, and the only first-class facility in the Eastern Province. Since it opened its doors in June 1979, the hospital went through two distinct operational stages.

First Stage (1979–1983)

Sheikh Abdulla Fouad had no experience or background in hospital administration, but he preferred to manage the hospital himself. Initially, he recruited a number of qualified doctors and medical assistants from the U.K. He also recruited some Saudi nationals to perform the administrative functions. During this stage, most of the patients were from Aramco, major companies, banks, and businessmen who were financially able to pay the medical fees.

The most important features of this formative stage were:

1) the high quality image of the hospital. It was instantly recognized as the only first-class facility in the Eastern Province and the second in Saudi Arabia;
2) the high operating costs caused by unusually high salaries of expatriate medical personnel;
3) average occupancy rate that ranged between 50–65 percent.

The combined bottom-line effect of the above-cited features is that the hospital was running in the red. It was simply too costly to build (SR 200 million) and to operate this facility. It appealed to corporate employees but was too costly for the average nonsponsored Saudi patient.

Second Stage (1984–1987)

The disappointing results of the first stage; the deep business recession, the decrease in number of expatriate patients, the expansion of Aramco hospital, and the construction of well-equipped government hospitals (i.e. the King Fahd University Hospital in Al-Khobar and the Medical Treatment Center in Dhahran), all have combined to force management to make various changes in its tactics. The objective of the second operational stage was to enable the hospital to meet its financial obligations and thus operate profitably.

With the beginning of the second stage, the following policies were adopted and implemented:

1) Because most area residents speak Arabic, it was apparent that an

Arabic-speaking medical staff was needed. The management recruited Arabic medical doctors to work in all departments within the hospital. Accordingly, the number of British medical staff dropped from 30 in 1983 to 5 in mid-1987.

2) Operating costs were reduced to enable the hospital to generate a reasonable profit. Various changes were made both in size and composition of the work force.

The Concept in Detail

The following points reflect specifics regarding the concepts on which AFH was developed:

1) The new hospital was to render the best medical services not only to the standards of the Eastern Region but also to those in the Kingdom.
2) The hospital was to acquire the latest medical and technological equipments for examination, testing, and treatment.
3) The hospital was to operate as a general medical center, covering all specialized medical services needed for the community.
4) The design of the buildings were to be convenient and comfortable for both patients and employees.
5) The hospital was to be equipped by all necessary facilities and services, such as complete drainage and sewage systems, a water supply system, an electrical system, a sanitation system, as well as employee accommodations and recreational facilities.
6) Operations were to be carried out by the best qualified medical staff from Britain and operated according to the British medical standards.
7) The capacity of the hospital was to be adequate to accommodate existing and future needs. The required present capacity was estimated at 300 beds.
8) From its inception, AFH's planners have targeted their services not only to the well-to-do Saudi nationals but to corporate patients as well.

Facilities

AFH is conveniently located in Dammam. Area residents can easily reach the hospital within ten minutes. Khobar and Dhahran residents can get to the hospital along two highways in less than fifteen minutes. Also, Ras Tanura, Qatif, Saihat, Jubail, Abqaiq, and Al-Hasa residents can easily reach the hospital.

AFH occupies a four-story building and several smaller adjacent buildings and villas. The unique architectural design and decor of the hospital suggests the idea of high class service within the minds of the visitors. Reception areas are spacious and comfortable. This also reassures visitors of high class service and quality treatment.

Although some areas of the hospital are comfortable and facilitating, others are not. Waiting areas are crowded with both male and female patients who stand near physicians' doors in small walkways. No forethought was given to the parking situation surrounding the hospital. Visitors experience difficulties in parking, and many park their cars on the streets around the hospital.

The Service Portfolio

AFH is a 310-bed general medical/surgical hospital, with an out-patient department consisting of 24 clinics covering all fields of medicine. In addition to fee for service treatment, the hospital offers various health care plans. The following information reflects specifics regarding these alternative health care plans.

Outpatient Plan

Exhibit 1 reflects the 12 specialist consultation fields offered by the outpatient plan at AFH and their respective department heads.

Exhibit 1   Fields of Specialization and Department Heads

Specialization	Head of Department
1. Medicine	Roohi A. Robb, MB, ChB, Ph.D. (West Germany)
2. Obst./Gyn.	E.M. El-Sayed, MB.Ch.B., M.R.C.O.G. (London)
3. Cardiology	Jamshehd Ahmed, MBBS (DOW), F.A.C.P. (USA)
4. Surgery	Donald L. Glen, MS, FRACS, FRCS (UK) FACS (USA)
5. Pediatrics	M. Chaudhry, MBBS, DCS (UK), MRCP (London)
6. Ophthalmology	M.H. Sheik, MBBS, DORCS, R.C.P. (Ireland)
7. Orthopedics	A. Salam Yousef, MB ChB, M.Ch. (Ortho) FICS (USA)
8. Dentistry	A. Rashed Qutb, B.Ch.D., D.O.S., MS (Dentistry)
9. Pathology	W.A. Ranasinghe, M.B.B.S., M.R.C. Path (London)
10. Radiology	Fouad S.D., Mohd, MBChB, MS, Ph.D. (Radiology)
11. Psychiatry	Mohd.A.R. Ghazi, MBChB, DPM(UK) MRCPsych (UK)
12. Dermatology	A. Abraham, MD (Dermatology/Venereology)

Inpatient Plan

The inpatient plan comprises of the following services: 1) Hospital room and board; and 2) inpatient physician care by any or all specialists.

Outpatient/Inpatient Combination Plan

This plan allows a patient to combine inpatient services along with outpatient service.

At Home Service Plan

This plan allows a patient to have one or more hours of general practitioner service at his home six days a week.

Accidents and Emergency Departments

This adequately staffed and equipped department is open on a 24-hour basis to deal with emergencies arising in the area; it also includes an ambulance service. The intensive care unit (I.C.U.) provides the patients with individualized medical care. It consists of a separate monitoring system for each patient and connection with the hospital's main monitor. This unit is matchless in its technical expertise.

The outpatient and inpatient departments are supported by the most modern and sophisticated laboratory and cardiological diagnostic equipment. This laboratory is one of the leading laboratories in the region, houseing its own blood bank.

The dental department offers complete dental services and is supported by qualified, experienced dental and oral surgeons, who are capable of carrying out any type of dental work. This department houses a dental laboratory and employs trained technicians who use state of the art dental equipment.

The hospital also offers numerous diagnostic and specialized services, which include ECGS, ECT, fundoscopy, spirometry, electrocardiography, and an infant intensive care unit. Hospital information is currently being computerized. Information regarding admission and discharge, payroll, inventory, patient billing, and other accounting functions has already been computerized. Other areas of the operation will soon be computerized.

Patient Classification and Its Impact on Clinics and Departments

The following sections provide information regarding patient classification and its affect upon the deliverance of clinics and departments' performance.

Patient Categories

Patients are classified in terms of payment method into two categories: cash patients and credit patients. The cash patients are those who pay before being issued a red sticker file and receive expected medical treatment. Credit patients are issued a green sticker file and are typically corporate sponsored. Their treatment is rendered, after a contract has been signed between the hospital and the sponsor. Payment is made by the sponsor.

Outpatient Clinics' Performance

Exhibits 2 and 3 provide comparative statistics relating to the performance of patient clinics during the period of 1982 to mid-1987.

Whereas the cash patients represented 28 % of the total patient load in 1983, this category increased to 60 % by 1986. Conversely, the share of credit patients dropped from 58 % in 1983 to only 38 % in 1986. Also, a sharp decline is noticed in the number of medical check-up patients who are mostly corporate employees transferred to the hospital by their sponsor so as to receive a medical check-up as part of their employment requirement. In general, the total number of patients visiting the outpatient clinics daily dropped from 450 patients in 1983 to 250 in 1986.

Nowadays, 70 % of the outpatients are well-to-do Saudi nationals living in the Dammam area. In the past, Saudis represented only 40 % of total patients. However, this does not mean that the number of Saudi patients has increased. As a matter of fact, their numbers have decreased by 6 % from 1983 to 1986.

Approximately 45 % of the patients visit the hospital between 8:30 a.m. and 12:00 noon, while the remaining 55 % prefer to show up between 4:00 p.m. and 7:00 p.m. Most of the morning patients are corporate employees, while the afternoon patients are drawn from family individuals. The majority of the patients visit the hospital in the beginning of the week (Saturday and Sunday) and on the weekend (Thursday). Seventy percent of the outpatients are repeat patients, and their share has increased by 10 % between 1983 and 1986. The remaining patients are new patients, as shown in Exhibit 2.

Exhibit 2   Outpatient Profile – Average Daily Patient Load by: Method of Payment, Nationality, Time of Day and Type of Patient

Category	1982 Jan–June	1982 July–Dec.	1983 Jan–June	1983 July–Dec.	1984 Jan–June	1984 July–Dec.	1985 Jan–June	1985 July–Dec.	1986 Jan–June	1986 July–Dec.	1987 Jan–April
Cash Patient	111	82	136	98	178	159	147	127	152	106	104
Credit-patient	138	120	275	232	211	177	119	101	83	87	67
staff	13	9	19	11	24	25	19	12	10	7	9
Med-check-up	–	–	42	53	22	12	4	3	5	1	1
Total	262	211	472	394	435	373	289	243	250	201	281
Nationality											
Saudi	45%	37%	40%	39%	40%	42%	53%	49%	66%	64%	72%
Non-Saudi	55%	63%	60%	61%	60%	58%	47%	51%	34%	36%	28%
Average Patient Per Clinic											
Morning	10	9	13	11	10	9	10	8	9	8	8
Evening	9	9	11	9	8	9	9	8	8	8	7
New patient	30%	29%	23%	22%	21%	24%	22%	24%	19%	15%	21%
Repeat patient	70%	71%	77%	78%	79%	76%	78%	76%	81%	85%	79%

Exhibit 3   Out Patient Clinic: Percentage of Sales Contributions

Clinic	1980	1981	1982	1983
Ped.	5	5	5	6
Ob-gyn.	11	10	10	10
ENT	7	6	6	5
Eye	4	5	4	3
Gen. medicine	24	23	19	23
Gen. Surgery	5	5	4	4
Urology	5	3.5	2	3
Orthopedics	8	7	9	8
Physiotherapy	3	4	4	4
Causality	21	17	8	8
Dental	7	7	7	7
Psychiatry	0.5	1.50	1	1.5
Referrals	–	3.50	19	15
Dermatology	–	3	2	2.5
Fracture clinic	–	–	–	–
Dietitian	–	–	–	–
Hematology	–	–	–	–
Medical check-up	–	–	–	–
Weight control clinic	–	–	–	–
	100	100	100	100

Source: Hospital records.

The majority of the outpatients (55 %) visit the hospital at an average of one visit a month. About 45 % are seen by a general practitioner, while the remainder are seen by specialists.

The percentage of outpatients visiting different clinics are shown in Exhibit 3. The general medicine clinic is most frequently visited followed by the OB-GYN, orthopedics, and pediatrics clinics.

Inpatient Departments Performance

As mentioned above, AFH is equipped with 310 beds, 273 of which are usable. Their distribution among the inpatient departments is shown in Exhibit 4:

The patients can select either a suite, private room, or semi-private room. For the corporate patient, the sponsor usually specifies the bed type in the contract for each class of its employees. About 85 % of the occupied beds are semi-private. The semi-private bed costs about SR 195 per day, whereas the private room costs SR 400. The suite costs SR 750 per day.

Exhibit 4   Distribution of Bedding Capacity by Speciality and Sex

Med.	28	Female	68	Male
Surg.	16		77	
Obst.	16			
Orth.	30			
Ped.	34			
Suites	2			
Total	126	+	145	= 271

In broad outline, the performance of the inpatient departments parallels that of the outpatient clinics (see Exhibit 5).

A bedding crisis is on hand. The bed occupancy rate has dropped from 70% in 1983 to only 44% in 1986. It is estimated that the average bed occupancy rate in 1987 will be around 40%. About 85% of the inpatients are admitted through outpatient clinics, whereas the remainder are admitted through the emergency room.

In contrast to the outpatient clinics, most of the inpatients are credit patients. In 1983, credit patients represented 65%, whereas in 1986 they represented 72% of the total patients. As shown in Exhibit 5, the majority of the patients are Saudi nationals.

The distribution of inpatients over different specialty areas is given in Exhibit 6. In the past general surgery was in the lead, now general medicine is in the lead.

Organization Structure

Sheikh Abdulla Fouad is the owner of AFH and the chairman of the board of directors. His son Fouad is the vice-president of the hospital as well as vice-president of other divisions within the corporation. Exhibit 7 reflects the organizational structure and hierarchy of AFH.

The hospital administrator, Mr. Yousef Sayadi, who is a Bahraini national holding a B.S. degree in business administration, looks after 8 supporting units: material services, financial accounting, log and general services, plant operations and maintenance, patients services, food services, nursing services, and personnel.

The medical director of the hospital, Dr. Abdul-Moniam-Hassanian, an Egyptian with management work experience, manages 4 units: surgery, medical, pediatrics, obstetrics, and gynaecology. Nine medical commit-

Exhibit 5 Inpatient Profile – Average Daily Patient Load by Method of Payment and Nationality

Category	1982 Jan– –June	July– –Dec.	1983 Jan– –June	July– –Dec.	1984 Jan– –June	July– –Dec.	1985 Jan– –June	July– –Dec.	1986 Jan– –June	July– –Dec.	1987 June– –Dec.
Cash patient	59	59	61	79	50	51	42	31	38	30	
Credit patient	124	91	128	128	120	122	111	89	86	89	
Staff	1	4	2	3	2	5	2	2	1	2	
Total	184	154	191	210	172	178	155	122	125	121	
Nationality											
Saudi	38%	42%	45%	33%	44%	47%	53%	58%	65%	66%	
Non-Saudi	62%	58%	55%	67%	56%	53%	47%	42%	35%	34%	
Bed-occupancy rate	67%	56%	70%	76%	63%	65%	56%	44%	45%	45%	40% (Expected)

Source: Hospital records.

Exhibit 6   Inpatient Department Percentage of Sales Contribution

	1980	1981	1982	1983
Ped	6	9	10	12
Gyn/female I	8	4	6.5	6
ENT	4	6.60	5.60	4
Eye	2	3	3	2
Gen. Medicine/Medical I	23	22	24	23.70
Gen. Surgery	24.30	22.16	19.5	18
Urology	4	4	3	5
Orthopedic	15	14	13	14
Obstet.	13	11	12	10.32
Psychiatry	0.70	3	3	3.30
Dental	–	0.10	0.27	0.38
Dermatology	–	0.14	0.13	0.16
C.C.U.	–	–	–	1.14
Female II	–	–	–	–
Nursery	–	–	–	–
Male Surgical II	–	–	–	–
Total	100	100	100	100

Source: Hospital records.

tees are found in the medical section. These support the medical units with advice, as well as participate in solving medical and operational problems.

Another committee is the executive committee of the medical staff, which holds at least one meeting per month. The executive committee may include in its monthly meetings agenda some important issues, such as planning procedures, financial procedures, purchasing procedures, and employment procedures. Occasionally, the chairman of the board participates in the executive committee of the medical staff meetings.

Hospital Personnel

Staff Size and Composition

The hospital staff profile is shown by nationality and profession in Exhibit 8. Most physicians during the formative years were British. In the current austere budget era, they have been replaced by Arabic-speaking physicians. The number of physicians in 1983 reached 50. By 1986, it had dropped to 36. In general, the majority of employees are from India, Pakistan, the Philippines, and Egypt.

The supporting staff represents 50% of the total manpower. Nurses represent 32% of the total hospital employees. The staff-bed ratio is 1.5 : 1. The total manpower was 588 employees in January 1983. The staff increased to reach 729 employees in May 1985. Since that time, management decided to trim the hospital manpower to match the existing work load. Thus, the total number of employees dropped to 672, and 473 in 1987 and 1986, respectively.

Recruitment and Selection Policy

Manpower represents the most critical area in any service organization. Employees are simply internal customers rather than external customers. Therefore, their recruitment and selection is given great consideration by the hospital's management team.

Hospital employees are carefully recruited through specialized recruiting agents in Asian and European countries. The recruiting agents will advertise the hospital's needs in local papers. They set up a preliminary selection interview. Then the interview results, along with the candidate file, are sent to the hospital for final selection. The candidate document is carefully checked by the concerned department's chief. If the candidate is selected, the agents will complete the employment formalities. Sometimes, the hospital recruits employees from the local market. A physician or any other qualified candidate who approaches the hospital or who is recommended by a friend is selected if he passes the interview.

Highly qualified medical personnel are always difficult to find. It takes one or two years' time to find and complete the recruitment process of a qualified physician. Moreover, some qualified physicians, working in Abdulla Fouad and other private hospitals, are raided by prestigious government hospitals. They provide them with salaries and working conditions that cannot be matched by private hospitals. As one hospital administrator complained, "We cannot compete with the administrators of government hospitals in this regard."

Training and Development Policy

The hospital maintains a medical library consisting of the latest medical books, journals, and magazines which give the hospital technicians and physicians current information regarding modern medicine. In addition, one week vacation with pay is offered to any physician who attends a medical seminar held locally or abroad. Also, nurses who do not speak the Arabic language are given training.

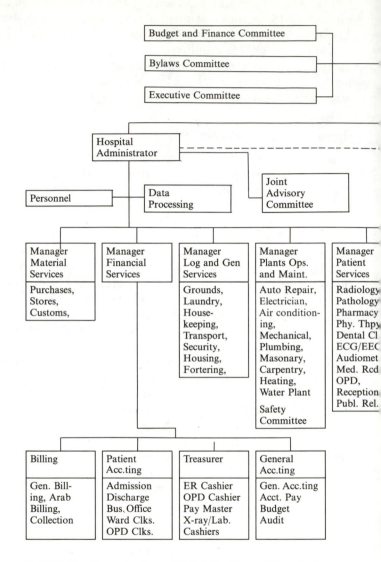

Exhibit 7   Organization of Abdulla Fouad Hospital

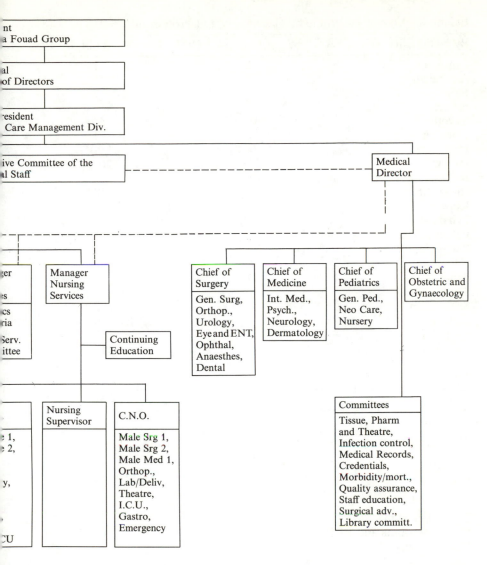

Exhibit 8   Manpower Profile by Nationality and Profession

By Nationality	As of 24.1.1983	As of 5.3.1982
American	2	1
Australian	1	1
Bahraini	7	3
British	31	5
Egyptian	38	44
Ghanian	1	1
Irish	–	1
Indian	231	205
Italian	1	–
Jordanian	5	4
Korean	3	1
Lebanese	1	1
Pakistani	165	87
Palestinian	1	1
Filipino	61	78
Saudi	5	6
Somali	–	–
Sri Lankan	3	2
Sudani	6	10
Syrian	1	2
Thailandi	21	12
Ugandan	1	–
Yemeni	3	3
Total	588	468

By Profession	As of 13.5.1987
Administrators and managers	7
Medical	36
Paremedical	38
Nurses	151
Pharmacist	2
Supporting staff	
Clerks, accounts and EDP	85
Housekeeping	63
Laundry	13
Transportation	14
Security	16
Gardening	5
Maintenance	43
Total	473

Source: Hospital records.

Compensation Policy

The salary of each individual in the hospital is determined mutually through negotiation during the selection process. The amount of the salary and other contract conditions depend on the physicians' circumstances at the employment time. Therefore, since there is no standard salary scale, variations in salaries were found within one employee category. For example, a driver or laborer who has worked at the hospital since 1979 may receive double the salary of his counterpart who joined the hospital a few years later. In general, a consultant or specialist physician is paid an average salary of SR 15,000 – SR 20,000 a month. A general practitioner is paid within the range of SR 8,000–SR 12,000 a month.

As a part of its retrenchment strategy, salaries of all employees, except physicians, were reduced between 15 and 40%. The amount of reduction was determined for each employee individually. Salaries of old, highly paid employees may be reduced by as much as 40%. The hospital's management team is trying hard to standardize the salary scale and to reduce high operating expenses. The expected savings in salaries as a result of this retrenchment strategy are estimated to be around 25% of the wage and salary budget for 1987. Few employees have rejected the reduction in their salary or terminated their contracts with the hospital.

Financial Issues

A quick look at the financial statements reflected in Exhibits 9 and 10 suggests that the hospital's income has experienced a sharp decline since 1983. The sources of income reflect both cash accounts.

The credit account represents 53% of the total income. Although the total income has dropped by almost 40%, the operating expenses have been decreased by only 10% from 1983 to 1985. Payroll is the main cost item, representing about 83% of the total operating expenses.

The hospital was able to generate operating profits during the years 1980, 1981, 1983, and 1984. The operation during the years 1982, 1985, and 1986 was not profitable. It is expected that the reductions in the following cost items may improve the hospital profitability by the end of 1987.

1) The hospital will save 3.5 million from payroll reductions.
2) Due to the Saudi government's resolution not to charge expatriates and their sponsors social security charges, the hospital will save about SR 1.12 million.
3) Other savings are expected from the reduction in electricity expenses. During 1985, electricity expenses were SR 679,210.22. However, all

Exhibit 9   Income Statement for the Years Ending December 31

	1983	1984	1985
Income			
General service	11,539,000	9,186,000	6,980,220
Special service	12,980,000	10,230,000	7,897,500
Total Income	24,519,000	19,416,000	14,877,720
Expenses			
Chemicals	590,300	589,400	404,650
Medicines	789,560	699,650	590,980
Wages and salaries	15,890,000	15,780,000	14,653,000
Rent	429,500	430,400	388,000
Utilities	529,250	499,000	379,500
Depreciation	480,000	480,000	480,000
Miscellaneous exp.	124,524	123,244	119,960
Total Expenses	18,833,134	18,601,694	17,021,090
Net Income (Loss)	5,685,866	814,306	(2,143,370)

Source: Hospital records.

service organizations, including the hospital, have benefitted from the resolution of fixing the electricity consumption charge at 5 halalas per kilow/w effective 9.4.1986. Since then, the electricity bill dropped to SR 302,879.32 during 1986. It is anticipated to fall to SR 180,000 by the end of 1987.

Competitive Analysis

Second to Jeddah, the private health care market in the Eastern Province is fiercely competitive. It is dominated by a numer of hospitals providing services to residents and guests of that region.

The major competitors of AFH are Dr. Fakhry Hospital and Al-Mana General Hospital. Both are located in Al-Khobar, and both are classified by the Ministry of Health as second-class hospitals. Both are well established and well-known, particularly among middle-class Saudi patients. Both offer lower prices and a similar quality of medical and nursing care as does Abdulla Fouad Hospital. As of late, both have started to provide luxurious accommodations to the upper middle-class segment of Saudi patients. AFH has the advantage of being the only general hospital in the Dammam area.

Exhibit 10   Balance Sheet for the Years Ending December 31 (in thousand Saudi Riyals)

	December 31 1983	1984	1985
Current assets			
Cash	158,418	159,000	156,324
Receivables	31,220	36,220	40,220
Medical supplies and Drugs	8,530	7,240	6,240
Prepaid expenses	420	420	435
Total current assets	198,588	202,880	203,219
Fixed assets			
Land	2,000	2,000	2,000
Building	24,000	24,000	24,000
Medical equipment	20,000	20,000	20,000
Laboratory equipment	12,000	12,000	12,000
Computer	1,500	1,500	1,500
Furniture	15,000	15,000	15,000
Ambulance and vehicles	5,000	5,000	5,000
Less depreciation	(3,120)	(3,600)	(4,080)
Total fixed assets	76,380	75,900	75,420
Total assets	274,968	278,782	278,639
Liabilities and owner's interest			
Current liabilities	62,000	65,000	71,000
Long-term government loan	50,000	50,000	50,000
Owner's equity	150,000	150,000	150,000
Retained earnings	12,968	13,782	7,639
Total liabilities	274,968	278,782	278,639

Source: Hospital records.

Other competitors of AFH are Aramco and King Fahd Teaching Hospitals. Access to the first one is restricted to Aramco personnel, while access to the second one is attained only by referrals from area clinics or hospitals. Both compete by offering their versions of modern medical technology and services. King Fahd Teaching Hospital offers its services free of charge. As might be expected, it tends to be overcrowded and offers its patients neither private rooms nor personalized treatment. Pregnant women are reluctant to give birth at this hospital because of the lack of privacy.

Price ceilings are determined and imposed by the Ministry of Health. The determined price is based on the class of each hospital. Since AFH is a first-class hospital, its prices are almost 30 % higher than those of the immediate competitors.

Lately, the hospital's management team has started to offer a 20 % discount for new corporate patients. Cash patients are charged full fare. However, a discount is sometimes granted to patients who are subject to a weak financial situation.

In addition to the surplus of beds already in the Eastern Province market, there are new hospitals under construction which will compound the bedding crisis and heighten competition among health care providers. The hospitals under construction and their projected capacities are listed in Exhibit 11.

Exhibit 11   New Hospitals Under Construction in the Eastern Province

Hospital	Capacity	Location
Gulf General Hospital	575 beds	Dammam
Al-Mana Hospital	300 beds	Dammam
Qatif Gen. Hospital	345 beds	Qatif
Jubail New Hospital	170 beds	Jubail
Hofuf Accident Hosp.	100 beds.	Hofuf
Al-Khaphji Hospital	100 beds	Al-Khaphji
Nuairiah Hospital	50 beds	Al-Nuairiah
Safwa Hospital	50 beds	Al-Safwa
Dhahran Gen. Hospital	200 beds	Dhahran
Medical Academic Hosp.	300 beds	–
Howasah Hosp. (priv.)	210 beds	Dammam
Al-Jazerah Hospital	200 beds	between Dammam and Khobar

Source: Primary; based on data compiled from the Ministry of Health in 1984.

The Future of Abdulla Fouad Hospital

The recession in the oil industry has affected all sectors of the Saudi economy. Nearly all business organization have reduced their manpower to save some money. Moreover, the government enacted a policy of expatriate manpower reduction. Two years ago, it assigned the Labor Office the task of supervising desired reductions in expatriate manpower. The Labor Office has implemented some regulations to significantly reduce the number of expatriates in the country. The ultimate effect of these regulations has been to drastically reduce the size of potential markets for private hospitals. A conference held in the Chamber of Commerce at

Dammam in 1985, and attended by the private hospital executives from the Eastern Province, has concluded that without economic recovery in the country, most of the private hospitals in the area will close their doors in the near future. AFH may very well be one of those facilities, if it does not act now to fill up its empty beds and underutilized facilities. The banks are threatening foreclosure unless management develops an effective plan to save the hospital from a financial collapse.

7.4   Green Crescent Health Services Clinic (GC)

M. Sami Kassem

Introduction

Green Crescent (GC) is a small health maintenance organization (HMO) located in Riyadh, the capital of Saudi Arabia. It is a wholly-owned and privately managed subsidiary of Saudi Medical Center. It opened its services to the public in August 1981. Since its inception, GC has developed a reputation for providing affordable personalized health care services backed by state of the art medical technology. It has developed a sizeable patient clientele in spite of the fact that the Riyadh metropolitan area has many high-quality, low-cost health care facilities among which potential customers may choose. With a typical patient load of about 250 to 300 persons a day, GC has demonstrated a demand for specialty clinics and referral services. GC has also demonstrated its ability to attract specialist physicians.

As of late, however, a number of exogenous and endogenous factors have threatened the viability of GC's original concept. A recessionary environment has eroded the core patient group – "subscribers" – who have switched to more affordable alternatives. Stiffening competition among area hospitals has resulted in operational losses and affected GC's ability to attract not only well-to-do patients but also high quality physicians.

In addition, there is a threat from within. The owners fell into disagreement. They agreed to submit their dispute to a court, which in 1987 ordered liquidation. Once liquidation is concluded, ownership will be transferred to another group that has not yet been determined. Two of the original founders might be tempted to buy the clinic. Whoever the new owners may be, they will have to decide whether to continue with the original concept or chart a new direction for the clinic.

Mission

The original mission of GC was to provide comprehensive, high quality ambulatory care to individuals who desire peace of mind and personalized attention for themselves and those for whom they are responsible. Specifically, GC aimed to:

1) participate together with the public and private sectors in providing advanced specialty medical services;
2) participate in health care education of Saudi society; and
3) provide complete medical protection and support for families, corporate patients, expatriates, franchised patients, and special referrals.

Current Strategy

1) Provide a wide range of specialized primary and secondary care services utilizing highly qualified specialists recruited from all over the world;
2) promote its services through the use of low-key tactics;
3) segment its market into two groups:
   - subscribers to its health maintenance program, targeted at married individuals, company managers, foreign embassies, and upper-income individuals;
   - non-subscribers, including the general public and other clinics and hospitals all billed on a "pay-as-you-go" basis.

Original Concept

As a health maintenance organization (HMO), GC was set up to provide medical services primarily to subscribers on a contractual basis. That is, to contract with an employer to provide a specified range of services (physicals, outpatient services, diagnostic services, inpatient services, etc.), for a certain fixed amount per employee, regardless of the degree to which its services would be utilized. The incentive to keep costs down under such an arrangement is that the HMO profit margin will increase. The incentive to maintain quality is that if it does not, it may lose the contract. When it was founded, about 90% of GC's patients were subscribers. This membership program is what differentiated GC from other hospitals and clinics. GC contracts covered primary care, preventive care, and cases involving simple operations or hospitalization of not more than one week. At the beginning of the contract, GC would conduct a general check of the subcribers' health and follow these physicals with quarterly checkups.
   The membership idea was new to Saudi Arabia.

Lately, the survival of this concept has been difficult for the following reasons:

– Most Saudi patients like to change doctors, clinics, and hospitals if they so desire.
– Most Saudis do not go to hospitals or clinics for preventive care, but only when they are seriously ill.
– Many potentical customers see no benefit in pre-paying for services which may not be required.

GC's quarters originally were not built as a clinic, and architectural design of the building falls short of modern requirements. However, top management regards the relative small size of the facility to be a plus.

GC Service Portfolio

1) specialized clinics (for details on these clinics and the range of medical services offered by GC, see Exhibit 1);
2) 24-hour emergency service;
3) house calls: GC offers house calls, a new idea in Saudi Arabia, to subscribers for a fee of SR 150 (US $ 40) per visit, compared with a normal charge for a clinic visit of SR 70. GC has encountered numerous difficulties in providing this unique service. For example, inaccurate directions have hampered GC's ability to easily locate patients' homes. In addition, government regulations regarding injuries stemming from family conflicts require that the police must be notified prior to any medical action beyond administering emergency first aid to the injured party. Further treatment requires that a government official be present to observe and record the events. Mandatory compliance with these regulations may discourage persons from seeking medical help in such cases and can impede actual treatment even if help is sought.

    There are also social restrictions that complicate the delivery of home medical care. For example, a female patient must have a male companion – usually her father or adult brother – present in the house when the physician calls and when she signs a document. Most families demand a female doctor to treat females in the house. There are additional social restrictions and regulations which limit the hospitals' ability to provide quick medical services to patients in their own homes.

    Despite these obstacles, GC has usually managed to provide good service to its subscribers, and it has a general practitioner and a specialist doctor on call at all times for house visits.

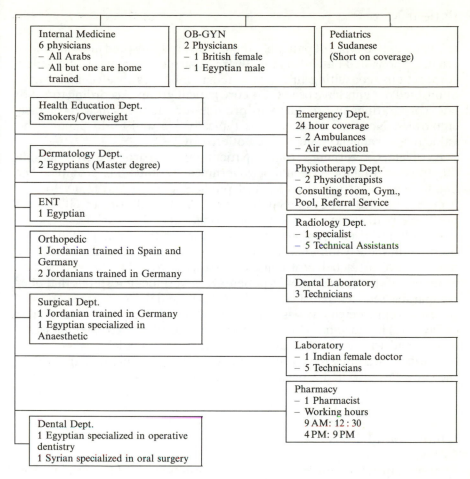

Internal Medicine	OB-GYN	Pediatrics
6 physicians	2 Physicians	1 Sudanese
– All Arabs	– 1 British female	(Short on coverage)
– All but one are home trained	– 1 Egyptian male	

Health Education Dept.
Smokers/Overweight

Emergency Dept.
24 hour coverage
– 2 Ambulances
– Air evacuation

Dermatology Dept.
2 Egyptians (Master degree)

Physiotherapy Dept.
– 2 Physiotherapists
Consulting room, Gym.,
Pool, Referral Service

ENT
1 Egyptian

Radiology Dept.
– 1 specialist
– 5 Technical Assistants

Orthopedic
1 Jordanian trained in Spain and Germany
2 Jordanians trained in Germany

Dental Laboratory
3 Technicians

Surgical Dept.
1 Jordanian trained in Germany
1 Egyptian specialized in Anaesthetic

Laboratory
– 1 Indian female doctor
– 5 Technicians

Pharmacy
– 1 Pharmacist
– Working hours
 9 AM: 12:30
 4 PM: 9 PM

Dental Dept.
1 Egyptian specialized in operative dentistry
1 Syrian specialized in oral surgery

Exhibit 1   Medical Team Chart

4) Systems Management: Hospital management contracts in Saudi Arabia are no longer monopolized by foreign firms. Wholly Saudi owned firms have started to enter the field with significant success.

GC has entered the hospital management field to diversify its sources of income and to help offset current losses from its other activities. GC has bid for management of the National Guard Hospital in Riyadh, and has provided pilgrim services for general medical security (medical automobiles).

Patient Mix

GC handles two types of patients – those who are sponsored and those who are not. Sponsored patients typically are expatriate employees of business corporations, consulting firms, or foreign embassies located in Riyadh. Sponsored patients have been GC's core patient group. According to Saudi law, corporations are required to provide for the medical care of their employees. Nonsponsored patients typically are well-to-do Saudis who value the convenience and privacy offered by GC.

As of late, GC revenues from its patient mix have dropped considerably due to several factors. Declining government revenue has prompted the Saudi government to cut its level of public spending, and many foreign firms have pulled out of the Saudi market. As a result, one of GC's most profitable patient segments – sponsored patients – has shrunk.

In addition, rise in competition with other health service providers has occurred in the Riyadh area. Lower prices and health care of comparable quality have attracted cost-conscious patients to other providers. For example, GC has lost some of its patients to government hospitals that offer comparable services free of charge. It is also bound to lose some sponsored patients from foreign embassies once the 200-bed Diplomat's Hospital is dedicated. This hospital is located on a prime site adjacent to the embassies' district and will offer the finest health care service available.

The dispute among the GC partners on the direction and management of the clinic has also had a negative impact of revenues.

Charges and Fees

Membership in GC entitles subscibers to various levels of service, but does not constitute a full-coverage health insurance.

Level 1 Subscribers

Family protection program Level 1 subscribers, and their families, are entitled to receive all outpatient medical services as prescribed or directed by GC physicians. Outpatient services include family practice clinics, as well as all specialty clinics and routine and emergency consultation (24 hours a day). Support diagnostic services include laboratory tests, X-ray studies, and physiotherapy. In addition, subscribers are provided with all necessary dressings, medications, plaster, casts, and injections as recommended by a GC physician.

Level 2 Subscribers

Family protection program Level 2 subscribers are entitled to Level 1 services plus inpatient services, i.e. hospitalization at GC, whether for diagnostic, therapeutic, or surgical purposes, and covers all costs normally associated with a hospital stay: food, medication, surgeon's fees, anesthetist's fees, nursing charges, operating room fees, casts, dressings, and so on.

Exclusions

Excluded under the familiy potection program for both levels are, for example, treatment of mental disorders, cosmetic surgery, dental treatment, house calls, use of an air ambulance, maternity care, and treatment of persons over 60 years of age.

Annual Individual Rates

Category of Individual	Level 1	Level 2
Male	SR 1,500	SR 2,200
Female	SR 1,800	SR 2,500
Child, 12 years and under	SR 1,600	SR 2,300

Annual Group Rates (per person)

Group Size	Level 1	Level 2
5 −10	SR 2,500	SR 2,200
11 −50	SR 1,400	SR 2,100
51 −100	SR 1,300	SR 2,000
101−250	SR 1,200	SR 1,900
251−500	SR 1,100	SR 1,800
500 and above	(negotiable)	

Non-Members Fees

First consultation	SR 100
1st specialist	SR 70
2nd specialist	SR 50

Follow-up visits within seven days are free of charge. Drop-in patients may pay SR 100 annually to become members, which entitles them to free check-up, excluding X-rays or laboratory tests.

Inpatient Labor and Delivery Charges

The normal delivery package includes one night in a shared room at SR 2000, with a deposit of SR 1000 due on arrival. If twins are delivered, an extra charge of SR 500 is levied. The normal delivery package includes also food, medical services, the delivery itself, and neonatal nursery care.

Accommodation in a private room with a private salon and bathroom is SR 300 per night. This fee is assessed if the patient stays beyond the one night covered by the package.

Private Room Fees

A private suite that includes a salon and bathroom costs SR 600 per day. In addition, a fee of SR 200 per day covers physician's attendance, nursing care, meals, and medication. If a family member wishes to stay with the patient, the cost is SR 200 per day including meals.

Management and Organization

The current organization of GC is shown in Exhibit 2. GC has a four-person board of directors and a president. The medical affairs section includes an outpatient department, radiology department, laboratory department, dental department, physiotheraphy department, operating room and anesthesia division, and pharmacies (internal and external). The presidency, the board chairmanship, and the directorate of medical affairs are combined in one and the same person: Dr. Wael Buraik. The administration and finance sections have various departments such as accounting, administrative services, purchasing and contracts, hospital management, and systems and planning.

Father and Son Roles in Management Operations

The father is a non-practicing physician. He is so busy with current operations that he does not have time for a strategy review and development of his Kingdom-wide HMO scheme.

The son is a trained systems engineer. He is in charge of developing systems records and procedures for GC and for other hospitals for a fee.

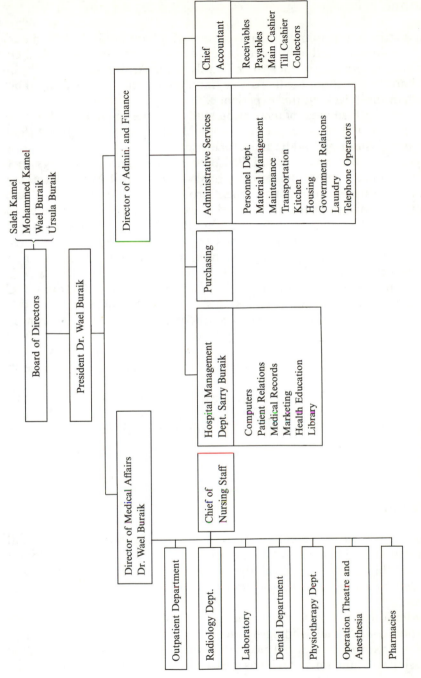

Exhibit 2   Green Crescent Organization Chart

Personnel

GC has striven to employ Arab physicians who have studied abroad and who have maintained a private practice elsewhere. Because of their experience in private practice, presumably these Arabic-speaking physicians know more about the fine art of handling patients and earning their trust than those lacking this experience.

GC has recruited most of its nursing staff from the Philippines. Filipino nurses are found to be cheaper, more reliable, and better disciplined than other Far Eastern or Middle Eastern nurses.

Highly qualified, well-credentialled medical personnel are always very difficult to find. Green Cresent policy has been to recruit Arabic-speaking doctors who have also practiced their profession in Europe. GC places recruitment advertisements in selected European newspapers. Interested doctors send their credentials to Dr. Wael Buraik, who reviews them and preliminarily selects those he believes to meet his standards. GC then contacts the prospects to arrange an interview with Dr. Buraik in their respective countries.

In addition to recruiting through ads in newspapers, some doctors at GC recommend current or former colleagues. Mr. Sary Buraik added that GC has been looking for a consulting physician for outpatient services for more than two years without success. They have not found anyone who meets GC standards. He said doctors with experience in public hospitals would not be suited for GC, which prefers to hire doctors with experience in private outpatient clinics.

GC recruitment for nursing is done by its agent in the Philippines. The agent selects those that meet GC requirements. Nurses work at GC on a two-year contract which can be renewed or terminated depending on the recruit's performance.

Marketing

Marketing is done by a committee which has a relatively low operational priority at GC. Hospitals and clinics advertise in local newspapers that a noted visiting physician is available. This is in line with the customary practice of most Arab hospitals and clinics in promoting their medical services.

In addition, GC promotes its services in a low-key fashion offering health education courses and sending newsletters to its customers. In the same vein, GC organizes specialized medical seminars to promote its image in the professional community. GC has passed the introductory stage of its services. It is estimated that about 70 % of the adult population of Riyadh know of GC and its services.

GC encourages its physicians to concentrate on short-stay operations whenever possible. Even then, GC has under-utilized bed capacity. In the years 1984, 1985, and 1986, average utilization declined from 79 % to 70 % to 53 %, respectively. In addition to the above-cited reasons, this sharp decline can be attributed to lack of training and aggressiveness on the part of the present management team. It is expected that bed utilization will further decline during the liquidation process.

Market Segments

Since GC opened its services to the public in August 1981, its major customers have been companies doing business in the Kingdom. Another major type of customer has been the middle-class married individual and others who sought top-class treatment irrespective of cost. In 1981, when the economy was strong, 90 % of GC's patients were members, while 10 % were casual or drop-in patients. Since 1983, the patient mix has actually been reversed: in 1987, 90 % of the patients were drop-in patients and only 10 % were members.

This decline is detailed in Exhibit 3. The decline in membership is due to the recession of the economy and the resultant departure of most of the companies who had purchased GC memberships for their employees. Moreover, as the Saudi public became more cost-conscious, it started going to public hospitals which are providing similar health care services free of charge.

GC is an anomaly. It is neither a clinic nor a hospital. According to government rules and regulations, a clinic must provide 24-hour emergency operation. Clinics do not have medical consultants, but have specialists and general practitioners. Moreover, clinics do not have beds for hospitaliz-ation. GC's most significant competitors are private and public hospitals, but clinics also represent a significant source of competition. Hospitals have a number of outpatient clinics that provide 24-hour emergency operation and have in excess of 50 beds. There are 165 national clinics, and 30 governmental clinics in the Riyadh area in 1987.

Competition

GC faces tough competition from the following public and private hospitals.

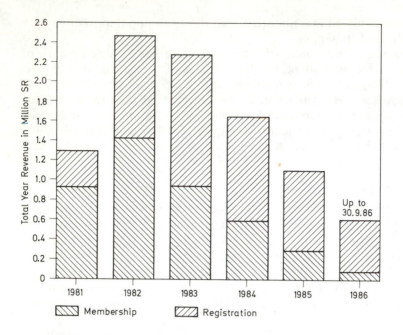

Exhibit 3   Changes in Patient Load Over Time
Source: GC records.

National Hospitals

These hospitals are for the national social security organization which is a quasi-governmental body providing medical services to its members.

Al-Hamadi Hospital

It is located near GC, and has a 217-bed capacity. Al-Hamadi is complaining that other medical organizations are copying their service delivery systems. Al-Hamadi is situated adjacent to the highly favored Ulaya project, which contains a prestigious residential development. The hospital is well-placed to draw clients from the diplomatic quarter and the surrounding area.

Al-Ali Hospital

This is a large and modern 315-bed hospital with Austrian management. The hospital has a relatively poor location on Al-Hijaz Road, about 20 kilometers from Riyadh, in the midst of a lower income area whose residents are willing to drive to government hospitals if the neighborhood facility is too expensive. This hospital, owned by Dr. Abdulrahman Al-Minshawi, has recently dedicated a new private maternity wing with a 220-bed capacity and advanced medical services. The maternity specialty hospital issues an elaborate birth certificate, and some patients may go there to get one of those fancy certificates for their children. GC corporate customers found that prices at Al-Ali hospital were initially cheaper than those at GC. GC thus lost 50 % to 60 % of its subscribers when Al-Ali first opened. However, most of those corporate subscribers have since returned to GC because they found that, comparatively, GC provides excellent services to its customers on credit, unlike other health care providers.

Al-Shumaisi Hospital (Central Hospital in Riyadh)

This is a government hospital with 1,500 beds plus a 300 bed maternity hospital wing. Many of its buildings have been closed due to deterioration and the possibility that they might collapse. Nevertheless, Al-Shumaisi is serving the public as a whole, including non-Arab and Arab expatriates living in Riyadh and other parts of the Kingdom. Despite Al-Shumaisi's old buildings, it is equipped with very sophisticated medical equipment. Al-Shumaisi provides high quality services and hospitalization to its patients free of charge.

Al-Shumaisi has an emergency department and an outpatient clinic plus all specialty clinics needed for treatment and operations. Al-Shumaisi also provides dental services through a new clinic dedicated to this purpose.

Response to complaints

The public relations section gathers patients' complaints and presents them to a committee consisting of two or three persons who discuss these grievances and analyze and formulate their possible remedies. For example, when the committee discovered that most patients were shocked upon receiving their unitemized bill, it recommended and implemented a new computerized system that itemizes expenses. And when it discovered that GC rates were higher than the competition's, the committee recommended bringing these rates in line with those of other health care providers.

Current Facilities

The present five-floor building was not specifically designed and built as a full service hospital. There is neither a private bath nor a sink for normal inpatients, unless the patient is willing to pay for a private suite at a cost of about SR 300 a day. The doors to patient rooms are too small for a portable bed or wheelchair to pass through. The surgical suites are separated, which requires duplication of equipment and waste of costly staff time. There is a small dietary department and a laundry facility.

Although the present facility is certainly adequate to meet the needs of the present volume, it is not equipped to handle growth in patient traffic or to compete with the new generation of super-luxury modern hospital facilities built in Riyadh over the last five years.

The inpatient facility includes an 18-bed female ward; an 18-bed male ward; a maternity ward with two delivery rooms, two labor rooms and one nursery; and an operating facility for general surgery and ophthalmic operations.

GC has 3 additional small buildings. They are used for physical therapy, dentistry, and administration and accounting. All of GC's buildings are rented. The landlord is not willing to lower the rent, even though similar facilities could be rented at much lower rates.

For its size, GC is well equipped with the latest diagnostic and laboratory equipment, including a CAT scanner. This equipment is utilized fairly efficiently (see Exhibits 4 and 5). In 1984 and 1985, this equipment yielded the highest of all other departmental income.

Finance

To encourage private ventures in the health care field, a range of financial inducements have been approved of by the government. Loans of up to SR 50 millions were made avaiable by the Ministry of Health. GC did not receive any loans from the governments, because its parent company profits were sufficient to establish GC. In its effort to promote private medicine, the Ministry of Health (MOH) can also contract for up to 15 % of the number of beds in private hospitals for emergency purposes. GC refused to reserve any beds for MOH. This refusal may have been ill-considered, because allocating beds to MOH would have guaranteed additional revenue. The decision was seemingly based on the desire of GC management to stay independent of government intervention.

GC rents buildings at very high rates. Its daily income is barely sufficient to cover daily expenditures. In 1985, GC reduced expenses by reducing

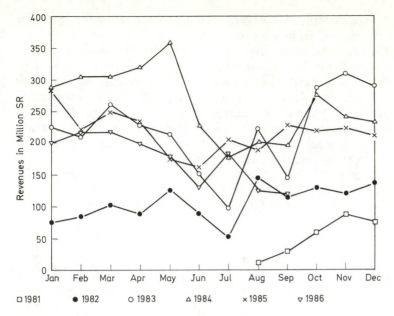

Exhibit 4   X-Ray Revenue Analysis (Year)

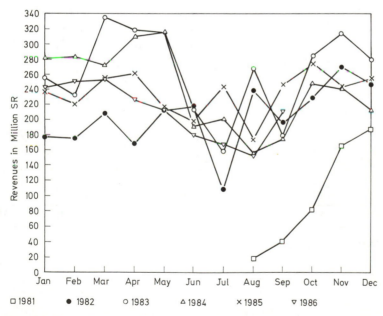

Exhibit 5   Laboratory Revenue Analysis (Year)

employees' fringe benefits. However, even this cost reduction was not sufficient to enable GC to break even.

By 1984, GC's annual expenditure was about SR 25.5 million, and its income was around SR 22 million (see Exhibit 6). If the economy had continued strong, GC could have escaped the inevitable initial losses associated with a business start-up. But in 1984, there was an unexpected drop in the number of patients. Attempts to cut costs without reducing the quality of service caused GC to reorganize purchasing and lower salaries. The continued decline in the patient load has lead to a reduction in GC's income and a decrease in equipment utilization.

GC currently has SR 3 million owed to it by its customers. Companies used to provide deposits, but do not any more. Since competitors do not require any insurance deposits, GC dropped its deposit requirements.

Exhibit 6   GC Income Statement 1984/1985

Income Source	1984 (SR)	1985 (SR)
ENT	442,505	245,717
OBH	131,011	339,662
Physiotherapy	294,351	146,373
OB & Gyn	732,747	691,492
Pediatric	481,110	624,750
Dental	2,995,002	2,832,968
Emergency room	912,140	965,543
Patients service	289,815	208,728
X-ray dept.	3,136,888	2,564,843
Laboratory	2,806,300	2,706,980
Internal medicine	2,482,723	1,984,057
Dermatology	558,571	601,601
In-patient	3,651,209	3,534,001
Maternity	2,666,508	1,806,985
Orthopedic	153,020	141,851
Urgent operations	346,980	328,675
Total income	22,080,880	19,724,226
Total expenses	25,645,835	22,610,716
Net income (loss)	(3,564,955)	(2,886,460)

Source: GC records.

Future Directions

Mr. Sary Buraik, the son of Dr. Wael Buraik and head of the administrative arm of the clinic, is convinced that Green Crescent can be a successful establishment, even though it is facing liquidation. Personal matters, more than anything else, have precipitated the liquidation of Green Crescent. He pointed out that Green Crescent, when offered for sale by the receivership, could be bought by one of the partners or a third party. The announcement of the sale has not yet been made, and no one can predict for sure the future of Green Crescent. But when asked what would be the first thing that his father would do if he bought GC, the younger Buraik answered,

"We would start cleaning up GC internally, and remodel its facilities. Moreover, we would continue the original idea of health maintenance that GC has pioneered."

Chapter 8
Strategic Management in Different Industries

8.1 Saudi Consulting House (SCH)

Ghazi M. Habib

Introduction

Saudi Consulting House (SCH) is a government-owned organization whose mission is to develop the consultancy industry in Saudi Arabia, render consulting services, and train Saudi nationals as consultants. Based in Riyadh, SCH is the only Saudi government institution which will have 50% of its ownership transferred to Saudi professionals 10 years after the date of its establishment.

SCH is unique in other respects. It gives higher priority to the training of Saudi nationals and the quality of its services than to profit. According to SCH officials, profit is not a chief objective at SCH, although achieving SCH's objectives and realizing a profit are not mutually exclusive. SCH is the only Saudi consulting firm which has a broad portfolio of services, encompassing engineering as well as economic and management related fields. For services beyond its capabilities and experience, SCH receives consulting support from Leo Daly Co. and Arthur D. Little International Inc. in engineering and management fields, respectively. In joint projects with foreign consulting partners, Saudi trainees are involved in all activities in order to gain experience and transfer knowledge.

SCH has estimated that American and European consultancy firms received about SR 5 billion (US $ 1.5 billion) worth of business in Saudi Arabia in 1977–1979, whereas less then 15% of total demand was satisfied by local firms. The total consulting business during the third development plan, which covers the period 1980–1985, was estimated at SR 10 billion. However, the total consulting business dropped to about SR 1 billion in 1986, with less than 10% secured by SCH.

Mr. Ahmed Al-Twaijri, vice-chairman and managing director of SCH, identified the difficulties facing SCH and other consulting firms in Saudi Arabia as:

1) fierce price competition among local and foreign firms, where low bids

are barely covering the salaries of the consultants involved, let alone other costs;
2) national firms such as SCH, which hire many Saudis, have higher payroll and benefits costs than their counterparts in the private sector, which employ a larger percentage of Third World nationals;
3) most Saudi consulting firms are owned by individuals and have limited capabilities and experience which may deny them complex and lucrative government contracts that are awarded to foreign consultants; and
4) lack of confidence in local consulting firms.

Mr. Al-Twaijri pointed out that despite the positive contribution of foreign consulting firms, they also have negative impacts, such as:

1) not hiring Saudi nationals except in minor jobs;
2) ignoring local materials and instead designing project specifications around material manufactured in the firms' country of origin;
3) to overcome a barrier to entry into the Saudi market, foreign firms pay a local firm a fee in exchange for sponsorship, without involving the local firm in the actual business of providing consultant services;
4) proliferating Western designs at the expense of Middle Eastern and Islamic designs; and
5) securing contracts for socio economic planning without the necessary background in Saudi culture and social background.

Objectives/Mission

According to SCH, the firm's objectives are:

1) develop national consulting services commensurate with the level of economic development and aimed at both the public and private sectors;
2) create and train national manpower while developing and improving their capabilities in accordance with the latest technology and modern standards to reduce dependency on foreign consultants; and
3) provide consulting services to various governmental and non-governmental organizations.

Exhibit 1 ranks the relative value placed on the firm's objectives by top SCH officials. It is interesting to note that profitability seems least important, and there was no unanimity on the most important objectives. However, training Saudis, growth, service quality, and efficiency were perceived by all three officials as relatively more important objectives.

Exhibit 1   Prioritization of Objectives (1 = most important, 13 = least important)

	Managing Director of SCH	Director General for Econ. Services	Director General for Eng'g Services
Profitability	13	13	4
Growth	1	5	6
Larger market share	8	12	8
Social responsibility	9	8	11
Employee welfare	10	7	13
Improving service quality	6	3	2
R & D	7	10	10
Diversification	2	9	5
Efficiency	5	4	1
Financial stability	11	2	7
Resources conservation	12	6	12
Management development	4	11	3
Saudi training	3	1	9

Source: Data collected by Tarek Al-Kohaji, a student of Dr. Ghazi Habib's MBA courses.

History

As late as 1966, there was still no ministry or specialized institution in charge of the industrial sector in Saudi Arabia. There were only about 35 factories in the Kingdom. King Faisal Ibn 'Abd Al-Aziz requested the United Nationals Industrial Development Organization (UNIDO) to prepare a plan for developing the industrial sector. UNIDO conducted a study and signed a 10-year contract with the Research and Industrial Development Center (RIDC), which was established explicitly to develop the industrial base.

The mission of RIDC was to:

1) study new projects;
2) conduct marketing studies;
3) conduct feasibility studies;
4) discover new investment opportunities;
5) prepare necessary facilities for new factories;
6) finance some selected small factories capitalized at no more than SR 100,000; and
7) establish maintenance workshops to help existing and new factories overcome repair problems.

RIDC helped increase the number of factories in the Kingdom to about 1,200 within 10 years of its establishment. However, RIDC was technically unable to cope with the fast development in other economic sectors. There was a great need to develop this center into a more diversified consultancy house that could supervise and guide technology transfer to Saudi Arabia.

In 1979, based on the recommendation of a committee composed of the Minister of Planning, the Minister of Finance and National Economy, the Minister of Commerce, and the Minister of Industry and Electricity, the Royal Decree Number M/17 announced the establishment of Saudi Consulting House (SCH). This organization was to provide consulting services in industrial, commercial, architectural, and other sectors on a commercial basis. Since its establishment, SCH has conducted many engineering, industrial, commercial, and economical studies for various governmental and private organizations. The industrial sector has accounted for about 30 % of its business.

SCH's Organization

Board of Directors

The board of directors of SCH is composed of 7 members; 6 of them are from the government sector and 1 from the private sector (see Exhibit 2). This board is headed by the Minister of Industry and Electricity.

The main responsibilities of the board of directors are to formulate all policies and guidelines of the organization and operation of the company. The Vice-chairman of the board is the firm's managing director. He is

Exhibit 2   Composition of the Board of Directors

1. Abdulaziz A. Al-Zamil Minister of Industry and Electricity	Chairman of the board
2. Ahmed S. Al-Twai jri Managing Director, SCH	Vice-chairman
3. Ibrahim A. Bin Salamah Vice-Chairman and Managing Director of SABIC	Member
4. Mahmoud Abdullah Taiba Governor of General Electricity Corporation	Member
5. Reda M. Abbar Businessman	Member
6. Mobarak A. Al-Khafrah Deputy Minister of Industrial Affairs Ministry of Industry and Electricity	Member
7. General Secretary of Royal Commission For Jubail and Yanbu	Member

responsible for managing and supervising all routine functions of the firm. He is also responsible for presenting periodic progress reports to the board.

Organizational Structure

Exhibit 3 shows that the administration and finance department, engineering services department, economic services department, information and public relations department, and Jeddah and Dammam branches all report directly to the vice-chairman and managing director. Exhibit 4 gives the names of senior management.

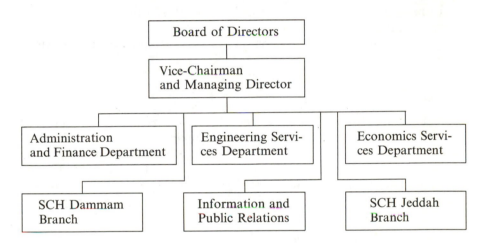

Exhibit 3 SCH's Structure

Source: SCH's brochure.

Exhibit 4   Senior Management

1. Abdul Hamid M. Al-Awadi	Director General for Engineering Services
2. Abdulaziz A. Al-Khathlan	Director General for Economic Services
3. Tajeddin Amin	Director General for Administration and Finance
4. Mahmoud M. N. Qutub	Head, Information and Public Relations Department
5. Siraj Qutah	Director SCH/Jeddah Branch
6. Abdullah Al-Salim	Director SCH/Dammam Branch

Finance and Administration Department

According to SCH's sixth annual report, the major duties and functions of this department are:

- to prepare annual budget estimates and quarterly financial reports;
- to adopt payment procedures;
- to provide cost analyses for the firm as a whole and for its departments;
- to control the current accounts of different professional associations working in cooperation with SCH, i.e. SCH/Leo a. Daly, SCH/Arthur D. Little Inc., SCH/Electricity Supply Board of Ireland and SCH/W. S. Atkins U. K.;
- to cooperate with controller general of the audit bureau for the annual audit of accounts of SCH;
- to make arrangements for the disbursement of funds to be spent on training programs; and
- to handle all administrative matters of SCH employees such as visas, accommodations, etc.

Engineering Services Department

This department is headed by a general director. He supervises 5 design teams, each consisting of experienced and qualified engineers in different disciplines, such as civil, structural, electrical, mechanical, and architectural engineering; and such technical trades as drafting. Exhibit 5 shows the portfolio of services rendered by the engineering and economics departments.

Economics Services Department

This department is headed by a general director. It consists of several teams of specialists in the fields of economics, accounting, business administration, statistics, and information systems. It is considered to be the second largest productive unit after the engineering consultancy department (see Exhibit 5).

Information and Public Relations Department

This department serves as a liaison office between SCH and potential investors, clients, businessmen, and industrialists both in the Kingdom and in other countries. The department maintains contracts with the information agencies of the Kingdom and the other Gulf Cooperation Council countries.

Jeddah and Dammam Branches

These 2 branches are each headed by a director. The responsibilities of these offices are to support headquarters by conducting economic and market surveys in their regions and to act as local points of contact for potential investors and clients. These offices also follow up SCH projects under execution in their regions.

Marketing

There is no marketing department at SCH. SCH officials contend that they use two techniques to market their services. First, the information and public relations department works as a communication agent (liaison) between SCH and potential clients inside and outside the Kingdom. It performs this task through publishing various guides (like *Guide to Industrial Management*), industrial bulletins and brochures (in Arabic and English), and research magazines (like Allam Al-Sinnaeh). SCH also participates in national and international exhibitions and seminars.

The second marketing vehicle is a committee that consists of different officials from each department within SCH. This committee is headed by an assistant manager, who communicates to public and private organizations who might have projects pending or need feasibility or other studies. The committee also contacts those who have received a license for certain projects but have not executed them to offer assistance in surmounting problems associated with project implementation. In addition, the two branches in Jeddah and Dammam function as advertising offices for SCH in their regions.

Exhibit 5   SCH Services Portfolio

Engineering Services

- Preparing architectural designs and engineering specifications for different construction projects like hospitals, commercial centers, schools, and other buildings for special purposes.
- Preparing engineering designs and specifications for causeways, bridges, water desalination plants, water network, sewage systems, and dams.
- Preparing designs for electrical power-generating stations and networks for transforming and distributing electricity.

- Supervising the execution of different projects and providing technical advice.
- Managing projects in different engineering fields.
- Analyzing and evaluating special proposals for establishing engineering projects.
- Preparing primary plans for engineering projects.
- Studying and designing industrial projects ancillary facilities.
- Preparing and revising plans for industrial complexes and factories and winning their approval.
- Providing civil, instrumentation, electrical, mechanical, and other engineering inspection services as well as maintenance consulting services.
- Providing consulting services for petrochemical factories, industrial complexes, and petroleum facilities with regard to application of industrial engineering systems and the separation of technical documents, designs, and drafts. Also supporting owners of projects in preparing contract specifications, executing the project, controlling quality, and inspecting and winning certification of manufacturing equipment and systems.
- Designing training programs for engineers, techicians, and administrators in different managerial, economic designs, and engineering fields.
- Preparing specifications for special medical projects and supervising the technical aspects during implementation.

Economics and Management Services

- Preparing feasibility and economic studies for industrial, commercial, agricultural projects, and projects in the services sector.
- Preparing marketing studies for new projects.
- Helping the established enterprises solve any marketing or managerial problems they might face.
- Preparing reports on different sectors and regional economic plans.
- Preparing feasibility studies for medical establishments and tourist facilities.
- Preparing special environmental studies.
- Providing advice on accounting, managerial, and technical systems and researching the costs of installing them.

Source: SCH Annual Report, 1986.

Customer Mix

SCH customers can be segmented into three groups. The first one consists of different ministries and companies owned wholly or partially by the government. Examples are the Ministry of Industry and Electricity, the Ministry of Health, the Ministry of Agriculture, the Saudi Arabian Basic Industries (SABIC), Petromin, and Saudia.

The second segment includes big, nongovernmental organizations like the Chambers of Commerce, which cooperate with SCH in preparing industrial studies and studies on companies that provide services to factories.

The third market segment includes private Saudi companies, Saudi-foreign joint ventures, Saudi investors, and foreign companies.

The first and second customer segments typically generate 60–70% of the total SCH revenue, whereas the third segment (private sector) generates about 30–40%. Furthermore, the first two market segments constitute about 70% of the total contracts handled by SCH's engineering department, versus about 50% of total contracts with the economics department.

The largest buyer of SCH services is the National Guard with total contracts of more than SR 50 million. Other large clients are the Saudi Retirement Funds Department, the Ministry of Health, the Ministry of Interior, and the Ministry of Industry and Electricity.

There are several reasons why the government prefers SCH to foreign consultants. First, because SCH is based locally, it can provide the government with ready follow-up support as well as continuity of service over time. Second, SCH may be better attuned to special government requirements, such as the need for secrecy or an understanding of Saudi society and culture. Third, SCH can provide a high quality of service at a relatively reasonable price.

Private Saudi firms have similar motives for choosing SCH over its foreign competition. The licensed Saudi distributor of General Motors products, for example, has employed SCH to conduct studies of the automobile market in Saudi Arabia.

SCH's Competitors

To be a consultant in engineering or business related fields requires a very high skill and experience. Most Saudi consulting firms offer this expertise through foreign partners or expatriate experts on their staffs. Large foreign consulting firms can perform such services at relatively low cost and thus at a competitive price.

The most intense competitors are those foreign consulting firms which are well-established, offer a high service quality, and are able to provide consulting in areas beyond the scope of local firms. Some examples of firms that have long experience in Saudi Arabia on projects are Bechtel, Phillips and Holsman, and Fluor Arabia. These foreign firms compete on huge government engineering projects – the main market of SCH. There are also some major foreign consulting firms that provide economic, organizational, and managerial services, including Arthur D. Little, Booz and Hamilton, William Bein, McKinsy and Partners. There are 97 foreign consulting firms, specializing in different engineering fields, doing business in the Kingdom.

Locally owned firms also compete with SCH. Although owned by Saudis, most of these firms are run by foreigners. There are more than 180 national consulting firms which provide engineering services in different regions of the Kingdom. Examples of large, well-established local firms are: Consulting Center, specializing in engineering and economic studies; the Saudi Office for Financial Consultancies; Dr. Faisal Al-Basheer Office; Mr. Saud Al-Ghurabi, marketing specialists; Engineer Tariq Al-Shawaf Office; and Al-Rasheed Office for Engineering.

A third group of competitors – new consulting offices that are owned and managed by Saudis – is small but growing.

The final group of competitors is of secondary importance. This group is made up of governmental research centers and institutions like the Research Institute at KFUPM, the Institute of Public Administration, and others. These institutes perform consulting services chiefly for governmental organizations and thus compete in the largest segment of SCH's market. Some of these institutes charge fees, like the Research Institute at KFUPM, while others do not.

Manpower Training

Developing Saudi manpower is one of the main objectives of SCH. This objective enjoys a high priority for two main reasons. First, it is in accordance with the national policy of the Saudi government. Second, skilled manpower is the chief asset of any technical consultancy.

Exhibit 6 shows SCH's employee mix over an eight-year period. It is quite conspicuous that the percentage of Saudi employees has declined over the time compared.

Exhibit 6 SCH's Employee Mix By Nationality and Department Affiliation

Year	Total	Nationality		Department Affiliation		
		Saudis	Non-Saudi	Engineering	Economics	Adminis-trative Services
1979–80	213	165	48	87	53	73
1980–81	213	165	48	87	54	72
1981–82	210	160	50	82	52	76
1982–83	252	151	101	113	59	80
1983–84	306	182	124	113	49	144
1984–85	327	173	154	204	51	72
1985–86	320	168	152	202	51	67
1986–87	307	158	149	194	49	64

Source: Compiled from SCH's Seventh Annual Report 1986.

Finance

Exhibits 7 and 8 show the comparative balance sheets and comparative income statements, respectively, of SCH for the period from 1980 to 1986. Accumulated net losses were SR 12,674,987 over the past seven years. Furthermore, expenses grew at a faster rate than revenue for all of the years except 1984 and 1985.

Challenges

The consulting industry in the Arab Gulf States is facing the following challenges:

1) Consulting services are very much tied to government spending. If the government pursues an expansionary monetary policy, this leads to a high growth rate in various economic sectors. However, declining oil revenues and the completion of the large infrastructure projects in most Gulf states diminished the amount of consultancy business tremendously. In Saudi Arabia alone, the value of engineering and management consulting business declined from about SR 4 billions in 1979 to about SR 1 billion in 2986.
2) Changes affecting consulting firms include:
   a) The general economic slowdown has caused oversupply and slack demand in the petroleum sector and many others.

Exhibit 7 Comparative Balance Sheet for SCH for the Last Six Years (in SR)

Item	1981	1982	1983	1984	1985	1986
1. *Current assets*						
Cash in vault and banks	33,196,602.21	77,583,422.10	562,909.00	301,775.51	5,453.00	40,332,075.70
Accts. rec. from joint	–	–	4,936,376.00	3,245,731.37	1,326,010.37	828,437.02
Accts. rec. from other	71,175,442.50	6,826,167.45	1,553,836.00	11,832,442.77	1,428,860.00	606,286.73
Inventory	126,581.95	95,310.00	198,447.00	163,710.91	141,198.00	154,046.43
Prepaid expense	1,335,954.75	1,979,715.25	3,356,788.0	2,618,967.25	3,181,907.00	11,752,064.62
Due earnings	283,666.67	3,557,599.16	8,501,658.00	36,856,886.92	23,752,469.00	24,360,847.30
Net contract under execution		–	7,394,361.00	5,438,480.22	3,380,343.00	11,367,036.37
L/C's Employees fund at SCH	212,718.00	200,000.00	339,000.00	437,000.00	437,000.00	437,000.00
Total current assets	106,332,078.10	90,301,113.96	26,551,665.00	51,047,994.95	92,128,273.00	79,837,794.17
Fixed assets after depreciation constructions	50,962,919.32	57,134,556.69	38,647,434.00	37,584,704.64	36,023,766.00	53,692,166.36
Deferred earnings – expenditure investments		–	5,261,686.00	14,554,700.15	18,278,050.00	–
Training expenditure			63,912,342.00	54,558,735.64	2,199,469.00	–
After amortizing	4,658,979.44	11,496,282.63	10,469,420.00	8,300,175.63	8,626,089.00	6,935,073.32
Total fixed assets	55,621,898.76	57,209,839.22	118,290,882.00	114,998,316.10	65,127,374.00	63,377,407.73

Credit for banks and investment Co.		2,439,557.70	3,080,000.00	2,000.000.00	8,039,327.00	
Credit accts. for joint foreign part.					285,015.00	
Credited accounts and other creditors	14,985,588.56	1,163,124.94	(1,254,921.00)	6,672,483.64	114,673.00	80,098.87
Deposits			1,044,167.00	153,941.21	–	57,478.41
Outstanding expenses (due)	197,794.36	1,187,853.89	1,599,563.00	5,921,082.84	4,178,855.00	3,407,938.76
Prepaid earnings	7,500.00	4,431.80	592,344.00	4,406.705.35	1,760,415.00	456,831.39
Employee funds (credits)						(100,000.00)
Appropriations			2,278,442.00	7,764,854.84		
Total current liabilities	15,190,882.92	5,794,968.33	7,259,595.00	26,919,066.88	14,378,285.00	3,902,347.43
b. Capital	163,000,000.00	163,000,000.00	163,000,000.00	163,000,000.00	163,000,000.00	163,000,000.00
Transferred losses from past years depreciation	(6,588,365.50)					
Net current year profit (loss)	(9,766,062.00)	(1,540,217.52)	(4,433,765.00)	(1,544,293.33)	81,725.00	(3,602,938.49)
Capital losses						(147,166.67)
Retirement allowance appropriation	3,052,505.95	3,052,505.95		3,668,393.00	3,668,393.00	2,849,010.10
Net current capital	146,645,572.50	146,645,572.50	114,842,547.00	139,127,244.30	142,877,362.00	138,307,874.50
Contract under execution (net)	1,450,692,225.00	114,842,547.00	21,155,678.00	22,600,157.01		
Contracts: letter of guarantee	117,521.00	(2,353,237.58)				
Total liabilities and capital	161,942,971.83	147,510,953.30	1,659,982.25	188,646,468.10	157,255,647.00	142,210,221.90

Source: SCH's Annual Report 1986.

Exhibit 8   Comparative Income Statements for SCH for the Last Six Years (in SR)

	1980	1981	1982	1983	1984	1985	1986
1. Revenue from productive dept. (OR)	7,630,765.00	10,509,106.00	24,850,114.00	37,374,443.00	80,044,887.00	46,313,927.00	48,057,295.00
2. Expenses of productive dept. (OE)	18,219,580.00	N.A.	14,968,475.00	23,458,175.00	63,542,386.00	35,688,038.00	48,390,133.00
3. Total revenues (TR)	15,591,025.00	20,803,483.00	36,034,571.00	46,092,167.00	87,909,122.00	56,144,301.00	53,207,327.00
4. Operating salaries (OS)	120,297,735.00	N.A.	13,596,855.00	15,060,994.00	75,988,823.00	10,049,909.00	33,467,582.00
5. Other salaries	8,428,977.00		5,256,824.00				
6. % of Op. salaries/No. – Ops	13,725,873.00	5,495,643.00	8,433,850.00	5,051,646.00	5,291,142.00	13,162,666.00	4,663,823.00
7. Operating and general and administrative expenses							
8. Total expenses (TE)	31,945,453.00	23,902,126.00	38,474,789.00	50,525,932.00	80,269,829.00	56,062,578.00	55,691,472.00
9. Operating profit	(10,588,814.00)	(7,887,377.00)	(5,190,824.00)	(5,767,255.00)	6,418,909.00	(2,536,777.00)	(332,838.00)
10. Net profit (loss) (NP)	(635,442.00)	(3,088,643.00)	(1,540,217.00)	(4,433,765.00)	1,544,293.00	81,725.00	(3,602,938.00)
11. Training after amortizing	4,658,979.00	N.A.	11,496,282.00	10,469,420.00	8,300,175.00	8,626,089.00	6,935,073.00
12. Total assets	161,953,976.00	N.A.	147,510,953.00	144,842,547.00	1,660,463.00	157,255,647.00	142,210,221.00
13. Total equities	147,809,117.00	N.A.	142,016,717.00	1,375,828,952.00	139,127,244.00	142,877,362.00	138,307,874.00
14. % OE/OR (2) (1)	2.38	N.A.	0.60	0.63	0.79	0.77	1.01
15. % OS/OE (4) (2)	0.66		0.45				
16. % TE/TR (8) (3)	2.05	1.15	1.04	1.10	0.91	1.00	1.05
17. % ROA (10) (12)					0.09	0.01	
18. % ROE (10) (13)					1.00	0.01	
19. Total no. of employees	213.00	210.00	252.00	306.00	327.00	320.00	307.00
20. TR per employee	73,197.00	99,064.00	146,566.00	150,628.00	268,835.00	175,451.00	173,314.00
21. NP per employee					4,723.00	255.39	
22. % of TR growth based on four years	33.0		78.00	25.00	91.00		
23. % of revenue from production	49.00	51.00	67.00	81.00	91.00	82.00	90.00
24. Units to total revenue							

Source: SCH's Annual Report 1986.

b) The phase involving the design and implementation of the infrastructure has given way to a new developmental phase, with stress on manpower training and maintenance.
c) Concern about the quality of work or place of origin has increasingly given way to concern about the lowest price.
d) Concern about how soon a particular job can be completed has given way to concern about how the work can be broken down into more phases, invoiced separately.

In addition to the general challenges facing the consulting industry in GCC countries, Saudi Consulting House faces these questions:

1) Are the objectives and charter of SCH still valid, given the changes that have taken place in the external environment?
2) Can SCH compete with profit oriented firms who employ less expensive Third World nationals, and incur no training costs?
3) Would Saudi professionals participate in the ownership of a firm that continues to lose money?
4) Should SCH reexamine its portfolio of services and narrow its focus to services, where it has distinctive expertise?
5) Should SCH make better use of its relationship with the Ministry of Industry, and, if so, how?

8.2 Saudi Arabian International School (SAIS) – "The Dhahran Academy"

*Gary Nosler and M. Sami Kassem**

Introduction

The Saudi Arabian International School (SAIS), better known as the Dhahran Academy, is an international school with an American curriculum covering grades one through nine. It serves the greater metropolitan area of Dhahran, Al-Khobar, and Dammam in Saudi Arabia.

Dr. Dan Brisbin, SAIS superintendent, is concerned by the dramatic downturn in the Saudi economy. He realizes that even as a non-profit organization, the Dhahran Academy cannot escape the forces of the marketplace. Lower oil production means fewer expatriates in the oil-producing region of the Eastern Province, and fewer students. Therefore, the Academy's strategic planners (Dr. Brisbin's cabinet and his board of trustees) are considering a number of strategic alternatives to cope with the enrollment crisis.

Expatriate Education in Saudi Arabia

When foreigners with dependent children come to Saudi Arabia, they usually seek the educational services of non-Saudi institutions. While some of them come from other Arab countries, the largest percentage are non-Arabic speakers, which rules out the Saudi government school system as a viable alternative for their children.

Even Arabic-speaking foreigners often send their children to non-Saudi schools. About 125 students, whose first language, is Arabic currently are enrolled at the Dhahran Academy. Their parents have chosen the Academy because they believe in the value of a Western style education, or because they are Christians and realize it would not be appropriate for their

---

* The original version of this case was prepared by Gary Nosler of Aramco, as a basis for class discussion. It has been extensively revised and edited by Professor Sami Kassem.

children to attend government schools where Islamic studies are mandatory.

A number of institutions have sprung up in Saudi Arabia to meet the special educational needs of foreigners. In the Dammam metropolitan area alone, there are private schools catering to Indian, Pakistani, German, Dutch, British, French, Italian, American, and even Arab preferences. Then why do all these nationalities attend the Academy?

History of the Academy

The historic development of the Dhahran Academy covers four distinct periods.

The Formative Stage: 1962–1968

In 1962, personnel of the American Consulate in Dhahran could not get their school age children admitted to the nearby school run by the Arabian American Oil Company (Aramco). They decided to pool their resources and open a small school of their own on the compound of the American consulate. Originally known as the Consulate Academy, the school covered grades one through six and employed 2 part-time teachers offering a standard American curriculum. The school was governed by a 5-person board with the consul general as chairman. The board effectively ran the school: it determined admission and graduation standards; recruited teachers and a headmaster; determined salaries; authorized the purchase of portable classroom buildings, books, and equipment; prepared the operating budget; and drafted a school constitution. Eventually, the size of the board grew to 10 members grouped into 4 standing committees: personnel, scholarships, plant and facilities, and language.

Quantitative Growth: 1968–1975

At the request of Aramco, the Academy prepared a master plan to cope with an expected influx of expatriate students into the greater Dhahran area during this period. Pending completion of the school's building expansion program, Aramco donated 4 portable buildings and classroom furniture. Maintenance and custodial problems skyrocketed. Enrollment jumped from 124 students in 1968 to 733 by 1975. To meet additional maintenance requirements, and administrative assistant to the headmaster was hired to supervise work of 2 Saudi custodians. To cope with the enrollment explosion, a priority system was devised for admitting prospective students according to available space. Tuition for the 1972–73 school year was set at US $ 1,100 plus $ 2,250 to defray the cost of the building expansion program.

In 1974, the Saudi government mandated that Dhahran Academy operate as an international school system for non-Muslim children throughout the Kingdom. The government was to provide land and money for buildings and furnishings, as well as a grant for maintenance and operations. The Dhahran Academy became the Saudi Arabian International School (SAIS) – Dhahran District. By 1975, the position of the headmaster was upgraded to superintendent and that of his assistant to principal. Whereas the former devoted his time to supervising the building program, the latter concentrated on developing curriculum and recruiting and supervising teachers.

Geographic Growth: 1976–1981

A number of area employers (including Aramco, Northrop, the US Army Corps of Engineers, and the Saudi Government's Royal Commission for the industrialization of Jubail and Yanbu), asked the Academy to operate schools on their behalf. This request put the Academy into the management contract segment of the school business. The Academy was to operate these satellite schools, utilizing its recruitment and purchasing expertise, on a cost-reimbursement basis.

Seizing this opportunity, the Academy sponsored 28 professional couples from the United States. A central office was formed at the Dhahran headquarters to assume the critical functions once performed by specialized committees appointed by the board of trustees. It was staffed by the superintendent; two deputies, one for personnel, the other for curriculum; and a director of finance. The Academy was split into two schools: a junior high and an elementary school, each one with its own principal and assistant principal. The board of trustees expanded from 10 to 12 members, including 8 representing sponsoring firms and 4 representing the Parent-Teachers Association. The consul general ceased to serve as the chairman of the board and became less involved in the day-to-day management of the Academy. Instead, his role is now confined to: (1) making strategic and policy decisions, (2) approving all hiring decisions and all budgets, and (3) selecting and evaluating the superintendent.

Qualitative Growth: 1981–1988

The key features of the current stage of the Academy development are:

a) a concern for improving the quality of instruction and the standing of the school via:
   - increased attention to curriculum development;
   - increased attention to the matter of training for the teachers;
   - seeking accreditation from the Middle States Association, which, in fact, the school has received;
b) a concern for "diversifying" the standard American curriculum to appeal to a broader segment of the student population. A British curriculum was launched at the Academy in 1981, followed by Dutch and German versions. This innovation – although costly – was later exported to the Jubail campus. However, it was not extended to cover other ethnic student segments such as Arabs, Pakistanis, or Japanese.

Dhahran Academy's Mission

The Academy is the sole source of a recognized and accredited American style educational curriculum in Dhahran which is available to anyone (or any company willing to pay the price), "within the guidelines established by the Saudi Arabian government." Importantly, these guidelines specify that the school is open to non-Arabic Muslim children ages 4 to 15, as well as to all non-Muslims (Green Book 1984).

Dhahran Academy's Purposes

1) to meet the growing and pressing needs of children of non-Muslim expatriate employees throughout the Kingdom;
2) to provide students with a liberal education at the elementary and intermediate levels and to train them in good citizenship and international understanding;
3) to prepare graduates to enter American or other secondary schools of high standards.

Customers' Analysis

If it were not for the fact that Aramco operates its own school system for the children of most of its expatriate professional employees, the

Exhibit 1   Student Nationalities – 1985–86 Academic Year

Nationality	Semester 1	Semester 2
American	536	508
British	219	217
Canadian	100	95
Egyptian	22	25
Filipino	107	107
Indian	130	130
Irish	22	22
Japanese	33	32
Jordanian	20	22
Korean	32	34
Lebanese	92	91
Pakistani	381	375
Syrian	11	11
Turkish	48	49
All others	205	198
Total	1958	1916

Academy's target market would be considerably larger. The students in the Aramco schools are primarily American. By contrast, the Academy's American nationals are outnumbered by more than 3 to 1.

Students of over 50 different nationalities are currently enrolled at the Academy. Their countries of origin range from Algeria to Zambia. Exhibit 1 lists the predominant nationalities attending during the 1985–86 academic year.

As mentioned previously, Aramco provides a school system for its professional level expatriate employees. Aramco expatriate employees whose children are ineligible to attend the company schools often turn to the Dhahran Academy. In fact, Aramco is by far the single largest source of students for the Academy. Currently, around 400 of the Academy's pupils are from Aramco families, and they represent nearly 21% of the entire student population. King Fahd University of Petroleum and Minerals (KFUPM), also located in Dhahran, is the second largest source of students, with about 130, or almost 7%. Others include Northrop (65 pupils), McDonnell-Douglas (60 pupils), Bell Canada (80 pupils), King Faisal University (50 pupils), and the U.S. military mission (15 pupils). The American Consulate provides 6–7 children to the Academy. Together these employers pay the tuition for about 60% of the Academy's students.

Enrollment at the academy grew steadily from 1962–63, when there were only 22 students, through 1978–79, when there were 1,261. Enrollment then leveled off, before increasing again in 1983–84. It peaked at 2020 students in 1983–84. Since then, it has declined. Exhibit 2 summarizes enrollment trends. It also tracks the size of the budget and staff, as well as the cost of tuition over a 24-year period.

Exhibit 2   Growth of the Dhahran Academy 1962–1987

Year	Enrollment	Budget	Teacher	Administrators	Tuition (SR) per Student	Cost per Student
1962–63	22	Unknown	4	1/2	–	N/A
1963–64	32	8,100	4	1/2	2,700	N/A
1964–65	45	114,000	7	1/2	N/A	N/A
1965–66	67	126,000	11	1/2	N/A	N/A
1966–67	68	186,000	15	1		N/A
1967–68	82	231,000	12	1		N/A
1968–69	124	291,000	17	1		N/A
1969–70	167	360,000	17	1		
1970–71	211	345,000	19	1		
1971–72	231	705,000	11	1		
1972–73	309	1,641,000	27	1	9,900	
1973–74	408	1,516,000	31	1		
1974–75	498	2,069,000	44	2		
1975–76	733	4,235,000	50	2	15,000	
1977–78	953	8,048,000	92	7		
1978–79	1261	9,400,000	101	7	16,000	N/A
1979–80	1173	11,434,000		10	15,000	N/A
1980–81	1202	13,002,000	96	9	18,000	13,030
1981–82	1329	21,608,000	101	10	18,000	15,089
1982–83	1586				16,000	15,931
1983–84	2020				15,000	17,425
1984–85	1899	31,699,093	199		7,500	20,445
1985–86	1877	25,458,642	160	18	14,200	17,479
1986–87	1450 (Est)	N/A	N/A	18	15,800	N/A

– US Dollar = 3.74 Saudi Riyals (Nov. 11, 1987)
– These figures represent the total originally approved by the board for the year indicated. The figures do not necessarily correspond to actual expenditures.
– Enrollment figures vary slightly depending on the source document and the time of the year they were recorded. The figures here represent a reasonable estimate of total enrollment at the middle of each academic year.

Source: Dhahran Academy files

Teachers and Staff

In order to satisfy customer expectations of quality and to meet its educational objectives, the Academy is, naturally, dependent on its ability to attract qualified teachers, administrators, and staff. To a great degree, the Academy's sustainable competitive advantage lies in its ability to impart a fully American education. Therefore, its teachers must be American, or non-Americans with at least a high proficiency in English, and a thorough familiarity with the American system.

Approximately 40 % of the teaching staff at the Academy comprises "sponsored" husband-wife teams; that is, they are recruited and hired for specific teaching positions and brought to Saudi Arabia. The other 60 % are "locals," generally spouses of employees from local businesses. Many of these are non-Americans, who speak English as a second language. The average salary for a sponsored teacher is SR 102,000 and for a local teacher SR 65,000. A similar strategy is employed by the area's other schools. For example, the Pakistani School recruits all of its teachers for its boy's school from Pakistan, whereas Pakistani spouses of employees in local businesses are the teachers in the girl's school.

Until recently, there were ample American teachers in the local labor pool. Now, however, that pool is dwindling as local businesses fold or scale back their operations, sending expatriates packing. The need for teachers at the Academy is also dropping, as Exhibit 2 indicates. Eventually, a point will be reached when the number of teachers cannot be reduced further without a retrenchment of course offers. Presently, subjects which are not considered vital to the curriculum (e. g., American history) are being dropped.

Governmental Regulation

Dhahran Academy is licensed by the Saudi Ministry of Education, which in principle, exercises full control over its affairs. Generally, however, there are very few restrictions on the Academy's operations. The Academy must offer courses in Arabic (culture, if not language), and it must refrain from religous instruction. Further, the school is not open to Arabic-speaking Muslim children, except with permission from the Ministry of Education. In fact, there are six such pupils (non-Saudi) currently in the Academy. Under no circumstances are Saudi children allowed at the Academy, though many Saudi parents have tried to obtain permission from the Ministry. A dress code is in effect which adheres to the Saudi standard of modesty.

Since its inception, the Academy has operated rent-free on land leased to it by the Saudi government. This lease or land grant expired in December 1986. With the sharp decline in government revenues, resulting from the pullback in the oil industry of the last few years, it is unclear to the Academy whether the government will charge a rental fee for the land, and if so, what the implication of that decision will be for tuition and enrollment.

Competitive Analysis

Exhibit 3 lists the dominant immediate competitors.

Dhahran Academy officials generally perceive no threat to their monopoly on American-style education in the Dhahran area. They effectively offer the only American curriculum outside the Aramco school system. That is not to say, however, that all Americans got for an American-style education. As Mr. Robert Findlay of the British Section of the Academy pointed out, some American children are in the British curriculum, because their parents favor a more international exposure for their children. These parents may also plan to send their children to schools in Britain, or other European countries, and they, therefore, feel it is important to prime their children for that type of experience.

As noted in Exhibit 1, Pakistanis are one of the largest contingents at the Academy (381 in 1985–86). In the past, many of these children would have been attending the Pakistani Community School, which charges tuition of just SR 1,300, against SR 15,800 at the Academy, were it not for the fact that Aramco paid parents with eligible school age children a stipend covering 100 % of the Academy's tuition. However, Aramco reduced that stipend to a maximum of SR 6,000 for every child entering school after November 1985. Eligible non-American employees at Aramco previously did not have to be concerned about the cost, today they are faced with some

Exhibit 3   Dharhan Academy's Competitors

School	Curriculum
1. The British School	British
2. Indian Embassy School	Indian Central School
3. Pakistani Community School	Federal Board of Islamabad
4. French School	French
5. Italian School	Italian
6. German Schools	West German

tough economic decisions. Thus, the Academy may find itself in more aggressive head-to-head competition with not only the Pakistani Community School, but also the Indian Embassy School.

The German, French, and Italian schools are so relatively small that they do not present any major competitive threat to the Academy. In fact, as the overall expatriate base diminishes, the survival of these schools will come more and more into question. This, in turn, could mean a small windfall of new students for the Academy.

Whether or not enrollments at the Academy remain at present levels will principally depend on the Pakistanis, Indians, and Arabs. They have a choice, and they will exercise their options, especially if they are financially pushed to the wall. Filipinos and other national students will continue at the Academy, mainly because they lack an effective substitute.

As the Pakistanis comprise the single largest contingent of non-Americans at the Academy, it is worthwhile noting that the Pakistani School provides transportation to and from the school with a fleet of 15 buses traveling to as far away as Jubail in the North and Abqaiq in the South. The Academy, on the other hand, provides no transportation.

What Does It Take to Succeed?

Given the international composition of the Dhahran area, the opportunity exists for a number of educational institutions to satisfy specific niches. The extent to which these niches comprise sufficient numbers of children in order to economically justify the existence of special schools will decide whether these educational enterprises will thrive. A key success factor, therefore, is to offer the educational menus demanded by target sectors of the community, and to have the appropriate staff for delivering them.

Without question, the availability of English language instruction is a strong magnet for most expatriate parents, whether the curriculum is American or not. Any organization that does not have a reputable English language program will find itself at a great disadvantage.

Opportunities and Threats

As Exhibit 2 and the accompanying explanation indicates, there is a tremendous interest in the Academy's American menu, but only, we may assume, if the price is right. While profit is not a motive, the linkage between fees charged and curriculum delivered cannot be flexed very much. It is safe, however, to assume that parents will respond favorably to a reduction in fees. One way of bringing about such an accommodating adjustment is by making the Academy's operation as efficient as possible, that is, by cutting costs.

So while the dwindling expatriate base very likely will mean a continuing decline in enrollment and heightened competition for those students that remain, it also presents an opportunity for the Academy to capitalize on its considerable competitive advantages.

Given the perceived value of its American curriculum, which no other comparable local institution outside Aramco offers, it should be possible for the Academy to maintain its viability by making strategic adjustments in its fee structure. Such a move might become inescapable in light of reduced company stipends for education. Reductions in employee salaries are occurring, too, as some businesses are exerting further pressure on the Academy to reduce fees. For example, Bechtel is instituting a 20% across-the-board cut in salaries, which will clearly arouse heightened concern about educational fees among Bechtel employees.

The British School represents a serious threat to the Academy's British section, particularly if its tuition remains substantially lower than the Academy's. The German and Dutch sections at the Academy are also especially vulnerable, not to competition as much as to economics. If the costs of these curricula are spread over an ever decreasing student body, parents may be forced to reconsider alternatives.

Inside Dhahran Academy

The Academy has never had an image problem. In fact, it has had, until recently, waiting lists of students because demand outstripped its ability to admit more.

The Academy's American curriculum is appealing to many non-Americans, in particular the Pakistani, Indian, and Arabic-speaking contingents, despite the fact that these nationalities have other educational alternatives. They seem to place a high value on the system of American education with its emphasis on learning by doing rather than by rote, and on individualized instruction.

Dhahran Academy, if it were in the United States, might well be confused with any of the many schools found in the Midwest or other rural environment. It consists of a library, containing 16,000 volumes, and roughly 35 other buildings, including a gymnasium, outdoor auditorium, and well-equipped classrooms (Schools Abroad 1985–86). Textbooks for the Academy come from the States, as do all standardized tests.

With the exception of a minuscule amount of interest earned on deposited funds, the only source of revenue to the Academy is tuition. Currently, this annual fee is SR 15,800 which compares favorably with other schools in the Kingdom and elsewhere (see Exhibit 4). A deferred payment plan is available on a semester basis which, if invoked by the parent, results in an additional charge of SR 500 per semester.

Exhibit 4   School Tuition Comparisons

Schools within Saudi Arabia	Tuition	Add'l Fees
Riyadh International Community School (RICS)	SR 15,200	SR 5,000
Dhahran Academy	15,800	
Parents Cooperative School (P. C. S.)	18,000	500
Yanbu	18,750	
Schools within the Arabian Peninsula		
The Sultan's School – Oman	14,100	5,634
American School of Kuwait	15,136	1,972
American Community School of Abu Dhabi	17,908	2,557
International School Sanaa – Yemen	21,000	3,750
Bahrain School	26,290	871
Jumairah American School – Dubai	26,375	
Schools in Africa, the Middle East, and Asia		
International School Bangkok – Thailand	14,100	
International Community School – Turkey	14,024	
International School Moshi – Tanzania	16,000	
Damascus Community School – Syria		
(Grades 1–6)	16,180	
(Grades 7–9)	18,560	
American Community School – Lebanon	16,300	
Lincoln School – Nepal	16,525	2,625
American International School – Bombay		
(Grades 1–6)	16,875	
American School of Tangier – Morocco	16,900	
American School of Mallorca	17,280	
American Embassy School – India	17,280	2,535
International School of Islamabad	17,840	2,253
American School of Madrid	18,480	
American Cooperative School – Liberia	18,540	
Jakarta International School – Indonesia	18,780	20,188
Khartoum American School – Sudan	19,343	
American Community School – Jordan	19,625	
International School of Kenya	20,800	
Schutz American School – Egypt	21,030	
Cairo American College – Egypt	21,412	4,875
American Cooperative School of Tunis	21,785	

SR 3.74 = $ 1.00 (Nov. 11, 1987)

Source: Dhahran Academy document.

Approximately 75% of revenues are paid out in the form of teachers' and administrators' salaries. The remaining 25% cover miscellaneous categories such as maintenance, supplies, and salaries of clerical and grounds personnel. As Exhibits 5 and 6 show, these percentages have held pretty uniformly in the recent past. As enrollment increased, so did teacher salaries. However, teacher salaries peaked in 1984; since then, they have been on the decline.

Exhibit 5   Budget Comparisons (1984–85 vs. 1985–86) in SR

Personnel Costs	1984–85	1985–86	Reduction
Salaries teachers, aides, and nurses	13,984,008	11,554,475	2,429,533
Salaries termination	1,000,452	689,920	310,532
Employee allowances	2,934,844	2,868,037	66,807
Shipment of pers. effects	66,829	45,492	21,337
Employee housing	4,042,463	3,422,145	620,318
Conferences	318,250	213,053	105,197
Travel	1,084,155	859,840	224,315
Supplies			
Office supplies	81,125	59,000	22,125
Instructional supplies	2,804,109	1,982,487	821,622
Equipment	267,634	119,914	147,720
Maintenance			
Building and grounds	2,195,500	921,800	1,273,700
Depreciation expenses	2,919,732	2,722,479	197,253

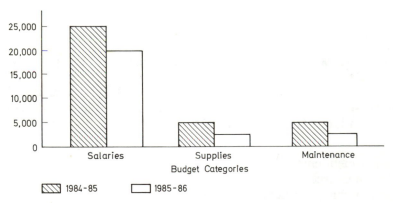

Exhibit 6   Budget Comparisons

Strengths and Weaknesses

Without question, the Academy's greatest competitive advantage is its American "connection". Rightly or wrongly, the perceived notion among the non-American community is that there is untold value in an American education for their children. One wonders how many parents have made great sacrifices to give their children this opportunity to obtain a diploma from an American institution. This document often is a ticket to a higher education in the U.S. Thanks to recent accreditation by the Middle State Association, the Academy can offer its graduates quick admittance to Stateside high schools, and – just as importantly - they are academically prepared to tackle the curricula there.

The Academy's solid reputation is not without foundation. Its students have consistently scored considerably above the US norms on the Stanford Achievement Test (SAT) in reading and mathematics. Moreover, the heterogeneity of its student body enriches the quality of the learning environment and provides the Academy with a unique edge over its competitors.

One of the weaknesses of the Academy is that it has not catered well enough to the special needs of its Arabic student body. Courses on Arabic language and Muslim culture are limited at best. Another weakness relates to the general appearance of the Dhahran campus. Although not the bleakest, it is not the prettiest of the private schools in the area. It is made up of a mixture of buildings that range from a single portable-type classroom to a modern two-story classroom building. Although landscaping is a difficult and costly proposition in a desert environment, the Academy seems derelict in this regard.

Organization Structure

The Dhahran Academy has developed what might be termed a divisionalized professional structure.

In theory, the entire expatriate community of the Kingdom elects 12 people to represent it on the Academy's board of trustees. The superintendent directs the affairs of the entire school system. He delegates powers to 5 assistants:

– 2 area superintendents;
– 1 assistant in charge of finance;
– 1 assistant in charge of personnel; and
– 1 assistant in charge of contracts and maintenance.

One of the duties of the area superintendent is to travel around to the various campuses and see how well the curriculum is being administered. Sometimes this involves actually sitting in classrooms and observing teacher performance. Any shortcomings are noted and passed on to the local principal/headmaster, who then implements the guidelines.

The superintendent together with his 5 assistants constitute the headquarter staff or the cabinet. This cabinet together with the board of trustees comprise the strategic apex of the Academy – the body officially in charge of making long-term strategic decisions.

There are 22 principals and vice-principals employed by the Academy. Regardless of how tiny the "campus" may be, it is staffed with at least one non-teaching principal or headmaster. (Interestingly, the headmaster of the Pakistani School, whose single campus would dwarf any one of most of the Academy's several campuses, has some teaching duties).

Outlook for the Future

Exhibit 2 shows that enrollment at the Academy began its decline after the 1983–84 school year. Further declines in enrollment can be expected. At least 5 alternatives are available to the Dhahran Academy for coping with the enrollment crisis.

1) Do nothing. While the Pakistani School offers some services (such as bussing), the Academy does not, but has a much lower fee structure, these factors are more accidental – or just fortuitous – than part of any particular organizational strategy. Field data suggest that management at both the Academy and Pakistani School falls pretty well into the do-nothing camp. Neither school voiced any concern about the threat of competition. By adhering to this reactive strategy, the Academy may likely experience a much faster decline in its non-American population than it expects.

2) The Academy could follow the lead of some European schools (such as TASIS of France and Aiglon of Switzerland) and engage in some promotional activities targeted at those nationalities most likely to consider substitutes. In such a campaign, all the Academy's competitive advantages could be emphasized, playing heavily on its American heritage, as well as the computer literacy it offers its students. It would be relatively inexpensive to distribute flyers, brochures, book markers, etc., as subtle and tasteful reminders about the Academy's educational benefits.

3) Without doing something about its present cost structure, it is unlikely

that any promotional effort, by itself, will be very successful for long. The Academy is simply pricing itself out of the market. A combination of cost-benefit and zero-base budgeting programs might help in cutting the direct and indirect cost per student to an acceptable minimum.

4) A market-oriented institutional planning approach could be implemented. By taking a closer look at its mission, its environment, and the preferences and behavior of its current and potential customers, the Academy would be in a better position to make decisions that improve student recruitment.

Such an analysis (conducted by existing staff members or by an outside consulting firm) might include studying the current student make-up, contacting local businesses to ascertain plans for future cutbacks, and polling non-captives (Pakistanis, Indians, and Arabs) to determine their preferences and economic inclinations. A closer look at the curriculum might reveal that some elective courses could be cut. On the other hand, others could be added to enhance the Academy's attractiveness.

5) The Academy is seriously considering operating a few satellite schools on a cost-reimbursement basis. This alternative would permit the Academy not only to exploit its recruitment and purchasing expertise but also to fulfill its chartered obligation as the sole source of approved American style education for the children of non-Muslim expatriates working in the Kingdom. Several contracts are open for bid including the Hofuf, Yanbu, Rabigh, and Hafr Al Batin.

According to Dr. Brisbin, superintendant of the SAIS-Dhahran system, the management contract alternative allows the Academy to benefit from economies of scale resulting from the allocation of costly central office staff over a larger student base. These economies are only potential; they must be balanced against diseconomies resulting from increases in the size and complexity of the school operation. Dr. Brisbin is quick to admit that managing a multi-site, multi-menu operation is much more difficult and challenging than managing a single-site, single-menu operation (such as that of SAIS-Riyadh).

References

Business Week. (1986): This is like stepping off the edge of a cliff. *Business Week*, April 14: 26.
Dhahran Academy handbook for parents. American Consulate General, Dhahran, Saudi Arabia.
Educational Research Service (ERS) (1986): *School staffing ratios*, 1986 Report.

The green book guide for living in Saudi Arabia (1984): Middle East Editorial Associates, 1984.

Saudi Arabia...A MEED practical guide (1983): London: Middle East Economic Digest, Ltd.

Schools abroad of interest to Americans (1985–86): Porter Sargent Publishers.

Weeks, A. E. (1982): *History of the Dhahran Academy*, unpublished report.

8.3 "Alpha Data Soft" (ADS)

Abdullah Al-Sharif and M. Sami Kassem*

History of "Alpha Data Soft"

In September 1984, Mr. Yousef Hamdan, a graduate of King Fahd University of Petroleum and Minerals, met with Mr. Yassin Sartawi, a civil engineer from King Faisal University. Both were working for computer firms, and they discussed the start-up of a new enterprise to supply customized computer software to businesses in the Eastern Province of Saudi Arabia. Both men had a fair amount of experience in programming. Mr. Hamdan's cousin, who owns Data Comm, a firm that sells IBM computers, pointed out that customers who buy computers need help to fully utilize them; they need guidance in peripherals and in software to tailor the computer equipment they buy to the needs peculiar to their particular business. Mr. Hamdan held many discussions with Mr. Sartawi about the possibility of launching a business to fill this need, and finally, they decided to push ahead and open a small office in downtown Dammam. They agreed to do the following:

1) to rent a small shop in downtown Dammam for SR 20,000 per year;
2) to buy an IBM XT personal computer for SR 6,000 and peripheral equipment for SR 4,000;**
3) to buy some office furniture for SR 4,000;
4) to apply for a license from the Commercial Licensing Office in the Ministry of Commerce and pay the fee of SR 50,000;
5) to obtain an assortment of software packages from the local market such as Dbase II and III and Lotus 1,2,3 at a total cost of SR 2,000.

Their initial investment totaled SR 86,000, or US $ 22,000. "Alpha Data Soft" opened for business. The development of the enterprise can be outlined in two phases.

---

* This case was prepared by Mr. Abdullah Al-Sharif under the direction of Professor M. Sami Kassem. All data are factual except the name of the firm and its owners. They have been changed in deference to their preference.

** At the time the case was written, US $ 1.00 equaled SR 3.76.

Phase I: Entering the Software Business

The partners generated business by personally calling on small firms and through the Data Comm connection. They received a SR 40,000 order from Saudi Fisheries, a company involved in selling fish to retailers throughout Saudi Arabia. The order involved setting up the computerized inventory, payroll, and order entry processes. A printing company, which also wanted customized programs became their second client. The business was rolling. Both partners worked very hard, and sometimes obtained outside help from part-time programmers.

Both partners cultivated the clients of their former employers and other business contacts to generate business. They found the demand for software to be strong. As a result, Alpha grew rapidly; its market niche quickly proved to be lucrative.

Phase II: Entering the Hardware Business

After six months of operation, Alpha received requests from potential clients for the complete range of computer equipment, instead of only software. Many small-sized firms requested turnkey service; they wanted to fully automate their office systems without having to worry about any intermediary steps. Examples of customers for this service were cold storage, spare parts retailers, and professional end-users. The partners decided to take on this new source of business, since a wide range of hardware already existed in the local market, and since they could obtain some types of hardware from Mr. Hamdan's cousin at Data Comm on lenient credit terms.

From this point onward, Alpha entered the hardware business. It started performing turnkey projects for small businesses by providing complete packages consisting of the computers, monitors, keyboards, printers, and plotters as needed, hard disks as needed, and software tailored to the client's needs.

The price for a turnkey project ranged from SR 30,000 to SR 70,000. Alpha relocated the business to a new showroom rented for SR 50,000 per year. The partners hired five programmers (1 part-time Saudi, 2 Jordanians, and 2 Filipinos). Mr. Hamda gave up programming to concentrate on the marketing side of the operation.

The partners decided to add the following 3 groups of products and services to their menu:

1) *CAD Soft*
   This hardware and software equipment is an aid to engineering graphics. A CAD Soft package costs the buyer about SR 70,000. Alpha's owners directed this product at local engineering consulting

offices and manufacturing firms with in-house engineering staffs. CAD Soft was obtained from large distributors in the local market. Later Alpha directly imported it from the United States.

2) *Bilingual Computers and Software*
   The owners perceived a strong need for Arabic software among potential clients. Thus, they developed, through straightforward manipulation of English programs, the "Arabic computer." The Arabic software was developed in-house. These new software products were directed at government offices and educational institutions, including private schools.

3) *Classroom Training*
   The partners believed that they should train potential customers to make them computer-literate, which would in turn help them appreciate the efficacy of Alpha's products and hopefully generate new business. This practice was first introduced in Saudi Arabia by IBM's general agent in the Kingdom (Juffalli). This firm had created training centers with the aid of IBM in all its stores throughout the country. Following Juffalli's lead, Alpha established a training classroom and hired a part-time instructor/programmer. Three courses were offered:

Training Course	Duration	SR
Introduction to personal computer	1 week	350
Introduction to software	2 weeks	700
Programming	3 weeks	1,200

Marketing

Marketing is Mr. Hamdan's most critical job. Being a literate Saudi in a Saudi market gives him an advantage over some other local computer firms. He specializes in large corporate accounts, leaving the small and medium-sized ones to his partner Mr. Sartawi. Mr. Hamdan is on the road most of the time, knocking on doors, talking to potential clients, answering their questions, and following up on leads.

Alpha does not advertise to promote its services. However, Mr. Hamdan does a great deal of business entertaining in his attractive Al-Khobar residence. These social functions have proved to be an effective method for promoting the business. In addition to personal selling, Alpha distributes an information packet to prospective clients that includes an attractive brochure. Mr. Hamdan's sales pitch is that Alpha matches its competitors' prices and quality.

Alpha's core client groups are:

1) engineering consulting firms;
2) government agencies;
3) medium and small firms such as cold stores and real estate firms;
4) private clinics; and
5) manufacturing firms, e. g., petrochemical enterprises.

CAD Soft and the Arabic computer are designed to serve these clients.

Operations

The 5 programmers are assigned to jobs on a project-by-project basis. When a client needs a customized software, Mr. Sartawi sees whether the job can be handled by 1 programmer or 2. Hardware selling is also handled by the programmers, according to Mr. Sartawi's instructions. Training is handled by the Saudi part-time instructor. Sometimes, Mr. Sartawi does programming when the work load is heavy.

Procurement

Initially, the partners purchased their hardware and software needs locally. Later on, as they got heavily involved in turnkey projects, they decided to bypass the local middle man. They import most of their hardware and peripheral equipment from Tatung of Taiwan. This strategy enables Alpha to be a low-cost bidder. It may hurt its image among clients who experience problems with their hardware, and who badmouth the firm in the market place. Choosy clients do insist on having brandname hardware such as IBM and NCR. To attract members of this minority camp, ADS entered into an agreement with NCR of Japan and EKJ (an IBM distributor in USA) to import computer hardware from them directly, and sell them without the required backup service for 10 % less than the local authorized dealer. Later on, those price-sensitive clients do get hurt when they experience problems with their hardware. In such eventuality, they will badmouth Alpha and boycott its products along with those sold by other "grey distributors".

Financial Profile

An estimated balance sheet and income statement prepared at the time this case was written are provided in Exhibits 1 and 2, respectively.

Exhibit 1 Estimated Balance Sheet in SR

Current assets		
Cash	150,000	
Account receivable	100,000	
Inventory	250,000	
Total current assets		500,000
Office equipment	50,000	
Office supplies	40,000	90,000
Total assets		590,000
Current liabilities		
Accounts payable (data comm)	20,000	
Utilities payable	5,000	
GOSI payable	1,500	
Total current liabilities		26,500
Equity		
Capital	90,000	
Retained earnings	473,500	563,500
Total liability and equity		590,000

Exhibit 2 Estimated Monthly Income Statement in SR

Sales		1,800,000
Cost of goods sold		720,000
Gross margin		1,080,000
Expenses		
Labor (7 employees)	300,000	
Rent	48,000	
Utilities	18,000	
Total expenses		366,000
Net income		714,000

Source: Primary; based on case writer's best estimates.

The following assumptions are made in constructing these statements:

1) Sales are 50 % hardware and 50 % software.
2) Alpha makes more money selling software than hardware. In software, most costs incurred are labor costs. With cheap Filipino and expatriate labor, Alpha realizes a higher profit margin from selling customized software.
3) The new product (CAD-SOFT) is priced at SR 70,000. Turn-key projects are priced from SR 30,000 to 60,000 depending upon required hardware and software.
4) All purchases from suppliers are made on a cash basis.
5) Alpha does not have any long-term debt, or unusual current liabilities.

Organization and Management

Alpha is a prototypical entrepreneurial firm. It has evolved a simple structure which is both organic and centralized at the same time. It is organic in the sense of being dynamic, fluid, and responsive to market conditions. It is centralized in the sense that key strategic (e. g., purchasing, bidding) and operating decisions are made by the partners themselves. Understandably, programming decisions are delegated to the program-mers themselves.

To succeed in this high-tech venture, Alpha's management must possess at least two of the following attributes. First, it must be client-oriented. Second, it must be innovative – capable of offering its clients something unique which they cannot get elsewhere. Third, it must be capable of responding rapidly to changes in the marketplace or elsewhere which are beyond its control.

The Computer Market in Saudi Arabia

In Saudi Arabia, the computer market is fairly large and dynamic. It has grown at an impressive rate in the last few years (see Exhibit 3). Mainframe sales grew an estimated 30 % per year through 1984 when they reached US $ 85 million. However, the mini-micro markets grew twice as fast – about 60 % per year from 1982 through 1984.

This disparity in growth rates can be explained as follows. The public sector has been a leader in computerization and still is the single most important end-user, representing about 50 % of the market. Whereas this

Exhibit 3   Computer Market in Saudi Arabia: Total Size and Major Sub-
             Categories (in US $ Million)

Year	Mainframe	Mini	Micro	Peripherals	Total
1980	34.5	9	11	2.5	57
1981	45	14	14	3.5	76.5
1982	50	18.5	21.5	4	94
1984	85	60	30	4.5	179.5
1986	100	85	45	10	230
1988	125	125	65	11	316

Source: Figures are compiled from different sources, primarily from Middle East
         Marketing Research Bureau, Nov. 1985.

sector is primarily mainframe-oriented and has the largest number of
mainframe installations in the Kingdom, the private sector is more prone to
utilize mini- or microprocessors. Microcomputers are relatively little used
in government offices. Since most mainframes are already in place in the
large government organizations, and since the Saudi economy is now in
recession, lower growth rates for all segments of the computer market,
particularly the mainframe segment, can be expected.

In addition to the slowed economy, many other factors will shape the
computer market in the next few years. These are listed below in order of
their importance.

1) Price/performance ration: the projected maturation of the Saudi
   economy will make computer demand increasingly sensitive to prices.
   The price/performance ratio, therefore, is becoming a major consideration.
2) Market competition: with the end-user becoming more price-conscious
   of relative prices, and the minicomputer segment of the market
   becoming more mature, competition will become more fierce. A
   competitive edge in marketing, service, support, and Arabization can be
   expected to figure more importantly in attracting and retaining
   customers.
3) Arabization and Arabic software: in government offices, computer
   Arabization is a must, since all official correspondence must be in
   Arabic. Arabization is also becoming important in other sectors. Saudi-
   oriented Arabic software packages are needed at all levels of the
   computer market. In the microcomputer market, for example, the end-
   user's knowledge of English tends to be very limited, so a clear need
   exists for Arabic programming.
4) Computer awareness: schools, the media, and computer exhibitions are

contributing to an increasing level of computer awareness in Saudi Arabia, which in turn can be expected to provide a boost and expand the microcomputer market with.

5) Staffing problems: local, Arabic-speaking personnel skilled in computers are in short supply. Currently, a large proportion of experienced staffers at computer firms are expatriates.

Presently, the minicomputer market is the most competitive market segment in Saudi Arabia. It is dominated by American suppliers, where 9 out of 10 installed minicomputer base are from the USA (IBM, DEC, WANG, Data General, NCR, HP, Burroughs). The price/performance ratio is the highest priority purchase criterion. Companies with a well-established local agent providing good and reliable engineering support, employing active marketing and promotional methods, and providing good Arabic-oriented software packages will continue to do well in this market.

In the personal computer or microcomputer market, IBM dominates, followed by Apple and a score of Japanese and Taiwanese imitations. This is the fastest growing market segment due to the influx of cheap imitations from the Far East, the proliferation of dealer networks, and the introduction of Arabic software. Competitive edge in this market will depend increasingly on two major factors: Arabization and price. Any supplier or dealer providing Arabic personal computers at competitive prices can be expected to do well in this competitive market segment.

Most computer dealers in the Kingdom at first were busy selling computers and not paying attention to the software needs of their customers. Later on, however, those dealers changed their strategies and began customizing software to the peculiar needs of each user. Indeed, software became a distinct segment within the computer market. In 1984, the total size of this segment in Saudi Arabia was estimated to be US $ 163 million.

Following are some key trends that characterize this developing market segment:

1) Saudi computer end-users are not properly trained to fully take advantage of their machines. It is estimated that the utiliztion rate was 37 % in 1981 and 44 % in 1984. Many first-time users are illiterate about computers. They need help without condescension by those who provide it.

2) In-house software development in Saudi Arabia accounts for about 7 % of total development in the Kingdom, compared to 69 % in the USA. Saudi firms depend largely on existing packages plus contracted software development. They would rather buy than make their own software, particularly if it is cheaper to buy.

3) Original software is costly to develop, but too cheap to copy, particularly in the Arab world. Copyrights are not a barrier for software developers in the Middle East, just as patents are not a barrier for hardware manufacturers of the Far East. For instace, Alpha can make a copy of an original software program for only SR 30 (US $ 8). After customizing it, Alpha can sell this copy for at least SR 18,000, depending on the complexity of the client's operation.

4) Few Saudi end-users are fluent in English. They get impatient reading the manuals and doing all the manipulations needed to play with the software. A small businessman told the case writer: "I don't have time to waste with this stupid disk; I want something ready so I can just push a few keys and use my computer." He obviously has a need for outside help in customizing his software. This kind of potential user represents the best market opportunity for companies like "Alpha Data Soft".

5) Arabization of existing hardware and software packages is here to stay. Hardware manufacturers and software developers who capitalize on this trend will have a definite advantage. The Ministry of Education is moving toward incorporating computer education in secondary, intermediate, and elementary schools. Arabic is the formal language of instruction in all Saudi schools and government offices.

Competition

The computer market in Saudi Arabia is fiercely competitive. It is flooded with dealers of all kinds, selling different products and services, while following different approaches to the market. Competitive advantage among these dealers is determined by price, availability, and reliability of support services, and the quality of hardware and software sold.

Alpha's competitors are of two types: local and national. Local dealers are self-made entrepreneurs with limited service portfolio and financial resources. Computers are their only business. National dealers, by contrast, are diversified business concerns, representing a brand name hardware manufacturer and offering a full range of computer services out of an extensive network of stores spread throughout the Kingdom. Following is a list of key competitors and their profiles.

Local Competitors

Gulf Computer

This firm operates in Al-Khobar and has about 10 programmers. It sells hardware as well as customized software. Its owner is not as agressive as his counterparts at Alpha. Most of the salespeople are Indians whose Arabic is at best limited. In addition, Gulf in going after large orders. This situation created an opportunity for Alpha to establish its own niche in the customized software business.

Al-Hamidi Computer Systems

The owner of this firm is a computer science graduate of KFUPM. This firm is a direct competitor of Alpha. It has a software department which is three years old. Its owner has two stores in Al-Khobar, and he concentrates on servicing customers there, a fact which has given Alpha opportunities in Dammam.

National Group for Computer Services

This six-year-old company is located in Al-Khobar. Its target market is Arabic-speaking computer users. The company develops and sells Arabic hardware and software and trains customers in their usage. It emphasizes its Arabic computer "RAED." This company competes with Alpha for Arabic computer business.

National Competitors

Jeraisy Computer Services

This is the most important competitor in both the hardware and the customized software business. It has many branches all over the Kingdom and is the Apple computer agent. The company serves medium to large businesses by catering to the full range of their computer needs. It is very strong financially.

Jaffalli Group

As the local IGM agent, Jaffali has a firm grip on the computer hardware market. It has stores in many locations and has a full-service approach to the market.

Saudi Computer Industries (SCI)

This company is chaired by Dr. Al-Thiga, previously the dean of graduate studies at KFUPM. This manufacturing firm makes Arabic computers (Al-Farabi) in addition to parallel Arabic software. The plant's capacity is 2,500 units per year and is located in Jeddah. This company is an important competitor to Alpha for Arabic computer business. SCI's target market is the public agencies, educational institutions, government agencies, and the private sector.

Abdulla Fouad and Sons

This Commodore computer agent has 12 stores in several cities of the Kingdom. The company emphasizes its Arabic computer "MANTECH." The company is financially stable, and MANTECH is an important competitor to Alpha's Arabic computer.

The Future

Alpha's owners are concerned about the challenges facing their firm. They admit that the present strategy of focusing on turnkey projects, while workable, is riskier than the original one of selling customized software to small- and medium-sized firms. Whereas the original strategy exposes the firm to the potential threat of the new software protection technology, the turnkey business strategy puts Alpha in competition with large full-service dealers. Although Alpha is not in any imminent danger, it still has to adopt a proactive posture if it is to prosper and grow. What sort of clients should it seek, and what sort of projects should it try to obtain? In short, what sort of dealer does Alpha want to be? Does it, for example, want to remain a full-service dealer (selling hardware, software, technical service, and training) or a self-service dealer (selling hardware only or hardware plus software with little or no backup support)?

The partners are contemplating the following alternatives:

1) Do Nothing:
   This strategy could lead to an erosion of business and depletion of the firms's financial resources in light of severe competition from larger firms.
2) Sell Only Copied Software:
   Total investment would be reduced in this case. However, the threat of software protection technology exists. This strategy could be profitable

in the short term, but lead to spotty business opportunities at best in the longer term.

3) Sell Only Customized Software (Original)

This strategy has more substance than the one above. However, it costs more to implement, and clients may be reluctant to pay the high cost of original software, particularly in hard times.

4) Sell original and copied software and enter an arrangement with Jaffali or Jeraisi to do consulting work for a commission on newly acquired customers. This strategy would require minimum capital and is thus not very risky. Customers can be provided original customized software or copied programs, depending on how much they can afford. The new mission of the firm would be only to provide either advice and software for hardware acquired by the client elsewhere. At the same time, brand-name hardware could be supplied through existing dealers for a commission.

Messrs. Hamdan and Sartawi have difficult choices to make. Being preoccupied with the day-to-day operation of their business, they have decided to seek the help of a former classmate who is a strategic planning consultant.

Reference

Middle East Marketing Research Bureau (1985): *Market Research Survey on Computers and Related Equipment in Saudi Arabia*, (November).

Part III
Summary and Conclusions

Chapter 9
Strategic Management: Arabian Style

M. Sami Kassem

Introduction

The 18 cases included in this book constitute a convenience sample of service organizations operating within the GCC states. Even though the bulk of these cases focus on enterprises in Saudi Arabia, and even though the sample size is admittedly small, our anthology is representative enough to tentatively answer important questions relating to strategic management in the Arab Gulf States. How do these organizations adapt themselves to their contextual environments? Do they plan their future, or do they just accept it as it comes? What are the sociological characteristics of the planners and the non-planners? Which type dominates the Gulf business environment and why? How organized are these firms? What type of structural configuration predominates? Finally, what are the implications of our findings for the practice and study of the strategic management process in the Arabian Gulf setting?

In this chapter, we concern ourselves with these questions, using a broad brush. Our theme is that while Western notions of business strategy and structure may be alien to many Gulf Arabs, businesmen in the Gulf region nevertheless plan, organize, and control their efforts in their own way.

Strategy Formulation

Based on our earlier presentation in Chapter 2, six discernible features of the Gulf business environment can be identified. These features constraint the behavior and limit the choices of Arab Gulf managers. Exhibit 1 contains a brief outline of the leading environmental factors influencing strategic management in the Arab Gulf States. This outline is neither new nor exhaustive. However, these six features are perhaps the most salient ones. In addition, they are unique to the region, and they all have been generally ignored in discussions of strategic management.

Exhibit 1   Environmental Constraints Affecting Strategic Management Practices in the Arabian Gulf States

Contextual Variables	Constraints	Generic Strategy	Consequences	Hypothesis for Further Testing

1) Heavy dependence of Gulf states on the outside world – to buy their oil, to provide them with modern technology, management, skilled labor, raw materials	– A single crop of "oil-based" economies which imports:
	  – labor
	  – management
	  – technology
	  – raw materials
		– Focus: e.g., government employees for airlines; corporate patients for private hospitals; business travelers for luxury hotels	– High dependence translates into high uncertainty
			– Condemned to operate with a built-in competitive disadvantage; i.e., high cost can't compete domestically or globally
				The heavy dependence of Arab Gulf managers on the outside world makes them:
				a) more helpless than their counterparts elsewhere,
				b) more prone to practice ad-hoc reactive planning

2) Heavy involvement of government in the economies of the Arab Gulf States	– Owner and operator of oil fields – Leading entrepreneur and biggest employer – Principal bank roller and protector of infant industries	– Focus on seeking the fat government contract, business, subsidies at all costs	– Cost-plus schemes encourage built-in inefficiencies – More prone to practice top down "centralized" strategic decision-making. Need to keep channels of contact with government limited*	Arab Gulf managers are more dependent on their governments than their counterparts elsewhere for indicating, supporting, and subsidizing their favorite investment projects – which they get implemented
3) Islamic "Sharia" or teachings	– A ban on "usury," pork, gambling, alcohol – An extremely common misconception about fate and free will	– Since "riba" or usury is haram or prohibited, growth has to be through internal financing – Banking, casinos, night	– Leveraging is haram. Partnership through venture capital is acceptable. – Resistance to long-range planning. The future belongs to Allah, not to man	Gulf managers are more committed to the Islamic code governing business transactions than their counterparts elsewhere, particularly, if they perceive that code as helpful and advantageous

ethnic sensitivities	capital, brains, and tourism to safe havens – Lack of distinctive competencies (strengths)	capital-intensive projects – and more prone to invest in short-term labor-itensive service ventures (e.g., operational maintenance)	security considerations – Higher insurance rates, and inability to benefit from sixth freedom traffic/transit traffic or to promote tourism – "Opportunism" and reactive planning is the norm	alries and ethnic sensitivities than their counterparts elsewhere – a fact which further limits the size of their domestic market, increases their operating costs, and prevents them from developing a strategic focus
5) Abundance of cheap capital and shortage of human capital	– Centralized ascriptive-based personnel systems	The use of capital – intensive technologies drive Arab service organizations to play a catchup game with their Western counterparts	– Over-emphasis on organizational imagery; on external evidence such as ultralavish modern buildings and equipment	The relative abundance of cheap capital and lack of internal competencies drive Arab Gulf managers to pay more attention to organizational imagery than to organizational functioning, to means rather than ends, to forms rather than substance
6) Thin, small domestic market segmented by ethnicity	– Cannot achieve economies of scale due to low load factor or high idle capacity	– Condemned to use focus strategy	– Unusually high costs of producing and marketing of services	The more Arab managers learn to pool their resources, expand the size of their local markets, the more they would be able to compete domestically and globally

* Luqmani, M., Habib, G. and Kassem, S. (1988) p. 56–67.

Source: Primary

The importance of the first feature listed in Exhibit 1 cannot be stressed enough, i.e., the dependence of the Arab Gulf States on the world economy. A decade ago, the world demand for oil was at its peak, and, as a result, the oil-rich states enjoyed a Seller's market. They were selling oil at nearly US $ 40 a barrel. Saudi Arabia was earning US $ 300 million a day, which made it possible for the Kingdom to finance the largest development program in modern history. Foreign labor was attracted from virtually all the corners of the earth to participate in building the country's infrastructure. The influx of foreign labor created untold opportunities for the country's fledging service sector. Long waiting lists and excessively high prices were common among hotels, hospitals, schools, and airline operators, particularly those who targeted their services to the foreign work force.

As oil prices plummeted and revenues from oil fell sharply to about one-tenth their peak level, the supply and demand situation for goods and services reversed itself. Fortunately, most of the large infrastructure projects had already been completed, some new ones were put on hold. The market for goods and services shrank. High prices began to decline. Expensive foreign workers were sent home in droves, being replaced partly by local nationals and partly by cheaper foreign substitutes. Many service firms experienced idle capacity (e. g., empty beds and unoccupied seats) for the first time. Many inefficient services operators were forced out of the market. Many of those that have remained are barely breaking even. This abrupt economic reversal hammered home the urgent necessity to diversify the economies of the Arab Gulf States away from oil wherever possible.

Another key feature of the region is that the size of the domestic market in all of the Arab Gulf States – execpt Saudi Arabia – is too small to support certain internally focused industries. For instance, while Kuwait can certainly afford to operate a topnotch flag carrier, it can only do so successfully if it serves regional and international markets, since there is virtually zero need or demand for domestic air service in tiny Kuwait. The GCC, with its goal of economic integration of its member states, could help offset this factor in the future.

It would be a mistake to leave the reader with a strictly gloomy portrait of the Gulf business environment. For one thing, this environment, unlike many others, is still loaded with opportunities, but they have to be found and researched. For another, even though the Gulf business environment has recently been littered with the wreckage of numerous businesses (see Habib and Abdeen 1987), many examples of successful service organizations can still be found. Why, given the same operating environment, do some firms flourish while others flounder or fail?

Motivation and Capacity

To answer this question, one needs to focus not only on the broader landscape, but also on the individual firm and particularly its motivation to adapt. There is a rich variety of adaptation strategies at work in the Gulf business scene; the common denominator characterizing firms that successfully employ these strategies may be motivation or the will to succeed.

Even in the most constraining business environment, an organization usually has at least several strategic choices it can make in adapting to change. However, without the will to adapt, the organization may never realize its true capacity for survival and success. For many organizations, the will and capacity to adapt go hand in hand. However, for some organizations, particularly in developing countries, no amount of will can overcome a lack of capacity, and no amount of capacity or resources can overcome the fatalism of a complete lack of will. An organism, or an organization, can be said to be "coping" with its environment when its will and capacity are operating in tandem.

Contrary to a common misconception, Islam teaches that God has endowed man (and by implication, organizations) with both the free will to make his own choices and the capacity to act upon them, for better or for worse. Open system theorists put it another way. They have suggested that organizations are characterized by equifinality, meaning that there are many solutions to a given problem. Consider the critical role of top management in making intelligent strategic choices. How else can we meaningfully explain the success of Singapore or Alia Airlines? Effective strategies are what bind the will and capacity of organizations and enable them to cope with their environments.

Patterns of Organizational Adaptation

Based on the preceding analysis and building on the recent work of Hrebiniak and Joyce (1985), it is possible to construct an organizational strategy matrix made up of two independent dimensions; the environment and the organism (firm). For simplicity of exposition, the two constructs making up the latter dimension – will and capacity – are combined in one process variable: coping. Each dimension will be regarded as a continuum ranging from low to high, yielding four distinct patterns or modes of adaptation, as shown in Exhibit 2.

Cell A basically reflects the conditions or assumptions underlying the Anglo-Saxon strategic management model. Proponents of that model argue that an organization, in order to be effective, must maximize the fit with its environment. It must influence its environment by being an efficient

Degree of Environmental Determinism

High

	Cell A: Prospectors	Cell B: Analyzers
Degree of Coping	... By design Proactive Innovators – high achieving entrepreneurs (2)	... Within severe constraints Despite the odds (4)
	Cell D: Reactors	Cell C: Defenders
	... By chance Reactive Lack strategic focus (7)	... By hook or by crook "Make or break" Bastion mentality (5)

Low   High

Exhibit 2   Organizational Adaptation Matrix

( )   = number of sampled organizations
...   = adaptation
: →   = the label given to each cell is not ours, but that of Miles and Snow (1978)

Source: Adapted from Hrebiniak and Joyce (1985): 339.

producer or an aggressive marketer or both. Only then can it be ahead of its competitors and in command of its destiny. Under these conditions, adaptation is made by design, not by accident.

Cell B involves a situation where environmental constraints are severe and the level of coping is high. While environmental constraints are as numerous and severe as in Cell C, the organization is blessed with superior distinctive competence, a strong will, or both. Instead of being resigned to an uncertain fate, it tries to survive despite the odds. This cell is typically populated by public utilities, conglomerates, and divisionalized organizations.

Cell C is the opposite of Cell A. It is populated by organizations which lack effective control over both their environment and their destiny. Typically, they sell undifferentiated commodities or services at the going market price in a market environment. Their management is rather passive. Faced with severe environmental constraints, such organizations become readily resigned to their fate. Under these conditions, where controls are in the hands of others (regulators, consumers, competitors), adaptation is determined from without. Organizations simply have to tough it out or die.

Cell D is characterized by both low environmental constraints and a low degree of coping. It is the opposite of Cell B. Organizations operating within this cell are typically young, inexperienced, and strategically inactive. Despite supportive government policies (e. g., subsidies, incentives, duty-free imports), these organizations are reluctant to exploit such opportunities. The clearest examples are the fly-by-night trading and contracting firms established during the boom of the 1970s. Lacking both distinctive competence and a strategic focus, these firms were the first ones to fail as recession hit the economies of the GCC states. Such firms sail for a while with the prevailing winds. Lacking a strategic focus, they are caught off guard when the economic winds shift.

Where do the 18 organizations sampled in this book fit on the matrix? An exercise for students would be to place each of them in the appropriate cell. Kassem put a group of his graduate students through this excercise. Exhibit 3 provides a tally of the results.

Exhibit 3   Distribution of 18 Sampled Organizations by Mode of Strategic Adaptation

Cell	Frequency	%	Constituent Organizations
A	2	11	A hospital and a large international bank
B	4	22	Two joint venture banks, two airlines
C	5	28	Two airlines, two hotels, and a local bank
D	7	39	Two hospitals, a private school, a consulting firm, a computer service firm, and two hotels
	18	100%	

A recent study (Kassem et al. 1987) of a larger sample of family-owned concerns operating in different lines of business in Saudi Arabia and Bahrain revealed a somewhat similar distribution (see Exhibit 4).

Exhibit 4   Family-Owned Firms in Saudia Arabia: Distribution of Respondents by Miles and Snow Strategic Type

Cell	Type	Frequency	Percentage
A	Prospectors	13	27
B	Analyzers	8	17
C	Defenders	20	40
D	Reactors	8	16
		49	100%

Source: Kassem et al., 1987

Results from our limited sample suggest that the *innovators* are the long-established, medium-sized, single-business entrepreneurial firms operating in a dynamic environment – usually with the help of a foreign partner who provides the management know-how. These firms usually have a well-defined strategic focus. Our research on family business shows that this group includes many of the old, well-established families who own and run diversified concerns (e. g., Al Gosaibi, Kanoo, Al Olayan, etc.).

The *analyzers* tend to be firms propelled by a high sense of purpose. They are very cautious, mature, and experienced firms operating in a complex dynamic environment full of adversities and constraints. Alia, the Royal Jordanian Airline, is one example.

The *defenders* tend to be large, old organizations, operating in a complex, dynamic, and deregulated environment in which they sell highly "standardized" services or commodities. These organizations depend on outside support, such as government subsidies in the case of airlines or non-interest-bearing deposits in the case of commercial banks.

Finally, the *reactors* of today are young and small organizations which use labor-intensive technologies and low levels of professional management. The reactors are usually owned by indigenous merchants. These merchants provide their name, contacts, and capital. Their foreign partners provide the direction, know-how, and day-to-day management of the firm.

Strategy formulation is a dynamic process. Organizations are not condemned forever to any particular position in the matrix. Instead, their position may shift as a result of changes in the external environment or in their capacity or motivation to cope. A historic analysis of strategic development in a larger sample of family-owned firms in Saudi Arabia confirmed this observation. Fifty-eight percent of that sample followed a deliberately proactive strategy during the pre-boom years, and 65% are currently repositioning themselves using strategies involving retrenchment and segmentation (Kassem et al. 1987).

Reactive Versus Proactive Planning

Only 6 of the 18 organizations covered in this book practice formal strategic planning described in Western management literature, and, if the 3 banks with foreign connections are excluded, the number drops to just 3 organizations of 18. The majority, by contrast, practices various forms of reactive, intuitive, and incremental planning.

There are a number of possible explanations for the dominance of reactive planning among our sampled organizations. As we have seen, the economies of the GCC states are highly dependent on world oil markets and thus highly susceptible to fluctuations in these markets. As we have also seen, the Arab Gulf States and their organizations have trouble predicting, comprehending, and responding to these fluctuaions. This handicap is perhaps due to the severe shortage of information required for strategic analysis. For instance, simple information related to the demographics, sociographics, and psychographics of Arab Gulf air travellers, patients, or bank customers in unavailable, and what little information is available is usually labeled confidential. One might argue that even in the West – where there is abundance of information – few predicted the oil crisis of 1973, the collapse of the auto industry in the mid-1970s, or the stock market crash of 1987. However, the difference between the GCC economies and Western economies is that the former are rather strictly oil-based, whereas the latter are diversified and hence less susceptible to sudden economic swings on the international scene.

The oil crisis of 1973 and the massive wealth it generated for the Gulf states brought untold opportunities for businessmen. These opportunities were so abundant and competition so slack that efficiency was only a minor consideration. Many a manger and businessman got away with making colossal mistakes. They could over-order the wrong items and wind up selling them at a profit. They could easily pass on cost increases and charge orders to willing customers. Today, the situation is completely reversed, and a major shake-out is taking place. The mortality rate among the region's business firms has been unusually high, particularly for newcomers, who jumped on yesterday's band wagon just before the music stopped playing. There is some evidence (e. g., Chandler 1962, Channon 1978, Miller and Friesen 1984, and Mintzberg 1987) that even in the industrialized West, major shifts in strategic and structural orientations occur only rarely and briefly in response to a crisis of one sort or another.[1]

Unlike many corporate managers in the West, Gulf Arabs are traders by tradition. They typically rely on market instincts, not on hard data. They also let others perform the technical functions, such as engineering and production, while they specialize in the commercial ones, such as the buying and selling. This "trading mentality" is focused on the short term. A streak of fatalism may also creep into this mind set, which runs something like this: planning involves dealing with the unknown – a domain which properly belongs to God, not man.[2] Moreover, Gulf Arabs tend to be

---

[1] The evidence that strategic and structural change tends to take place in relatively sharp discontinuities comes from two sources. First there is the historical evidence of the sort reported by Chandler 1962 on American business and Channon (1978) on British Service industries. Second, there is recent empirical evidence derived from longitudinal study of strategy and structure in few North American organizations. For example, Mintzberg (1987) questions the assumptions of the traditional strategic management model which basically assumes that change is continuous and that organizations are adapting all the time. He argues, instead, that major strategic changes happen in brief quantum leaps.

[2] In Islam, there is a delicate balance between free will and predestination, between the will of man and the will of Allah. There are texts in the Quran which clearly assert that man is responsible for his own actions, though the majority of texts – in both the Quran and Hadith – seem to assert that they are definitely decreed. Yet, this balance seems to be tilted in favor of predestination, leading to a rampant attitude of fatalism, particularly in the minds of the

traditionalists at heart. They idealize the past and distrust the future. They prefer the tried and true to the untried. Field research conducted by Learner (1963) and Kassem and Al Modaifer (1987) confirms this cultural orientation.

The above explanation of the dominance of reactive planning in the Arab Gulf States is not intended as an apology for real inadequacies, but instead to suggest the subjectivity and probable bias of the traditional Western model of strategy formulation. This model grew out of the relatively stable industrial environment of the West which is dominated by large firms and governed by the logic of efficiency and profitability. It prescibes the strategy-formulation process as involving activities such as: establishing goals, monitoring the environment assessing internal capabilities, searching for and evaluating alternative strategies, and choosing the best strategy for the organization (e. g., Andrews 1971, Hofer and Schendel 1978, Pearce and Robinson 1988, Steiner 1979). It assumes free competition, that strategies are always deliberate and that

... the firm speaks with a unitary voice or can be composed of omnipotent, even heroic general managers or chief executives, looking at known and consistent preferences and assessing them with voluminous and presumably opposite information which can be organized into clear input-output relationships, (Pettigrew 1985: 276).

Thus, criticism of strategic management practices in the Arab Gulf States should be tempered by the realization of the cultural biases of the particular model used in the analysis. One should be mindful, too, that Arab organizations in the Gulf operate in an entirely different environment.[3]

Organizational Structure

Formulating a strategy and adjusting the organizational structure are important aspects of the strategic management process. Both involve making difficult choices.

---

ignorant segment of the population. In as much as everything is decreed, it is idle for man to make any effort or to map out any plan. Carried to excess, this popular misconception has obvious dangers to the life of an individual, an organization or a nation. It explains, in part, the reluctance of Arab executives to engage in proactive strategic planning. On this point, see Exhibit 2 in this chapter and Muna (1980: 93–98).

[3] For a detailed critique of the conventional strategic management model see Quinn, J. B., Mintzberg, H., and Roberts, R. M. (1988), where they question the assumptions and expose the limitations of that model thoughout their work. They argue that strategies are not deliberately formulated but rather formed, and that their formation and implementation occur simultaneously – not sequentially – within a context.

We have concluded that strategies followed by the majority of our sampled organizations are seldom proactive, as idealized by textbooks on strategic management. Instead, they are the outcomes of many ad hoc decisions intended to deal with immediate problems. We have argued that such decisions are constrained by a broad set of impersonal environmental factors and equally influenced by the culturally determined values of the organizations' top decision makers.

Decisions about how to structure organizations in the Gulf context follow a similar pattern. Our message is that the Gulf Arab executive of today – if he is to succeed as an architect of organization design – has to be flexible. He should strive for an organic structure that can take advantage of changing conditions. Both the Gulf Air and Alia cases drive that lesson home.

Forms Follow Functions

Conventional wisdom in both architecture and organizational design dictates that one has to decide on a desirable destination well before planning how to get there. Identifying goals is one of the first steps of successful design. However, one feature of Arab organizations is that the actual objectives may not be the stated ones.

The No-System System: Organized Anarchy

Conventional organization theory states that organizations have to develop rules, standards, and policies to spell out expectations, reduce uncertainty, and ensure fairness with regard to clients and employees.

Given their cultural aversion to uncertainty, most Arab organizations have developed their own system of rules. These rules are often written in such a way as to delimit the authority of the boss. The Arab boss learns to customize and personalize rules in a system of favoritism. "We swallow the mistakes of those we like, but those we don't like have to account for theirs," this statement aptly describes the Arab sensibility. Formal rules in Arab organizations tend to apply to Arab employees who are in disfavor or to expatriates. By contrast, informal rules are specially "engineered" for the in-group of favored Arab employees in such a way as to encourage loyalty. A skilled Arab manager can invoke either set of rules at any particular moment in order to achieve his ends.

Desert Democracy

Organizations, by their very nature, are small societies of unequals. In both East and West, organizations have managers and the managed, leaders and followers.

Arab culture is characterized by a high degree of power distance demanding respect for both elders and those in positions of authority.[4] This suggests that if the Arab manager is to be successful in the use of his power, he has to concentrate it in his hands as much as possible. It comes as no surprise that most Arab managers do not delegate authority. The few who try to involve their subordinates do not involve them as individuals, but as groups in the decision-making process. They form a lot of committees or task forces in the belief that this is consistent both with Arab culture, with its emphasis on consensus, and with modern management theory. However, they may find that their subordinates are not really interested in sharing power with them. As a matter of fact, those reluctant subordinates, ever mindful of authority, may question the intentions of their superiors. This skepticism about participative management is quite common in the Arab East, as it is in the West.[5]

There is some evidence to support the conclusion that the Arabs wrote the book on "management by committees." To implement its recently formulated retrenchment strategy, a major Gulf carrier, reported in this book formed over a dozen committees. These committee members, especially those in charge of administrative expenses, balked at cutting the real fat – their own salaries and benefits.

Needed: Better Systems, Not Better People

There exists a myth in the Arab Gulf States that a lack of indigenous talent is what is slowing down the development process. Perhaps this was the case 20 years ago, but no longer today. There is considerable native talent in most fields, but it stays hidden and underutilized. One pillar of the Weberian bureaucratic model is that personnel decisions should be made on the basis of merit. Regrettably, this principle is not always followed in the Arab world – even though Islamic teachings warn against violating this rule. In practice, the most qualified person does not always get the job, and the most productive employees do not always end up with the top reward. Furthermore, often the job occupant is not delegated the requisite

---

[4] Arabic culture derives a great many of its ideals and values from the teachings of Islam. The latter puts a heavy emphasis on obedience to superiors and, at the same time, demands that superiors consult with their subordinates on matters that directly affect their welfare.

[5] The debate about how much power a leader should share with his subordinates continues to be fruitless unless one specifies the nature of the task, subordinates, and contextual situation, including the demands of the larger culture. On the latter dimension, it is clear from the research reviewed in Chaptere 2 that the Arab culture is inherently less participative. For more evidence, see Schein (1980): 132–135, Chackerian and Shadukhi (1983), and Saud (1985).

authority. For instance, loan officers in many Gulf banks are not authorized to approve even minor loans on their own.

To the outsider, this set of managerial practices may seem as a depreciation of human assets. However, a culturally more sensitive observer might evaluate the situation differently. The Arab manager is pulled in different directions. He is pulled by his cultural heritage which expects him to take care of his own people: "A tree whose shade does not cover its seedlings deserves to be uprooted." He is also pulled by his own feelings of insecurity and inadequacy: "Better to have a donkey to ride than a horse that rides you." He is pulled by public policy, which asks him to give nationals preferential treatment. Finally, he is pulled by the organizational need for efficiency. Almost every Arab Gulf manager experiences these conflicting pulls. How he and his colleagues resolve them depends to a large extent on their inner strength and interpersonal flexibility and skill.

Our reading is that the above-cited contradictions or departures from the Weberian model do not reflect on the competence of Arab managers. Since these contradictions are culturally induced, they seem to suggest that there should be an alternative organizational model to better describe the reality of the Arab manager's situation. This model can be called "bedoaucracy."

We are not the first ones to discover the model,[6] but we are the first ones to identify and detail its parameters and compare it with its bureaucratic counterpart (see Exhibit 5). In this connection, it should be emphasized that bedoaucracy is a construct. As such, it may not describe any particular organization that actually exists.[7] But it does describe central tendencies likely to be shared by most Arab Gulf organizations.

---

[6] Just as it was natural for Max Weber to discover bureaucracy and develop its sociological indicators, so it was for Saudi students of Public Administration to discover bedoaucracy. Al Awaji (1971), Abdul Rahman (1982), Al Nimr and Palmer (1982), and Al Hegelan and Palmer (1985) have all developed the theme that Saudi Arabia is a transitional society. Despite the introduction of modern organizations and methods, the administrative behavior is still highly traditional. Consequently, overlapping of modern and traditional elements is a major feature of present-day Saudi bureaucracy. Other features include over-centralization of authority, overstaffing, personalization, formalization, nepotism, and corruption. These features continue to prevail, because they are functional both to leaders and followers alike.

[7] This model is a composite which is based on the writings of students of Arab management such as Badawy (1980), Muna (1980), Al Nimr and Palmer (1982), Al Hegelan and Palmer (1985), Saud (1985), and Kassem and Al Mudaifer (1987).

Exhibit 5   Bureaucracy and Bedoaucracy Compared

Organizing Principle	Bureaucracy	Bedoaucracy
Key part of organization:	Technostructure	Executive council
Specialization:	One-man, one-job	One-man, several jobs
Integration:	One-man, one-boss	One-man, one-boss
Type of authority:	Direct authority	Consensus, mutual adjustment Representative democracy
Base of authority:	Rational/Legal: Knowledge; expertise merit	Traditional: Age, social status, religosity, income, education
– flow of authority:	significant throughout	often top-down
– informal communication:	discouraged	encouraged
– flow of decision-making:	top down	mixed: top down (autocratic) and bottom up: (upward delegation)
Formalization:	High Impersonal rules	Low Personal/informal rules
Centralization:	Low Horizontal decentralization to experts	High
– Motivation: inducement to contribute:	Calculative	Loyalities: saving face to the clan
– Membership orientation:	Cosmopolitan	Local
– Organizational goals:	Relatively stable	Relatively dynamic: they change with change in leadership
– Organizations are:	Well-oiled machines	People
– Orientation:	Business is business	Business is people
– Criteria for measuring organizational effectiveness:	Efficiency	Satisfaction/welfare of the tribe at large
Contingency variables:		
Age:	Old	Varies
Size:	Lean	Fat/large (too many chiefs/few indians)
Culture:	Low: Power distance, uncertainty avoidance High: Individualism and masculinity	High power distance, uncertainty avoidance and collectivism Low: masculinity
Environment:	Simple, stable	Simple, stable
Power:	Technocrats/experts	Chief of tribe or the head of the organization

For a similar attempt at comparing Islamic with Western organizations, see Moore and Delener (1986): 80–84.

Typology of Service Organizations

If the bedoaucratic model fits the Arabian Gulf landscape more than its bureaucratic counterpart, the fact still remains that, within the service sector, some organizations are more centralized than others; some are more democratic than others; some are more formalized than others; still some are more hierarchical than others.

The theme of this concluding chapter is that organizations are not all alike. Their environments and strategies differ, and so do their technologies and structures. As strategy is contingent upon the environment, so structure is upon technology.

There are many competing typologies that can be used to classify the structure of the 18 sampled organizations. The most useful one for our purposes is that of Schmenner (1986). For one thing, his typology specifically applies to service organizations. For another, it helps us diagnose the special problems associated with each type of service business and map out appropriate solutions.

Schmenner's typology has two dimensions which together describe the technology employed in the service delivery process. The first dimension is labor intensity, defined as the ratio of labor costs to the value of the plant and equipment. A labor-intensive business involves little capitalization per worker and a high payroll. By contrast, capital-intensive business has a low wage bill relative to capitaliztion per worker. The other key dimension is customization of the service (or its counterpart, standardization). A highly customized service can meet individual preferences and tastes. By contrast, highly standardized service treats customers as cases or numbers – as if all their tastes and preferences were alike.

As Exhibit 6 shows, this model yields a two-by-two matrix with 4 types of firms: the service factory, mass service, professional service, and service shop.

Cell A is made up of service organizations which combine a high degree of labor intensity with low customization. Five cases reported in this book belong to this cell: 3 commercial banks, a private school, and a computer software firm. The special challenge facing the heads of these firms is how to personalize their services.

As the bulk of expatriates left for home, competition for local customers increased and automation became widespread in order to increase operating efficiency. At this juncture, appealing to individual and cultural differences becomes a wise strategy for some firms, particularly commercial banks. In the status-conscious Arab culture, personalized banking could make a comeback. Success may come to those banks that are aggressive in using internal and external marketing tools. Joint-venture banks who attract young Arab talent, put them in front of customers, train them well,

Degree of Customization

	High		
Labor Intensity High	Cell A: Mass Service 3 – Commercial banks 1 – School 1 – Computer service (5)	Cell B: Professional Service 1 – Consulting firm 2 – Investment banks (3)	
Low	Cell D: Service factory 4 – Airlines 3 – Hotels (7)	Cell C: Service Shop 3 – Hospitals (3)	High

Exhibit 6   Organization Structure Matrix
( ) = number of sampled organizations

Source: Adapted from Schmenner (1986): 25

give them the requisite decision-making authority, and reward them on the basis of performance will be in a better competitive position than their counterparts who continue down the road of further automation and standardization.

Cell B is the pure case of professional service firms, where both customization and labor intensity are equally high. Three organizations in our sample belong to this cell: a consulting firm and 2 investment banks. Typically, these organizations are staffed by expatriates who acquired their expertise outside their organizations. These professionals approach each client as if it is a unique case requiring individualized diagnosis and treatment.

Throughout the Arab Gulf States, professional service firms are typically managed by young, talented, but inexperienced Gulf nationals. When these managers cannot resist the temptation to interfere in the work of their more experienced and self-motivated professional subordinates, this meddling tends to generate more heat than light. It dampens professionalism, upsets delicate client relationships, and can stifle innovation. In such context, management may be best when it manages least.

Cell C is the opposite of Cell A. It is populated by service organizations which offer a high degree of customization but are not very labor intensive. The three health service organizations reported in this book belong to this cell. They all employ various kinds of medical personnel working with modern equipments to diagnose patients' ailments and treat them. Patients pay dearly to get the undivided attention of the physician serving them.

Whereas managing human assets is the toughest challenge facing executives of professional service firms, managing capital assets is the toughest challenge facing the service shops executives. This is not to imply that managing medical personnel is unimportant in a hospital quite the contrary. Our argument is simply this: a critical problem for a private modern hospital is whether to invest in new capital equipment. The latest CAT-scan machine can cost US $ 1 million. Should a hospital have its own blood bank or its own kidney dialysis machine? Such capital budgeting decisions ware awesome. The consequences of a wrong decision can affect the fate of a hospital for years thereafter.

Cell D is the opposite of Cell B. It is populated by service factories, which do not offer customized service and are not labor-intensive. Seven of our sampled organizations belong to this cell: four airlines and three hotels. They are classic examples of what Mintzberg (1979) terms the "machine bureaucracy." Their tasks are simple, repetitive, and routine: as a result, their work is highly standardized, differentiated, and integrated. It is the service factory that develops the tallest hierarchy. For instance, at Kuwait Airways, there are 7 levels of management separating the chief executive from the lowest level manager.

The general manger of a service factory faces a twin challenge. On the one hand, he has to treat his own employees as individuals, not as robots. Performing simple, routine tasks all day long can take its toll on productivity. Experimenting with some of the latest work-redesign methods might help reduce the boredom and increase job satisfaction. On the other hand, customers are people, too. They, too, prefer "warm," individualized attention.

Because of their operational orientation and cultural heritage (i.e., large power distance and high uncertainty avoidance), chief executives of Arab service factories become so enmeshed in operating problems that they tend to lose sight of strategic destinations. To compound their difficulties, the service factory is ill-suited to any change in strategic direction. Not unlike a machine, it is designed for special purposes and cannot be easily redirected.

Using The Model

The preceding analysis clearly suggests that service organizations are not all alike. As Exhibit 6 demonstrates, they do differ in the type of technology used in the delivery of their service. Differences (in labor intensity and customization) do have implications for organizational design and strategic action.

We admit that our typology, like many others, is not a perfect one. It may not neatly fit the case of a given organization. For instance, where in our matrix does an avant-garde men's tailor shop belong? Similarly, does the

Green Crescent Clinic properly belong in Cell B or C? Really, it does not matter that much. What is important is to realize the relative merits of increasing or decreasing the degree of customization. Offering more customized service costs money and effort. But it should not cost too much. Otherwise, customers may switch to cheaper, more affordable alternatives. That is exactly what happened when some patients in the Gulf region switched from private to public hospitals when faced with rising fees and recessionary pressures.

Ten of the 18 organizations covered in this book are capital-intensive. This comes as no surprise. After all, the Arab Gulf States are rich in capital and short on labor. We have seen that Arab service organizations operate with a built-in competitive disadvantage: namely, a high cost-structure. This problem could be converted into an opportunity if serious consideration were given to the customization issue. Unreported field data about Arab consumer behavior clearly shows that most Arabs prefer first-class to economy-class treatment. At major GCC airports, the demand for first-class seats exceeds the available supply. In hotels and hospitals throughout the region, the same situation prevails. As a matter of fact, private hospitals were the first ones to capitalize on this trend. Some were quick to reposition themselves, so they could offer expectant Arab mothers luxury hotel-style accommodation. Again, however, it must be stressed that customization strategies run the risk of pricing the service out of the market.

Managing people also represents a challenge for executives of Arab service organizations that are operating in the labor-short GCC states – especially those firms that are highly labor-intensive and customized. As change agents, they have to welcome their foreign workers, inspire and train local employees, and mold both groups together well into well-functioning teams. Managing professional employees is especially delicate, because generally they are not intimidated by authority and respect competence more than position.

Finally, the management of service organizations that are low on customization requires the development and enforcement of customer service standards. This is where management contract firms have made their greatest contribution. Moreover, aggressive and imaginative marketing is urgently needed to restore and capitalize on the personal touch – which Arabs are famous for.

In concluding this section, it is reasonable to assume that service organizations that conform to the organizing logic peculiar to their cell in the matrix will tend to outperform those that do not. However, the technological imperative hypothesis remains untested.

Practical Implications

The lackluster performance of the service section of the GCC states is due to a combination of factors. We have singled out the dependence of this region on the world economy – on oil exports for revenue and on imports for most of its factor inputs. The effect of this dependency is two-fold. First, it puts the fate of the GCC economies into the hands of foreign powers. Second, the situation favors foreign producers of goods and services whose average unit cost is much lower than that of their Arab counterparts. The completion of major infrastructure projects and the return of guest workers to their homeland in the wake of declining oil revenues are factors which have cut the demand for goods and services in the GCC states.

In addition, certain endogenous factors, reported in some detail in the case studies contained in this book, have contributed to the weak performance of the service sector. Most of the service establishments reported in this book are organized and managed as tribes, not as modern businesses. Just as a tribe perceives its right to exist without ever considering why, so it is with Arab service organizations. Their ends and means are seldom explicitly stated. The owner/manager seldom involves his employees meaningfully in formulating business strategies. In summary, Arab service organizations generally:

1) lack a strategic focus;
2) lack the ability to adapt to changing conditions; the manager simply becomes accustomed to surprises; and
3) fail to involve and motivate workers (i. e. customers-contact personnel), which translates into indifference to customers and their needs.

Just as a tribe cannot function on the basis of impersonal rules and standards, so it is for the Arab service establishment. Even in old and large Arab organizations, lack of formalization is the rule, not the exception.

If our diagnosis is correct, then how can a turnaround be engineered? In our opinion, nothing less than a massive re-education of owners, managers, employees, and customers are needed. This task, which involves the changing of cultural values will take a few generations. It requires a few courageous horsemen and a few good Arabian stallions to get started.

What is urgently needed is a critical mass of innovative entrepreneurs – leaders with a clear strategic vision, a strong sense of direction and mission, and clear strategies. Fortunately, our experience with the Gulf business scene tells us that the minimum required leadership is available locally within the ranks of existing organizations. In our interviews, we have seen quite a few boxed-in horsemen who qualify for executive leadership positions. They need to be discovered, groomed, and put where they belong.

Good horesemen alone are not enough. They need good horses to be effective. They need to create efficient and adaptive structures where every employee:

1) has a well-defined job;
2) is given the requisite authority to accomplish his job;
3) is rewarded for his performance, not his conformity or loyalty; and
4) is informed of what is happening in his relevant segment of the environment, so he can adjust his acts accordingly.

Shrewd management is a must if Arab service firms are to compete successfully with their local and international rivals. The new management has to be skilled in:

1) cutting costs without feeling remorse;
2) raising productivity intelligently;
3) responding to customer needs swiftly; and,
4) practicing internal and external marketing imaginatively.

Obviously, this is a tall order that will take years to achieve. However, there are already a few service organizations in the Arab world which are leading the way.

Theoretical Implications

Although the data reported here in this book is incomplete to warrant such a conclusion, impressionistic evidence from interviews, observation, and recent literature (e.g., Hofstede 1980, Quinn et al. 1988) suggests two things:

First: There are, *at least*, two models of organizational adaptation: the Western and the Eastern. Likewise; there are two models of organizational structure: the bureaucratic and the bedoaucratic.

Second: These organizational models work well – in their respective environmental contexts. They are not exportable, in whole or in part, without risking some unexpected negative results.

References

Abdul Rahman, O. (1982): *Oil bureaucracy and the development dilemma*, Kuwait: National Council for Culture, Arts, and Humanities.

Abdul Rahmann, O. (1986): *The dilemma of development in the Arabian peninsula*, Kent, England: Croom-Helm.

Al Awaji, I. (1971): Bureaucracy and society in Saudi Arabia, Unpublished Ph. D. Dissertation, University of Virginia.

Al Hegelan, A. and Palmer, M. (1985): Bureaucracy and development in Saudi Arabia, *The Middle East Journal*, 39, 1: 48–68.

Ali, A. and Swiercz, P. (1985): Managerial decision styles and work satisfaction in Saudi Arabia, *Management Decision*, 23, 2: 33–42.

Al Jaffary, A. and Hollingsworth, A. T. (1983): An exploratory study of management practices in the Arabian Gulf, *Journal of International Business Studies*, Fall: 143–152.

Almaney, A. J. (1981): Cultural traits of the Arabs: Growing interest for international management, *Management International Review*, 21: 10–18.

Al Nimr and Palmer, M. (1982): Bureaucracy and development in Saudi Arabia: A behavioral analysis, *Public Administration and Development*, 2: 93–104.

Al Qobaisi, A. (1985): Toward a comparative administration study of the Arabian Gulf States, *Journal of the Gulf and Arabian Peninsula Studies*, 42: 75–94.

Anastos, D. et al. (1980): The development of modern management practices in Saudi Arabia, *Columbia Journal of World Business*, (Summer), 15, 2: 81–91.

Andrews, K. (1971): *The concept of corporate strategy*, Homewood Ill.: Richard Irwin.

Badawy, M. K. (1980): Styles of Middle Eastern managers, *California Management Review*, 21: 51–58.

Badran, M. and Hinings, C. R (1981): Strategies, administrative controls and contexual constraints in a less developed country: The case of Egyptian public enterprise, in: Lammers, C. J., Hickson, D. J., and MacMillan, C. J. (Eds.): *Organizations and nation*, Aldershot: Gower.

Chackerian, R. and Shadukhi, S. (1983): Public bureaucracy in Saudi Arabia, *International Review of Administrative Services*, 49, 3: 319–322.

Chandler, A. D. (1962): *Strategy and structure*, Cambridge, Mass.: M.I.T. Press.

Channon, D. F. (1978): *Service industries*, London: The Macmillan Press, 260.

Economist (1986): The GCC countries: A survey, *The Economist*, February 8: 6.

Habib, G.M. and Abdeen, A. (1987): Bankruptcy of some Saudi firms: Cause and solutions, *Arab Journal of Administration*, 11: 2: 147–165.

Hofer, C. and Schendel, D. (1978): *Strategy formulation: Analytical concepts*, St. Paul, MN: West.

Hofstede, G. (1980): *Culture's consequences*, London: Sage Publications.

Hofstede, G. (1983): The cultural relativity of organizational practices and theories, *Journal of International Business*, (Fall): 75–89.

Hrebiniak, L. and Joyce, W. (1985): Organizational adaptation: Strategic choice and environmental determinism, *Administrative Science Quarterly*, 30: 336–349.

Johany, A., Berne, M., and Mixon, W. (1987): *The Saudi Arabian economy*, Baltimore, Md.: Johns Hopkins University Press.

Kassem, M. and Al Modaifer, K. (1987): Bureaucracy and society in the Arab world: A replication and extension of Hofstede's value survey model, *Working Paper*, King Fahd University of Petroleum and Minerals.

Kassem, M. and others (1987): The strategy and structure of family firms in the GCC states: An exploratory study, *Working Paper*, King Fahd University of Petroleum and Minerals

Learner, D. (1958): *The passing of traditional society: Modernizing the Middle East*, Glencoe, Ill: The Free Press.

Luqmani, M., Habib, G., and Kassem, S. (1988): Marketing to LDC's governments, *International Marketing Review*, special issue, 5, 1: 56–67.

Mackey, S. (1987): *The Saudis*, Boston: Houghton Mifflin.

Miles, R. and Snow, C. (1978): *Organizational Strategy, structure, and process*, New York: McGraw-Hill.

Miller, D. and Friesen, P. (1984): *Organizations: A quantum view*, Englewood Cliffs, N.J.: Prentice-Hall.

Mintzberg, H. (1987): Crafting strategy, *Harvard Business Review*, July-August, 65, 4: 66–75.

Moore, R.M. and Delener, N. (1986): Islam and work, in: G. Roukis and P.J. Montana (Eds.), *Workforce management in the Arabian peninsula*, Westport, CT: Greenwood Press.

Muna, F.A. (1980): *The Arab executive*, London: Macmillan.

Norman, R. (1984): *Service management: Strategy and leadership in services businesses*, New York: Wiley.

Pearce, J. and Robinson, R. (1988): *Formulation and implementation of competitive strategy*, Homewood, Ill.: Richard Irwin.

Pettigrew, A. (1985): Examining changes in the long term context of culture and politics, in: *Organizational strategy and change*, J.M. Pennings and Associates (Eds.), San Francisco: Jossey-Bass, 269–318.

Pezeshkpur, C. (1978): Challenges to management in the Arab world, *Business Horizons*, 21, 4: 47–55.

Powell, L, Geib, M., and Spengler, A. (1975): *Atlas of the Middle East*, Dubuque, Iowa: Kendall, Hunt.

Quinn, J.B., Mintzberg, H., and Roberts, R.M. (1988): *The strategy process*, Englewood Cliffs, N.J.: Prentice-Hall.

Rosen, G. (1980): *Western economists and eastern societies*, Baltimore, Md.: The Johns Hopkins University Press.

Roukis, G. and Montana, P. (1986): *Workforce management in the Arabian Peninsula: Forces affecting development*, Westport, CT: Greenwood Press.

Saud, S. F. (1985): Management and Leadership: Styles of American, Arab, and Southeast Asia Managers. Unpublished Dissertation, United States International University.

Sayiegh, Y. (1978): *The economics of the Arab world*, New York: St. Martin Press.

Schein, E. (1980): *Organizational psychology*, 3rd ed., Englewood Cliffs, N.J.: Prentice Hall.

Schmenner, R. W. (1986): How can service businesses survive and prosper?, *Sloan Management Review*, 27, 3 (Spring): 31–32.

Shabon, A. (1981): *The political, economic and labor climate in the countries of the Arabian peninsula*, Philadelphia: The Wharton School, University of Pennsylvania.

Steiner, G. (1979): *Strategic planning: What every manager must know*, New York: McGraw Hill.

Wright, P. (1981): Organizational behavior in Islamic firms, *Management International Review*, 21: 86–93.

Appendix A
A Guide to The Case Method

Theory

The case method is a proven learning tool. Its purpose is not to offer solutions to the particular problems you will discuss in class, but is to train the student in a systematic approach to problem solving which can be applied to all situations. The specifics of the problems and corresponding solutions are relatively immaterial. What is important is the ability to work with specific facts, analyze those facts, use your business knowledge to arrive at a workable solution, and argue the merits of your solution. Note: in approaching a case, it pays to remember that, "It is the hard exercise that counts rather than reaching the right answer."

The usefulness of the case method is increased, if both the teacher and students understand their respective roles.

Role Of The Teacher

As Dooley and Skinner (1977) make abundantly clear in their detailed discussion of case teaching, there are as many roles an instructor can play as there are case teachers. Depending on preferences, convictions, talents, and educational objectives, instructors may act as facilitator, coach, quarterback, demonstrator, choreographer, referee, judge, conductor, or as evangelist. But once you have made these strategic choices, you still have to make different tactical choices relating to the "how-to" of the following issues:

1) Prepare for class; plan the questions to be raised and the reactions to be sought.
2) Lead off the class and draw students into discussion.
3) Keep students on the topic.
4) Play the devil's advocate.
5) Call on and respond to students.
6) Help students see the big picture.
7) Challenge their imagination.
8) Summarize and end a discussion.

Role Of Students

1) Attend class regularly.
2) Read the assigned case thoroughly a few times. Analyze the problem and be prepared to present and defend your analysis before your peers and teacher. Without this thorough preparation you will be a free-rider, ill-equipped to get actively involved in classroom discussion or in group brainstorming sessions.
3) In analyzing the case, put yourself: (a) in the role of the chief executive officer of the firm at hand – or of its management consultant; (b) in the time frame when the case was written.

Guidelines For Case Analysis

A case is nothing more than a problem presented in the context of a business setting. Therefore, the approach to solving a case is similar to a general problem-solving technique.

1) Define the strategic problem. Read the case as many times as necessary until you become familiar with its content. After this, you should have a general feeling as to what the problem area(s) is/are. Briefly list as many problems as you can identify. Rank those problems in order of importance. *Note*: There is a difference between a problem and a symptom. Be sure you have only listed the problems. Choose the first two or three problems to focus your report on. Typically, these are referred to in the first or concluding paragraph of the case. Defining the problem in strategic terms calls for making a factual judgment, i.e., judgment as to the facts of the case. The corresponding question here is "What is happening that is unusual? What business is the company in? What is its competitive advantage?"
2) Gather data describing the problem. Analyze the data offered in the case which pertains to the problems you have identified as being the most important. There is data that is relevant and other that is irrelevant; you have to decide which is which. Consult all the exhibits. Analyze both quantitative and subjective data pertaining to the firm at hand, its industry, its competitors, and its clients. There may be a point where you think not enough information is supplied to fully analyze the problem; that is no good excuse for quitting. Make logical assumptions when necessary, but be sure to state them and the reasoning behind them.
3) Identify strategic alternatives. Feel free to write down any sensible alternative that comes to mind, no matter how absurd you think it sounds. You may use some part of it in the actual solution. Focus on company strategic, objectives, environment, etc.
4) Evaluate the alternatives. Does the alternative solve the problem(s),

either independently or along with other alternatives? What other areas might this solution affect (i. e., environment, organization, society, etc.)? Weigh the cost/benefit of each solution. Does it solve more problems than it creates? Develop evaluation criteria which can measure the potential effectiveness of each alternative. It is best to base these on quantitative data when possible to support your argument. These are all pertinent questions you should ask during the evaluation process.

5) Select the best alternative. Based on the evaluation of each alternative, this is the next logical step. It involves making a value judgment, so do your best. For instance, you may be required to recommend what business company X should be in and what market it should serve – given its contextual environment and resource profile.

6) Implement the solution. Choosing the best alternative alone will not solve the problem. It is necessary for the solution to be implemented. This step involves making an action judgment; the corresponding question here is, what is required to move from the present to the preferred situation. Outline the basic steps necessary to put your plan into action. These steps should be logical, well-ordered, concise, complete, and clear.

7) Follow up in order to assure that the solution is effective. Performance is the ultimate test of any solution. Though it is not physically possible to implement a solution, it is reasonable to include a logical discussion of how your solution would be expected to perform. Base the discussion on the question of how it would solve the problems you identified earlier.

Report Format

The report format is mostly the same as the problem-solving approach described earlier, except for minor changes in order. Here, the decision follows the statement of the problem and precedes the analysis. A discussion of the five important sections follows below.

Summary of Important Facts

This is not a summary of the entire case. Only identify those facts which are particularly relevant to the problems you identified earlier. This is a set-up for the identification of the problem.

Problem

This section is used to identify and describe the problem in strategic terms. It should be concise, complete, and clear. Describe the problem in order to set up the remainder of the paper. This discussion is in general terms. Think along the lines of the organization – structure, management, technology, etc.

Decision

This is your recommendation to the company. Be concise and clear. This is not the place to discuss how the solution works or how to implement it. Simply state your recommendation and the effects of it. There should be one decision for each problem identified in the preceding section.

Analysis

This is the most important section in the report. Here you demonstrate your ability to solve problems. Include discussions of your alternatives, evaluation criteria, and the advantages and disadvantages of each alternative. Also, be sure to include a discussion of any assumptions you may have made. These play a major role in following your problem-solving logic. It is important to be persuasive – you are selling your idea as a viable solution. Include, whenever possible, the analysis of quantitative data. Facts and figures provide better proof than superlatives and generalities.

Conclusion

The conclusion is the part where you summarize how your decision solves the problem. Be precise and exact. Again, do not speak in vague phrases. Also, include a discussion of how to implement your decision. Be concise, complete, and clear.

Lesson(s) Learned

In the concluding section, do not forget to mention the lesson(s) learned from handling the assigned case, and link that lesson with the concepts and theories learned in the policy and prior courses.

Do's

1) Address yourself to the assignment.
2) Be concise – make your point and move on.
3) Lead from one point to the next with some transition.
4) Consider the kinds of criticism your analysis will be subject to.
5) Check quantitative data to make sure it is correct.
6) Comprehend teaching points of the case.

Don'ts

1) Rehash facts of the case. Your teacher has read them.
2) Use lack of facts as excuse for solution. Make assumptions when necessary.
3) Try to solve all the problems. Address the two or three most important problems.
4) Over-suggest liquidation as a viable solution. It is usually a cop-out.
5) Rely on suppositions or assumptions. Base your arguments on facts presented in the case.
6) Assume your solution will be accepted by all those involved. There is no right answer.

References

Dooley, A. and Skinner, W. (1977): Casing case method, *Academy of Management Review*, April.

Edge, A.G. (1982): *The guide to case analysis and reporting*, Honolulu: System Logistics.

McLeod, R.Jr. (1986): *Management information systems*, 3rd ed., Chicago: Science Research Associates, 115.

McNair, M.P. (Ed.) (1954): *The case method at the Harvard Business School*, New York: McGraw-Hill.

Wernette, J.Ph. (1965): The theory of the case method, *Michigan Business Review*, 17, 1, January: 21–24.

Appendix B
Questions for Discussion and Teaching Notes

Chapter 1

1) Arab policy makers have been debating the merit of various strategies to reduce the dependency of their economies on oil.
   a. Do you share their heavy emphasis on manufacturing? Why or why not?
   b. Do you agree that services offer a better choice?
   c. Does it offer real hope in terms of raising the Gross Domestic Product (GDP) as well as creating jobs?
2) Make a case for and against:
   a. The pro-service bias of this book.
   b. The pro-case bias of its authors.
3) Is it possible for an economy to based entirely on services?

Chapter 2

1) Why do governments play larger roles in the economies of the GCC states?
2) Do you think American management concepts can be successfully applied in Arabian settings?
3) In your opinion, what explains the relative absence of Arab multinational corporations?
4) What are the forces making for the formation of the GCC? What are the benefits of such a union for the member states and for the rank and file Gulf Arab?
5) In your opinion, what common characteristics do Arab business executives have that might make their joint-ventures with their American counterparts problematic?
6) What are the distinctive features of:
   a. Arab management?
   b. Arab organizations?

Chapter 3

1) Explain why a manager of a service operation may face a more complex and difficult task than a manager of a manufacturing operation.
2) What are the distinguishing characteristics of services in Arabia?
3) What are the chances that Saudi Arabia can become a truly service-oriented society compared to the likes of Singapore or Switzerland?
4) Are economies-of-scale possible in services?
5) What are some possible measures of performance for a university? For a private hospital? For a flag-carrier?
6) Do the GCC states have what it takes to revitalize their service sector?

Chapter 4
4.1   The Arab Airline Industry

Introduction

The Arab Gulf states need a sound airline industry. To develop, maintain, and manage such an industry requires a thorough understanding of economic, financial, and marketing factors as well as relevant social and political considerations. This note addresses many key concerns and offers considerable insights into the structure and operation of the Arab airline industry.

Briefly, the note suggests that the industry is going through a major structural change. It operates in an exceedingly inhospitable environment characterized by recession brought about by a decline in the Arab oil revenues, excess capacity, fierce competition, fare wars, high operating costs, and political instability. This note exposes students to the logic of industry analysis as developed by Michael Porter (1980). It provides a useful background for understanding the strategic issues facing selected Arab carriers such as Saudia, Gulf Air, Kuwait Airways and Alia.

Teaching Strategy

Two class periods are necessary for teaching the industry note. The first period is devoted to identifying each of Porter's "five-force" typology and the key success factors (i.e., traffic rights, control of labor, fuel cost, superior service, and aggressive marketing). The second class period is spent analyzing and tracking key changes in these strategic dimensions and their likely impact on the future structure of the industry.

Questions for Class Discussion

1) Use Porter's "five forces typology" to analyze the Arab Airline industry.
2) Which characteristics appear to be promoting competition within the industry? Why?
3) Of the five forces identified in (1), which ones appear most important in influencing the competitive dynamics of the industry? Why?
4) Differentiate between a mere flag carrier and a true national carrier (Hint: the latter has an obligation to achieve socioeconomic changes (e.g., to be a source of hard currency, employment, and technical training). The former's only obligation is to be a symbol of national prestige and pride.)
5) How is this industry segmented? Why has this segmentation occurred? Which segment will be most profitable by 1990?
6) Will Arab carriers ever be profitable? Will they ever be able to compete with major foreign flag carriers such as AF, LH, or SR? Why, or why not? What does it take to enhance the competitiveness of the Arab carriers? Hint: read Levine (1987) and Kasper (1988).
7) Explain the "empty-seats" phenomenon. Would lower fares be the answer to such a phenomenon?
8) Is the overcapacity in the airline industry a cyclical event or a major shift?
9) What diversification is taking place in the industry? Why? (Although the note is silent on this point, the cases suggest that Arab carriers are diversifying into hotels, catering, fleet maintenance, aircraft rental, and management contract, ground handling activities).
10) Is privatization the answer to the problems facing Arab carriers? Why or why not?
11) Is regional cooperation among Arab carriers the answer to their individual problems? Under what conditions would such scheme as joint flights, joint maintenance, and training facilities work best?
12) How important computerized reservation systems are to Arab airlines? How should they proceed to acquire such systems?

References

Kasper, Daniel (1988): *Deregulation and globalization*, Cambridge, Mass.: Ballinger.
Levine, M. E. (1987) "Airline Competition in deregulated markets: theory, firm strategy and public policy" *Yale Journal of Regulation*, 4: 393–494.
Porter, M. E. (1980): *Competitive strategy*, New York: Free Press.

4.2   Saudi Arabian Airlines "SAUDIA"

Introduction

Saudia, headquartered in Jeddah, is the national flag carrier of Saudi Arabia, and one of the world's argest airlines. It owns and operates a fleet of 106 modern aircraft, employs a labor force of 26,000 employees, and serves about 12 million passengers. It was created and operated by the government to serve as a tool for engineering the socioeconomic development of the Kingdom. As such, it was regarded by top Saudi government officials as a favorite "infant child", whose needs are always accommodated, irrespective of costs.

As of late, however, Saudia has been encountering a number of turbulences, not in its skies – but on the ground, such as:
- the deregulation of the world airline industry;
- the sharp decline in Arab oil-revenues and the massive exodus of expatriate workers, the traditional core passenger segment for Saudia;
- the excess capacity in the market place and the resultant fare wars waged by Saudia competitors.

These trends together, with a sluggish corporate culture, have adversely affected the capacity of Saudia to cope with its new market environment and improve its passenger service.

Selected Strategic Issues

1) The goal-setting and goal-achievement processes within the context of state-owned and state-managed enterprises:
   - the distinction between a mere flag carrier and a truly national carrier;
   - what sort of carrier is Saudia? What sort of carrier does it want to be?
   - the relative importance of profitability and public welfare in state-owned enterprises;
   - the make up, functions, and effectiveness of the board of directors of state-owned enterprises.
2) Segmentation within the dominant passenger market:
   - The dangers inherent in being dependent on a huge but declining captive "labor traffic". What will happen when this segment eventually dries up?
   - Should Saudia chase the discount passenger? The Umra passenger? The vacation passenger? (Leisure or discretionary travelers)
3) Market maturity and niche encroachment.
4) Privatization as a possible cure for Saudia's ailments.
   Hint: read *The Promise of Privatization*. Raymond Vernon (Editor). New York: Council for Foreign Relations: 1988.

5) Engineering a successful turnaround in a hostile environment:
   – what sort of turnaround is needed the most: strategic or operational?
   – what functional area needs to be emphasized the most? Why?
6) Difficulties involved in implementing strategic turnaround plans.

Questions for Discussion

1) What does Saudia sell in the international market place?
2) Why is the current shift in strategic emphasis from extensive to intensive development taking place? From routes and services to manpower development and cost containment? Operational efficiency?
3) What are Saudia's stated goals? What about its operative goals?
4) What explains the drop in passenger traffic and load factors in the early 1980s?
5) Is it impracticable to expect Saudia's management to be answerable to *both* the market place and to Saudi government?
6) Why does Saudia's organization structure approximate Weber's machine bureaucracy (i.e., tall, rigid inflexible pyramid with layers upon layers of supervision and obsession control)? (Hint: Consider Woodward's mass production technology, importance of standardization of the work of the operating core; scheduling service delivery...centralization of accountability, customer services decisions).
7) Is Saudia's present structure responsive to current market conditions? Why or why not?
8) Can Saudia afford to be unresponsive to the needs of its captive market segment?
9) The Saudization goal is an ambitious one. Could Saudia ever be totally Saudized? What implication will such a policy have for:
   a) the quality of service delivery;
   b) labor cost;
   c) employee morale?
10) Why does Saudia's in-flight service consistently get a better rating than its preflight service?
11) Why is Saudia's international network a moneymaker while its domestic network a money loser?
12) Some critics claim that Saudia is loosing money because it is basically a "dry carrier". Comment.
13) What is happening in Saudia's environment? What opportunities and threats are being created by this environment?
14) Saudia is a sleeping giant who is being attacked on its international network – by both the giant carriers of the Western and Far Eastern worlds and the lean and mean carriers of the Arab world.

a) Identify current product market strategy of Saudia.

b) What are the inherent weaknesses in current Saudia's strategy?

15) Could Saudia ever be a moneymaker? What does it take to engineer such a strategic turnaround? What choices does it have to survive in the short term and to prosper in the long term?

16) What does Saudia have to do *now*:

a) to protect its "natural traffic" from aggressive foreign competition;

b) to capitalize on opportunities offered by its environment?

17) Given your answer to the above question, and given what you know about Saudia's corporate culture, how would you propose to implement your recommended turnaround strategy?

4.3   Kuwait Airways Corp (KAC)

Synopsis

KAC is the national carrier of the State of Kuwait. It has been established by the government to implement a number of national socioeconomic goals. Yet, as a public enterprise, it is expected to be run on a commercial basis and not to be a drain on the state treasury. The company is in the process of becoming a truly national carrier, serving as a school for training natives in aviation related skills, providing lucrative jobs for Kuwaitis, and carring the state flag.

As of late KAC, like its Arab sisters, started reflecting the pains of a rapidly deteriorating environmental scenario: sharp declines in oil revenues, escalation of the Gulf war, continuation of civil strife in Lebanon, domestic instability, and the tightening of security measures including visa restrictions. These environmental conditions negatively impacted on the passenger traffic into and out of Kuwait and have adversely affected KAC's maneuverability. KAC's management response to the crisis took the form of pork-chopping, price-discounting, and selling excess aircraft.

Major Strategic Issues

– Corporate goals and national goals in a state-owned enterprise.
– Distinction between mere flag and truly national carriers.
– The case for and against uncontrolled growth: infrastructural projects.
– Retrenchment strategy.
– Barriers and gateways to regional cooperation.
– Trimming the fat – reorganizing for survival.

Questions for Discussion

1) What sort of airline is KAC? Is it a sixth freedom carrier? A regional/international carrier?
2) What strategies has KAC followed successfully?
3) What strategies has it followed unsuccessfully?
4) KAC is more than an airline. Rather, it is a total institution in the service of national, political, social, and economic goals. Can you quantify the rate of return on manpower training for Kuwaiti nationals, being a good host for incoming carriers (e. g., SASCO) and creating jobs for nationals?
5) Some critics believe that KAC would have been better off investing its capital in the financial markets. Do you agree? Why?
6) Which strategy has it followed presently? With what success?
7) What type of organizational structure does KAC have? Does its structure fit its current environment, its culture, its people, its tasks?
8) What sort of functions does KAC perform well?
9) What is KAC's distinctive competitive advantage? Competitive disadvantage?
10) Many Kuwaiti nationals at one time flew KAC. And today, KAC seems as favorite an airline as British Airways, Air France, and Lufthansa were yesterday. Explain why KAC seems to be the favorite choice of many Kuwaiti nationals?
11) KAC is an aggressive discounter. Yet, it failed to be a sixth freedom carrier. Why?
12) It has been said that management should first focus its attention on achieving optimum efficiency from core airline operations before diversifying into ancillary activities. Do you agree or disagree?
13) KAC is a victim of deteriorating environmental scenario.
    a) Identify those environmental conditions that threaten the growth of passenger air traffic in the Arabian Gulf region.
    b) Which ones of these conditions cuts heavily against KAC?
14) How can a competitor's organization chart and officers' titles aid in understanding your competition? What advantages might be given by knowledge of the background and personal values of your competitor's top managers?
15) Evaluate the current cost-containment program. Will it ease the pressure on KAC's profitability? How about its social responsibility toward its labor force?
16) What additional measures are needed to cope with the current excess capacity and declining traffic?

References

Porter, M. E. (1980): *Competitive strategy*, New York: Free Press.

4.4   Gulf Air (GF)

Introduction

GF is a household name in the Arabian Gulf, if not in the Middle East. It is owned by the governments of Oman, Bahrain, Qatar, and Abu Dhabi, and serves as a successful example of regional cooperation. It is bent on going private and becoming a full-fledged international carrier. As of late, it has added Frankfurt and Nairobi to its busy schedule. Presently, it is considering adding either New York or Tokyo to round out its route network. The decision to add either destination will inevitably bring the novice carrier into the harsher world of international competition. After all, North Atlantic I (New York) and North Atlantic II (Gulf-Far East) are the busiest and most heavily discounted air routes on the globe. Hence, this decision requires much careful analysis, sound judgment, and imagination on the part of GF strategic planners.

Major Strategic Issues

1) Distinguish between the industry-specific and firm-specific key success factors.
2) High operating costs as a built-in competitive disadvantage for Gulf carriers.
3) Regionalism vs. internationalism in commercial aviation: the Atlas, SAS, and the Arab experiences.
4) Route planning – the cornerstone of airline planning:
   a) compare with programming for commercial TV networks;
   b) economic vs. noneconomic criteria for new routes (destinations);
   c) role of pricing, scheduling, and fleet planning in the success of new routes.
5) Privatization strategy: risks and rewards.
6) Role of structure and strategy in explaining the successful performance of GF.

Questions for Discussion

1) Identify GF's past success formula. What role does strategy play in it? (*Hint*: Read Toby Odone, The rise and rise of Gulf Air, *Middle East Economic Digest (MEED)*; February 8, 1985, pp. 24–25.)
2) GF has recently been reorganized to meet the demands of its turbulent environment. What is so remarkable about its new structure? How does the carrier ensure coordination among its three divisions?
3) Identify the strategy of the shareholding states to depoliticize management and run the carrier as a business concern.
4) Cooperation is key to understanding the unusual success of Gulf Air. Comment.
5) Gulf Air's environment is turbulent and unfriendly. Comment.
6) High operating costs put Arabian Gulf carriers at a competitive disadvantage. Yet these carriers have to become global to survive.
   a) What explains the high cost structure of Gulf Carriers?
   b) Given this built-in disadvantage, can Gulf carriers successfully compete with the giant carriers of the Far East and Western Europe?
7) How are corporate plans formulated at GF? Use route planning as a case in point.
8) Which criteria does GF use to decide on new routes?
9) Which additional criteria – other than those mentioned in Exhibit 12 (in GF Air chapter) – might be used for choosing among New York or Tokyo? (*Hint:* Some of the factors that might be considered in planning a new route are: the service needed by the traveling public; the benefits accruing to the national economy, national pride, and prestige; the presence or potential of a market to justify the operation; and the incremental effect on the present network taken as a whole.)
10) Entering Tokyo or New York markets through joint ventures is the best strategy to test the potential of these markets with little or no investment. Comment.
11) Should GF fly to Tokyo or New York? What do the numbers suggest? What about your own judgment?

4.5   Alia: The Royal Jordanian Airline

Synopsis

Alia is an unusual airline. It is the leanest and most aggressive carrier in the Arab world. In contrast to its Arab sisters who serve as mere flag carriers, Alia is a truly national carrier capable of competing with giant international carriers, making a positive contribution to the public treasury, neutralizing adversities, and converting environmental threats into opportunities. To illustrate its tenacity: the Arab-Israeli wars of 1967 and 1973 resulted in the destruction of its fleet and the cessation of the Holy Land traffic – its core passenger segment. Alia more than made up for these losses by capitalizing on the labor traffic to and from the oil-producing countries. It also used the deregulation act of 1979 as an opportunity to innovate low fares, expand its route network first to North America, then to Europe and the Far East, and to champion the cause of regional cooperation in commercial aviation.

Alia is not just an airline. It is a total institution entrusted with the job of serving as Jordan's roving ambassador to the rest of the world. It carries the very best of Arab culture (art, music, fashion, dance) to other countries and carries much of other cultures to Jordan, thereby promoting tourism and trade.

After two decades of nonstop growth and more than a decade of profitability, Alia's performance took a nose dive. A recession in the neighboring oil-rich countries; the escalation of the Gulf war; the continuation of the civil war in Lebanon; the stiffening of competition from neighboring airports and sister Arab carriers; staggering costs of financing new aircrafts; and the heavy dependence on low-yield discount passenger have all combined to adversely affect the carrier's profitability and increase its vulnerabilities. The challenge facing Alia's strategic planners is captured by the comment made by its VP for planning.

"We have an oversized modern fleet for a country like Jordan, given its national size, geopolitics, and national resources. Putting that fleet into productive use is the toughest challenge facing us."

Strategic Issues

- Proactive strategic planning in the Arab world: is Alia the rule or the exception?
- Environmental and managerial determinants of strategic adaptation process.
- Strategic importance of the royal connection in setting the tone – the corporate charter – and providing the moral support needed for route expansion and capital acquisition. Can we justifiably consider this connection as a political strategy?
- The multiple role of the chief executive as a strategist, organization builder, an ambassador.
- Role of experience and longevity in explaining corporate success.
- Distinction between mere flag carriers and truly national carriers.

– Social and public responsibility of Alia in promoting tourism and trade and in serving as a cultural bridge.
– Managing decline.

Questions for Discussion

1) Alia is an airline that made it in spite of the odds. Both Alia and its environment are equally obstinate. Explain in detail the sources of Alia's success.
2) Why does Alia outperform its Arab sisters?
3) Which strategies has Alia successfully followed?
4) Which strategy is it presently following? With what success? What sort of airline is Alia? What is its corporate mission?
5) Bruce Henderson of the Boston Consultive Group states that business has only financial objectives in the final analysis. What does he mean? Would you agree with him if you were Ali Ghandour?
6) What are the strengths and weaknesses of Alia? What sort of functions does Alia perform well?
7) Could Alia have succeeded without: (a) the support of King Hussein? (b) the vision, leadership, and the longevity of its CEO-Mr. Ghandour?
8) What do Alia and Singapore Airlines have in common? Can their success be replicated elsewhere in the developing world? Under what condition?
9) Knowing what you know about the Arab airline industry (see Chapter 4), what opportunities and challenges do you see developing for Alia? What is the worst that could happen to Alia? What is a bad dream for Ali Ghandour?
10) How much of Alia's income is derived from airline operations? How much from ancillary operations? Do you recommend that Alia ignore the recent experience of United Airlines and continue with its present diversification strategy or would you rather urge Ghandour to focus on airline operations?
11) Ali Ghandour is the architect and spokesman for regional cooperation among Arab carriers. What are the merits of his case? What are the barriers?
12) Which organizational structure would best suit a company like Alia? Why? (mechanistic vs. organic)
13) Alia focused its turnaround strategy on the business traveler, rounding out its route network and increasing the number of flights to each destination, projecting a new image for Alia, and revamping the organization structure. Is this an adequate cure for Alia's current ailments? If not, what specific measures would you recommend to Ghandour? How would you sell them to him?

Chapter 5
5.1 A Note on the Banking Industry

Introduction

This note utilizes Porter's five factor framework to describe environmental aspects driving competition in the banking industry. The note provides the various stages of historical developments in the Arab Gulf banking industry since the colonial era of the British mandate until recent times.

The declining demand for OPEC oil has caused a decline in oil revenue accruing to the Arab Gulf States from a peak of US $ 165 billion in 1981 to less than US $ 40 billion in 1988. This has led the Gulf governments to substantially reduce its expenditure, creating a slowdown in economic activity. This in turn has made the Gulf banking more competitive and has given Gulf banks new inputs to further their involvement in international financial market operations.

Teaching Strategy

This note may stand alone as an exercise in competitive industry analysis or may be used as background material for the bank cases in this Chapter.

Questions for Discussion

1) Use Porter's framework to analyze the forces driving competition in the Gulf banking industry.
2) What are the objectives of commercial banks? How do they differ from the objectives of their substitutes such Islamic banks, and governmental funds?
3) What are the key success factors in:
   a) The commercial banking industry?
   b) The Islamic banking segment?
4) How is this industry segmented?
5) What are the major factors that led to the nationalization of foreign banks in the Gulf region?
6) What are the implications of the Gulf citizens' negative predisposition towards commercial banks, vis-a-vis Islamic banks?
7) Compare the strategy and structure of endogenous banks (such as NCB and Al Rajhi) with those of nationalized banks (such as SAMB and the Saudi French).
8) What are the key trends in the Arab banking industry? Do these trends cut differently for different segments? How so?
9) What are the strategic implications of the above-cited trends?

10) What does it take to revitalize this industry?
    Hint: read, *Changing money: financial innovations in developing countries*. Marcello de Cecco (Ed.) N.Y.: Basil Blackwell, 1987.

5.2   National Commercial Bank (NCB)

Case Summary

NCB was the first bank to be established in Saudi Arabia. It is the only private bank in Saudi Arabia. It has 169 local branches in addition to three foreign branches. NCB and Riyadh banks attract about 60% of government deposits.

NCB is managed by the sons of the owner Bin Mahfouz and assisted by a number of deputy general managers. The ferocity of competition in the Saudi banking industry is intensifying due to dwindling opportunities and the sophistication of major NCB competitors such as Saudi American Bank which is managed by Citibank and is known for pioneering technological banking innovations in the market.

NCB received the approval of the Saudi Monetary Agency to branch out into the international financial market for market diversification and growth.

Teaching Strategy

This case can be used to focus on the appraisal and diagnosis phase of the strategic management process. NCB is at a phase of searching the external environment and diagnosing changes and how to adapt to them and establish a new fit, in light of its internal resources and objectives.

Questions for Discussion

1) Why has NCB been so successful? Identify the elements of its success formula.
2) Who are the major and minor competitors of NCB? How could NCB outcompete them?
3) Is it prudent to maintain NCB as the only private bank in Saudi market?
4) What are the key trends in the GCC banking industry?
5) Should NCB move its headquarter to the capital Riyadh?
6) Should NCB Saudize (put nationals) in all of its key managerial positions? Should it at least Saudize its corporate culture?
7) Was it prudent to venture out into the highly competitive international financial market?

5.3   Saudi American Bank (SAMBA)

Case Summary

SAMBA is an aggressive and progressive bank. It is a pioneer in introducing technological banking innovations such as electronic and voice banking and linking all its branches in Saudi Arabia through a centralized computer network.

SAMBA is a joint stock company 60% owned by the Saudi public and 40% owned by Citibank. Citibank is managing SAMBA in a Western professional impersonal management style.

Since its inception in 1980, SAMBA has targeted corporate banking as the thrust of its business. This strategy has translated into a limited number of 30 branches all over Saudi Arabia.

As of late, corporate business and investment opportunities in the Saudi market have declined and SAMBA reported a net profit decline of 53.8% in 1986.

Teaching Strategy

Track I:
Prepare a thorough evaluation of the thrust of SAMBA's banking strategy and its fitness to the prevailing market conditions in the Saudi market.
Track II:
This case can be used to demonstrate the inevitable transformation of international entities operating in developing countries to nationalized entities managed by nationals. It also can be used to demonstrate the importance of long-term orientation and adaptability to prevailing social and cultural norms and practices.

Questions for discussion

1) Who are the major and minor competitors of SAMBA. How does SAMBA compete?
2) How could SAMBA change its image as the bank of the rich and the foreign contractors?
3) Should SAMBA maintain its current Western, professional, and impersonal management style? Why? What do you suggest?
4) Should Citibank's plan phase down its role in SAMBA? How?
5) Should Citibank phase out from the Saudi market? Why?

5.4   Saudi French Bank

Case Summary

Saudi French Bank (BSF) the most aggressive of the Saudized banks. It focused on corporate clients, invited them to deposit their money at a cheap rate and provided them with loans at a higher rate. Its loan policy was liberal, aggressive, and Kingdom-oriented. It borrowed from other banks to finance clients, expand its market, share and improve its profit picture. When clients were hit hard by the recession, they defaulted and the bank performance suffered. To cope with the prevailing recessionary environment, BSF redefined its market to include retail customers and modified its organization to include units responsible for corporate planning, private and retail banking (PRB). It also centralized loan approval decisions at the regional level.

Teaching Strategy

BSF demonstrates the significance of dynamic strategy development. The aggressive loan policy followed by the bank has been successful only in good times (i. e., during the boom). However, it has proved to be risky and unsuccessful in hard times. Borrowers failed to pay the interest and the principal. The case points out that a periodic review of strategy must be conducted, and that yesterday's strategies must be updated to fit today's conditions.

The case also raises the issue of effective implementation of strategies. Repositioning to focus on the retail customer appears to be inconsistent with the BSF capability profile. The bank does not offer a hospitable environment to attract to and retain Saudi middle managers who are badly needed to implement the new retail strategy.

Questions for Discussion

Track I: Thought-provoking, open-ended question:
"Prepare a report for the board of directors outlining survival strategies for the remaining 1980's and their implementation. You are Yves Max."
Track II:

1) Why was BSF so successful? Was its success a random or deliberate event (i. e., a product of blind luck or hard work)? What was its success formula?
2) What are the trends that characterize the Saudi banking scene? What kind of opportunities do they offer? What kind of challenges do they pose?

3) Do the above-cited opportunities and threats apply similarly to different banks? Specifically, how do they apply to BSF?
4) Prepare a capability profile for BSF.
   - What are its strenghts (its substainable competitive advantages)?
   - What are its weaknesses?
5) Evaluate BSF's diversification strategy.
   - Is it congruent with environmental trends?
   - Is it congruent with internal capabilities?
   - Is it congruent with organizational culture?
6) Evaluate the new organization:
   a) Does it answer the human problems of the operating core?
   b) Does it answer the turnover problems of the middle line managers?
   c) What problems does it create? For whom?
7) What additional changes would you recommend with respect to BSF's
   a) strategy,
   b) structure?

5.5   Gulf International Bank (GIB)

Gase Summary

GIB is an offshore wholesale and investment bank incorporated in Bahrain. It was formed by the seven Arab Gulf States of Bahrain, Iraq, Kuwait, Oman, Qatar, Saudi Arabia, and United Arab Emirates in 1976, with equal shares. GIB was established to serve the banking interests of the share holding states and to capitalize on the new petrodollar wealth accumulated in 1974 and beyond. GIB's board and senior management are provided from the shareholding state with equal representation. In addition, many experienced expatriates are also employed in every unit in the bank. GIB's charted corporate mission emphasizes commitment to the training Arabian Gulf nationals in the banking industry.

Teaching Strategy

The GIB case can be used to demonstrate the choice and implementation phases of the strategic management process. The bank is faced with choices related to the hiring policy of inexperienced national vs. experienced expatriate in a highly competitive banking region; choices related to commitment to the region vs. diversifying into other international markets, given the declining opportunities in the Gulf region.

Questions for Discussion

Track I:
Prepare a report for the board of directors outlining the strategic choices and implementation strategies for GIB survival in the late 1980s and beyond.

Track II:
Respond to the questions and challenges facing the banking industry in the Gulf in general, and GIB in particular (refer to the section on challenges).

Chapter 6
6.1   A Note on the Lodging Industry

Introduction

The hotel industry enjoyed a sizable growth rate since 1973 to meet the requirements of the massive influx of customers attracted by government investments in building infrastructure. The Gulf governments enticed the private sector to invest in hotel development to meet the shortage of hotel accommodations by providing generous financial support and incentives.

Hotel construction and operating costs in the Arab Gulf States have been very high. While a cost of $ 100,000 to $ 150,000 per room is the international norm, a cost of $ 500,000 per room was not uncommon in the Gulf states. One manager of a luxury Gulf hotel reported that his hotel needs an occupancy rate of 56 % to break even.

Currently, the hotel market in the Gulf states is characterized by excess capacity, declining demand, and keen competition and pricing wars.

Teaching Strategy

This note can be used to provide background for the cases on the hotel industry.

Questions for Discussion

1) Use Porter's framework to analyze the Gulf hotel industry.
2) How is this industry segmented?
3) Could the hotel industry have started without government support?
4) Evaluate the competitiveness of each of key player in the industry.
5) How does the cost and revenue structure of the hotel industry compare with its counterpart in the West?

6) How does the composition of sales (Exhibit 9) compare with its counterpart in the West?
7) What are the key trends in the lodging industry? Do these cut differently for different segments? For different countries?
8) What does it take to revitalize the lodging industry?

6.2   The Gulf Meridien

Main Thrust of the Case

Unlike its competitors in the luxury category, the Gulf Meridien has not been a victim of the recessionary environment that plagued the economies of the Gulf states. Its occupancy rate is the highest and its costs are not rising. While the opening of the Bahrain-Khobar Causeway in 1987 and the relocation of the present Dhahran Airport 60 miles from the GM are likely to hurt the occupancy rate and the profitability of the hotel, GM management does not believe these occurrences will have a major impact on their success.

Selected Strategic Issues

1) The hotel industry: yesterday and today
   – identification of opportunities and threats nationwide/regionwide (Eastern Province).
2) The Gulf Meridien:
   – identification of strengths and weaknesses.
3) Identification of GM's special success formula, its most critical success factor: is it the name of the Meridien chain or name of the owners.
4) Hotel management firms:
   – costs vs. benefits
   – the importance of selecting the right firm.
5) Environmental threats:
   – Can a firm succeed in sealing itself permanently from its environment?

Questions for Discussion

1) What are the major trends in the hotel industry in Saudi Arabia?
2) What are the factors that depress the profitability of the luxury class hotels in the Eastern Province? (the recession in oil markets; oversupply of rooms; the opening of the Bahrain-Khobar Causeway;

many companies have their own guest compounds; among other factors).

3) Would the relocation of the Dhahran Airport adversely affect occupancy rates? For what hotels? How about the withdrawal of major carriers out of Dhahran?

4) Why has GM been so successful in comparison with its competitors?

5) Identify the elements of the GM's success formula. (the importance of selecting the right location; the right management firm; the right timing; of having the right connection, etc).

6) Do you forese any problem with GM's way of operating?

7) What are the implications for future success of a reactive strategic orientation?

8) Does the organizational structure of the Meridien approximate a hierarchy, a machine, or a tribe? What are the implications one way or the other?

9) The owners of GM are growing impatient with the present French managements lack of a proactive strategy. They are contemplating replacing the present, more costly, less aggressive management firm by another, as did their counterparts in Jeddah. Would you advise them for this move or against it?

10) What can be done to:
   a) revitalize the present management team?
   b) neutralize the opening of the Causeway and the relocation of the airport?

6.3   Al Gosaibi Hotel

Synopsis

Al Gosaibi is a family-owned 5-star hotel conveniently located in Al-Khobar, on the Arabian Gulf, near the Dhahran International Airport and the Dammam seaport. It has 300 rooms, 37 suites, 25 villas, the usual assortment of amenities, and a huge exhibition hall. It is the oldest luxury hotel in the area. It suffered the most as the business recession hit; its occupancy rate declined sharply. The relocation of the airport 80 kilometers away from town and the opening of a permanent exhibition facility are likely to affect the future of the hotel adversely. A former general manager of the hotel, Munir Tadros, was offered the challenging assignment of stepping in again to save the business for its owners and jobs for its employees.

Strategic Issues

1) The role of the general manager as a change agent.
2) The promise, possible pitfalls, and mechanics of using a turnaround strategy.
3) The costs and benefits of using management contracts.
4) Reentering a system: methods and strategies for diagnosing the health of the business and improving its performance.
5) Negotiating a successful reentry.

Questions for Discussion

You are Munir Tadros:
1) How do you go about collecting data about the hotel?
2) What is your diagnosis?
   a) What ails the hotel the most?
   b) Is it worth saving?
   c) Is it operationally strong and strategically well-positioned?
3) If your answer to 2c is negative, which of the following strategies would you use?
   a) Generate more revenue.
   b) Liquidate assets.
   c) Cut costs.
   d) A combination of the above.
4) What problems will you face?
   a) How are you going to change the culture of the Al Gosaibi organization?
   b) How would your employees feel about you, about the changes your are about to implement? How are you going to earn their trust and cooperation?
   c) How would your home office superiors feel about you? About your moves?
   d) How would you handle your clients?
   e) How would you handle your immediate competitors?
   f) How would you handle your peers?
5) What are your goals?
6) What do the home office executives think? What is their job? Their objectives?
7) What do the owners want? What are their objectives?
8) How do the owners feel about management contracts? Why do they feel that way?
9) How do you learn about your job?
10) Should you accept the job offer? If so, under which conditions?

Teaching Strategy

This case can be used in two ways. First, it can be used very early in a business management course to illustrate the dual role of the general manager as a strategist and organization builder. Alternatively, it can be used at the end of a policy course to illustrate the interrelatedness of the strategy-formulation and implementation process. The latter approach provides an opportunity to illustrate the role of luck, environmental uncertainty, and leadership in the strategy-making and implementation processes. The case can be introduced with an open-ended question along these lines:

You are Mr. Tadros. You just received a telex offering you the job of general manager of the Al Gosaibi Hotel. You have walked this territory before. After a relaxing dinner you want to discuss the offer with your wife. Your wife is tired of temporary living situations abroad. What would you tell her? How would you decide? Do you have what it takes to succeed in the new job? If you decide to take the position, how do you convince your wife that this is the best course?

6.4   Al-Hamra Hotel

Case Summary

Al-Hamra is a budgeted hotel established in 1980 in the middle of Dammam business centers. It is managed by an experienced Swiss hotelier who managed to attract Western businessmen through reasonable prices and home atmosphere. They accounted for about 31% of European customers in 1985. Al-Hamra has not been as successful as some of his budget class competitors in attracting other nationalities, particularly Saudi and Far Eastern nationals.

Lately, the hotel owners and management have been concerned about the continuous decline in room occupancy.

Teaching Strategy

The case provides plenty of data that can be analyzed for formulating an optimal strategy for survival and growth.

Questions for Discussion

1) Evaluate the changes in the external environment that affected Al-Hamra Hotel.

2) Evaluate the internal resources and assets that Al-Hamra possesses. Are they adequate under prevailing conditions?
3) Does Al-Hamra hotel have a clear strategy? What is it? Should it be changed? How?
4) How are the major competitors of Al-Hamra performing? What is the core of their strategy?
5) If you became the manager of the hotel, what changes would you introduce? Can they afford it? What strategy would you formulate? How would you implement it? How would you control it?

Chapter 7
7.1   A Note on the Health Care Industry

This note describes economic and environmental aspects of competition in the health care industry. Both public (for free) and private (for fee) sectors of the industry are considered, along with intraregional differences. The note utilizes Porter's five factor framework for analyzing the industry, understanding its structure, and diagnosing its current problems.

As of late, the Arab Gulf States have developed a health care industry that is almost second to none. Their citizens, who used to travel abroad in search of medical treatment, are now provided with the finest and cheapest treatment found anywhere. For those choosy and wealthy patients, there is a spectrum of private health care facilities to consider.

Currently, this capital-intensive industry, like many others, has been caught by a recessionary fever characterized by a declining occupancy rate and rising costs. Its private segment is fighting a survival battle. With the exodus of expatriates, it must compete with government hospitals in the attraction of native patients, but must do so without charging enormous prices for their services.

Questions for Discussion

1) Use Porter's "five forces typology" to analyze the Arab health care industry.
2) How is this industry segmented? Why has this segmentation occurred?
3) What are the objectives of public hospitals? How do these differ from their private counterparts?
4) Why has the private sector not made heavy inroads into the health care industry despite lucrative government incentives?
5) Could private hospitals have started without government help?

6) What are the KSF (Key Success Factors) in the private segment of the health care industry?
7) What trends are evident in hospital revenues and costs? What are the implications of these trends for staffing and financing the purchase of major equipment and operating expenses?
8) The departure of expatriates – the core market segment of private hospitals – suggests entering into stiff competition with public hospitals for endogenous patients. What are the difficulties inherent in such a repositioning strategy?
9) Private hospitals have been criticized lately by consumers in Saudi Arabia for overcharging patients, employing less competent medical staff, and using obsolete equipment. Evaluate the merit of this argument.
10) If you were a physician, would you prefer to work for a government or a private hospital in Saudi Arabia? Why?
11) Are there any bright spots? What opportunities do you see in the private segment of the health care industry? (*Hint:* consider the market for management contract, equipment maintenance, building maintenance, medical emergencies.)

Suggested Use of the Note

This Note may stand alone as an exercise in competitive industry analysis or may be used as a background for any or all three of the private sector hospitals offered in this segment (Abdulla Fouad, Al-Mana, and Green Crescent). In either use, the forces which affect and shape the nature of competition in the industry should be identified, changes and trends should be described, and the implications of these trends should be considered.

7.2   Al-Mana Hospital

This case traces the strategy and describes the organization, management style, and functional policies of a family-owned hospital operating in the oil-producing province of Saudi Arabia.

Main Thrust of the Case

In Saudi Arabia, family firms predominate the business scene. They are subject to many misconceptions among which the most important are: (a) they are not large enough to survive; (b) they are not professionally managed, particularly at the top where managers are skilled in almost everything except marketing; and (c) they often lack an explicit strategy.

The objective of this case is twofold. First, it shows how a family-owned hospital has survived in the recessionary and competitive environment of the post-oil boom era. Second, the case beautifully illustrates the concept of social responsibility as practiced in an Eastern society. It also illustrates Mintzberg's distinction between intended and emergent strategy. The former is what Sheikh Al-Mana designed to accomplish – an eye and dental clinic. The latter is what his sons saw as a market opportunity to convert their clinic into a full-fledged general hospital.

Strategic Issues

1) Strategy formulation and implementation in an entrepreneurial firm.
2) The practice of social responsibility in an Islamic society.
3) Pattern of opportunity identification and strategy formulation in first and second generation family business.
4) The decision to broaden and limit service portfolis in a hospital setting (i.e., the educated sons of the owners decided to create a general hospital instead of keeping it a specialized eye clinic during the boom time, and then decided to concentrate on maternity during the current recession.)

Questions for Discussion

1) Identify the past and present strategy of Al-Mana Hospital.
2) Identify the strengths and weaknesses of Al-Mana Hospital.
3) Sheikh Al-Mana was an institution. He was a true entrepreneur, but he also was a writer and a philanthropist. How has the development of the hospital been brought about by his childhood attitudes and beliefs?
4) What were Sheikh Al-Mana's goals and objectives in establishing his clinic?
5) Which characteristics appear to predominate in the Al-Mana family? Would you expect this characteristic to survive the death of the head of the family?
6) The death of the founder did not have an adverse effect on the hospital. How did the sons engineer a smooth succession and prevent possible dissent within their ranks?
7) How have the sons performed as strategists? As executives? What are their accomplishments? Their credentials?
8) What problems did they inherit?
9) Evaluate their decision to concentrate on maternity. What are the risks involved? What are the rewards?
10) Which environmental challenges does the Al-Mana face?
11) Which specific strategic and policy changes would you recommend and why?

7.3   Abdulla Fouad Hospital

Main Thrust of the Case

When AFH was established in 1979, it was by far the one and only private hospital in Dammam, and the second best in Saudi Arabia. Times were good and occupancy rates were high – about 78 %. Its founder, Sheikh Abdulla Fouad, viewed it as another SBU, which he could manage by remote control. However, when the recession hit, AFH was plagued with various problems. Due to the exodus of expatriates, the customer base of private hospitals, and the building of new government and private hospitals, occupancy rates dropped from 70 % in 1983 to 44 % in 1986. Earnings dropped by 40 % over the same period, while expenses dropped by only 10 %. Occupancy rates were expected to decline further. AFH was facing the problem of managing contraction: How to fill the empty beds?

The case provides insights into the plights of an investor-owned hospital, and the environment in which its administrators operate. It offers an opportunity to examine a highly capital and labor-intensive and competitive industry. It also offers an opportunity to explore alternative strategies to manage contraction.

Selected Strategic Issues

1) Abdulla Fouad as an entrepreneur:
   – a dreamer or a realist;
   – as a strategist and as a hospital administrator.
2) The market for private hospitals in the Eastern Province: yesterday and today:
   – opportunities and threats.
3) Hospital management contract market in Saudi Arabia:
   – managing a hospital: the dual authority structure,
   – the job of the management firm: cost-benefit analysis.
4) Coping with the bedding crisis:
   a) revise fee structure;
   b) Reposition:
      – What kind of hospital does AFH want to be?
      – A general hospital?
      – A specialist hospital?
      – In which field?
      – What kind of patient should it target?
   c) Sell out? To Whom? Businessmen? Physicians?
   d) Declare bankruptcy.

Questions for Discussion

1) How does one account for the initial success of AFH? What is its special success formula?
2) Could AFH have achieved its initial success without:
   a) Mr. Fouad's reputation;
   b) Government's soft loan and incentives?
3) What were Mr. Fouad's goals and objectives in establishing his hospital?
4) What is your assessment of the market of private hospitals in the Kingdom? In the Eastern Province? Is it still growing or is it maturing? Are there still opportunities in it? For whom? What are the risks involved?
5) What are the strengths and weaknesses of AFH?
6) Which challenges does AFH face?
7) Can AFH continue its present strategy of being a first class gerneral hospital? How can it finance the purchase of new medical equipment and retain its present medical staff in the face of the current bedding crisis?
8) Which actions would you suggest to meet the challenges identified above?
   a) What must AFH do *now* to survive the current crisis?
   b) What must AFH do to fulfill the owner's goals and expectations identified above?

External Analysis

Opportunity

Due to the low standard of health care services provided by Dammam Central Hospital, and since there is no other hospital in the city except AFH, it is a true opportunity for the hospital to attract Saudi patients residing in the Dammam area. To accomplish this, they can offer them high quality medical service at reasonable rates. The good location and reputation of AFH will facilitate the task.

Threats

1) Continuous reduction in the number of expatriates working in the country.
2) The excess capacity of beds in the existing hospitals may lead to a price war between private hospitals.
3) Hospitals under construction will add another 1,890 beds to the available beds.

4) Continuous development and improvement in the nonprofit hospital attracts more Saudi patients.

Internal Analysis

Strengths

1) The hospital has the advantage of modern equipment in the labs, surgery, and treatment section.
2) The hospital has qualified physicians, i.e., consultants and specialists.
3) The hospital is clean and organized.

Weaknesses

1) The hospital is lacking a mosque and parking area.
2) Women patients do not have a separate waiting place.
3) Hospital employees are discouraged by salary reductions.
4) Hospital patients' records and data are not completely organized.
5) The hospital is in need of patients and a public affairs department.
6) Patients' follow-up at home by telephone is not existing, rather, they are required to visit the hospital for follow-up. The patients go through a long procedure of retrieving their file and waiting in a long line with other patients.
7) The hospital is over-staffed by the supporting staff. They represent 50% of the total employees, whereas Al-Mana Hospital's supporting staff represents 26% and is 40% at Dr. Fakkri's hospital.

Recommendations

It appears that AFH has gained prominence in the Dammam community in maternity and general surgery. It should continue to strengthen this part of the operation by attracting and retaining qualified female Arabic-speaking physicians.

At the same time, AFH should strive to add more specialties related to this capability, such as pediatrics or neonatal care units. Due to rising costs of medical equipment and competition from local government and private hospitals, AFH cannot continue to be a general hospital. It would have to specialize in some medical service or else find itself bombarded by overcapacity plus mounting losses.

Confronting the uncertainties of future changes, local hospital overcapacity, plus internal constraints in management, marketing, and finance, AFH has the immediate task of increasing occupancy and stabilizing operations in order to survive in a recessionary environment.

7.4   Green Crescent Clinic

Synopsis

Green Crescent is an innovative multi-specialty private clinic that happened to be a victim of a deteriorating environment. Its founder, Dr. Buraik, imported its concept from the U.S., and introduced it with some slight modifications in the over-crowded market of Riyadh, the capital city of Saudi Arabia in 1981. The idea was to provide first-class personalized health care services to a select group of subscribers. The majority of those were expatriate corporate employees; the minority, self-paying private Saudi patients. A severe business recession meant the exodus of the former and stiff competition for the latter. Consequently, the core patient group of the Green Crescent subscribers has virtually disappeared. Besides, a feud among the owners reached the courts, which decreed liquidation.

Strategic Issues

1) Medical entrepreneurship: striking a balance between the role of the entrepreneur as a strategist and his role as an administrator.
2) Plant location as a strategic weapon.
3) Problems of the transfer of American ideas, such as HMO, to Arab lands.
4) Identifying:
   a) sustainable competitive advantage;
   b) strengths and weaknesses;
   c) market opportunities and threats.
5) Distinction between: deliberate and emergent strategy.
6) Liquidation: conditions for its optimal use as an endgame strategy.
7) Strategies for managing liquidation:
   a) how to overcome employees negative reaction to liquidation;
   b) managerial tasks required for managing the liquidation process;
   c) managerial dilemmas in the management of liquidation.
8) Turnaround strategy: strategic and operational. Which type to use when? When to use insiders and when to use outsiders as CEO's? When to step down and when to stay on top of the helm? [Hint: Read Manfred Kets de Vries, "The Dark Side of CEO Succession," *Harvard Business Review* (Jan.–Feb. 1988): 56–60].

Questions for Discussion

1) Identify Green Crescent's initial strategy. What business is it in? What services does it provide? to whom? What market niche does it serve?

2) Identify Green Crescent's competitive advantage.
3) What does Green Crescent offer by way of utility? What is "value" to its customers?
4) Identify Green Crescent's strengths and weaknesses.
5) What is your assessment of the health care market in the Riyadh Metropolitan area? What are the existing opportunities and threats?
6) Would Green Crescent's fate have been different had it located elsewhere in Saudi Arabia, such as Jeddah or Dammam?
7) Who are Green Crescent's competitors? How do they compete?
8) Should Green Crescent retain the present customer segmentation scheme (i.e., subscribers vs. nonsubscribers)? If yes, how should it differentiate its offerings to each segment? If not, why?
9) Speculate why the court ordered liquidation? Does its reasoning coincide with conditions for using endgame strategies.
10) Although liquidation hurts Dr. Buraik's pride, it still offers the owners the best way out of their current stalemate. Discuss.
11) What other endgame strategies might have been pursued? Should Dr. Buraik resign? Should the partners look for an outside successor?
12) You are an associate editor of *Saudi Business*. You have just learned about the court decision to liquidate Green Crescent. Write the obituary.
13) Speculate on the reaction of GC employees to the court decision.
14) If you were appointed by the court to be in charge of liquidation, how do you go about managing the transition?
15) What sort of dilemmas are you likely to encounter and how do you go about resolving them? (Hint: read Robert Sutton, "Managing Organizational Death," *Human Resource Management*, 22, 4, Winter 1983).
16) The Buraiks, have expressed a desire to take over Green Crescent. They think it is viable and worth saving. What are their motives? Are they sentimental fools or hardheaded businessmen? Could they engineer a successful turnaround? With or without Dr. Wael, the founder? What are their assets? Their competitive advantage? As a strategic planning consultant, do you advise the Buraiks to retain their original business definition or abandon it?

Chapter 8
8.1   Saudi Consulting House (SCH)

Case Summary

Saudi Consulting House (SCH) is a government – owned organization designed to train Saudi nationals as consultants and to render consulting services to the government and the public. SCH renders a portfolio of engineering and economic services in cooperation with some international consultancy houses.

SCH faces keen competition for local as well as established multinational consulting houses. The problem is further compounded by sharp declines in the consulting business, the low market share of SCH, and the image of a national firm operating in the field which has always been the exclusive domain of multinational consulting firms.

Teaching Strategy

Philip Kotler identified four marketing competitive strategies for the market: leaders, challengers, followers, and nichers. This case can be used as an exercise in market strategy analysis.

A second track is to use the case to develop a strategic plan that evaluates the historical charted objectives mission for SCH and whether they still maintain a viable fit between SCH's resources and its environmental opportunities and threats.

Questions for Discussion

1) Are the objectives and charted mission of SCH still valid? What do you suggest?
2) How does SCH compete? What is its distinctive competence? How does it compare with its key competitors?
3) Evaluate SCH's organization structure? Do they need a marketing department?
4) If you were put in charge of managing SCH, what changes would you make? What is your new marketing plan? What is your long-term strategic plan?
5) What do you think of the idea of Selling the businesses to its employees? Hint: Read Blasi, Joseph R. (1988). *Employee ownership: revolution or ripoff?* Cambridge, Mass.: Ballinger.

8.2   The Saudi Arabian International School "The Dhahran Academy"

Case Summary

The Dhahran Academy was founded in 1962 as a result of the need of the American consulate general personnel. It was expanded during the oil-boom to include many of the children of the non-Muslim expatriate communities spread throughout the Kingdom. To attract non-American pupils, the school broadened its basically American menu "curriculum" to include British, Dutch, and German menus. As of late, the Academy has been experiencing an enrollment crisis brought about by an economic recession. Lower oil production meant fewer expatriates resulting in fewer students. As area employees began trimming the fat (employee salaries, educational allowance for dependent children), and as competition for non-American students increased from other ethnic schools, the Academy was left with a high cost structure and a tenuous financial position. The case requires an analysis of the Academy's strenghts, weaknesses, and strategies in determining how it can best overcome major industry and internal obstacles in meeting its goals.

Teaching Strategy

The Dhahran Academy case can be used in different ways to illustrate important business policy concepts.

1) The case may be used early in the course to isolate and highlight the school's mission and to identify strategy elements in each of the school's major functional areas (student admission, recruitment of teaching and administrative staff, curriculum planning, etc.).
2) The case can also be used to determine product market opportunities and future threats to the firm or industry (catering to non-American students and contracting to manage far away schools).
3) The case can also be used to illustrate Porter's five factor framework for industry analysis.
4) The case is an excellent example of what it takes to run a large, decentralized, non-profit professional organization.
5) The case also illustrates other concepts such as:
   a) the benefits and pitfalls of luck in the local economy;
   b) the strategic functions of the board of directors;
   c) the competitiveness of American industry in world markets;
   d) the intelligent use of a focus strategy.

Strategic Issues

- Government regulation;
- the effects of a "boomtown" bust;
- dealing with success and complacency;
- organizational goals in the not-for-profit sector;
- redefinition of the school business;
- the parochial perceptions of management; and
- strategic management in hard times.

Questions for Discussion

1) What was the original mission of the Dhahran Academy? What is it now?
2) What was the original strategy? What is it now?
3) Use Porter's framework to analyze the attractiveness of private schools to private investors in Saudi Arabia. What does it take to succeed in such an industry?
4) Is the Dhahran Academy a success story?
5) What is happening in its external environment?
6) Evaluate the Academy's organizational structure. How would you propose to improve it if you were in charge?
7) What is the role and function of the board of trustees? What should it be?
8) In light of your answer to 5), what should the Academy strategy be now, and how should it go about implementing it?
9) The political process inherent in strategy formulation at the Academy prevents its officials from choosing the correct response to the enrollment crisis and guarantees that the organization suffers from groupthink. Explain in detail.

8.3   Alpha Data Soft

Synopsis

Two young University graduates with some minor experience in the computer business, detected a niche in the fast developing computer market in Saudi Arabia. They formed a company that originally specialized in customizing software to fit the peculiar needs of small-sized firms. Later, the company entered the hardware business by providing complete packages consisting of hardware and software tailored to clients' needs.

Although Alpha is not in imminent danger, it realizes the risks involved in its present and past strategies. Whereas the original strategy exposes Alpha to the potential threat of the new software protection technology, its present strategy to the real risks of competing with large full-service and full-time computer dealers. Given this risk, Alpha has to decide what sort of a dealer does it want to be? Should it sell copied software, customized software, either or both, plus hardware?

Key Strategic Issues

1) Entrepreneurship in the high technology field.
2) Identification of firm-specific key success factors.
3) Identification of competitive advantage.
4) Distinction between deliberate and emergent strategy.
5) Identification of key trends in the computer marketplace and detecting opportunities and threats as they concern a small dynamic player.
6) Organizing and managing an entrepreneurial firm.
7) Evaluation and analysis of strategic alternatives.

Questions for Discussion

1) Identify Alpha Data Soft's past and present strategy.
2) Identify ADS's competitive advantage. How does it compete in its chosen niche?
3) How do the partners divide work among themselves? What functions does each personally perform and what functions do they delegate to their subordinates? Do you see merit in their design?
4) The computer market in Saudi Arabia is fiercely competitive.
   a) How is this market segmented?
   b) How do the players compete in it?
   c) What are the key trends in this market?
   d) What does it take to succeed in this business?
5) Identify key opportunities and threats in the computer market in Arabia. Are these opportunities and threats viewed similarly by all players?
6) Who are ADS's direct competitors? How do they compete?
7) What's the worst that could happen to ADS?
8) What are ADS's objectives? What are its assets and limitations?
9) As a consultant, how do you help the partners evaluate and choose among the four alternatives listed at the end of the case? How do you help them redefine their business?

Chapter 9

1) Bedoaucracy and bureaucracy are ideal types. Is it possible for Arab managers to change their practices and operate somewhere in the middle? If so, what do they have to gain and what do they have to lose?
2) Using Schmenner's two dimensions – degree of labor intensity – and degree of customization – apply these dimensions to help Arab managers operate their businesses more effectively.
3) Some Arab organizations have a low degree of coping with their environment. Make suggestions as to how formal planning could help managers become more responsive to the needs of their environments.
4) The Arab business environment is characterized by a high-cost structure. Suggest strategies to help reduce these costs.
5) What explains the lackluster performance of Arab service firms? What would it take to revitalize them?
6) What explains the Arab aversion to formal strategic planning? Are the Arabs unique in this regard or are they in the company of others?
   Hint: read Reiger, Fritz (1987). "The influence of national culture on organization structure, process and decision-making." Unpublished doctoral dissertation. Montreal: McGill University.
7) Dostojewski in his "The Brothers Karamazov" made the following comment:
   "Reforms, when the ground has not been prepared for them, especially if they are institutions copied from abroad, do nothing but mischief."
   How relevant is the above quotation to the teaching and practice of strategic management in the Arab world?

Appendix C
Major GCC Currencies and Their
Exchange Rates as of 11/11/1987

One U.S. Dollar equals:

- – 3.74 Saudi Riyals (SR)
- – 3.63 Rialys Qatari (QR)
- –   .385 Oman Dinar (RO)
- –   .377 Bahraini Dinar (BD)
- –   .277 Kuwaiti Dinar (KD)
- – 3.69 UAE Dirham

Appendix D
List of Abbreviations

AACO	= Arab Air Carriers Organization		HCIMA	= Hotel Catering and Institutional Management Association
ABC	= Arab Banking Corporation			
ADS	= Alpha Data Soft		HMO	= Health Maintenance Organization
AF	= Air France			
AFH	= Abdulla Fouad Hospital		IATA	= International Air Transport Association
Aramco	= Arab American Oil Company		ICAO	= International Civil Aviation Organization
ASK	= Available Seat Kilometer		ICU	= Intensive Care Unit
ATK	= Available Tonne Kilometer		IHG	= International Hospital Groups
ATM	= Automatic Teller Machine		JD	= Jordanian Dinar
			JET	= Jordan Express Travel
BBME	= British Bank of the Middle East		JETT	= Jordan Express Tourist Transport
BOAC	= British Overseas Airways		KAC	= Kuwait Airways Corporation
BSF	= Saudi French Bank			
CEO	= Chief Executive Officer		KASCO	= Kuwait Aviation Service Company
C.C.U.	= Coronary Care Unit			
CTO	= City Ticket Offices		KD	= Kuwait Dinar
DBM	= Data Base Management		KFUPM	= King Fahd University of Petroleum and Minerals
DH	= U.A.E. Dirham			
ENT	= Ear, Nose, Throat		KLM	= Royal Dutch Airlines
GC	= Green Crescent (Health Services Clinic)		KSF	= Key Success Factors
			LH	= Lufthansa
GCC	= Gulf Cooperation Council		MEED	= Middle East Economic Digest
GF	= Gulf Air		MODA	= Ministry of Defense and Aviation
GIB	= Gulf International Bank			
GM	= Gulf Meridien		MOH	= Ministry of Health
GMH	= Grand Metropolitan Hotel		MOHE	= Ministry of Higher Education
GOSI	= Government Organization for Social Insurance		NCB	= National Commercial Bank (of Saudi Arabia)
GSA	= General Sales Agent		OBU	= Offshore Banking Unit

PIF	= Public Investment Fund	SAMA	= Saudi Arabian Monetary Agency
PSC	= Public Services Commission (Interior Ministry)	SANG	= Saudi Arabian National Guard
QR	= Rialys Qatari	SAS	= Scandinavian Airline System
RCJY	= Royal Commission for Jubail and Yanbu	SASCO	= Saudi Auto Service Corporation
REDF	= Real Estate Developing Fund (Saudi Arabia)	SBU	= Strategic Business Unit
RIDC	= Research and Industrial Development Center	SCH	= Saudi Consulting House
RO	= Oman Dinar	SIDF	= Saudi Industrial Development Fund
RPK	= Revenue Passenger Kilometer	SR	= Saudi Riyal
RTK	= Revenue Tonne Kilometer	SR	= Swissair
SAAB	= Saudi Arabian Agriculture Bank	SV	= Saudia
SABIC	= Saudi Arabian Basic Industries	TOP	= Temporary Operating Permit
SAIS	= Saudi Arabian International School	U.A.E.	= United Arabian Emirates
SAMBA	= Saudi American Bank	UNIDO	= United Nationals Industrial Development Organization
		UWS	= Universal Work Station

About the Authors

M. Sami Kassem is professor of management in the College of Business Administration, The University of Toledo, Ohio. He degree received his B. Com. from Ain Shams University (Cairo), did graduate work at the University of Chicago, and obtained his MBA and Ph.D. degrees in management from New York University.

Dr. Kassem has taught at several American and overseas universities. He served as a visiting professor at the European Institute of Business Administration (INSEAD) and the European Center of Permanent Education (CEDEP) in France from 1972 to 1975, and at King Fahd University of Petroleum and Minerals in Saudi Arabia from 1984 to 1987. While in Europe, he worked closely with Geert Hofstede in producing *European Contribution to Organization Theory* (Van Gorcum, 1976), and while in Saudi Arabia, he did the field work for this book. He has published in a number of professional and academic journals. He is active in the management development field, having designed and conducted a number of executive training programs in Europe, the Middle East, and the United States.

Dr. Kassem was the recipient of the 1970 Outstanding Teacher Award at The University of Toledo and was awarded a Fulbright Research Scholarship to Romania in 1983.

Ghazi Habib is an associate professor of marketing at King Fahd University of Petroleum and Minerals in Dhahran, Saudi Arabia.

He received his B.Sc. degree in Mechanical Engineering with honors from The University of Petroleum and Minerals in 1985, his MBA in Technology Management from the University of California in 1978, and received a Doctor of Administration degree from Texas Tech University in 1983.

He was the recipient of the Outstanding Teacher Award at KFUPM in 1985. Dr. Habib is very active in the field of management development, and coordinates a program of marketing in service organization and for commercial banks. He is also active as a writer and as a management consultant.

Dr. Habib is a member of the American Marketing Association, the American Management Association, and the International Academy of Business in the USA. His numerous articles appeared in the Academy of

Management Journal, International Marketing Review, and the International Journal of Bank Management.

de Gruyter Studies in Organization

An international series by internationally known authors presenting current research in organization

Vol. 1
The Japanese Industrial System
By *Charles J. McMillan*
2nd revised edition
1985. 15.5 x 23 cm. XII, 356 pages. Cloth. ISBN 3 11 010410 5; 0-89925-005-X (U.S.)

Vol. 2
Political Management
Redefining the Public Sphere
By *H. T. Wilson*
1984. 15.5 x 23 cm. X, 316 pages. Cloth. ISBN 3 11 009902 0

Vol. 3
Limits to Bureaucratic Growth
By *Marshall W. Meyer* in Association with *William Stevenson* and *Stephen Webster*
1985. 15.5 x 23 cm. X, 228 pages. Cloth. ISBN 3 11 009865 2; 0-89925-003-3 (U.S.)

Vol. 4
Guidance, Control and Evaluation in the Public Sector
Edited by *F. X. Kaufmann, G. Majone, V. Ostrom*
1985. 17 x 24 cm. XIV, 830 pages. Cloth. ISBN 3 11 009707 9; 0-89925-020-3 (U.S.)

Vol. 5
International Business in the Middle East
Edited by *Erdener Kaynak*
1986. 15.5 x 23 cm. XVI, 278 pages. Cloth. ISBN 3 11 010321 4; 0-89925-021-1 (U.S.)

Vol. 6
The American Samurai
Blending American and Japanese Managerial Practice
By *Jon P. Alston*
1986. 15.5 x 23 cm. XII, 368 pages. Cloth. ISBN 3 11 010619 1; 0-89925-063-7 (U.S.)

Vol. 7
Organizing Industrial Development
Edited by *Rolf Wolff*
1986. 15.5 x 23 cm. XI, 391 pages. Cloth. ISBN 3 11 010669 8; 0-89925-168-4 (U.S.)

Vol. 8
Organization Theory and Technocratic Consciousness
Rationality, Ideology, and Quality of Work
By *Mats Alvesson*
1987. 15.5 x 23 cm. X, 286 pages. Cloth. ISBN 3 11 010574 8; 0-89925-165-X (U.S.)

Vol. 9

Anglo-American Innovation
By *Peter A. Clark*
1987. 15.5 x 23 cm. X, 404 pages. Cloth. ISBN 3 11 010572 1; 0-89925-164-1 (U.S.)

Vol. 10

Unemployment: Theory, Policy and Structure
Edited by *Peder J. Pedersen* and *Reinhard Lund*
1987. 15.5 x 23 cm. XX, 358 pages. Cloth. ISBN 3 11 011071 7; 0-89925-277-X (U.S.)

Vol. 11

Organization of Innovation
East-West-Perspectives
Edited by *John Child* and *Paul Bate*
1987. 15.5 x 23 cm. X, 238 pages. Cloth. ISBN 3 11 010700 7; 0-89925-167-6 (U.S.)

Vol. 12

Management in China during and after Mao in Enterprises, Government, and Party
By *Oiva Laaksonen*
1988. 15.5 x 23 cm. X, 379 pages. Cloth. ISBN 3 11 009958 6; 0-89925-025-4 (U.S.)

Vol. 13

Innovation and Management
International Comparisons
Edited by *Kuniyoshi Urabe, John Child* and *Tadao Kagono*
1988. 15.5 x 23 cm. XX, 371 pages. Cloth. ISBN 3 11 011007 5; 0-89925-294-X (U.S.)

Vol. 14

Leadership and Management in Universities:
Britain and Nigeria
By *Titus Oshagbemi*
1988. 15.5 x 23 cm. XX, 249 pages. Cloth. ISBN 3 11 011514 X; 0-89925-426-8 (U.S.)

Vol. 15

Boards of Directors under Public Ownership:
A Comparative Perspective
By *Miriam Dornstein*
1988. 15.5 x 23 cm. X, 165 pages. Cloth. ISBN 3 11 011740 1; 0-89925-496-9 (U.S.)

WALTER DE GRUYTER · BERLIN · NEW YORK
Genthiner Straße 13, D-1000 Berlin 30, Phone (0 30) 2 60 05-0, Telex 1 83 027
200 Saw Mill River Road, Hawthorne, N.Y. 10532, Phone (914) 747-0110, Telex 646677